ERRATA

The illustration on page 217 of *Review of Research in Education 5* should appear, instead, on page 218 with the caption for Figure 2.

The illustration on page 218 should appear, instead, on page 217 with the caption for Figure 1.

In Table 3, page 374, in the first equation in the middle column, symbols u and n are defined as follows:

u = ordinate of unit normal
distribution
n = total sample size

REVIEW
OF
RESEARCH

CONTRIBUTORS

GEORGE W. McCONKIE

MICHAEL MacDONALD-ROSS

REBECCA BARR

ROBERT DREEBEN

WALTER DOYLE

VINCENT TINTO

MARTIN BURLINGAME

MICHAEL J. SUBKOVIAK

FRANK B. BAKER

DAVID HAMILTON

GENE V GLASS

IN EDUCATION

5

1977

LEE S. SHULMAN
Editor
Michigan State University

Assistant Editor
SUSAN MOWRY

F. E. PEACOCK PUBLISHERS, INC., ITASCA, ILLINOIS

A PUBLICATION OF THE

AMERICAN EDUCATIONAL RESEARCH ASSOCIATION

Editorial Board

John B. Carroll

T. Anne Cleary

Laurence Iannaccone

William G. Spady

Kenneth Strike

Decker F. Walker

Statement from the Editor

Learning from text has remained a constant feature of formal schooling and non-formal education for many years. The first section of this volume is devoted to reviews of research on learning from the two major forms of text—prose and graphics.

Recently educational research has devoted as much attention to the study of teaching as has traditionally been assigned to investigations of learning. Two chapters review research on teaching in the present volume from social psychological and sociological perspectives not typically brought to bear on this rapidly developing field.

Research related to educational policy decisions has emerged rapidly since the Coleman Report as a major focus for educational inquiries. Two areas of policy research are examined in Section III. The first is the perennial question of the value of schooling for life success. A second is the analysis of how policy decisions achieve their effects on schools and school personnel.

Section IV examines two important areas of measurement and evaluation: test theory and curriculum evaluation. The former reviews recent research developments in test theory emerging out of the controversies over criterion-referenced and norm-referenced testing, as well as other important topics in measurement. A historical perspective is provided for examining the rapidly changing field of curriculum evaluation in the second chapter of that section.

The final section, on Methodology, critically examines approaches to accumulating the findings of studies conducted by different researchers in disparate settings. A number of methods have been developed to generalize across individual investigations in order to reach conclusions more firmly grounded than can be derived from any single study. These are reviewed in Section V.

LEE S. SHULMAN
Editor

Contents

I

LEARNING FROM TEXT

1

Learning from Text

GEORGE W. McCONKIE
Cornell University

One of the most important goals of educational institutions in Western culture (as well as many other cultures) is to help students learn how to acquire information from written text. The person who can read well has a means of obtaining knowledge on almost any topic, with little assistance from anyone else. However, an equal burden falls on the writer, since characteristics of a passage, quite apart from the complexity of the content, greatly influence what readers understand and retain from it. An understanding of the psychological processes involved in learning from text should provide a basis for assisting people to become more effective readers and communicators.

No book, let alone a single chapter, could adequately review all the research related to learning from text. Any comprehensive attempt would include research in many fields, including rhetoric, communication, education, artificial intelligence, and areas of linguistics and psychology as well as branches of philosophy and neurology. Thus this chapter must be sharply limited in its scope of review.

Since Carroll (1971) has reviewed the literature related to learning from text through 1970, our focus is on publications in the first half of the present decade. We primarily consider studies involving prose, that is, connected discourse consisting of more than a single sentence. The studies included typically involved competent learners (usually adults) who read or heard individual short passages. Thus questions about the development of reading or listening competence, or about learning from more extended texts (for

---

JOHN B. CARROLL, University of North Carolina, was the editorial consultant for this chapter.

Note: The preparation of this review was partially supported under Grant no. NIE-G-74-0018 from the National Institute of Education. Carl H. Frederiksen aided greatly in the initial planning of the review, and Diana Dee-Lucas carried out much of the literature search.

instance, a series of lessons or an entire book) have been largely ignored. The review deals much more with what is retained from passages than with the details of how the information is comprehended. It summarizes much of the empirical research and points the reader to the more relevant theoretical work from the fields of linguistics and computer science.

We begin by dealing with the two problems Frase (1975) has identified as having held back research on learning from text: the complexity of the stimulus—the text—and the difficulty of analyzing the complex behaviors which reveal what has been learned. We then consider the nature of the cognitive representation of textual information and examine three sources of control over language-processing activities in reading and listening: textual controls, task structure controls, and the effects of extratextual information. Other sections deal with retrieval processes and effects of individual differences on learning from text, and the final section suggests some possibilities for the future.

THE NATURE OF TEXT

Why Analyze Text?

In earlier research on learning and retention, characteristics of the text used in presenting the information were largely ignored. There was little basis for selecting a particular passage for use in an experiment other than to make sure that it was of an appropriate reading level, and it communicated new information to the reader which could be fairly readily tested. It was generally hoped that the results obtained would be relatively passage-free and would generalize to some unspecified, fairly large set of passages typically encountered by readers.

Today there is a greater concern for making a thorough analysis of the text itself, for the following reasons, among others. First, in order to study what is and is not retained from a passage, a logical prerequisite is some description of the information communicated by the passage. Second, the development of techniques for assessing what information a person has acquired from the text must be based on an analysis of the information communicated by the text, whether questions, free recall, or some other technique is used in making the assessment. Third, since many characteristics of the text probably influence what is retained from it, the text must be analyzed to identify the controlling or influencing characteristics. And fourth, assuming that at least some experimental results will not hold for all passages, the nature of the texts used in a study must be understood in order to know the domain to which the results may be generalized.

A "Layered" View of Text Structure

It is common in psychology to make a distinction between text content and text form. Linguists have made a great deal of progress in describing the syntactic aspects of sentences and, more recently, a number have turned their attention to discourse analysis, or the analysis of larger segments of text. Grimes (1975) provides an excellent summary of much of their work (also see Petofi & Reiser, 1973; Van Dijk & Kintsch, in press). He describes three types of organization or structure in passages: the content structure, the cohesion structure, and the staging structure. The content is the semantic or meaning structure. The cohesion provides the means for signaling to the reader what information is new and how it relates to information previously stated. The staging gives the writer's perspective on what is being said, communicating what the passage is about, what it is placing at center stage, as it were. Hence the staging communicates the relative importance of different aspects of the text, from the writer's point of view.

A framework for integrating these aspects of text structure into a more unified view might present them as being layered, as in Figure 1. At the top layer, the Knowledge Base, is the semantic content to be communicated in the passage. This may be thought of as a semantic network; it is some portion of the writer's total knowledge. At the second layer is the content that is in fact to be represented in the passage; this subset of the Knowledge Base is titled here the Passage Base. This distinction is made to recognize that the writer does not directly express much of the information which is part of the domain of knowledge being communicated. Some information is not important for the purpose of the passage, some is already likely to be known to the reader, and other information can be inferred and therefore need not be directly stated.

The Knowledge and Passage Base structures are presumably not linear, whereas the text is. In order to convert the Passage Base to actual text, an

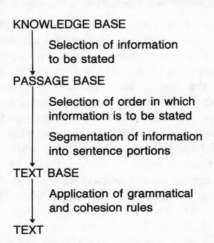

Figure 1.   A "layered" view of text structure, suggested by C. H. Frederiksen (personal communication).

additional step is required, that of selecting a beginning point and a path through the structure, or an order in which the information is to be expressed. The segments of the structure which are to appear as sentences must also be delimited. This step appears to coincide with the process of establishing the staging of the text. These decisions are actually motivated by more basic decisions concerning the writer's intent and point of view in writing the passage. Following Kintsch (1974), this sequenced and segmented structure is referred to as the Text Base; it is assumed to contain all the information necessary to result uniquely in the text itself, which is the final layer. The grammar is all that is necessary to map from Text Base to Text.

From this brief description, it can be seen that there are many Passage Bases which could be derived from a Knowledge Base, depending on the degree of completeness of information to be communicated, what the likely readers are assumed to know, and so on. Given a Passage Base, there are many possible Text Bases which might be produced, depending on such factors as the writer's viewpoint and what is to be stressed. Much of the author's style of expression may be involved in the decisions made at this point. However, once these decisions are made, there remains little or no freedom in the application of the grammatical rules in the production of the text. Much of the cohesion structure may be just as automatic, and it can be developed below the level of the Text Base as well. While the Knowledge Base may indicate the content to be communicated in the passage, decisions involved in deriving other levels have important effects on what aspects of the passage are likely to be retained. Evidence on this point will be reviewed later.

Representing the Content Structure of a Passage

Typically, the goal of the educational or psychological researcher has been to investigate what aspects of the passage content are retained. This has led to a desire for a representation of something like the Passage Base for a passage. Early attempts at this goal involved writing out a set of relations to be expressed in the passage and then producing one or more passages which expressed those relations (as well as other relations not included in the original structure). Thus the initial structure provided a partial representation of the information in the passage, the part that was to be assessed. Recently, attempts have been made to develop more complete structures representing the content of existing passages. Forms of representation which have been used for these purposes include set relations (Dawes, 1966), linear relationship structures (Frase, 1973), propositions (Frederiksen, 1975c; Kintsch, 1974) and networks (J. R. Anderson, 1976; Anderson & Bower, 1973; Crothers, 1975; Meyer, 1975; Rumelhart, Lindsay, & Norman, 1972). At present, except for work with limited problems, networks and propositions (including propositional networks) appear to be the most general and most widely adopted forms for representing the Passage Base. Simmons and Bruce (1971) have demonstrated the equivalence of these two forms of representation.

Frederiksen (1975c) conceives of the content of a passage as consisting of a set of concepts (objects, actions, or attributes) which serve as nodes, together with a set of labeled relations among them which form a semantic network structure. Such a structure has several levels of units. At the lowest level is the concept, which may be further decomposed, as in Schank (1972), or left complex. The next level is the triple, the smallest unit containing relational information. Above this is the proposition, which consists of one or more triples. Propositions themselves can be rank shifted (Winograd, 1972) to function as nodes in other propositions, thus making the structure recursive. There are also logical relations which take propositions as elements to be related and are capable of relating sets of related propositions. Finally, the passage as a whole may be taken as a unit. Frederiksen breaks the relations into three classes: role relations (Fillmore, 1968), stative relations, and logical relations. Each relation is defined according to the characteristics of the elements that it can relate. This general pattern is quite common to most work in the area, though the specific natures of the nodes and relations may differ.

Content structures of different passages vary in a number of ways, including the types of relations that occur most frequently; the degree of cohesiveness of various sorts (e.g., the degree of interrelationship among the propositions); general pattern of structure (e.g., some are quite linear, and others are highly branching or interrelating); and number of objects included (Kintsch, Kozminsky, Streby, McKoon, & Keenan, 1975). To date, while these differences have been recognized, no one has developed an adequate set of descriptors for communicating general differences among these structures.

Recently there has been a concern for identifying functional units between the proposition and the passage level, such as an episode in a story. Schank (1975) deals with the problem of attempting to identify episodes, and Rumelhart (1975) has formulated a story grammar which includes such categories as setting and episode. The means of identifying these larger units and the question of whether text structure at this level requires a different set of relations than it does at lower levels are problems yet to be resolved.

Other Aspects of Passage Structure

According to Grimes (1975), the staging component of passage structure is realized through such characteristics of the passage as what is taken as the point of departure, what is fronted or in other ways given emphasis in sentences (see Chafe, 1970), and how the techniques of subordination and embedding of information are used. Clements (1976) has made an initial attempt at putting these concepts into a set of rules for analyzing a passage to yield a staging hierarchy of the passage, which can be used in psychological research. Linguistic work in this area has shown that much of the variation in language which some psychologists have treated as free variation, such as differences in voice (active vs. passive) or the relative placement of phrases in a sentence, is actually rule governed at the discourse level. These character-istics probably have important psychological effects in terms of signaling the relative importance of different parts of the text from the writer's point of view.

In discussing cohesion characteristics of text, or the means provided to aid the reader to follow the thread of discourse, Grimes discusses how the passage content is segmented into information blocks (Halliday, 1967, 1968), each having a center, the place where new information is placed. In a common structure in English, the old information is fronted in a sentence and new information is given later, though by means of stress patterns the structures can be much more complex than this. Grimes also discusses the use of pro-nominalization and other referential devices which aid the reader to keep track of reference. Chafe (1970) points out the use of definite and indefinite forms as a means of signaling to the reader whether the object being discussed is assumed to be already known (i.e., previously introduced in the passage or assumed to be common knowledge).

Psychological and educational researchers should be acquainted with the present linguistic knowledge about discourse, both because it suggests many variables whose effects on language processing and learning ought to be ex-plored, and because they need to be aware of the linguistic effects of text manipulations in their studies. The types of text used in many studies have so violated the natural patterns of English discourse that it is questionable whether learning from "connected discourse" was being studied after all.

ASSESSMENT OF LEARNING AND RETENTION

The second great deterrent to research on learning from text has been the difficulty of finding adequate means of assessing what has been learned. Carroll (1971) summarizes the various techniques that have been employed, most of which can be classed as either question-oriented techniques, in which the subject responds to specific questions, or free-recall techniques, in which the subject is asked to reproduce part or all of the information from the passage. There have been recent significant advancements in both of these types of assessment.

Question-Oriented Techniques

The difficulty of attempting to assess exactly what information is retained (a multidimensional problem) has led researchers to be satisfied with exploring the question of how much is retained (a unidimensional problem). Questions are typically generated on an intuitive basis by the experimenter and are treated as a random selection from a much larger set of questions which would cover most or all of the information communicated in the passage. Bormuth (1970) and R. C. Anderson (1972) have criticized the procedures usually involved in generating questions, indicating that since these procedures are not explicitly defined, it is not clear to what population of questions the results might be generalized. They attempt to overcome this problem by proposing an algorithmic approach to the generation of questions. The test questions used are then a sample of all questions that could be generated by the same algorithm, thus making clear the domain from which they came. Finn (1975) has developed an algorithm for question generation in this manner. Bormuth, Manning, Carr, and Pearson (1970) have demonstrated that the form of the question (the nature of the algorithm used to generate it from the text) has a substantial effect on the likelihood that it will be answered correctly.

The approach advocated by Bormuth involves sampling sentences from the text on a random basis, or on the basis of some clear principle; deleting a certain part, such as the subject or object; and then performing certain grammatical transformations on the sentences to produce questions of the appropriate form. This process has two characteristics which I feel are undesirable: It is syntax based rather than semantics based, and it continues the emphasis on estimating the amount retained from a passage rather than identifying what is recalled. Both can be eliminated while keeping an algorithmic approach, however.

The recent development of content structures for passages makes it possible to begin to identify what aspects of the information in a passage a particular question is interrogating. It is possible to select a question and then attempt to identify which propositions, or parts of the semantic network, would need to be intact for the question to be answered correctly, and even what information not in the passage would be required in order for an adequate answer to be given. A question generated from a single sentence, in the manner suggested by Bormuth (1970), can often be answered on the basis of any of several propositions in the content structure; in fact, deletion of the source sentence from the passage would have very little effect on the likelihood that such a question could be answered. Other questions, however, can only be answered on the basis of information in their source sentences.

This approach to question analysis, or even generation, is in harmony with Bormuth's suggestions, but it is semantics based rather than strictly syntax based. Questions can be classified on the basis of semantic characteristics of the information in the passage which is being interrogated, rather than on syntactic characteristics of the questions themselves. Work in computer science dealing with question-answering algorithms, matching question structures against semantic networks (for an introduction, see Hunt, 1975), has laid an excellent base for work on this problem. While no such system for analyzing or generating questions has yet been published, this is an area in which some significant work can be expected during the next decade.

Free-recall–Oriented Techniques

Free-recall data have been even more difficult to deal with than the question-oriented approaches to assessment. One approach was simply to count the number of words (sometimes just the content words) or word sequences in the subject's recall which were present in the original passage, and assume that this produces an index of total amount of information retained. In spite of substantial efforts by Cofer (1941) and later by King (1960, 1961) to develop a psychometric basis for this type of scoring, it has never been widely adopted.

A long history of scoring free recalls for meaning typically has involved segmenting the passage in some manner (according to sentences, clauses, etc.) and then judging whether each segment is represented in the recall. This yields a score indicating the number of "idea units" recalled from the passage (see Meyer, 1975, for a review). However, this procedure was often viewed as deficient, both in the subjective manner in which the text was segmented and in the subjective basis for decisions about whether the text segments were represented in recall. Still, this approach typically yielded good reliability between scorers; for instance, Royer and Cable (1975) report correlations of .98, and Todd and Kessler (1971), of .99. It also seemed to come closer to indicating the amount of the meaning of the original passage that was recalled than did simple word counts, though these two measures tended to be correlated (e.g., Todd & Kessler report a correlation of .93 or higher).

Johnson (1970) suggested that an objective procedure for the segmentation process would be to break the text at those points where speakers typically pause. Two problems exist with this and other segmentation methods. One is that it is affected by strictly syntactic factors; with one syntactic construction, a clause may be left intact as a single unit, but with another it may be broken into two or more units. Segmentation of the passage should be made on the basis of semantic considerations rather than procedures which depend heavily on syntax. This concern led Bransford and Johnson (1973) and Schallert (1975) to restate the text information as simple sentences, thus grouping related information, and then to use clauses and phrases as the scoring units. Aiken, Thomas, and Shennum (1975) used a similar approach.

A second problem is judging whether enough of the information from a unit is present in the recall to justify checking it as being recalled. It is common to find that some elements of the segment have been included in the recall but others have not. Thus it would be desirable to have more elementary units which can be scored independently.

Content structures of passages (described earlier) provide a basis for improving this type of scoring. They provide a representation of the information expressed in the passage which can be checked at any level of specificity desired, whether it be recall of individual concepts and relations, of triples, of propositions, or even of larger structures if desired. It is also possible to note, in many cases, what specific parts of the information in the passage have been changed by a subject and the nature of the change. While no manual for this type of scoring presently exists, examples can be found in Kintsch (1974), Frederiksen (1975c), and Meyer (1975). A somewhat related approach is described by Spencer (1973).

It is important in working with free recall to carefully distinguish between what is retained and what is expressed. Meyer and McConkie (1973) reported that when subjects recalled the same passage twice in immediate succession, only 72% of the "idea units" recalled were present in both free recalls. In a single recall, subjects are not able to exhaust their knowledge concerning a passage. In the long run, it may be desirable to augment free recall with questions in order to explore further what information is retained from a passage.

NATURE OF THE COGNITIVE REPRESENTATION

What Is Retained?

For decades it has been said that people tend to remember the meaning or content of a message rather than its form. Sachs (1967) demonstrated this by showing that within seconds after reading a sentence in a passage, a person is not able to detect changes in the sentence which do not modify its meaning. Jarvella (1971; Jarvella & Herman, 1972) showed that memory for the form of a sentence in text is largely confined to the sentence one is presently encountering. Bransford and Franks (1971) found that subjects who hear a subset of the possible set of sentences which might be used in describing a scene could not later identify which specific sentences they had actually heard. Such studies have provided convincing evidence that the reader/hearer is using the form of the sentence in establishing an abstract cognitive representation of the content or meaning, and this meaning is primarily what is retained.

However, this generalization needs several qualifications. First, even if the generalization is accurate, it must be recognized that all content is not equally well retained. Studies involving free recall consistently find a great variation in the number of subjects recalling different elements of the original passage (Bartlett, 1932; Meyer, 1975; Spencer, 1973; Thorndyke, 1975). Some elements are recalled by almost everyone; others by no one. An important goal of research in learning from text is to be able to specify what aspects of the content are most and least likely to be retained under various conditions, and to give a theoretical accounting of these results.

The second qualification is that much information other than pure content is retained. Subjects are often able to specify the region of the page on which particular information appeared, though this docs not seem to be useful for information retrieval (Rothkopf, 1971; Zechmeister & McKillip, 1972; Zechmeister, McKillip, Pasko, & Bespalec, 1975). Clark (1972) reports that subjects retain information which might be thought of as staging (i.e., whether a sentence mentions that the star is above the circle or the circle below the star), and this influences the facility with which they can answer different questions about the relative placement of the objects. Bilingual persons tend to remember in which language a sentence was presented (Kolers, 1974; Rose, Rose, King, & Perez, 1975). File and Jew (1973) presented instructions to airline passengers in various forms (varying in voice and negation-affirmation) and found a substantial tendency for the subjects to recall the instructions in the same syntactic form as they were presented (although the most frequent recall form was active-affirmative). Even studies which have demonstrated the abstract nature of the cognitive representation have tended to show retention of various aspects of form (e.g., Barclay, 1973; Bransford & Franks, 1972). Katz (1973; Katz, Atkeson, & Lee, 1974) replicated the Bransford and Franks (1971) studies and found that if all the sentences presented to the subject are active, or are very simple (stating a single relation), sentences different in form presented during testing are usually identified as being new. Singer and Rosenberg (1973) applied regression analysis to data from a replication of the Bransford and Franks (1971) study and found a large effect for a syntactic component determining responses in a recognition test. The amount and type of the nonsemantic information that is retained is undoubtedly a function of the nature of the task set for the subject. At present, no one has seriously attempted to describe the cognitive representation for information of these sorts. However, it should be pointed out that such representation may be quite abstract in nature. While some memory for form (as opposed to content) may consist of a lingering residue from the sentences themselves, there are also other possibilities. For instance, the reader may gain a sense of the general theme of the passage, and this may suggest which components of a sentence are most likely to be fronted in sentences or paragraphs. Thus the fact that a reader may be able to pick out sentences which differ in form from the original is not necessarily evidence that the specific form of the original sentences was retained.

A third qualification relates to the fact that people often retain information which was not directly stated in the passage but was apparently inferred from it.

Representation of Semantic Information

The way the researcher conceptualizes what people retain from reading a passage, the form of their cognitive representation of the semantic information obtained, greatly influences the types of studies conducted and what is looked for in the data. The nature of this representation is one of the central questions in the field. Yet there is not much research data to place substantial constraints on theories of the cognitive representation of semantic information. Most present theorizing is being done on the basis of arguments of adequacy, that is, whether the representation system adopted in a given model is capable of supporting activity assumed to be common in human cognition. Still prominent in the field is the work of Bartlett (1932), who demonstrated that what people recall from a passage can be quite different from what was initially presented. He argued that a Gestalt-type schema was constructed in the process of reading which undergoes transformations over time paralleling the Gestaltists' perceptual laws. At recall, the person must attempt to reconstruct the passage, as far as possible, from this somewhat distorted representation. However, Gauld and Stephenson (1967) found that after recalling a passage subjects can identify quite well which parts of their free recalls did not come from the original passage. Thus it appears that much of the rich variation which Bartlett observed was knowingly inserted into the recalls by his subjects in order to make them more coherent. This finding led Zangwill (1972; see also Spencer, 1973) to claim that retention and recall are abstractive rather than constructive.

A number of recent studies has supported the position that the cognitive representation of textual information is much more abstract than being simply a representation of the sentences seen or heard. Bransford and Franks (1971) demonstrated that subjects are not able to distinguish which sentences out of a set describing a scene were the actual sentences heard during the experiment (see also Griggs, 1974b; Katz, 1973; Singer & Rosenberg, 1973b). Later studies demonstrated that this abstract representation need not be an "image," or isomorph to a scene, since similar phenomena were found with very abstract sentences (Bransford & Franks, 1972) and even nonsense sentences (Katz & Gruenewald, 1974). Bransford, Barclay, and Franks (1972) demonstrated that information not stated in the text but reasonably inferable from it, on the basis of common usage or spatial relations, is frequently misrecognized as having been stated (see also Johnson, Bransford, & Solomon, 1973).

There is the question of whether such inferences should be viewed as "generated propositions," that is, as segments of cognitive structure which are generated at the time of reading and thus specifically added to the representation, or whether, when a structure is developed to represent the stated information, this unstated information is a natural part of the representation. An argument for the latter position can be derived from the work of Potts (1973, 1976) and Griggs (1974a), who have studied the retention of short paragraphs describing linear orders ("Jim is taller than John, John is taller than Ralph," etc.). A subject who has read a paragraph asserting such an ordering typically is able to identify logical inferences from it (Jim is taller than Ralph) with more accuracy than the stated relations and is able to verify such sentences faster than sentences containing information directly stated in the passage. In fact, actually stating these inferential relations in the text has no effect either on the likelihood of responding correctly or on the verification response times, indicating that the information is just as much present in the representation when it is not actually stated in the passage as when it is. At least in this straightforward situation, and perhaps in others, it seems reasonable to assume that unstated information is directly given in the cognitive structure produced to represent the actually stated information.

In theorizing efforts about the form of cognitive representations, they typically are assumed to be in the form of images, propositional or semantic networks, procedures, or more global entities referred to as frames or schemas. Begg and Paivio (1969) reported an experiment in which it was shown that concrete information in sentences is more likely to be retained than abstract information, and they argued for two forms of representation, images and nonimages, with the former being more efficient in terms of retention. However, Pezdek and Royer (1974) found that abstract information can be retained at least as well as concrete information if appropriate context is provided for clearly identifying the text meaning. This two-factor approach to cognitive representation has been challenged by the claim that the type of information typically thought of as being characteristic of images (i.e., spatial representation of visual scenes) can be represented in discrete forms, such as by networks (Anderson & Bower, 1973; Pylyshyn, 1973). This, of course, provides a discrete representation of essentially continuous information, and it smacks of the old all-or-none vs. continuous-strength debate in learning theory. Bobrow (1975) provides an excellent discussion of different forms of representation, showing how the "analogical vs. propositional" (continuous vs. discrete representation) dispute can lead to polarization rather than clarification of issues. At present, those who are attempting specifically to model the cognitive representation via a computer typically choose a semantic network or proposition list (J. R. Anderson, 1976; Anderson & Bower, 1973; Frederiksen, 1975c; Kintsch, 1974; Norman, Rumelhart, & LNR Research Group, 1975; Schank, 1972; Simmons, 1973). Anderson and Bower (1973) and Anderson (1976) have useful introductions to this sort of representation, and an excellent collection of examples is provided by Schank and Colby (1973).

A related approach to the representation of knowledge is referred to as procedural semantics (Winograd, 1972). Here, meaning is represented in terms of actions to be taken. Thus, in computer languages, the meaning of *move* is an action which is taken when that word is encountered. In the same way, for humans meanings can be represented in terms of the action (perceptual, mental, or physical) which results or may result when the meaning is activated. J. R. Anderson (1976) describes how such procedural information can be readily modeled in the form of production systems (Newell, 1973), and Miller and Johnson-Laird (1976) take a more thoroughgoing procedural approach.

A more global form of representation is exemplified by Minsky's (1975) notion of frames. Knowledge is assumed to be organized into frames which can be instantiated under appropriate conditions and which by themselves provide much useful information about those conditions. For instance, common knowledge about restaurants is organized into a family of frames. When reading about a restaurant, for example, the appropriate frame is activated, providing a context of knowledge about what is normal in this situation and what sorts of questions one normally has about it (aspects of the situation which are so variable that they have no normal condition). The normal conditions are assumed to hold as defaults unless contradicted by the text, thus accounting for some sorts of inferences readers typically make, and the frame defines what might be taken to be normal vs. surprising in this situation. It also guides the reader in terms of what information typically is sought when reading about this situation. This concept has not yet been fully developed, but such larger organizing concepts seem necessary to account for many aspects of our language processing, and they will probably become more and more important in theories of learning from text.

Although work on knowledge representation is moving rapidly at the present time, many words of caution are being expressed. Woods (1975) points out a number of problems which have not been solved in the development of semantic networks. J. R. Anderson (1976) suggests that rather than dealing with forms of cognitive representation in isolation, researchers should deal with representation-retrieval pairs. The properties of a system depend as heavily on the way the retrieval processes are assumed to interact with the knowledge representation as on the nature of the representation itself.

Forms of human cognitive representation are undoubtedly much more complex and abstract than have yet been envisioned (Franks, 1974; Weimer, 1974). Surely the models of today will look primitive in future years. For the present, which form of representation is found to be most satisfactory for a particular study may well depend upon the characteristics of the information being asserted by the passages used in the study (logical relations, spatial relations, procedural information, etc.) and the nature of the assessment task used. This should be an area of lively research interest during the next decade.

TEXTUAL CONTROLS ON COMPREHENSION AND RETENTION

Cohesion

The task of the reader/hearer is to build a cognitive representation of certain information stated in the passage, that is, to identify the concepts being discussed and perceive the patterns of relations which, it is asserted, hold among them (Bransford & McCarrell, 1974; Kintsch, 1976). The reader has two sources of information as a guide: the text, with its syntactic and discourse cues, and the reader's own knowledge of the subject matter being discussed. There are many features of our language to aid the person in perceiving the continuity within the text. There are also many ways in which it is possible to delete or misuse these textual patterns, thus making it more difficult to integrate each new proposition into the structure being built and thereby reducing comprehension and test performance. Several of these have been demonstrated in experiments.

The detrimental effects of scrambling or reordering sentences have been documented by Frase (1970), Thorndyke (1975), Wolk (1974), Bruning (1970), and Meyers and Boldrick (1975), among others. A problem with these studies is that the reordering of sentences in a passage is an extremely gross manipulation which can have a number of different effects depending on the nature of the passage. Such reordering typically disrupts the old-new information structure of the passage, as well as other cohesion devices; it destroys some of the passage content typically communicated by sentence order, such as temporal and causal relations (Goetz, 1975); it disrupts reference; and it distributes related information farther apart in the passage, so it is impossible to add each new bit of information incrementally to a growing, coherent structure. As would be expected, Kissler and Lloyd (1973; see also Goetz, 1975) found that the amount of performance decrement produced by reordering sentences depends upon both the nature of the passage (its cohesion pattern, in this case) and the nature of the test (the degree to which it requires knowledge only of fragments of the passage structure which are communicated by individual sentences). Perhaps future studies will be more delicate in manipulating specific aspects of the cohesion pattern in text and will observe the particular effects produced in retention.

It is also possible to make reference in the passage so ambiguous that the reader cannot establish a coherent representation; the referents of nouns and the verb senses can be left ambiguous, and it can be unclear that two nouns in the passage are referring to the same concept. Bransford (Bransford & Johnson, 1973; Bransford & McCarrell, 1974; Johnson, Doll, Bransford, & Lapinski, 1974) and Dooling (Dooling & Lachman, 1971; Dooling & Mullet, 1973) have carried out studies involving passages of this type and have found very poor recall. However, when a picture or title is given which provides the information necessary to specify reference and to identify the proper sense for parts of speech, the person, given some prior knowledge of the situation or event, has a feeling of comprehension, and test performance rises dramatically.

DeVilliers (1974) presented a list of sentences in a manner in which some people perceived them as a story and others did not. He found that when the sentences were perceived as a story, information most closely related to the theme was retained best, but when it was perceived as an unrelated list of sentences the imagery value of the sentences and their serial position were most closely related to recall.

In general, textual manipulations which reduce information useful to the reader in building a coherent representation of the content can be expected to reduce comprehension of the passage. In some cases, the reader's prior knowledge will compensate for loss of textual information, or relations may be identified on a problem-solving basis requiring greater reading time. In fact, the mental activity required in doing this may actually improve recall (Schumacher, Liebert, & Fass, 1975). The fact that syntactic complexity can result in slower reading probably has the same basis (Kintsch & Monk, 1972).

It should be noted that text variations designed to manipulate other variables may produce their effects because cohesion patterns in the text are being disrupted. Frase (1970) found poorer retention of a linear ordering when the text presented the elements in reverse order. This manipulation was achieved by simply reordering the sentences from the original passage. In the resulting passage, the topic of each sentence contained new information and the comment was a reference to old information; this is an extremely deviant discourse pattern and may be what produced the drop in retention. Manipulations of syntactic form can produce the same difficulty; for instance, changing the voice of sentences in a passage (Blount & Johnson, 1972) is likely to disrupt normal cohesion patterns, unless the passage has only minimal structure. Frase (1973) reports that subjects produced more confusions in recall when his text manipulation (made for another purpose) caused sentence topics to be inconsistent with the theme of the paragraph. Future research involving text manipulations must be much more sophisticated in controlling for discourse characteristics of the texts.

Staging

As indicated earlier, the same content can be written in the form of different texts which "stage" different parts of the content at higher or lower levels. Several studies have shown that this hierarchical characteristic of text structure is related to what people tend to retain. Meyer and McConkie (1973) used an outlining approach to reveal the hierarchical structure of a passage. They found that information higher in the structure was better retained and more stable from recall to recall, and co-occurrence among immediate neighbors in the structure was high (see also McKoon, cited by Kintsch, 1976). However, there was no relation between structural position and amount of increment produced by additional presentations of the passage.

Meyer (1975) took the further step of producing different passages which contained the same paragraph in the same physical location, but with information from that paragraph staged high in one passage and low in another. Total recall from the two passages was similar, but the target paragraph was recalled much better when staged high. This study overcomes Goetz's

(1975) criticism that the effect of staging position on recall may result from different types of content typically being staged high or low in a passage. Johnson (1970) established "structural importance" on the basis of a deletion scheme and found this related to recall, even with reading time controlled (also see Rickards & August, 1975).

Kintsch's (1974) technique for analyzing passages yields a hierarchical structure, and he has found that both within sentences (Kintsch & Keenan, 1973) and within a passage (Kintsch, 1976; Kintsch et al., 1975), higher elements tend to be better recalled. Clements (1976) separately tested the effects of three devices proposed by Grimes (1975) as producing staging variations—order of first mention, topic/comment sentence structure, and embedding—and found each to have a significant effect on both the likelihood of recalling the information and the likelihood of answering a question probing for the information.

Sasson (1971) organized sentences according to temporal sequence (according to date), name sequence (grouping together statements dealing with the same person), or thematic sequence (grouping sentences dealing with mental illness or light). The type of information around which the sentence list was organized tended to be recalled best.

There seems to be good evidence, then, that the staging of information in a passage has a substantial effect on what subjects tend to retain from it. A simple explanation might be that the staging features alert the reader to what is important in the passage, and this determines what a sophisticated reader retains (given that the reading is not being done with some other purpose in mind). However, Clements (1976) and Cohen (1973) failed to find a relation between staging and subjects' ratings of importance of passage segments. Meyer & McConkie (1973) found a relation for one passage but not for another. Johnson found such a relation with narrative texts (1970) but not for nonnarrative texts (1973). A striking aspect of these data is the degree of variability among subjects in the ratings given by them to the same passage segments. The mechanism by which staging produces its effect on retention has not yet been discovered.

Another set of studies manipulates the form of a passage while keeping the content constant, and then examines the effect this has on what is retained. These studies have employed simple passages which provide information about several objects of the same class (countries, sailing vessels, chessmen, etc.). Each sentence provides one fact about one of the objects. Related facts are given concerning each of the objects; that is, the passage indicates the typical weather of each country, its main agricultural crop, and so on. These facts are typically referred to as "attributes" by these researchers. Three versions of the passage are then constructed by reordering the sentences. In one version (object organization), sentences giving facts about the same object are grouped together to form each paragraph. In a second version (attribute organization), sentences stating related facts are grouped together into paragraphs; one paragraph may indicate the typical climate of each country, and the next may give the major industry of each. A third version (random organization) is produced by randomizing the sentences.

These studies have attempted to determine whether one form of sentence organization produces higher recall than another. Their results have been complex, but the following generalizations seem to have emerged. First, people prefer organizing the information by object rather than attribute (DiVesta, Schultz, & Dangel, 1973; Myers, et al., 1973; Perlmutter & Royer, 1973; Schultz & DiVesta, 1972). Second, although all three versions assert the same content structure, the nature of the cognitive representation of the information is heavily determined by the way the sentences are grouped (Frase, 1973; Myers, et al., 1973; Perlmutter & Royer, 1973). Third, while the presence of either type of organization has typically facilitated performance in comparison to random organization (see Myers et al., 1973, for an exception), the difference between object and attribute organization has not been consistent. In most studies, attribute organization has been found superior (Myers, et al.; Perlmutter & Royer; Schultz & DiVesta) though DiVesta et al. (1973) found this to interact with instructions given to the subject, and Frase (1973) found that under slightly different conditions object organization produced best performance.

In summary, there is sufficient evidence to indicate that the staging characteristics of a normal passage have a strong influence on what is retained from it. Information that is placed at higher levels in the staging structure is recalled substantially better.

Content

It has often been said that one tends to retain the "gist" of a passage, and researchers today may be coming closer to being able to identify the nature of the gist. A content structure representation of a passage tends to show some information as being central in maintaining the story line or theme of the passage, and other information as being more peripheral and not leading to further aspects of the content. Schank (1975) describes the more central strand as the causal chain and presents a beginning set of rules to define what will and will not be well recalled, based on content structure characteristics. Van Dijk and Kintsch (in press) speak of the macrostructure of the passage, believing this is what is contained in what would be accepted as a summary of the passage. It has typically been reported that attributive information is not retained as well as other aspects of the passage, such as names, actions, or causal relations (Gomulicki, 1956; Kintsch & Keenan, 1973; Meyer, 1975; Spencer, 1973). Since attributive information is ordinarily not part of the causal chain or central linking material in most passages, it is not clear whether its poor recall is due to the nature of the content or the structural position it typically occupies.

Characteristics of the content structure can also influence the likelihood that information not directly stated in the passage will be recalled or identified as being in it. Schank (1975) describes how gaps in the structure of the passage must be filled in on the basis of prior knowledge in order to make almost any passage comprehensible. Thorndyke (1975) has shown that unstated information which is needed to explain an occurrence later in the passage is likely to be identified as being stated in the passage (see also Bransford & McCarrell, 1974; Kintsch, 1976).

Schank (1975) also points out that where gaps the reader is unable to bridge exist in the content structure, the information is likely either to be ignored (see the poor recall of an unrelated sentence in a passage used by Bransford & McCarrell, 1974, p. 207), or to be marked with a "peculiarity marking" which makes it particularly well recalled. (Schank cites two parts of Bartlett's story "War of the Ghosts" which are probably well recalled on this basis.)

It seems likely that the investigation of content structure effects on retention and recall will be an active research area during the next decade, although it may prove difficult to separate entirely content effects from the effects of how the content is staged. It is also likely that the higher levels of text structure previously described (text grammars, episodic structure, etc.) will be found to be important in determining what is recalled; for examples, see Kintsch (1976), Gentner (1976), and Thorndyke (1975).

Certain aspects of the content itself, aside from its structure, have been found to affect what is retained. Information judged to be more concrete (Johnson, 1974; Philipchalk, 1972), more image-arousing (De Villiers, 1974; Morris & Reid, 1972; Paivio, 1971; Thorndyke, 1975), more specific in denotation (Johnson, 1974), and rated higher in interest value (Johnson, 1974) tend to be better recalled. Further investigation is needed to reveal the reasons for such effects.

Finally, the amount of information in a passage influences the likelihood of recalling any particular element in it. An element is less likely to be recalled from a longer passage (Newsom & Gaite, 1971; Spencer, 1973; Todd & Kessler, 1971). Having relatively more propositions in text of the same physical length slows reading (Kintsch & Keenan, 1973), and increasing density of new knowledge in the passage reduces the probability of recalling an element (Aiken, Thomas, & Shennum, 1975). With the number of propositions in a passage held constant but with more different arguments in these propositions, reading slows and retention drops (Kintsch et al., 1975).

Serial Position Effects

There has been a continuing interest in whether serial position effects (greater recall of information at the beginning and end of the passage) are found in learning from text as they have been in list learning. Meyer & McConkie (1973) and Goetz (1975) conclude that serial position effects are more likely to occur with passages showing minimal text structure. That is, the more the passage appears to be a list of relatively independent sentences, the more likely it is that consistent serial position effects will be found (e.g., see Russell & Sewall, 1972; Schumacher, Liebert, & Fass, 1975). The question of serial position effects is difficult to answer with more normal texts, since serial position is related to staging (Clements, 1976), and the type of information placed at the beginning and end of a passage often differs from that placed in the center (Goetz, 1975). Kintsch et al. (1975) found a primacy effect in their data which disappeared when height in the passage hierarchy was controlled. If a serial position effect is typical of retention from normal texts, it seems safe to say that it is small in comparison to the effects of various staging and content structure variables.

TASK STRUCTURE EFFECTS ON PROCESSING

Most of the studies reported during the period covered in this review have investigated the effects of various task variables on what people retain from a passage. In order to give some perspective to this research, we will now outline a more general framework within which to examine the research.

What a person retains from some learning task is a function of the task structure, the strategies adopted by the person to deal with the task, and the person's own skills and abilities. Among other things, the task structure consists of the constraints within which the person is acting (he can or cannot take notes, he is supposed to attempt to form images, etc.), the aspects of his performance which will be evaluated, and the relative weight given to these different aspects in coming to a final performance evaluation (whether it is more important to read quickly or to remember all the details). Researchers try to establish a task which will produce a particular type of behavior, and then they observe the results. In general, the subjects are very cooperative and try to maximize their own performance with respect to their perception of the task structure. In learning tasks, the results of the evaluations are usually taken as indices of the subjects' abilities or skills. People who recall more are assumed to have a better memory or a more effective encoding strategy.

There are several reasons why this assumption may be incorrect. First, the task structure may not be clear. In the face of ambiguity, different subjects are likely to adopt different strategies, essentially attempting to maximize behavior for different task structures. Thus the data patterns will reflect the distribution of strategies taken by the subjects, in addition to their skills and abilities, and this will add variability to the results. This phenomenon has been noted by Carver (1972) and Sanders (1973). Second, it may take a while for the subjects to develop their strategies. Thus task variables often do not have their full effect on the first trial or two (McConkie & Rayner, 1974). Third, subjects may not respond to the task structure in the way the experimenter anticipates, even when it is clear. Subjects undoubtedly differ in their willingness to abide by rules established by the experimenter, especially when they are perceived as inhibiting maximum performance on the outcome measures. Finally, subjects may have expectations which are not part of the task as defined by the experimenter. For instance, test-sophisticated subjects expect to be tested and usually have some notion of the type of test they might receive. Their expectations are important, of course, because they provide part of the perceived task structure within which the subjects attempt to maximize their behavior. The most critical part of defining an unambiguous task structure is making clear the basis for ultimate evaluation of the subjects' performance and convincing them that this is the goal toward which they should maximize their behavior.

The main point of this discussion is that the effect of variables in learning studies will depend primarily on their roles in the perceived task structure, rather than on their physical descriptions. For instance, researchers investigating the effects of adjunct questions, instructional objectives, underlining, or notetaking are likely to find that each factor has quite different effects under different conditions, depending on its perceived role in the task structure. In fact, one of the most serious flaws in much of the research on learning from text is that the role of many of these "adjunct aids" has been left ambiguous, allowing different subjects to make different assumptions about the roles they play, and thus they treat them in different ways (Carver, 1972). In designing learning studies it is necessary to decide whether the attempt is to study the subjects' best performance in a well-defined task situation, or how the subject tends to define the task for himself within the ambiguity left by the experimenter.

In reviewing the studies investigating the effects of task variables on learning from text, they will be grouped according to various manipulations of task structure which can be produced.

Modifying the Person's Expectations Concerning Evaluation

In studying learning from text, typically three aspects of performance may be evaluated: reading time, performance on some task during the learning period (e.g., answers to adjunct questions), and performance on some sort of final test. Final-test performance is the basis for evaluation used most often and probably the one that is most expected by subjects. Often there is no concurrent task providing a basis for evaluation, and time may be held constant in the study. Even though time is not mentioned to participants in a study, there is an expectation that subjects will not take more time than is necessary. Good readers are expected to read rather quickly, and subjects do not use extra time for such purposes as actually memorizing the passage.

In many studies nothing is said to the subjects about the nature of the evaluation; sometimes they are simply told to prepare for a test and are given no information about its nature. This, of course, introduces exactly the type of ambiguity in studies which was described earlier. Even when the experimenter explicitly attempts to describe the basis for evaluation, verbal instructions frequently fail to communicate effectively. It is difficult to indicate verbally the exact nature of the questions that will be in the test, or how fast one must read to finish a 500-word passage in three minutes. In addition, it is quite likely that the subjects will suspect some form of deception in such instructions. Even though they are told they will be tested only on information targeted by certain instructional objectives, they may suspect that retention of other information also will be tested, which may well be true.

A more effective technique for establishing the expectations desired is to have the subjects participate in the experiment several times under constant conditions (for instance, consistently being tested only on information targeted by the objectives). This would allow them to identify the nature of the task structure more precisely and give them a basis for adjusting their activities to maximize their performance. Once the desired set has been well established, the subject is tested on the last passage read in all the ways desired for the study.

Few studies of this type have actually been done, but the available examples are quite instructive. McConkie and Rayner (1974) and McConkie and Meyer (1974) demonstrated people's willingness and ability to increase their reading speed when they knew that was part of the evaluation. McConkie, Rayner, and Wilson (1973) demonstrated that subjects anticipating different types of tests (e.g., recognition of words and phrases, or questions interrogating explicitly stated information, "higher order" information, or structural information) read at different rates and obtained different information from the same passages. However, they did not always perform best on the types of questions they anticipated. Watts and Anderson (1971) demonstrated that subjects can acquire information necessary to identify new instances of a principle when they anticipated a test of this sort. This task is performed much more poorly by those who expect to be asked to recognize names or examples used in the text.

In another study involving repeated testing, Frederiksen (1975a) had subjects read and free recall a passage four times. One group had been told that they would later be asked to apply the information in the passage to the solution of a particular problem. While there was little difference among the groups in the amount of accurate information recalled from the passage, there was a substantial difference in the amount of modified and intruded information contained in their recalls. Anticipating the problem-solving task changed the degree to which the subjects produced inferences and related textual information to other knowledge.

A basic problem with most of the studies to be described from here on is that they engaged the subjects in the task only once or twice. Since the task structure therefore undoubtedly failed to exert its full possible effect, underestimation of the possible power of the experimental manipulations was likely.

A second way of manipulating what subjects will anticipate being evaluated on is to tell them the basis for evaluation in the study. This can be done by such devices as providing a list of objectives or indicating that they will be tested only on underlined information (Crouse & Idstein, 1972). The unanimous finding of these studies is that subjects perform better on tests interrogating this "targeted" information than on those questioning other information in the passage, and better than subjects for whom no information was targeted (Crouse & Idstein, 1972; Frase & Kreitzberg, 1975; Kaplan, 1974; Kaplan & Rothkopf, 1974; Kaplan & Simmons, 1974). In various studies acquisition of the nontargeted information by subjects, compared to a control group, has been facilitated, inhibited, or unaffected. These differences undoubtedly reflect characteristics of the individual studies. For example, if it is not easy to find the targeted information, the subject will probably reread the passage more times in searching for it, and this is likely to increase retention of nontarget information. It is likely that if the targeted information is easily identifiable, and the subjects are convinced that other information is irrelevant to the task, they will be selective in their learning. Increased retention of the targeted information will then be at the expense of the other information presented in the text.

Several variables have been found to influence the likelihood that a question interrogating information targeted by an objective will be answered correctly. If a larger number of sentences has been targeted, this reduces the likelihood that any particular question will be answered correctly (Crouse & Idstein; Kaplan & Rothkopf), though passage length itself has no effect. And the more general the objective, the smaller the effect. Objectives can be made more general in two ways: they can specify only one element in the passage but be stated in a general manner (Frase & Kreitzberg), or they can be broadened to specify multiple elements (Kaplan & Rothkopf). The former probably makes it more difficult to find the relevant information, and the latter makes it more likely the subject will unknowingly fail to find all the relevant elements. When objectives relevant to individual segments of the text are placed just before individual segments of the passage rather than being grouped together at the beginning, the normal facilitation still occurs and may even be enhanced (Kaplan, 1974). When objectives state the information being targeted ("Find that Columbus discovered America" vs. "Find who discovered America"), they are less effective when placed at the beginning of the passage, since they reduce the need to read it, and more effective when placed at the end, probably because they call for extra review of the information.

It should be pointed out that most of the objectives used in these studies so far have been of a very low-level type, typically targeting a specific phrase in a particular sentence. In fact, the lists of objectives can become practically as long as the passages (Kaplan & Rothkopf). In these studies there is an almost perfect correlation between the test performance and the amount of time the groups of subjects spend in reading the passage.

Two studies have investigated the effects of having certain parts of the text underlined but not informing the subjects about the reason for the underlining. Fowler and Barker (1974) found better retention of the underlined information, but Rickards and August (1975) did not. It is not surprising that people do not consistently retain underlined information better than other information when they do not know whether it is more likely to be tested.

A large number of studies have investigated the effect of placing questions prior to or following the text, without specifying the role of the questions in the task structure. This makes the results difficult to interpret and should lead to differences in subject strategies and in results of the studies.

Anderson and Biddle (1975), who reviewed a number of these studies, reported that questions placed prior to the text (called prequestions) consistently led to increased performance on these or closely related questions, and often to decreased performance on other questions (see also Boker, 1974; Boyd, 1973; Bull & Dizney, 1973; Frase, 1975; Felker & Dapra, 1975; Hiller, 1974; Sanders, 1973; Shavelson, Berliner, Ravitch, & Loeding, 1974; Swenson & Kulhavy, 1974). These results suggest that many subjects base their reading on the assumption that these questions are especially likely to occur once again in a final test, and thus they serve much the same function as the objectives discussed earlier. At the very least, they are probably taken to indicate the type of information to be tested. Felker and Dapra (1975) reported that questions worded similarly to the text ("verbatim" questions) produced greater facilitation than questions in paraphrased language, though this was not found with children (Swenson & Kulhavy, 1974). Whether questions were "higher order" or "lower order" in nature had no effect, and there was no transfer to other questions of the same type; facilitation was found only on those questions that appeared with the text (Shavelson et al., 1974). Questions designed specifically to arouse curiosity may have a particularly facilitative effect (Bull & Dizney, 1973).

Questions which follow relevant sections of the text (called postquestions) cannot direct subjects to specific text content with the same precision as prequestions or instructional objectives given before reading can. Still, they might be expected to have several effects. Most obviously, they provide a review of the specific information being interrogated and greatly enhance the likelihood it will be retained on a later test (Anderson & Biddle, 1975; Boker, 1974; Boyd, 1973; Eischens, Gaite, & Kumar, 1972; Frase, 1975; Frase & Schwartz, 1975; Koran & Koran, 1975; LaPorte & Voss, 1975;

Rothkopf & Billington, 1974; Rothkopf & Bloom, 1970; Sanders, 1973; Swenson & Kulhavy, 1974; Walker, 1974; and many others). Felker and Dapra (1975) showed that performance on questions usually missed could be greatly improved this way; Hiller (1974) found that students preferred studying without questions; and Snowman and Cunningham (1975) found the same effect when students draw pictures to answer questions rather than writing the answers out. These results of the use of postquestions are typically referred to as the backward effect of questions.

If postquestions are consistently of the same identifiable type, they also could indicate to subjects the nature of the information which seems to be of most interest to the experimenter and thus is most likely to be tested. This would of course influence the type of information subjects would seek from passages they encounter later. Such questions could also provide a quality control check whereby the reader could determine whether her or his reading strategy is providing the information necessary to answer questions of this sort. Such effects as these are referred to as the forward effects of questions, since processing on later materials is being affected.

Anderson and Biddle (1975) report inconsistent results from study to study with respect to whether the postquestioning technique facilitates performance on test questions other than those that appeared in the text. A majority of the studies they reviewed showed a facilitation effect. However, most of the studies since 1970 which have appeared in the journals have found an inhibitory effect, in comparison with an appropriate no-question control group. The ambiguity in the task structure (as previously explained) and the fact that subjects typically participated only once in the task suggest that these studies do not reveal the full effects which the presence of postquestions is capable of exerting. I am confident that with proper structuring of the task and of the relation between postquestions and questions on the final test, substantial effects of either a facilitative or inhibitory nature could be produced.

The type and location of postquestions have been found to influence learning in some studies. These influences have usually been limited to performance on the same questions appearing later on the test rather than other questions. It might be expected that postquestions of a higher order type, requiring some integration of passage information, would produce more general facilitation than questions directly interrogating information presented in individual sentences, but neither Allen (1970) nor Shavelson et al. (1974) found such an effect. Felker and Dapra (1975) did find an effect on a problem-solving task using information from the passage, but not on test questions themselves. Sanders (1973) found no facilitation at all from his "general" postquestions. In the same vein, it might be expected that postquestions which are almost verbatim from the text (but converted into question form) might be less facilitative than those that are in paraphrase form and perhaps require added processing of the text in order to answer. Swenson and Kulhavy (1974) found no such effect, and Anderson and Biddle (1975) found verbatim postquestions to be most effective, but only on later testing of those same questions. This point will be discussed more fully below. How frequently questions are inserted in the text has not been found to have an effect on test performance for new questions which do not occur in the text (Anderson & Biddle, 1975; Eischens et al., 1972; Koran & Koran, 1975).

Notetaking and underlining might be seen as tasks in which subjects reveal to the experimenter the information they expect is most likely to be tested. Rickards and August (1975) report that subjects tend to underline information of high structural importance, which (as indicated in an earlier section) is the information most likely to be recalled. A related finding is that when various subjects are asked to write questions on a passage, they all tend to produce questions that interrogate the same information from the text.

In summary, it appears that subjects (most of whom are college undergraduates) have expectations about what type of information is likely to be tested and the likely basis for evaluation in the experiment. However, these expectations can be readily modified by giving subjects experience in a particular task structure, telling them what will be tested, or giving the task characteristics which might be thought to indicate the nature of the later evaluation. Subjects seem quite willing and able to change their learning strategies in response to task structure characteristics. Such changes are reflected in terms of reading time and in what and how much is retained from a passage.

Modifying Perceptions of the Relative Weights of Different Outcomes

In addition to modifying subjects' expectations of what they are to be evaluated on, it is possible to manipulate the relative value placed on different aspects of their performance. When greater weight is given to reading speed, the result is much faster reading. Interestingly enough, speeding up reading can have very little effect on test performance on questions of the type subjects expect (Himelstein & Greenberg, 1974; McConkie & Meyer, 1974; McConkie & Rayner, 1974), but performance is reduced on other types of questions and on questions testing complex logical material (Keesey, 1973; McConkie et al., 1973). Under normal testing situations, subjects apparently tend to give greater weight to test performance than to reading speed (McConkie & Rayner, 1974). If greater weight is placed on the ability to answer postquestions by requiring that they be answered orally to the experimenter (Rothkopf & Bloom, 1970) or be written out and thus available to public inspection rather than simply thought about (Anderson & Biddle, 1975), the effects of postquestions on performance are increased.

Recent psychological research has frequently found that asking subjects to give more weight to one aspect of a task results in poorer performance on another. This finding has led to the notion of limited channel capacities,

but Spelke, Hirst, and Neisser (in press) have voiced a warning in this literature. Their study showed that with sufficient practice, subjects can learn to
write down one message while reading another, and without producing a
drop in their retention of the passage read. Researchers must be careful
not to assume fixed limitations in their subjects before they have been given
the opportunity to develop the strategies and abilities necessary to carry
out complex tasks.

Modifying the Expected Result of the Evaluation

Research is greatly simplified by the willingness of most people to try to
maximize their performance according to the structure defined by the experimenter. Attempting to increase general motivation by paying people for their
performance tends to have very little effect under these conditions (McConkie
& Rayner, 1974; McConkie & Meyer, 1974), though the effect may be greater
in experiments that engage the subjects in groups or over longer periods of
time. Of course, what it is that people are paid for can exert a great effect,
since this helps define the structure of the task.

An excellent example of what happens when subjects are not willing to
exert their best effort is provided by Lahey, McNees, & Brown (1973). Two
sixth-graders who read orally at the sixth-grade level but whose comprehension was substantially below that level were compared with two other sixth-
graders whose oral reading and comprehension levels were both at grade
level. Each pair of students read a series of passages and was tested after
each one. The poor comprehenders consistently scored much lower than
the other students, and this established the baseline level for comprehension.
Next the students were "reinforced" with praise and a penny for each correct
answer. Immediately the performance of the poor comprehenders rose to
the level of the good comprehenders, who showed no similar rise. After a
number of passages, the reinforcement was withdrawn, and within a few
passages the performance of the poor comprehenders had dropped almost
to baseline level once again. Again no change occurred with the other students.
When reinforcement was reinstituted, the two pairs of subjects again were
indistinguishable. Thus, the poor comprehenders were simply students who
were unwilling to abide by the normal rules of the testing situation; as a
result, they were improperly described as having poor comprehension ability.
How widespread this problem is in our schools, we do not know.

Besides making sure that the task is well defined for the subjects, it is
important for the researcher to ensure that their cooperation has been engaged
if their best performance in the situation is to be secured. In general, this
is not a problem for short-term laboratory research studies using adult volunteers, though it may in fact be the major problem of education in the normal
school situation.

Modifying the Nature of the Task

A principle which has become commonplace in psychological theorizing is that what one retains from a stimulus can more profitably be conceived as some encoding of the stimulus, rather than as a copy of the stimulus itself (Tulving & Thomson, 1973). For instance, the title of an ambiguous passage can bias one's interpretation of the meaning of the passage and thus affect what is retained from it (Schallert, 1975). Craik and Lockhart (1972) have suggested that what subjects retain from carrying out a task is determined by the requirements of the task; in particular the task may require different levels of processing. Tasks that require subjects to attend primarily to surface characteristics of the text typically result in poorer retention of the message (Howe, Ormond, & Singer, 1974; Schallert, 1975), while tasks that require finer semantic distinctions to be made are likely to result in increased recall (Frase, 1975).

The task can also influence the frequency with which particular information in a passage will be encountered (Frase, 1969, 1970, and studies described earlier dealing with postquestions), and how long certain information must be kept in mind in order to meet the task requirements (Frase & Silbiger, 1970). These characteristics of the task affect the likelihood that different aspects of the passage will be retained.

It has been thought that the type of processing required in underlining while reading or notetaking while listening might improve retention. DiVesta and Gray (1972, 1973) described and provided evidence for two possible facilitating effects of notetaking: to aid encoding of information when it is encountered, and to provide a basis for later review. Aiken et al. (1975) reviewed studies on notetaking while listening and indicated that its facilitating effects are generally restricted to studies in which subjects could use the notes for review. These researchers, together with Fisher & Harris (1974a, 1974b), reported no facilitative effects when review was not permitted, and Peters (1972) documented an interfering effect from notetaking. Schultz and DiVesta (1972) found that when subjects were allowed to make notes while reading, the tendency to organize information cognitively in the same form it was presented in the text was reduced; thus notetaking can facilitate cognitive reorganization of information during reading or listening. Underlining during reading, with opportunity for review prior to the test, has a facilitative effect (Fowler & Barker, 1974). However, any general facilitative effect from underlining is probably due not simply to the act of underlining itself but to the type of processing required for carrying out the task. Rickards and August (1975) report that underlining substantially increased reading time (from 9 to 16 minutes), and asking subjects to underline sentences stating information that was low in structural importance depressed general recall of the passage. Much remains to be learned about the effects of these common learning-aid practices.

It is clear that the type of task subjects engage in can substantially influence what they are likely to remember. The obvious relevance of this fact to practical problems of education should motivate considerable research to explore this phenomenon further. However, detailed data will be required to provide a basis for theorizing about the processes characteristic of different tasks involving learning from text. Changes in scores on a single achievement test will usually not be very revealing. Detailed analysis of what was retained, or of fine-grained characteristics of the subjects' behavior as they are learning, has not been typical of past research on learning from text.

Modifying the Nature and Timing of Information Presented

Repeated presentations of a passage increase the amount of information retained from it (Meyer & McConkie, 1973; Meyers & Boldrick, 1975). Gentner (1976) attempted to identify on which trial a previously unrecalled segment of a passage is most likely to be recalled. He found that this tends to occur when one of its neighbors (either serially in the passage, or in a story-grammar structure) has been recalled previously. The notion that successive presentations result in a gradually growing, cohesive cognitive representation of the information from the passage is an appealing one and needs further investigation.

Frederiksen (1975a, 1975b) has shown that the types of errors subjects make change over passage repetitions. He reports that in free recalls some types of changes tend to increase in frequency with passage repetitions and are probably occurring during encoding of the passage. Other changes, notably intrusions and elaborations, tend to decrease and are probably occurring during the recall process itself. Howe (1970) also noted a tendency for certain types of errors made on one recall to perseverate on later recalls, even when subjects received additional presentations of the text during the interval. Simply encountering the original information again is not always sufficient to cause a person to recognize and correct errors in his cognitive representation.

Presenting specific segments of information from a previously read text provides a review of that information and increases its likelihood of being retained (see Anderson & Biddle, 1975). The increment is generally specific to the repeated information, though Rothkopf and Billington (1974) found some increment for other information that was adjacent in the passage and closely related semantically. Postquestions following a passage can provide such a review, if the subjects can recall the answers when seeing the questions. Anderson and Biddle report that two factors influence the likelihood of post-questions being answered correctly: question timing and question wording. Decreasing the time between when subjects encounter the information and receive the postquestions increases the likelihood a correct answer will be given, and thus the enhancement the postquestions will produce on a later test is increased. Wording postquestions in a manner similar to the text also increases the likelihood they will be answered correctly, and this also increases scores on a later test.

It is not always necessary to depend on the subjects' abilities to answer questions. A statement of the information can be presented instead of a question, but Anderson and Biddle report this has less effect than questions (see also Kaplan & Simmons, 1974). Or the correct answer to the question can be provided after the subject's response; Rothkopf and Bloom (1970) found this greatly increases correct answers on a later test. LaPorte and Voss (1975) found that such feedback has no effect on questions initially answered correctly, and only those initially answered incorrectly are enhanced; thus this effect is primarily corrective in nature. Delaying the feedback concerning correct answers to questions also facilitates later test scores (see Sassenrath, 1975); this is a case where immediate feedback has no advantage over delayed feedback (Sassenrath & Spartz, 1972). Sturges (1972) reports that the nature of the feedback and the way subjects respond to it also produce effects.

King (1971, 1972, 1973, 1974) has investigated whether the amount retained from a passage (typically in terms of specific words and word sequences) is a direct function of the amount of learning time available, regardless of how that time is distributed. King's results have sometimes supported the total-time hypothesis (Cooper & Pantle, 1967) and sometimes have not. Studies have also attempted to determine whether oral or visual presentation of textual materials results in superior learning. Again, the results have been mixed (File & Jew, 1973; Sanders, 1973).

In summary, the beneficial effects of review have been demonstrated repeatedly, but we still have much to learn about the mechanisms by which it occurs and how to maximize its effects.

Asking Subjects to Adopt Different Strategies

A large amount of research has been conducted with word lists and other materials which ask subjects to employ various strategies (e.g., forming images or using various mnemonic techniques) in their learning. These studies have found substantial differences in what is retained. In learning from text, the primary manipulation of this sort has been to ask subjects to form mental images of the information in the text. Anderson and Kulhavy (1972), Montague and Carter (1973), and Lesgold, McCormick, and Golinkoff (1975) report no facilitation from imagery instructions, though the first of these studies found that subjects who reported using imagery to a greater extent recalled somewhat more information. Rasco, Tennyson, and Boutwell (1975) did find facilitation, and Levin (1973) found it for some readers but not others. Lesgold et al. trained third- and fourth-graders to draw stick-figure cartoons about a passage, in an attempt to increase visual imagery for passage information. This training produced no general facilitation of retention from a later passage, but when trained subjects were told to use imagery, their retention rose considerably. Steingart (1975) found that whether instructions to form images facilitated retention depended upon the way the passage was structured.

Apparently, instructions to form images during reading or listening can produce differences in what information is stored, or perhaps in the form of the representation. To foreshadow a theme to be developed later, it would probably be more useful in the long run to investigate the nature of the changes in what people retain from a passage, which are produced by imagery instructions, rather than to continue to conduct studies which simply ask whether imagery instructions result in better performance on a general retention test.

Comments Concerning Task Structure Effects

The studies which have been reviewed in this section reveal the reader/listener to be an active processor of information, rather than simply a receiver and storer of a copy of the stimulus. We encounter the text and adjust our processing activities in response to the task structure provided by the experimenter. We are quite able to modify both our reading speed and the operations we perform on the text as required to meet the demands of the task. The nature of these activities determines what is retained by affecting what is encoded, whether certain information receives repeated exposures, what information we attempt to retain, how much time is given to the task, and so on. When we are reading/listening for text meaning, we can primarily attend to certain parts of the message rather than others if we want to. There is still much to learn about the mechanisms by which these activities are accomplished, but the knowledge gained so far about the general effects of task characteristics on performance seem to have many practical applications.

In studying learning from text, as in all research, it is important to be clear about the goal of the research, and two distinctions must be kept in mind. The first is whether the research is aimed at directly identifying which combination of variables maximizes learning of some particular sort or at revealing information about the mental processes involved in the learning. The former may be called the educational goal of research and the latter the psychological goal. While the two contribute to each other, they often require somewhat different approaches to the research. If the educational goal is adopted, as seems to have been the case with many of the studies on effects of questions, objectives, imagery, and so on, it is critical for the experimenter to give careful consideration to the nature of the objective toward which he is attempting to maximize performance. If nonimportant objectives are used and his research shows how to maximize behavior with respect to them, he will have accomplished very little. Many tests used in such research seem to assume that the objective is for the person to know equally well every assertion stated in the passage. A critical need for this type of research is to give more consideration to what it is important to retain from the passages studied, for various educational purposes.

If the psychological goal for the research is adopted (which I believe will contribute to the educational goal in the long run), the second distinction to be made is whether the experimenter wishes to understand the subjects' "normal" processing (if such exists) or what they do when they are maximally motivated. I suspect that most of our research is not appropriate for investigating what people normally do as they read and listen. If people respond so readily to task structure variables as has been suggested above, then the very fact that they are engaged in a study will affect their performance. To investigate normal performance will require great ingenuity to find task structure conditions similar to those that hold in normal life situations. Certainly just asking someone to "read the way you normally do" falls far short of providing a normal task structure for the subject who knows that his behavior is being monitored and that he will undoubtedly be tested for retention on what he is reading.

Thus, the question which can most readily be investigated when subjects are aware that they are participating in a study concerns the nature of their mental activities when carrying out a task to the best of their ability: the study of their maximal performance. To do this well the researcher must take into account two considerations. First, to encourage participants to show their maximal performance, a clear, unambiguous task structure must be used. Second, the measures used must be capable of providing information about the nature of the subjects' mental activities. This means that test questions should be carefully selected to reveal something about the cognitive processing, or a data source should be used, such as free recall, which provides sufficiently rich information to make it possible to discern patterns related to cognitive processing. A study yielding only one mean score for each of two or three groups does not provide much information and is useful only if it is carefully designed to provide exactly the information needed to bear on some specific issue concerning the cognitive processes.

INFLUENCE OF EXTRATEXTUAL INFORMATION
ON PROCESSING AND RETENTION

Besides the factors which define the task for the subject (instructions, etc., as discussed in the preceding section), there is other, extratextual information which plays an important role in the processing and retention of information from text. This can include such specific factors as related information the reader/hearer might have previously read or heard or may read or hear later, or it may be as general as the textual patterns characteristic of the culture. Rumelhart's story grammars are an attempt to demonstrate the influences of such cultural factors, as was Meyers and Boldrick's (1975) study of how the Americanization of an Eskimo story failed to improve retention.

The reader's prior knowledge provides an important part of the "context" for a passage. How the information communicated meshes with the person's existing knowledge must play a most important role in determining what is retained. If a passage is said to be about a well-known person (e.g., Hitler, Keller), subjects show poorer recognition of sentences from it, and false positive recognition errors are made on sentences which are not from the passage but which describe commonly known information about the person (Sulin & Dooling, 1974). Passage information which is generally consistent with what one already knows on some topic becomes integrated with existing knowledge and may be difficult to separate from it during the test. Readers also tend to select as accurate those sentences that are so worded as to be biased in the direction presumed to be typical of the speaker (Wertsch, 1975). Whether this reflects a difference in what is understood from the passage or the use of all available information during the test is not presently known. But knowledge of the source certainly affects what the subject later identifies as coming from the passage.

Studies investigating general transfer effects from the learning of one set of materials to the learning of another have met with varied degrees of success. In one of the most extensive studies, Deno, Jenkins, and Marsey (1971) found little nonspecific transfer from extensive training about EKG patterns and the types of abnormalities they signal to retention from a related passage. Other studies failing to find a general transfer effect include Voss (1974) and Wulf (1974). Royer and Cable (1975) report that reading a concrete passage facilitated retention from an abstract passage relating the same information, but there was no facilitation from the abstract to the concrete. While effects of advanced organizers (Ausubel, 1968) are still being reported, they seem to interact with individual differences in ways that are not consistent across studies (Allen, 1970; Proger, Taylor, Mann, Coulson, & Bayuk, 1973).

Researchers have tended to be more successful in demonstrating specific transfer effects, based on carefully designed specific similarities between passages, than in obtaining general transfer effects. Thorndyke (1975) reports that when people read two passages with the same plot structure, recall of the second is depressed, whereas if two passages have the same set of participants, recall of the second is enhanced, in comparison to appropriate control conditions. A number of studies have demonstrated retroactive inhibition with learning from text. Some of these are reviewed by Cunningham (1972), who points out that the critical factor in whether retroactive inhibition is produced is the nature of the similarity between the passages. Similarity in

topic or paragraph headings is not sufficient (Wong, 1970), though this sometimes produces inhibition (Jensen & Anderson, 1970). Gillman (1970) found
retroactive inhibition with passages judged by subjects to be on similar topics.
However, most studies have followed the example of Crouse (1970, 1971)
and have used passages which explicitly provide different answers to the
same questions. Reading a second such passage consistently reduces retention
of the first (Andre, 1972; Van Mondfrans, Hiscox, & Gibson, 1973); Kalbaugh
and Walls (1973) also demonstrated proactive inhibition. Anderson and Myrow (1971) and Bower (1974) demonstrated both retroactive inhibition and retroactive facilitation, depending on whether the passages provided
identical or incompatible answers to questions (see also Walker, 1974). Myrow
and Anderson (1972) report the disappearance of retroactive inhibition when
the alternatives in multiple-choice questions did not include information from
the interfering passage, suggesting that the results are of a response-competi-
tion sort. However, these researchers also expressed doubts about the importance of RI in learning from text if it is found only under such restricted
circumstances (Myrow & Anderson, 1972).

In a paper which will likely spawn a flurry of studies, Spiro (1975) reported
that information provided in an offhand manner by the experimenter to subjects who had just read a passage had a substantial influence on their later
recall if they did not expect a test, but little effect if they did. Subjects
who expected a test apparently succeeded in keeping this additional information distinct from that in the passage itself. Spiro claims that the learning
set typically induced in laboratory research is highly artificial, in that the
person seeks to keep the information learned separate from his normal knowledge structures. Thus, Spiro claims, virtually all research which has been
done on learning from text has failed to investigate the normal knowledge
acquisition processes.

When the dust has settled on this issue, we will likely appreciate more
fully the fact that learners can vary in the degree to which they attempt to
remember the source of information they receive. Further, retention of this
source influences what information they attempt to integrate into free recall
or the generation of an answer to a question. It seems unlikely that either
attempting or not attempting to retain the source of the information will
be found to be a more "natural" condition.

RETRIEVAL PROCESSES

What people retrieve from their cognitive representation of information
from a passage depends, of course, not only on what is retained but also
upon the nature of the cues provided. The free-recall task typically provides
the least cue information, and hence it produces the lowest recall levels for
specific information from a passage (Sehulster & Crouse, 1972).

In the free-recall task the subject is engaged in language generation from his Knowledge Base, so many characteristics of the recalls reflect this generation process. Sentences are likely to occur in more common syntactic forms (Bock & Brewer, 1974; File & Jew, 1973). If cues are provided, they are likely to be fronted, or placed in topic position, in the sentences (Perfetti & Goldman, 1975). Thus changes of form from the original passage to recall may reflect any of a number of different factors, such as a change in emphasis, syntactic changes required due to information loss (if the agent is forgotten, the sentence is likely to appear in passive form), or a change in the cohesion pattern required by a modification in the order in which information is being recalled. Similarity between passage and recall does not necessarily indicate that the syntactic structure was retained; it may simply indicate that the information retained, together with the emphasis and cohesion patterns adopted, were similar to those of the original writer.

It has already been noted that questions using the exact wording of the text are more effective as cues than are paraphrased questions, but this difference tends to disappear with time (Anderson & Biddle, 1975). This indicates the loss of effectiveness of textual surface structure characteristics as retrieval cues.

In general we know very little about the retrieval processes involved in accessing information from complex cognitive structures such as those required to represent information from normal passages. Of particular interest is the possibility that specific retrieval or more general free recall of a passage is being directed by a general conception of the structure of the information, such as the information represented in Rumelhart's (1975) text grammar categories or Van Dijk's (1973) macrostructures.

EFFECTS OF INDIVIDUAL DIFFERENCES ON WHAT IS RETAINED

Many studies investigating learning from text have included measures of the subjects' IQ's, verbal abilities, or reading abilities. Practically all have found better test performance for higher ability subjects. In addition, higher verbal ability subjects benefit more from feedback on questions initially answered incorrectly (Surber & Anderson, 1974). There is a higher correlation between verbal ability and immediate test performance for paraphrase than for "verbatim" questions (Anderson & Biddle, 1975). Better readers produce longer free recalls containing more idea units, more identical words, and more eight-word sequences from the original passage (Todd & Kessler, 1971).

Higher self-confidence is related to better retention (Hiller, 1974), and subjects tend to score higher on tests for those passages on which they indicate a greater interest (Howe & Evans, 1973). Howe and Evans also note the many problems with this type of research. The effects of anxiety have been mixed: Hiller found "facilitating anxiety" to be positively correlated with retention test scores, and "debilitating anxiety" to be negatively correlated, but Johnsen, Hohn, & Dunbar (1973) did not find that trait anxiety affected test performance or interacted with task difficulty.

Ausubel and Schwartz (1972) identified the degree to which subjects tended to write down general principles rather than examples of the principles when asked to indicate what they obtained from a passage. Using this score to separate subjects into generalizers vs. particularizers, they found generalizers scored highest on a multiple-choice test on questions interrogating specific details in the passage and those dealing with inferences and interpretive information. Contrary to what one might expect, the generalizers scored particularly well on detail questions; particularizers scored equally well on both types.

Rohwer and Harris (1975) conducted an extensive study investigating what media forms produce best retention with children of high and low socioeconomic status (SES) backgrounds, comparing written, oral, and picture presentations in all combinations. Low–SES children showed highest scores on all types of tests when a combination oral and picture presentation was used, but high–SES children showed different patterns, depending on the nature of the test.

Several studies have been conducted in an attempt to find out which students would benefit from having questions interspersed in the text. Sanders (1973) found that students having high rather than low grade point averages benefited most from questions occurring immediately after the text, though this difference was not maintained on a delayed test. Shavelson et al. (1974) found no aptitude-treatment interaction with a hidden-figure test, letter span, anxiety test, or ability to remember and transform verbal information. However, subjects obtaining a low score on a vocabulary test (which correlates with verbal ability) were aided by higher order questions following test segments, while the same questions lowered retention for students having high vocabulary scores. In studies cited by Shavelson et al., Berliner (1971) found that inserting questions in the text raised test scores for subjects with low memory ability, but not for those with high memory ability, and Hollen (1970) reported retention to be positively related to memory ability when there were no questions, but negatively related when questions were present. Koran and Koran (1975) report an aptitude-treatment interaction between vocabulary and associative memory scores and question placement, for information not related to the inserted questions. No such effect was found for question-relevant information. It appears that a great deal of basic research on distinguishing types of questions, characteristics of passages, effects of task conditions, and processes involved in obtaining and retrieving information from text will be necessary before we can make much sense of many of these results.

In such a complex area, it is particularly important to attempt to understand the full effects of the variables, rather than simply investigating their effects on a particular test score. Frederiksen (1975b) provides an example of such an attempt. He measured a number of abilities in his subjects which he thought to be related to different aspects of text processing. His subjects were given one of three tasks: reading a passage to recall it, reading it in preparation for solving a specific problem, or both. He then analyzed their free recalls, obtaining indexes of the amount of information correctly recalled and the frequency of several types of modifications (overgeneralization, inference, elaboration, and pseudodiscrimination). His results are very complex, seeming to argue against the existence of a single comprehension ability and for highly specific processes involved in learning from text. Different abilities come into play to varying degrees when subjects carry out different tasks, and over repetitions of the same task, and these abilities are also related to different response measures. One consistent finding in Fredericksen's data is that reasoning ability is positively related to the amount of veridical information produced in free recall and negatively related to the amount of elaborative material produced. Thus, comprehending and retrieving the information without distortion seems to be a task highly dependent on one's reasoning ability and is not a simple copying-reproduction process.

A GLIMPSE AT THE FUTURE

The study of learning from text is rapidly becoming a more complex, and a much more interesting, domain for investigation. Today it finds itself right in the center of a newly developing coalition among the fields of education, psychology, linguistics, and computer science. Attempts are being made to bring forth a new discipline called cognitive science in which concern for language processing and learning in man and machine is one focus of activity (see Bobrow & Collins, 1975). Thus concerns which were previously the domain of educational psychologists are now being carefully studied by people from several disciplines. Each is making its unique contribution, and there is real cross-disciplinary interaction. It seems obvious that the primary beneficiary of the advancement of knowledge about language processing and learning will be the field of education, whether the research comes from psychology, linguistics, or artificial intelligence.

Much of the initial impetus for these new directions has come from linguists and computer scientists. Now, however, there is a need for empirical, descriptive studies which yield detailed facts about people as they learn and retrieve information from text, facts which will put constraints on what may be taken as acceptable theories. Much of the research of the past has avoided this type of information and has instead relentlessly sought individual methods of increasing retention, while bypassing understanding of the nature of the mental activity involved. Hundreds of studies of this sort can be carried out without making a significant contribution to our understanding of the mental processes involved in learning from text. Instead, we end up with a box score indicating how many studies found that a particular manipulation makes some improvement in people's scores on a general retention test. This reveals practically nothing about the nature of the learning processes, and it even provides little information about the conditions under which the manipulation used might be expected to produce a fairly reliable positive effect.

The promise offered by the new directions being taken in research on learning from text is the possibility of coming to understand the mental activities involved in comprehension and learning. Such knowledge will permit us to make wise decisions about preparing materials for educating people and for teaching them how to gain information from text efficiently. Research on the cognitive processes involved in learning from text will quickly make contact with work on reading and on instruction and should contribute to these areas. In fact, there is a renewed recognition of the importance of the "ecological validity" of the types of tasks studied by psychologists, who in the past have often spurned the need for research to have potential applications (see comments made by Restle, 1974; J. R. Anderson, 1976; and Neisser, 1976). This view of research is drawing more researchers toward a concern for the types of issues that previously were almost exclusively the domain of education. This broadening of psychology will make it more likely that the knowledge gained will have real potential for useful application. All this portends well for the study of learning from text, and for the likelihood of producing knowledge which will be beneficial to the educator.

REFERENCES

Aiken, E. G., Thomas, G. S., & Shennum, W. A. Memory for a lecture: Effects of notes, lecture rate and informational density. *Journal of Educational Psychology,* 1975, *67,* 439-444.

Allen, D. I. Some effects of advance organizers and level of question on the learning and retention of written social studies material. *Journal of Educational Psychology,* 1970, *61,* 333-339.

Anderson, J. R. *Language, memory and thought.* Hillsdale, N.J.: Lawrence Erlbaum Associates, 1976.

Anderson, J. R., & Bower, G. H. *Human associative memory.* Washington: Winston & Sons, 1973.

Anderson, R. C. How to construct achievement tests to assess comprehension. *Review of Educational Research,* 1972, *42,* 145-170.

Anderson, R. C., & Biddle, W. B. On asking people questions about what they are reading. *Psychology of learning and motivation* (Vol. 9). New York: Academic Press, 1975.

Anderson, R. C., & Kulhavy, R. W. Imagery and prose learning. *Journal of Educational Psychology,* 1972, *63,* 242-243.

Anderson, R. C., & Myrow, D. L. Retroactive inhibition of meaningful discourse. *Journal of Educational Psychology,* 1971, *62,* 81-94.

Andre, T. Retroactive inhibition of prose and change in physical or organizational context. *Psychological Reports,* 1972, *32,* 781-782.

Ausubel, D. P. *Educational psychology: A cognitive view.* New York: Holt, Rinehart & Winston, 1968.

Ausubel, D. P., & Schwartz, F. G. The effects of a generalizing-particularizing dimension of cognitive style on the retention of prose material. *Journal of General Psychology,* 1972, *87,* 55-58.

Barclay, J. R. The role of comprehension in remembering sentences. *Cognitive Psychology,* 1973, *4,* 229-254.

Bartlett, F. C. *Remembering: A study in experimental and social psychology.* Cambridge: Cambridge University Press, 1932.

Begg, I., & Paivio, A. Concreteness and imagery in sentence meaning. *Journal of Verbal Learning and Verbal Behavior,* 1969, *8,* 821-827.

Berliner, D. C. Aptitude-treatment interaction in two studies in learning from lecture instruction. 1971. (ERIC Document Reproduction Service No. ED 046 249).

Blount, H. P., & Johnson, R. E. *The influence of imagery on the recall of sentences in prose.* Paper presented at the meeting at the American Educational Research Association, Chicago, February 1972.

Bobrow, D. G. Dimensions of representation. In D. G. Bobrow & A. Collins (Eds.), *Representation and understanding: Studies in cognitive science.* New York: Academic Press, 1975.

Bobrow, D. G., & Collins, A. *Representation and understanding: Studies in cognitive science.* New York: Academic Press, 1975.

Bock, J. K., & Brewer, W. F. Reconstructive recall in sentences with alternative surface structures. *Journal of Experimental Psychology,* 1974, *103,* 837-843.

Boker, J. R. Immediate and delayed retention effects of interspersing questions in written instructional passages. *Journal of Educational Psychology,* 1974, *66,* 96-98.

Bormuth, J. R. *On the theory of achievement test items.* Chicago: University of Chicago Press, 1970.

Bormuth, J. R., Manning, J., Carr, J., & Pearson, D. Children's comprehension of between- and within-sentence syntactic structures. *Journal of Educational Psychology,* 1970, *61,* 349-357.

Bower, G. H. Selective facilitation and interference in retention of prose. *Journal of Educational Psychology,* 1974, *66,* 1-8.

Boyd, W. M. Repeating questions in prose learning. *Journal of Educational Psychology,* 1973, *64,* 31-38.

Bransford, J. D., Barclay, J. R., & Franks, J. J. Sentence memory: A constructive versus interpretive approach. *Cognitive Psychology,* 1972, *3,* 193-209.

Bransford, J. D., & Franks, J. J. Abstraction of linguistic ideas. *Cognitive Psychology,* 1971, *2,* 331-350.

Bransford, J. D., & Franks, J. J. The abstraction of linguistic ideas: A review. *Cognition,* 1972, *1,* 211-249.

Bransford, J. D., & Johnson, M. K. Considerations of some problems of comprehension. In W. G. Chase (Ed.), *Visual information processing.* New York: Academic Press, 1973.

Bransford, J. D., & McCarrell, N. S. A sketch of a cognitive approach to comprehension: Some thoughts about understanding what it means to comprehend. In W. B. Weimer & D. S. Palermo (Eds.), *Cognition and the symbolic processes.* Hillsdale, N.J.: Lawrence Erlbaum Associates, 1974.

Bruning, R. H. Short-term retention of specific factual information in prose contexts of varying organization and relevance. *Journal of Educational Psychology,* 1970, *61,* 186-192.

Bull, S. G., & Dizney, H. F. Epistemic curiosity-arousing prequestions: Their effect on long-term retention. *Journal of Educational Psychology,* 1973, *65,* 45-49.

Carroll, J. B. Learning from verbal discourse in educational media: A review of the literature. 1971 (ERIC Document Reproduction Service No. ED 058 771).

Carver, R. P. A critical review of mathemagenic behaviors and the effect of questions upon the retention of prose materials. *Journal of Reading Behavior,* 1972, *4,* 93-119.

Chafe, W. L. *Meaning and structure of language.* Chicago: University of Chicago Press, 1970.

Clark, H. H. Difficulties people have in answering the question "Where is it?" *Journal of Verbal Learning and Verbal Behavior,* 1972, *11,* 265-277.

Clements, P. *The effects of staging on recall from prose.* Unpublished doctoral dissertation, Cornell University, 1976.

Cofer, C. N. A comparison of logical and verbatim learning of prose passages of different lengths. *American Journal of Psychology,* 1941, *54,* 1-20.

Cohen, F. P. *The effects of different instructional sets on ratings of importance and recall from prose passages.* Master's thesis, Cornell University, 1973.

Cooper, E. C. & Pantle, A. J. The total time hypothesis in verbal learning. *Psychological Bulletin,* 1967, *68,* 221-234.

Craik, F. I. M., & Lockhart, R. S. Levels of processing: A framework for memory research. *Journal of Verbal Learning and Verbal Behavior,* 1972, *11,* 671-684.

Crothers, E. J. *Paragraph structure description* (Report No. 40). Boulder, Colo.: Program on Cognitive Factors in Human Learning and Memory, University of Colorado. 1975.

Crouse. J. H. Transfer and retroaction in prose learning. *Journal of Educational Psychology,* 1970, *61,* 226-228.

Crouse, J. H. Retroactive interference in reading prose materials. *Journal of Educational Psychology,* 1971, *62,* 39-44.

Crouse, J. H., & Idstein, P. Effects of encoding cues on prose learning. *Journal of Educational Psychology,* 1972, *63,* 309-313.

Cunningham, D. J. The retention of connected discourse: A review. *Review of Educational Research,* 1972, *42,* 47-71.

Dawes, R. M. Memory and distortion of meaningful written material. *British Journal of Psychology,* 1966, *57,* 77-86.

Deno, S. L., Jenkins, J. R., & Marsey, J. Transfer variables and sequence effects in subject-matter learning. *Journal of Educational Psychology,* 1971, *62,* 365-370.

De Villiers, P. A. Imagery and theme in recall of connected discourse. *Journal of Experimental Psychology,* 1974, *103,* 263-268.

DiVesta, F. J., & Gray, G. S. Listening and notetaking. *Journal of Educational Psychology,* 1972, *63,* 8-14.

DiVesta, F. J., & Gray, G. S. Listening and note taking: II. Immediate and delayed recall as functions of variations in thematic continuity, note taking, and length of listening-review intervals. *Journal of Educational Psychology,* 1973, *64,* 278-287.

DiVesta, F. J., Schultz, C. B., & Dangel, T. R. Passage organization and imposed learning strategies in comprehension and recall of connected discourse. *Memory and Cognition,* 1973, *1,* 471-476.

Dooling, D. J., & Lachman, R. Effects of comprehension on retention of prose. *Journal of Experimental Psychology,* 1971, *88,* 216-222.

Dooling, D. J., & Mullet, R. L. Locus of thematic effects in retention of prose. *Journal of Experimental Psychology,* 1973, *97,* 404-406.

Eischens, R. R., Gaite, A. J. H., & Kumar, V. K. Prose learning: Effects of question position and informational load interactions on retention of low signal value information. *Journal of Psychology,* 1972, *81,* 7-12.

Felker, D. B., & Dapra, R. A. Effects of question type and question placement on problem-solving ability from prose material. *Journal of Educational Psychology,* 1975, *67,* 380-384.

File, S. E., & Jew, A. Syntax and the recall of instructions in a realistic situation. *British Journal of Psychology,* 1973, *64,* 65-70.

Fillmore, C. J. The case for case. In E. Back and R. T. Harms (Eds.), *Universals in linguistic theory.* New York: Holt, Rinehart & Winston, 1968.

Finn, P. J. A question writing algorithm. *Journal of Reading Behavior,* 1975, *7,* 341-367.

Fisher, J. L., & Harris, M. B. Effect of note-taking preference and type of notes taken on memory. *Psychological Reports,* 1974, *35,* 384-386.

Fisher, J. L., & Harris, M. B. Note taking and recall. *Journal of Educational Research,* 1974, *67,* 291-292.

Fowler, R. L., & Barker, A. S. Effectiveness of highlighting for retention of text material. *Journal of Applied Psychology,* 1974, *59,* 358-364.

Franks, J. J. Toward understanding understanding. In W. B. Weimer & D. S. Palermo (Eds.), *Cognition and the symbolic processes.* Hillsdale, N. J.: Lawrence Erlbaum Associates, 1974.

Frase, L. T. Structural analysis of the knowledge that results from thinking about text. *Journal of Educational Psychology Monograph,* 1969, *60,* 1-16.

Frase, L. T. Influence of sentence order and amount of higher level text processing upon reproductive and productive memory. *American Education Research Journal,* 1970, *7,* 307-319.

Frase, L. T. Integration of written text. *Journal of Educational Psychology,* 1973, *65,* 252-261.

Frase, L. T. Prose processing. *Psychology of learning and motivation* (Vol. 9). New York: Academic Press, 1975.

Frase, L. T., & Kreitzberg, V. S. Effects of topical and indirect learning directions on prose recall. *Journal of Educational Psychology,* 1975, *67,* 320-324.

Frase, L. T., & Schwartz, B. J. Effect of question production and answering on prose recall. *Journal of Educational Psychology,* 1975, 67, 628-635.

Frase, L. T., & Silbiger, F. Some adaptive consequences of searching for information in a text. *American Educational Research Journal,* 1970, *7,* 553-560.

Frederiksen, C. H. Acquisition of semantic information from discourse: Effects of repeated exposures. *Journal of Verbal Learning and Verbal Behavior,* 1975, *14,* 158-169.

Frederiksen, C. H. Effects of context-induced processing operations on semantic information acquired from discourse. *Cognitive Psychology,* 1975, *7,* 139-166.

Frederiksen, C. H. Representing logical and semantic structure of knowledge acquired from discourse. *Cognitive Psychology,* 1975, *7,* 371-458.

Gauld, A., & Stephenson, G. M. Some experiments relating to Bartlett's theory of remembering. *British Journal of Psychology,* 1967, *58,* 39-44.

Gentner, D. R. The structure and recall of narrative prose. *Journal of Verbal Learning and Verbal Behavior,* 1976, *15,* 411-418.

Gillman, S. I. Retroactive inhibition in meaningful verbal learning as a function of similarity and review of interpolated material. *Journal of General Psychology,* 1970, *82,* 51-56.

Goetz, E. T. *Sentences in lists and in connected discourse* (Tech. Rep. 3). Urbana, Ill.: University of Illinois, Laboratory for Cognitive Studies in Education, 1975.

Gomulicki, B. R. Recall as an abstractive process. *Acta Psychologica,* 1956, *12,* 77-94.

Griggs, R. A. Logical errors in comprehending set inclusion relations in meaningful text (Rep. 74-7). (Bloomington: Indiana Mathematical Psychology Program, Department of Psychology, Indiana University, 1974.)

Griggs, R. A. The recall of linguistic ideas. *Journal of Experimental Psychology,* 1974, *103,* 807-809.

Grimes, J. *The thread of discourse.* The Hague: Mouton, 1975.

Halliday, M. A. K. Notes on transitivity and theme in English, Pts. 1 and 2. *Journal of Linguistics,* 1967, *3,* 37-81, 199-244.

Halliday, M. A. K. Notes on transitivity and theme in English, Pt. 3. *Journal of Linguistics,* 1968, *4,* 179-215.

Hiller, J. H. Learning from prose text: Effects of readability level, inserted question difficulty, and individual differences. *Journal of Educational Psychology,* 1974, *66,* 202-211.

Himelstein, H. C., & Greenberg, G. The effect of increased reading rate on comprehension. *Journal of Psychology,* 1974, *86,* 251-259.

Hollen, T. T. *Interaction of individual abilities with the presence and position of adjunct questions in learning from prose materials.* Unpublished doctoral dissertation, University of Texas at Austin, 1970.

Howe, M. J. A. Repeated presentation and recall of meaningful prose. *Journal of Educational Psychology,* 1970, *61,* 214-219.

Howe, M. J. A., & Evans, L. Role of task interest in learning from prose passages. *Perceptual and Motor Skills,* 1973, *36,* 951-957.

Howe, M. J. A., Ormond, V., & Singer, L. Recording activities and recall of information. *Perceptual and Motor Skills,* 1974, *39,* 309-310.

Hunt, E. B. *Artificial intelligence.* New York, Academic Press, 1975.

Jarvella, R. J. Syntactic processing of connected speech. *Journal of Verbal Learning and Verbal Behavior,* 1971, *10,* 409-416.

Jarvella, R. J., & Herman, S. J. Clause structure of sentences and speech processing. *Perception and Psychophysics,* 1972, *11,* 381-384.

Jensen, L., & Anderson, D. C. Retroactive inhibition of difficult and unfamiliar prose. *Journal of Educational Psychology,* 1970, *61* (4, Pt. 1), 305-309.

Johnsen, E. P., Hohn, R. L., & Dunbar, K. R. The relationship of state-trait anxiety and task difficulty to learning from written discourse. *Bulletin of the Psychonomic Society,* 1973, *2,* 89-90.

Johnson, M. K., Bransford, J. D., & Solomon, S. K. Memory for tacit implications of sentences. *Journal of Experimental Psychology,* 1973, *98,* 203-205.

Johnson, M. K., Doll, T. J., Bransford, J. D., & Lapinski, R. H. Context effects in sentence memory. *Journal of Experimental Psychology,* 1974, *103,* 358-360.

Johnson, R. E. Recall of prose as a function of the structural importance of the linguistic unit. *Journal of Verbal Learning and Verbal Behavior,* 1970, *9,* 12-20.

Johnson, R. E. Abstractive processes in the remembering of prose. *Journal of Educational Psychology,* 1974, *66,* 772-779.

Johnson, R. E. *Dimensions of textual prose and remembering.* Paper presented to the meeting of the American Educational Research Association. New Orleans, February 1973.

Kalbaugh, G. L., & Walls, R. T. Retroactive and proactive interference in prose learning of biographical and science materials. *Journal of Educational Psychology,* 1973, *65,* 244-251.

Kaplan, R. Effects of learning prose with part vs. whole presentations of instructional objectives. *Journal of Educational Psychology,* 1974, *66,* 787-792.

Kaplan, R., & Rothkopf, E. Z. Instructional objectives as directions to learners: Effect of passage length and amount of objective-relevant content. *Journal of Educational Psychology,* 1974, *66,* 448-456.

Kaplan, R., & Simmons, F. G. Effects of instructional objectives used as orienting stimuli or as summary review upon prose learning. *Journal of Educational Psychology,* 1974, *66,* 614-622.

Katz, S. Role of instructions in abstraction of linguistic ideas. *Journal of Experimental Psychology,* 1973, *98,* 79-84.

Katz, S., Atkeson, B., & Lee, J. The Bransford-Franks linear effect: Integration or artifact? *Memory and Cognition,* 1974, *2,* 709-713.

Katz, S., & Gruenewald, P. The abstraction of linguistic ideas in "meaningless" sentences. *Memory and Cognition,* 1974, *2,* 737-741.

Keesey, J. C. Memory for logical structure and verbal units in prose material at increased rates of presentaton. *Psychological Reports,* 1973, *33,* 419-428.

King, D. J. On the accuracy of written recall: A scaling and factor analytic study. *Psychological Record,* 1960, *10,* 113-122.

King, D. J. Scaling the accuracy of recall of stories in the absence of objective criteria. *Psychological Record,* 1961, *11,* 87-90.

King, D. J. Influence of interitem interval in the learning of connected discourse. *Journal of Experimental Psychology,* 1971, *87,* 132-134.

King, D. J. Temporal factors involved in the learning of connected discourse. *Journal of General Psychology,* 1972, *87,* 187-194.

King, D. J. Presentation time and method of reading in the learning of connected discourse. *Journal of General Psychology,* 1973, *88,* 283-289.

King, D. J. Total presentation time and total learning time in connected discourse learning. *Journal of Experimental Psychology,* 1974, *10,* 586-589.

Kintsch, W. Memory for prose. In E. Tulving & W. Donaldson (Eds.), *The organization of memory.* New York: Academic Press, 1972.

Kintsch, W. *The representation of meaning in memory.* Hillsdale, N.J.: Lawrence Erlbaum Associates, 1974.

Kintsch, W. Memory for prose. In C. N. Cofer (Ed.), *The structure of human memory.* San Francisco: W. H. Freeman, 1976.

Kintsch, W., & Keenan, J. Reading rate and retention as a function of the number of propositions in the base structure of sentences. *Cognitive Psychology,* 1973, *5,* 257-274.

Kintsch, W., Kozminsky, E., Streby, W. J., McKoon, G., & Keenan, J. M. Comprehension and recall of text as a function of content variables. *Journal of Verbal Learning and Verbal Behavior,* 1975, *14,* 196-214.

Kintsch, W., & Monk, D. Storage of complex information in memory: Some implications of the speed with which inferences can be made. *Journal of Experimental Psychology,* 1972, *94,* 25-32.

Kissler, G. R., & Lloyd, K. E. Effect of sentence interrelation and scrambling on the recall of factual information. *Journal of Educational Psychology,* 1973, *64,* 187-190.

Kolers, P. A. Remembering trivia. *Language and Speech,* 1974, *17,* 324-336.

Koran, M. L., & Koran, J. J. Interaction of learner aptitudes with question pacing in learning from prose. *Journal of Educational Psychology,* 1975, *65,* 76-82.

Lahey, B. B., McNees, M. P., & Brown, C. C. Modification of deficits in reading for comprehension. *Journal of Applied Behavior Analysis,* 1973 *(6),* 475-480.

LaPorte, R. E., & Voss, J. F. Retention of prose materials as a function of postacquisition testing. *Journal of Educational Psychology,* 1975, *67,* 259-266.

Lesgold, A. M., McCormick, C., & Golinkoff, R. M. Imagery training and children's prose learning. *Journal of Educational Psychology,* 1975, *67,* 663-667.

Levin, J. K. Inducing comprehension in poor readers: A test of a recent model. *Journal of Educational Psychology,* 1973, 65, 19-24.

McConkie, G. W., & Meyer, B. J. F. Investigation of reading strategies: II. A replication of payoff condition effects. *Journal of Reading Behavior,* 1974, *6,* 151-158.

McConkie, G. W., & Rayner, K. Investigation of reading strategies: I. Manipulating strategies through payoff conditions. *Journal of Reading Behavior,* 1974, *6,* 9-18.

McConkie, G. W., Rayner, K., & Wilson, S. J. Experimental manipulation of reading strategies. *Journal of Educational Psychology,* 1973, *65,* 1-8.

Meyer, B. J. F. *The organization of prose and its effect on memory.* The Hague: Mouton, 1975.

Meyer, B. J. F., & McConkie, G. W. What is recalled after hearing a passage? *Journal of Educational Psychology,* 1973, *65,* 109-117.

Meyers, L. S., & Boldrick, D. Memory for meaningful connected discourse. *Journal of Experimental Psychology: Human Learning and Memory,* 1975, *1,* 584-591.

Miller, G. A., & Johnson-Laird, P. N. *Language and perception.* Cambridge: Harvard University Press, 1976.

Minsky, M. A framework for representing knowledge. In P. H. Winston (Ed.), *The psychology of computer vision.* New York: McGraw-Hill, 1975.

Montague, W. E., & Carter, J. F. Vividness of imagery in recalling connected discourse. *Journal of Educational Psychology,* 1973, *64,* 72-75.

Morris, P. E., & Reid, R. L. Imagery and the recall of adjectives and nouns from meaningful prose. *Psychonomic Science,* 1972, *27,* 117-118.

Myers, J. L, Pezdek, K., & Coulson, D. Effect of prose organization upon free recall. *Journal of Educational Psychology,* 1973, *65,* 313-320.

Myrow, D. L., & Anderson, R. C. Retroactive inhibition of prose as a function of the type of test. *Journal of Educational Psychology,* 1972, *63,* 303-308.

Neisser, U. *Cognition and reality: Principles and implications of cognitive psychology.* San Francisco: W. H. Freeman, 1976.

Newell, A. Production systems: Models of control structures. In W. G. Chase (Ed.), *Visual information processing.* New York: Academic Press, 1973.

Newsom, R. S., & Gaite, J. H. Prose learning: Effects of pretesting and reduction of passage length. *Psychological Reports,* 1971, *28,* 123-129.

Norman, D. A., Rumelhart, D. E., & the LNR Research Group. *Explorations in cognition.* San Francisco: W. H. Freeman, 1975.

Paivio, A. *Imagery and verbal processes.* New York: Holt, Rinehart & Winston, 1971.

Perfetti, C. A., & Goldman, S. R. Discourse functions of thematization and topicalization. *Journal of Psycholinguistic Research,* 1975, *4,* 257-271.

Perlmutter, J., & Royer, J. M. Organization of prose materials: Stimulus, storage, and retrieval. *Canadian Journal of Psychology,* 1973, *27,* 200-209.

Peters, D. L. Effects of note taking and rate of presentation on short-term objective test performance. *Journal of Educational Psychology,* 1972, *63,* 276-280.

Petofi, J. S., & Reiser, H. *Studies in text grammar.* Dordrecht, Netherlands: Reidel, 1973.

Pezdek, K., & Royer, J. M. The role of comprehension in learning concrete and abstract sentences. *Journal of Verbal Learning and Verbal Behavior,* 1974, *13,* 551-558.

Philipchalk, R. P. Thematicity, abstractness, and the long-term recall of connected discourse. *Psychonomic Science,* 1972, *27,* 361-362.

Potts, G. R. Memory for redundant information. *Memory and Cognition,* 1973, *1,* 467-470.

Potts, G. R. Artificial logical relations and their relevance to semantic memory. *Journal of Experimental Psychology,* 1976, *2,* 746-758.

Proger, B. B., Taylor, R. G., Mann, L., Coulson, J. M., & Bayuk, R. J. Conceptual prestructuring for detailed verbal passages. *Journal of Educational Research,* 1970, *64,* 28-34.

Pylyshyn, Z. W. What the mind's eye tells the mind's brain: A critique of mental imagery. *Psychological Bulletin,* 1973, *80,* 1-24.

Rasco, R. W., Tennyson, R. D., & Boutwell, R. C. Imagery instructions and drawings in learning prose. *Journal of Educational Psychology,* 1975, *67,* 188-192.

Restle, F. Critique of pure memory. In R. L. Solso (Ed.), *Theories in cognitive psychology: The Loyola Symposium.* Hillsdale, N.J.: Lawrence Erlbaum Associates, 1974.

Rickards, J. P., & August, G. J. Generative underlining strategies in prose recall. *Journal of Educational Psychology,* 1975, *67,* 860-865.

Rohwer, W. D., Jr., & Harris, W. J. Media effects on prose learning in two populations of children. *Journal of Educational Psychology,* 1975, *67,* 651-657.

Rose, R. G., Rose, P. R., King, N., & Perez, A. Bilingual memory for related and unrelated sentences. *Journal of Experimental Psychology: Human Learning and Memory,* 1975, *1,* 599-606.

Rothkopf, E. Z. Incidental memory for location of information in text. *Journal of Verbal Learning and Verbal Behavior,* 1971, *10,* 608-613.

Rothkopf, E. Z., & Billington, M. J. Indirect review and priming through questions. *Journal of Educational Psychology,* 1974, *66,* 669-679.

Rothkopf, E. Z., & Bloom, R. D. Effects of interpersonal interaction on the instructional value of adjunct questions in learning from written material. *Journal of Educational Psychology,* 1970, *61* (6, Pt. 1), 417-422.

Royer, J. M., & Cable, G. W. Facilitated learning in connected discourse. *Journal of Educational Psychology,* 1975, *67,* 116-123.

Rumelhart, D. Notes on a schema for stories. In D. Bobrow and A. Collins (Eds.), *Representation and understanding: Studies in cognitive science.* New York: Academic Press, 1975.

Rumelhart, D. E., Lindsay, P., & Norman, D. A. A process model for long-term memory. In E. Tulving and W. Donaldson (Eds.), *Organization of memory.* New York: Academic Press, 1972.

Russell, G. W., & Sewall, E. C. Serial-position effect and organization of recall of connected meaningful verbal material. *Psychological Reports,* 1972, *30,* 443-446.

Sachs, J. S. Recognition memory for syntactic and semantic aspects of connected discourse. *Perception and Psychophysics,* 1967, *2,* 437-442.

Sanders, J. R. Retention effects of adjunct questions in written and aural discourse. *Journal of Educational Psychology,* 1973, *65,* 181-186.

Sassenrath, J. M. Theory and results on feedback and retention. *Journal of Educational Psychology,* 1975, *67,* 894-899.

Sassenrath, J. M., & Spartz, L. R. Retention of reading material as a function of feedback time and testing. *California Journal of Educational Research*, 1972, *23*, 182-187.

Sasson, R. Y. Semantic organizations and memory for related sentences. *American Journal of Psychology*, 1971, *84*, 253-267.

Schallert, D. L. *Improving memory for prose: The relationship between depth of processing and context* (Tech. Rep. 5). Urbana, Ill.: University of Illinois, Laboratory for Cognitive Studies in Education, 1975.

Schank, R. C. Conceptual dependency: A theory of natural language understanding. *Cognitive Psychology*, 1972, *3*, 552-631.

Schank, R. C. The structure of episodes in memory. In D. G. Bobrow & A. Collins (Eds.), *Representation and understanding: Studies in cognitive science*. New York: Academic Press, 1975.

Schank, R. C., & Colby, K. M. *Computer models of thought and language*. San Francisco: W. H. Freeman, 1973.

Schultz, C. B., & DiVesta, F. J. Effects of passage organization and note taking in the selection of clustering strategies and on recall of textual materials. *Journal of Educational Psychology*, 1972, *63*, 244-252.

Schumacher, G. M., Liebert, D. & Fass, W. Textual organization, advance organizers and retention of prose material. *Journal of Reading Behavior*, 1975, *7*, 173-180.

Sehulster, J. R., & Crouse, J. H. Storage and retrieval of prose material. *Psychological Reports*, 1972, *30*, 435-439.

Shavelson, R. J., Berliner, D. C., Ravitch, M. M., & Loeding, D. Effects of position and type of question on learning from prose material: Interaction of treatments with individual differences. *Journal of Educational Psychology*, 1974, *66*, 40-48.

Simmons, R. F. Semantic networks: Their computation and use for understanding English sentences. In R. C. Schank and K. M. Colby (Eds.), *Computer models of thought and language*. San Francisco: W. H. Freeman, 1973.

Simmons, R. F., & Bruce, B. C. Some relations between predicate calculus and semantic net representations of discourse. *Proceedings of the Second Joint International Conference on Artificial Intelligence*, MITRE Corp., 1971.

Singer, M., & Rosenberg, S. T. The role of grammatical relations in the abstraction of linguistic ideas. *Journal of Verbal Learning and Verbal Behavior*, 1973, *12*, (3), 273-284.

Snowman, J., & Cunningham, D. J. A comparison of pictorial and written adjunct aids in learning from text. *Journal of Educational Psychology*, 1975, *67*, 307-311.

Spelke, E., Hirst, W., & Neisser, U. Skills of divided attention. *Cognition*, in press.

Spencer, N. J. *Changes in representation and memory of prose*. Unpublished doctoral dissertation, Pennsylvania State University, 1973.

Spiro, R. J. Inferential reconstruction in memory for connected discourse (Tech. Rep. 2). Urbana, Ill.: University of Illinois, Laboratory for Cognitive Studies in Education, 1975.

Steingart, S. K. *The effects of image and text structure on what is learned from reading a passage*. Unpublished doctoral dissertation, Cornell University, 1975.

Sturges, P. T. Effect of instructions and form of informative feedback on retention of meaningful material. *Journal of Educational Psychology*, 1972, *63*, 99-102.

Sulin, R. A., & Dooling, D. J. Intrusion of a thematic idea in retention of prose. *Journal of Experimental Psychology*, 1974, *103*, 255-262.

Surber, J. R., & Anderson, R. C. The delay-retention effect in natural classroom settings. *Journal of Educational Psychology*, 1975, *67*, 170-173.

Swenson, I., & Kulhavy, R. W. Adjunct questions and the comprehension of prose by children. *Journal of Educational Psychology,* 1974, *66,* 212-215.

Thorndyke, P. W. *Cognitive structures in human story comprehension and memory.* Unpublished doctoral dissertation, Stanford University, 1975.

Todd, W. B., & Kessler, C. C., III. Influence of response mode, sex, reading ability, and level of difficulty on four measures of recall of meaningful written material. *Journal of Educational Psychology,* 1971, *62,* 229-234.

Tulving, E., & Thomson, D. M. Encoding specificity and retrieval processes in episodic memory. *Psychological Review,* 1973, *80,* 352-373.

Van Dijk, T. A. Text grammar and text logic. In J. S. Petofi & H. Reiser (Eds.), *Studies in text grammar.* Dordrecht, Netherlands: Reidel, 1973.

Van Dijk, T. A. *Text and context: Explorations in the semantics and pragmatics of discourse.* London: Longmans, 1977.

Van Dijk, T. A., & Kintsch, W. Cognitive psychology and discourse: Recalling and summarizing stories. In W. U. Dressler (Ed.), *Trends in text-linguistics.* Berlin: deGruyter, in press.

Van Mondfrans, A. P., Hiscox, S. B., & Gibson, G. L. Response requirement and nature of interpolated stories in retroactive inhibition in prose. *Journal of Experimental Education,* 1973, *42,* 85-87.

Voss, J. F. Acquisition and nonspecific transfer effects in prose learning as a function of question form. *Journal of Educational Psychology,* 1974, *66,* 736-740.

Walker, B. S. Effects of inserted questions on retroactive inhibition in meaningful verbal learning. *Journal of Educational Psychology,* 1974, *66,* 486-490.

Watts, G. H., & Anderson, R. C. Effects of three types of inserted questions on learning from prose. *Journal of Educational Psychology,* 1971, *62,* 387-394.

Weimer, W. B. Overview of a cognitive conspiracy: Reflections on the volume. In W. B. Weimer and D. S. Palermo (Eds.), *Cognition and the symbolic processes.* Hillsdale, N.J.: Lawrence Erlbaum Associates, 1974.

Wertsch, J. V. The influence of listener perception of the speaker on recognition memory. *Journal of Psycholinguistic Research,* 1975, *4,* 89-98.

Winograd, T. Understanding natural language. *Cognitive Psychology,* 1972, *3,* 1-191.

Wolk, S. The influence of meaningfulness upon intentional and incidental learning of verbal material. *Memory and Cognition,* 1974, *2,* 189-193.

Wong, M. R. Retroactive inhibition in meaningful verbal learning. *Journal of Educational Psychology,* 1970, *61,* 410-415.

Woods, W. A. What's in a link: Foundations for semantic networks. In D. G. Bobrow and A. Collins (Eds.), *Representation and understanding: Studies in cognitive science.* New York: Academic Press, 1975.

Wulf, K. M. A study of Ausubel's proactive hypothesis. *The Journal of Psychology,* 1974, *86,* 3-11.

Zangwill, O. L. *Remembering* revisited. *Quarterly Journal of Experimental Psychology,* 1972, *24,* 123-128.

Zechmeister, E. B., & McKillip, J. Recall of place on the page. *Journal of Educational Psychology,* 1972, *63,* 446-453.

Zechmeister, E. B., McKillip, J., Pasko, S., & Bespalec, D. Visual memory for place on the page. *Journal of General Psychology,* 1975, *92,* 43-52.

2

Graphics in Texts

Michael Macdonald-Ross
The Open University

To the scientific mind it is most annoying to have to deal with phenomena that cannot be formulated in a way that is satisfactory to intellect and logic.

Carl Jung

INTRODUCTION

The purpose of this review is to summarize what is known about the effective use of graphic devices in texts and other instructional materials. Information about graphic devices comes mainly from two sources: the experience of skilled graphic communicators and the formal laboratory experiments of applied psychologists. Both these sources have been consulted for this review. To keep it to a reasonable length I discuss what I think are the central issues and leave other questions untouched. It may be useful for researchers to consult the recent bibliography by Macdonald-Ross and Smith (1977), which lists all the relevant research known to me as I write this review.

Graphic devices have been invented by humans to help represent, explain, and control the world in which they live. Ordinary language (verbal and gestural) is our primary means of communication, but there are many tasks for which it is ill-suited. We cannot do without mathematical and musical notations, scientific diagrams, tables, and maps. Some such systems of representation are essential to us, as they have been to all civilized cultures since

LAWRENCE T. FRASE, National Institute of Education, and GEORGE R. KLARE, Ohio University, were the editorial consultants for this chapter.

I would like to thank Professor Brian Lewis and Dr. Tom Sticht for their helpful suggestions.

the first city-states. The relationship between language and graphics is complex and subtle; it deserves much more attention from scholars than it has so far received. Gombrich (1972) has spelled out some of the basic issues, and the broad history of graphic communication is given in Hogben (1949).

The first sentence of this review introduced some key terms that need clarification: *texts, graphic devices,* and *effective use.* A text is a printed or written book or document: marks on paper. The interest lies in what is being said (the content), how it is interpreted and used by readers, and how the organization of the content affects the reader. Thus this review deals with a matter of great general interest (how we communicate information to each other) in a special setting (the printed text and its reader). Much of the review also applies, with certain qualifications, to other media such as film, television, and computer graphics, though these connections will not be spelled out explicitly.

The term *graphics* is not exact, but it is still the best word to describe alternatives to prose. In this review *graphics* is meant to exclude ordinary language and its derivatives (such as poetry and Basic English). Also this review does not deal with decorative illustration, fine art, or advertisements. Many of the graphic devices dealt with here are pleasing to the eye, and no doubt this does help to attract attention and motivate the reader. However, the prime purpose of the devices discussed is to display conceptual information: numerical, logical, spatial, and temporal data. There is a world of culture that has been left out of this review, especially the classic arts of the book illustrator (Beardsley, 1893, and Rackham, 1911, are two superb examples; Bland, 1958, is a standard history of book illustration), and newspaper and magazine advertisements and wall posters. Comic strips are mentioned briefly, but the space accorded them scarcely does justice to their cultural significance. The body of the review deals with those graphs, charts, diagrams, notations, and other devices which are specially adapted for presenting scientific, technical, social, and commercial information.

The term *graphic device* refers to a particular diagram; the term *graphic format* refers to a family of devices, such as Cartesian graphs. The phrase *system of representation* refers to the context and rules of procedure associated with a graphic format: not just the marks on paper, but also the rules for construction and interpretation (whether explicit or implicit). Such rules include ways to decide whether a particular subject matter can be represented legitimately by a particular format. The area of legitimate use of a format is its *domain.* These brief definitions need further development; for example, the status of language associated with graphic devices has not been spelled out. Also, it should be noted that some graphic formats make use of more than one system of representation. These subtleties would need teasing out in any comprehensive theory of graphic communication.

The third key term to be clarified is *effective use.* Since the decorative connotations of graphics are considered here in a secondary role, fairly strong criteria of effectiveness can be adopted. For some graphic formats a straight-forward behavioral definition will do: The device is effective if and only if the user can perform some well-specified operation with its aid. Nomograms and algorithms are two such cases. Other formats aim at comprehension; the reader is meant to see general trends and relationships. Many scientific diagrams and tables of social statistics are of this type. In some cases the format is strongly directive (algorithms; Isotypes), but other formats allow the reader to interpret or use them in different ways (many maps and tables). This state of affairs is depicted in the simple 2 × 2 table presented as Table 1.

The test-items corresponding to the four cells, I, II, III, and IV, in Table 1, would have these characteristics:

Cell I. Items of high validity derived from task analysis; all items to be attempted by subjects; criterion test with pass mark set at an appropriately exacting level.

Cell II. Same as cell I, but subjects attempt only those items that are relevant to their purpose.

Cell III. Items of lower validity derived from experts; all items to be attempted by subjects; if criterion-based, pass level may be lower than in cells I and II; may be marked competitively in some cases.

Cell IV. Same as cell III, but subjects attempt only items relevant to their purpose.

Experimenters often try to raise the reliability of items in cells III and IV by setting rote-recall tasks. This seems unwise, for it makes it difficult to draw general inferences which would be useful in practical situations. It is worth remembering that the most usual purpose of graphic devices in cells III and IV is to display some general trend or other relationship; exact recall of numerical or other data is rarely required. This problem is familiar to those who construct comprehension tests in education: the tradeoffs between reliability and content validity are difficult to handle. To summarize: in some

TABLE 1
A Simple 2 × 2 Classification of Test Items

Control		AIMS Tasks	AIMS Comprehension
	Directive	I	III
	Reader selects	II	IV

cases the effectiveness of a graphic device can be tested rigorously and the results interpreted unambiguously (cells I and II), whereas in other cases the question of effectiveness may be less easy to decide (cells III and IV). This is important for the design of experiments and their interpretation by the practitioner.

The empirical studies to be discussed in this review have been tested against a severe criterion: Can practical communicators use the results, and can other researchers build upon them? These demands are met if work is directed toward a relevant question, valid in design and execution, properly reported, and robust when applied in the field. Since many experiments fail one or more of these tests, some work which others have taken at face value does get more skeptical treatment in this review.

The review also makes use of the tacit skills of expert graphic communicators, which constitute a valuable reservoir of prescientific knowledge. I have discussed the ideas in this review with many applied psychologists and graphic designers. It seems some psychologists believe that the only reliable source of knowledge is the controlled laboratory experiment, while designers often reject the idea of systematic empirical testing. However, it may be more useful to see these two traditions as complementary (see comments in Macdonald-Ross, 1977, Macdonald-Ross & Smith, 1977, and Macdonald-Ross & Waller, 1975a). An understanding of the practical art of graphic design can guide the researcher toward fruitful experiments and away from certain kinds of costly mistakes. The designer also has much to gain from empirical research; too often he fails to get usable feedback about the effect of his work, and he may unwittingly copy the bad practices of other designers.

According to certain books on methodology, one tests to eliminate false hypotheses but this does presuppose that one has grounds for generating the hypotheses in the first place. At this stage in the progress of graphic communication it is no easy matter to decide which hypotheses are crucial, or even to decide what the key variables are in a graphic device. Perhaps a more cogent reason for conducting tests is to *externalize* the hitherto tacit know-how of the acknowledged expert (the master performer) so that it can be talked about, criticized, and improved.

VISUAL PERCEPTION

Percepts are guesses.
Gregory

Research into visual perception has a long and distinguished history, so it is not unreasonable to hope that the results might be of some use to practising graphic designers. In an effort to cover such a broad field it is useful to make two simple distinctions. One can choose to look mainly at the established *results* of a science or at the *methods* of that science. Furthermore, one can look at the most *general* or universal aspect of a science or at its *particular* aspects.

These distinctions must be used with some circumspection, for a particular world-view will condition the researcher's choice of problem, and often it will determine the methods used to tackle the problem. Provided this is borne in mind, we can say that research into visual perception can contribute to the practice of instruction by providing for:

1*a*. Universal prescriptions based on the results.

1*b*. Particular prescriptions based on results of research into limited problems.

2*a*. General research methods useful for a wide range of problems.

2*b*. Special-purpose research methods for the solution of particular problems.

Universal Prescriptions

Under category 1*a* the work of Abercrombie (1960), Fleming (1970), and Travers (1970) should be noted. Abercrombie used Gestalt theory as the basis for a series of seminars designed to help medical students with their learning problems. These problems included both perceptual learning (e.g., diagnosing X-rays) and conceptual learning (e.g., meaning of key terms in clinical medicine). Abercrombie's book is full of examples taken from these seminars, with edited transcripts of the group discussions. It is the work of an inspired teacher. Nevertheless, we must ask an interesting question: Did this teacher's seminars derive from the prescriptive force of Gestalt psychology, or did they come from her experience and intuition, with the framework of theory added as a post hoc justification?

The book-length review by Travers (1970) covers in detail the contribution made by Shannon's information theory (Shannon & Weaver, 1949) to our knowledge of the human perceptual system. This is a valuable survey, but despite its subtitle—*A Primer for Media Specialists and Educational Technologists*—it is by no means clear how practitioners can use this knowledge. Take as one example the work on sensory channel capacity, which is one of the more fruitful contributions of information theory to psychology. In order to make use of information theory experiments must be designed to allow fairly rigorous quantitative inferences to be drawn. To achieve this end it is essential to eliminate the effects of prior knowledge and experience; hence the use of letters, numbers, and nonsense syllables as the raw "information." The experimenter's justification is the reasonable hope that the ultimate limits of channel capacity cannot be transcended, and these methods will discover those limits.

The trouble with this reasoning is that the notion of information is being used with two meanings (Weaver recognised this; see his discussion of three levels of communication in Shannon and Weaver, 1949; see also Green & Courtis, 1966; Johnson & Klare, 1961). No one doubts that there is a limit to the rate of transmission of nerve impulses and a limit to the rate these impulses can be decoded by the cortex. However, there is a huge difference in the significance of such a message according to the set and prior knowledge of the individual subjects. This commonsense observation was brought home with great force by the work of de Groot (1965, 1966) and is put thus by Simon (1969): "We now know that meaningfulness is a variable of great importance." Similar problems arise with the work on short-term memory, since the concept of "chunk" is so embarrassingly dependent on the subject's prior experience of the problem domain.

For our purposes, however, it is not necessary to reach any definite conclusions about the information-theoretic approach to perception research. It is sufficient to recognize that translation of the results into prescriptions is a nontrivial task which is fraught with pitfalls and difficulties. Is it reasonable to expect practical communicators to make that translation? I suspect not, and so does Travers, who cautions the reader not to expect to "receive the kind of help that research rarely can give." In Travers's opinion, basic research can give these benefits to the practitioner:

1. Provide a *vocabulary* so that practical problems can be discussed with more precision.
2. Enable the practitioner to *think more intelligently* about the problems he encounters.

Of course, a technical framework biases the way problems are selected and interpreted—with great benefit if the framework is appropriate, and with much wasted effort if it turns out to be inappropriate.

Fleming's Detailed Review. Fleming (1970) gives a detailed review of perception research and provides advice for the designers of instructional materials. This valuable source includes 61 research findings in eight chapters—a huge body of advice. Some issues are selected for comment below, though it is essential for serious students to consult the original review for detailed references.

Fleming's first chapter ("Man as Perceiver") covers these principles:

1. Man's perception is relative.
2. Man's perception is selective, organized, and influenced by set.
3. Stable individual differences in perception do exist.

In general, people do not perceive absolutes. However, our perceptual system is especially well adapted to making comparisons and distinctions. Such comparisons can be *explicit* (presented together side by side, as in Isotype charts) or *implicit* (the learner compares new knowledge with a similar situation drawn from memory). This is a good example of researchers and practitioners reaching the same solution independently, which naturally increases our confidence in the conclusion. The Isotype system is discussed later, but it is worth summarizing here Otto Neurath's central ideas on visual communication:

1. All visual communication is based on comparisons.
2. A visual statement is an explicit visual comparison.
3. A visual argument is a set of comparisons selected to make a teaching point.

These ideas are completely consistent with Fleming's first principle, though they were not derived from formal experiments in perception. Fleming's second and third principles are well treated in the standard textbooks, and they are made specific for the designer by Fleming in later chapters.

Fleming's second chapter ("Attention and Preattention") tackles an important subject, but the author runs into some difficult problems. "Man's attention is drawn to what is novel" is certainly true in some sense, but there is an apparent conflict with a previous principle, "Man perceives what he expects." Also, "Man's attention is drawn and held by complexity" runs counter to "The organization of a stimulus markedly influences the speed and accuracy of perception." I do not think Fleming succeeds in resolving these problems, and I am also not impressed by Vernon's solution: "In directing his attention, man seeks a balance between novelty and familiarity, between complexity and simplicity, between uncertainty and certainty" (Fleming's summary of Vernon, 1952).

The notion of "balance" used here by Vernon is, I suggest, a nonexplanation. People do attend sometimes to the novel and sometimes to the familiar; but apparently we do not have at present a satisfactory account of these differences in behavior. To get to the bottom of questions like this researchers should test not universal (yes/no) hypotheses but more limited when/when not questions. The practitioner needs to know *in what situations* a particular method is appropriate. Lacking such information, Fleming partially retrieves the situation with common sense: "Change or novelty should direct attention to the most relevant ideas in a message rather than the marginal or superficial."

Fleming's third and fourth chapters ("Perceptual Elements and Processing" and "Perception of Objects, Pictures and Words") deal with the processes that follow attention:

1. Apparent brightness and color can be influenced by adjacent brightness and color.
2. Magnitude of stimulus and magnitude of perceived effect are related, but not in simple linear form (see Weber's and Fechner's psychophysical laws of perception).

3. Certain stimulus features (contours, straight lines) are accentuated in perception, while others (uniform areas) are not.
4. Gestalt qualities (such as good figure) will be preferentially perceived.
5. Objects and pictures of objects are remembered better than their names, and concrete words are remembered better than abstract words.

These principles, which are well handled by Fleming, coincide with the kind of informal advice which is often given to teacher trainees and fledgling designers. For example, the maxim "Go from the concrete to the abstract, from the simple to the complex, and from the familiar to the unfamiliar" is a homely old recipe which is remarkably useful.

In his fourth chapter ("Objects, Pictures and Words"), Fleming runs into two further difficulties. The first concerns modalities, that is, the strengths and weaknesses of sight and hearing. Fleming's exact words are: "Vision is a sense that is superb for representing spatial distinctions but relatively poor for temporal. Audition is a sense that is superb for representing temporal distinctions but relatively poor for spatial." (p. 22.) Part of this generalization seems true: It is difficult to represent spatial knowledge in sound (probably no practical designer would try to do so). On the other hand, the passage of time can be shown quite well (as sequence, order, succession) in texts and on film and television. For example, displays of social data (tables and Isotype charts) often show temporal trends; graphs are plotted with time as the independent variable; processes are shown stage by stage. Continuous movement is obviously well handled on film or television, and speech can be represented as printed words. An audio message does have some special qualities; for example, it can "pace" the learner, it can represent some things superbly well (e.g., spoken language and music), and audio tapes are cheap and simple to change. Apparently, Fleming's account of sense modality is too general and too symmetrical.

The second difficulty is caused by the decision to split signs into two classes, *digital* (words and numbers) and *iconic* (all pictures and diagrams). This distinction goes back to Morris (1938, 1946, 1964) and has been adopted by many audiovisual researchers, including Gibson (1954) and Knowlton (1966); see also Bruner (1966). Here are the original definitions from Morris (1938):

A characterizing sign characterizes that which it can denote. Such a sign may do this by exhibiting in itself the properties an object must have to be denoted by it, and in this case the characterizing sign is called an *icon;* if this is not so, the characterizing sign may be called a *symbol.* A photograph, a star chart, a model, a chemical diagram are icons, while the word "photograph," the names of the stars and of the chemical elements are symbols (p. 24).

This definition contains two noteworthy presuppositions, one inside the other. First, it assumes that the primary source of knowledge and therefore of communication is a world full of objects. This view of the world is pure logical atomism; Wittgenstein's *Tractatus* (1922) includes these dictums:

2.021 Objects make up the substance of the world.
2.12 A picture is a model of reality.
2.131 In a picture the elements of the picture are the representatives of objects.

Later in his life Wittgenstein came to believe that his *Tractatus* was profoundly wrong in building upon "primary elements" (i.e., objects). This change of mind, incidentally, caused him to reclassify diagrams as language games (Wittgenstein, 1953).

This dramatic shift of opinion by a great philosopher cannot be taken lightly; at the least it shows we should not accept Morris's definitions at face value. Suppose we recast the definition of iconic to bring it closer to its use in ordinary language, as follows: "An icon is an image or portrait of an object or person." This makes good sense but does not cover diagrams, indeed it does not cover any abstract graphic formats. Now it becomes clear that most of the graphic formats listed by Morris and Fleming are not iconic in this sense: not chemical diagrams (a chemical element is certainly not an "object" in any straightforward sense), not geometric figures, and perhaps not even maps (this is the second presupposition). Too much is included under Fleming's *iconic,* and his advice on digital versus iconic messages should be used warily.

Fleming's fifth chapter ("Perceptual Capacity") raises the same issues as did Travers's review discussed above. Chapters 6 and 7 deal with the perception of sets, time, space, and motion. Some key principles are:

1. Similar objects or objects placed close together will be perceived as related.
2. Familiar objects exhibit perceptual constancy.
3. Common themes, patterns, and structures assist the process of interpretation.
4. The spatial arrangement of a picture or diagram affects the process of interpretation.
5. Words in support of graphics can aid learning.
6. Perception of depth is influenced by relative size of familiar objects, perspective, texture, superimposition, and various qualities of light.
7. Perceptions of size, motion, and time duration may be aided by providing appropriate frames of reference or comparisons.

These are expansions of the basic themes in the first chapter.

The final chapter ("Perception and Cognition") is rather thin by present-day standards; for example, the crucial works by de Groot and Simon, though published before 1970, were not consulted by Fleming. Fleming's use of standard textbooks as his original sources led to a sound account of the traditional research in perception but one which missed out on the modern rebirth of cognitive psychology (see Lindsay & Norman, 1972; Newell & Simon, 1972, and Pylyshyn, 1973). Overall this is a review of impressive scope and sound common sense. Its major conclusions (as listed above in shortened form) could help designers to improve their work, providing the pitfalls mentioned are given due attention. However, since the conclusions are rather too generalized for direct practical application (again the need for when/when not research), perhaps a skilled intermediary is needed to link practitioner and researcher. This link is the "transformer" (Macdonald-Ross & Waller, 1976), or instructional technologist.

This discussion of perception research has so far looked at the possibility of universal prescriptions derived from research. The three sources chosen (Abercrombie, Travers, and Fleming) give a fair idea of what perception research has to offer. There are, however, other worthwhile sources which may be consulted. Gibson (1954) offered a theory of pictorial perception based mainly on the realism dimension. This has been an influential paper, though it suffers from the same weakness as Morris's theory of signs. A diagram as a surrogate for reality is Gibson's idea; contrast that with a diagram as a way of representing problems, or with diagrams as language games. Another important paper is Gerbner's (1956) general model of communication, based on the Shannon-Weaver model of communication, which, as discussed above, has its limitations.

Gropper (1963) looks at graphic communication through the spectacles of behaviorism: "The general aim of instruction is to increase what was an initially low probability of occurrence to a high probability of occurrence. When this happens, responses are said to be under the control of stimuli" (p. 76). For graphics which have a strong task orientation, this may be a useful conception. Knowlton (1966) gives an interesting discussion of the definition of *picture,* though once again Morris's unsatisfactory theory of signs has a corrosive effect.

Particular Prescriptions

Category 1*b* includes particular prescriptions based on the results of research into limited problems. Most of the empirical evidence for the later sections of this review comes from this kind of limited research, and examples will be given in the appropriate places.

General Research Methods

Research methods are categorized as general and special purpose in categories 2*a* and 2*b*. We shall briefly consider three approaches to general research methods:

The physicalist model. Laboratory experiments with simplified stimulus material and close control of variables.

The pragmatic model. Field experiments with realistic stimulus material (ergonomics–human factors).

Theory-driven research. An example is the artificial intelligence–problem-solving model.

None of these models is exclusive, and a broad research program might use them all. In practice, however, researchers do tend to specialize in one of the three.

The physicalist model has often been used, but its relevance to graphic communication is problematic. The model uses simplified stimulus material and attempts to control each variable in standard laboratory conditions. Though copied from the physical sciences, this model lacks any strong theoretical components. Hypotheses are tested, but it is often unclear how they were selected in the first place. The experiments by Tinker (1963) into typography are regarded as classic examples of this approach; they will be discussed later in this review.

The pragmatic model used in human factors research has been quite successful and offers a plausible alternative to the physicalist approach. The pragmatic model also avoids any deep commitment to theory, but it conducts tests in realistic situations with stimulus material of full complexity. Of necessity this means that only the chief variables can be controlled. Coherent alternatives can be tested, with the aim of achieving large improvements that are robust under field conditions. Statistically significant improvements may not be sufficient, and, contrariwise, results of no significant differences may mask differences which are significant in the real world (see Johnson & Klare, 1961). (This is also one of the key problems with the physicalist model.) Important sources for the pragmatic approach are Baker and Grether (1954), Chapanis (1959, 1966; Chapanis, Garner, & Morgan, 1949), and Bartlett and Mackworth (1950). Most of this work has been done on the ergonomics of radar displays, aircraft cockpits, instrument panels, and road signs. Therefore it is the research methods rather than the results that are most useful in this setting.

The invasion of cognitive psychology by ideas drawn from artificial intelligence is certainly one of the most important developments in modern psychology. Its significance for a theory of graphic communication is as follows. One of the key steps in solving a problem is to represent it "so as to make the solution transparent" (Simon, 1969); in other words, to fit the task onto the strategies available for its solution. This means that *a graphic format is a canonical representation for problems of a certain class;* the format allows people to manage certain tasks that would be impossible or difficult if posed in words alone. Such a theory makes sense of the majority of graphic formats:

all mathematical diagrams are clearly designed to facilitate problem solving (see Hogben, 1960; Polya, 1945; Wertheimer, 1945); so are most scientific diagrams (see discussion in Toulmin, 1953), as well as tables, nomograms, algorithms, and most of the other devices reviewed in this chapter. Even the diagrams in anatomy textbooks could be considered as problem-solving tools for dissection and surgery. The work of Kennedy (1974) on picture perception is quite interesting, but might have been improved if Kennedy had made connection with current work on pattern recognition and scene analysis (for which see Minsky & Papert, 1969, 1972: Winston, 1970). The key sources for the "graphic device as problem representation" are Bobrow and Collins (1975), de Groot (1965), Kleinmutz (1966), Newell and Simon (1972) and Simon (1969). Interesting precursors to this idea can be found in the work of the Gestalt school (Koffka, 1935; Wertheimer, 1945).

Special-Purpose Research Methods

The field of research into perception is remarkable for the variety of instruments and methods available to the researcher. Some of these (for example eye-movement recorders, tachistoscopes) can be used on a fairly wide range of problems; others (such as the Ishikawa color test) are used for one purpose only. These instruments tend to condition the way researchers look at problems, and usually for the better, for the effect is to suggest ways of translating research questions into action.

To summarize: the field of perception research can offer both *results* and *experimental methods* for use by graphic communicators. The review by Fleming (1970) was selected for detailed analysis, and a shortened version of his principles was given. Two models of research which I believe are worth special attention are:

The artificial intelligence–problem-solving model, whereby a graphic device is seen as a canonical form for representing certain kinds of problems.

The human factors–ergonomics model for conducting realistic experiments on applied problems.

PRESENTING QUANTITATIVE DATA

If it can't be counted, it isn't science.
Lord Kelvin (attrib.)
All social facts are statistical.
Otto Neurath

The two quotations that head this section illustrate the great importance of quantitative data in our scientific-industrial age. As a matter of fact, both statements are rather contentious; such extreme positivism is rare in present-day philosophers of science. Nevertheless, adequate collection, organization, and presentation of numerical data are essential in our world. In this review there is no space to deal with the collection and analysis of data, though it must be said that a good communicator needs to understand the conceptual foundations of the graphic devices he uses. To design a chart or table the designer may need to go back to source documents to check the definition of key terms, the sampling procedures, and so on. This does require some basic familiarity with research methods, and it may be that the training of graphic designers could be improved in this respect.

There are two major reviews of the graphic presentation of quantitative data (Funkhouser, 1937, and Macdonald-Ross, 1977). Wright's broad survey (1977) also includes a discussion of quantitative data. Funkhouser's historical survey is a splendid piece of scholarship which describes the origin and development of all the graphic formats which are used for presenting data. This survey shows how a graphic format is invented to meet some need that existing formats could not satisfy, how the original idea is improved (in an erratic, piecemeal manner), and finally how it is standardized.

Tables

Until recently the design of tables for presenting statistics has been an arcane art, understood well by few people. Now, work by Ehrenberg (1977) has clarified the process by showing how application of a few simple principles can markedly improve the design of tables:

1. Round numbers to two significant digits. This facilitates mental arithmetic.
2. Provide row and/or column averages. They are reference points.
3. Figures are easier to compare in columns; so use columns for the most important comparisons.
4. Order rows and columns by size of numbers and not, for example, by alphabetical order of the labels.
5. Columns and rows should be set compactly, not artificially spaced out to fit the page. Space can be used to distinguish relevant blocks of figures.

Ehrenberg's rules are supported by examples (one of which is shown here in Figure 1), by some informal trials and formal tests, and by detailed discussion of the objections his fellow scientists have raised in discussion. For example, if two-digit rounding is criticized for "losing data," Ehrenberg points out that much precision is spurious, and, furthermore, errors of rounding are usually trivial in effect. Moreover, the rule has a distinct benefit for the user: We can see, manipulate, and communicate data more easily in this

TABLE A

Table from "Facts in Focus" (London: Penguin, 1974). As published, it breaks most of Ehrenberg's rules.

Unemployment in Great Britain

	1966	1968	1970	1973
Total unemployed (thousands)	330.9	549.4	582.2	597.9
Males	259.6	460.7	495.3	499.4
Females	71.3	88.8	86.9	98.5

Source: *Facts in Focus*

TABLE B

The same data as Table A, but with rows and columns interchanged and numbers rounded and placed in decreasing order of size. Visual comparisons and mental arithmetic are now straightforward. The effects of such rearrangements are even more marked with complex tables.

Unemployment in Great Britain

GB	Unemployed (000's)		
	Total	Male	Female
1973 (D)	600	500	99
'70 (B)	580	500	87
'68 (A)	550	460	89
'66 (C)	330	260	71
Average	520	430	86

TABLE C

The same data arranged to show the deleterious effect of artificial spacing-out to fit the page.

Unemployment in Great Britain

	Total	Unemployed Male	Female
1973	600	500	99
'70	580	500	87
'68	550	460	89
'66	330	260	71

Figure 1. Examples of Ehrenberg's rules applied to a simple table.

simplified form. The rule is also consistent with the limitations of short-term memory: "If any task, however simple, is interposed between [the subject] hearing the items and his repeating them, the number he can retain drops to two" (Simon, 1969, pp. 39–40). According to Ehrenberg, the reading of a table is a self-interrupting task, which fits Simon's description quite closely.

The main benefit of tabular presentation is its compactness; a great deal of data can be put on a single page. Also, even with the two-digit restriction a table presents numbers more exactly than bar or pie charts do. Therefore it seems likely that tables will remain the preferred format for professional users. The great weakness of tables is their abstract nature. A table consists entirely of abstract symbols—words and numbers. For example, 333 and 999 occupy the same space, and it takes an act of cognition to make sense of them. When hundreds of numbers are arrayed in a complex table most people find it difficult to sort out the significant features; indeed, there are many who cannot interpret even the simplest tables. No doubt it would help if such skills were taught in schools, but they are not, and the practising communicator has to take people as they are. Therefore it is common practice to use charts for a general readership. Bar charts show quantity by length, and Isotype charts show quantity by rows of standard symbols. In effect this reduces the need for abstract cognition and offers the data as a series of visual comparisons (this/that, here/there, now/then).

Charts and Graphs

The relative effectiveness of bar charts, circle charts, pie charts, and graphs has been a subject of some controversy. Experimental studies have gradually sorted out the main issues, though several researchers made the mistake of using poor-quality stimulus material and inappropriate tasks. A detailed review of this work has recently been completed (Macdonald-Ross, 1977). The main conclusions are:

1. The quantity and the logical and visual arrangement of data have an important effect on learning (Washburne, 1927).
2. No form is more effective in all respects than all other forms (Washburne, 1927).
3. Bar charts are generally superior to circle charts (Croxton & Stein, 1932) and to line graphs (Culbertson & Powers, 1959).
4. Circles (or squares) of differing sizes should be avoided; if used they should be range-graded (in stepped sizes) and a key provided to show the number represented by each step (Meihoefer, 1969, 1973).
5. Where possible, labels should be placed directly on bars or lines; they should not be indirectly keyed (Culbertson & Powers, 1959).

6. For general use, horizontal bar charts were understood better than tables, and tables were understood better than text (Feliciano, Powers, & Kearl, 1963).
7. Use text to support charts and tables (Washburne, 1927; Feliciano et al., 1963).
8. If pie charts are used, avoid fine angular discrimination (E. Hoch, personal communication).
9. In general, the advice given by expert designers has been vindicated by subsequent empirical tests (Macdonald-Ross, 1977).
10. Any graphic format can be executed well, or poorly, for a particular purpose. This is often a more significant variable than the choice of format (Macdonald-Ross, 1977).

The Isotype Chart. An important graphic format for general readers is the pictorial chart, in particular the Isotype system developed by Otto Neurath

Figure 2. A typical isotype chart.

(1936). The Isotype system is especially adapted for presenting social statistics to the general public and is the main alternative to bar charts for this purpose (see Figure 2). The main principles of the Isotype system are:

1. The subject matter is represented by standard iconic signs.
2. Each sign stands for a given quantity or percent.
3. To show larger quantities, use more signs (*not* larger signs).
4. Arrange the signs to make a "visual argument."

The last principle needs some clarification, for it introduces a new term, *visual argument,* to which Neurath attached a great deal of weight. Neurath assumed that communication was for a purpose: The statistics were not just displayed, they were organized to get a message across. In the Isotype system, the graphic communicator is called a "transformer" to express his role as an intermediary between the source and the reader. Since the transformer is in a position of control he must be, according to Neurath, an educated person of impeccable integrity. Neurath said, "The transformer is the trustee of the public"—a splendid way to express the relationship.

The heart of a visual argument is an explicit comparison or a series of comparisons, for example:

Imports and exports
  of corn and steel
    into and out of the U.S.A. and the U.S.S.R.
    in 1910, 1930, 1950, and 1970.

This kind of data would provide the basis for an Isotype chart, many hundreds of which were produced during the lifetime of the Isotype Institute. The use of visual comparisons is fully consistent with Fleming's (1970) first principle, discussed above. Neurath wrote only one formal account of his system (O. Neurath, 1936), so to see the full scope one has to look at the product. The social atlas (O. Neurath, 1930) and the social history (O. Neurath, 1939) are beautiful sources, worth many hours of study. Other accounts worth consulting are Marie Neurath's history of the Isotype Institute (M. Neurath, 1974), and the books by Koberstein (1973) and Modley (1937).

In the early days of the Isotype Institute charts were informally tested on groups of schoolchildren, but these trials were never reported in journals. This lack of documentation is quite normal with formative evaluation, but it does lay the practitioner open to the charge that the graphic methods used are just "a matter of opinion," and from time to time a skeptical researcher puts the question to an empirical test. A case in point is the series of experiments on pictorial charts, bar charts, graphs, and tables by M. D.

Vernon (1946, 1950, 1953, 1962). A fair summary of Vernon's conclusions would be: Differences in format make little or no difference to the performance of subjects; especially, "No all-round advantage is gained by using pictorial charts."

If Vernon's conclusion could be sustained graphic communication would have received a severe blow, for what is the point of graphic ideas like Isotype if they cannot be read with greater facility than tables or graphs? A good deal of expertise is needed to produce charts, and they are therefore relatively costly. However, there is no reason to accept Vernon's no-difference results at face value. Her experimental design contains some serious flaws, and her graphic devices were incompetently designed. A test of a table that has been fairly well set in type against a poor graph or a dreadful pictorial chart is invalid; no general conclusions can be drawn. For reasons of this kind the inferences Vernon drew from her results were not justified (see discussion in Macdonald-Ross, 1977).

Nomograms. Nomograms are graphic devices for representing equations on a plane surface. They are widely used in engineering design and to a lesser extent in the social and physical sciences. Nomograms can be divided into two classes, or distinct graphic formats:

Abac. Equation drawn as a graph on Cartesian or logarithmic coordinates.
Alignment chart. Three or more scales arranged so that a straight line joining two known values cuts the third scale to give the required value.

These two formats are logically identical but psychologically quite different, as Figures 3 and 4 show. As mentioned earlier, a basic tenet of the general theory of problem solving is that the way a problem is represented can affect the ease and manner of its solution. This is a case in point, for there is widespread testimony from expert users that alignment charts are much easier to use than abacs. Engineers have often conducted comparative tests for their immediate practical purposes, though few of these tests have found their way into the literature of education or psychology. Basic references are Allcock and Jones (1932), Douglass (1970), D'Ocagne (1899), Ford (1969) and Griffin (1932). Beeby and Taylor (1973) is a recent example of the systematic formative testing of an abac; unfortunately, they did not try out the alignment chart format on this occasion. D'Ocagne is the inventor of the alignment chart, one of the most recent additions to the range of graphic alternatives and one of the most important.

Since the chief purpose of the nomogram is to make exact data available for operational use, its chief competitor is the table. Operational tables may break Ehrenberg's two-digit rule, since they are not used to detect general trends but to provide exact data for some operational purpose. The choice

Graph for Estimating Reliability

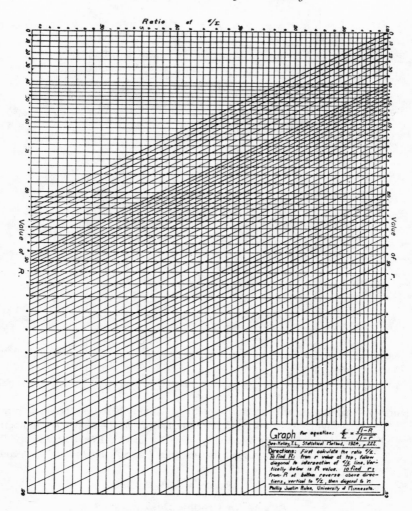

Figure 3. An abac for estimating reliability. (From P. J. Rulon, "A Graph for Estimating Reliability in One Range Knowing It in Another," *Journal of Educational Psychology,* 1930, *21,* 140–142.)

between nomogram and table involves a complex tradeoff among cost, space, convenience, accuracy, and speed. These tradeoff situations provide one good reason why no one graphic format is suitable for all purposes. Of course, there can be good methods (satisficing solutions) for particular cases.

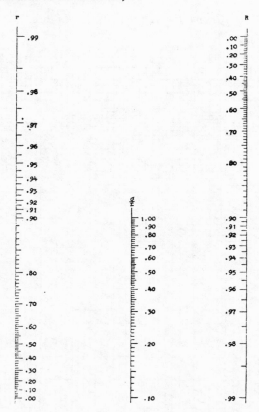

Figure 4.   An alignment chart for estimating reliability based on the same formula
as Figure 3. From E. E. Cureton and J. W. Dunlap, "A Nomograph
for Estimating the Reliability of a Test in One Range of Talent When
Its Reliability Is Known in Another Range," *Journal of Educational
Psychology,* 1929, *20,* 537–538.

Advice for Graphic Designers

For practical graphic designers the following advice is the best that can
be offered at present:

1. For showing general trends and relationships to:
   a. The general public, use *horizontal bar charts* or *Isotype* charts. Bar
   charts are easier to construct, but Isotype charts are more likely
   to attract and motivate the reader. Avoid change for the sake of
   change.
   b. The professional, use *tables,* and follow Ehrenberg's guidelines.

2. For presenting exact data:
   a. To show the results of experiments or investigations, use *graphs* (on Cartesian or logarithmic scales) or *tables*.
   b. To present exact data for operational purposes, use *nomograms* (especially alignment charts) and *tables* (the two-digit rule does not apply to these tables).

Other graphic devices may be used, but variation for its own sake is not advisable. These systems of representation are partly or wholly symbolic, embodying codes that must be learned by the user. Switches in the format therefore entail switches in the user's interpretive procedures, thus increasing the risk of misinterpretation. The advice Neurath gave on this score was "Everything in a chart should have a meaning; and nothing should be changed without a reason." This also applies to charts in series.

Another caveat: It is not always possible to see whether the users should be classified as *general public* or *professional.* Indeed, these terms were deliberately chosen for their broad denotations. For example, high school students and beginning university students may be regarded as untrained for this purpose and treated as members of the general public; graduate students, however, should be treated as professionals. Categories 1*b,* 2*a,* and 2*b* above are mainly for the trained professional user, but again this guideline must be used with common sense. A high school student may be able to handle simple graphs and tables with just a short training session, and teachers should be encouraged to regard graphic interpretation as a basic reading skill.

The use of Cartesian and other graphs for displaying experimental data is ubiquitous in science and technology, so it is included under 2*a.* This practice has not been researched extensively by applied psychologists but has developed over many years by a process of gradual, piecemeal evolution. Therefore, there is a prima facie case for assuming that graphs do display such data fairly effectively, and in any event the practice is so deeply entrenched that it will last. At the start of this review, two sources of knowledge were listed: formal tests and expert practitioners. Ideally, these sources coincide and reinforce each other, but sometimes one must make do with whatever knowledge is available.

SCIENTIFIC AND TECHNICAL DIAGRAMS

Scientific discourse consists of ordinary language, technical terms, diagrams, equations, and special notations; this is the apparatus used by scientists to describe their subject matter. A study of how these linguistic and graphic systems work together would be important and interesting and would certainly help us understand the central issues of graphic communication. No such enterprise has yet been attempted, and even partial studies covering particular subject matters or particular types of diagrams are quite rare.

There *has* been continuing interest in the kind of technical diagrams used for maintaining, operating, and troubleshooting complex equipment, however. This section therefore discusses two types of diagrams:

Scientific diagrams used to help explain and illustrate.

Technical or operational diagrams which help the user to carry out tasks.

The section *omits* the types of diagrams discussed elsewhere, such as the graphs and nomograms described in the preceding section.

One consequence of using a simple iconic-symbolic distinction to classify graphic formats (as discussed above) is that too many kinds of diagrams are lumped together as "iconic," including many that are in no way images of objects. As an alternative, I suggest a simple list of *purposes* which could be used to develop a more sophisticated classification:

Iconic purpose. Here the purpose is to show what an object looks like, and to identify and label key parts.

Data display purpose. Here the purpose is to display the results of empirical observations.

Explanatory purpose. Here the purpose is to show the logical relationships between key ideas.

Operational purpose. Here the purpose is to help the reader to perform some well-specified task.

Some diagrams have a single purpose, but others combine two or more. For example, mathematical diagrams can be both explanatory and operational; biological diagrams can be both iconic and explanatory; engineering drawings can be both iconic and operational. These purposes are achieved by the use of rules or codes which, in effect, specify how the diagrams shall be constructed and interpreted. Sometimes these rules are explicit and are taught formally to students (e.g., graphs in physics), and sometimes the rules remain tacit and not articulated, in which case they are picked up in an informal fashion (e.g., medical illustrations). This raises the possibility that diagrams could be separated into families according to the kinds of interpretive rules they embody. Such a classification would make it much easier to design valid experiments to test their effectiveness.

Although in general scientists are not aware of the role diagrams play in their work, there are some notable exceptions. Allweis (1971) is a magnificent survey of the role played by systems diagrams in physiology; Hogben's (1960) history of mathematics pays full attention to the development of mathematical notations and diagrams, and both Meredith (1961) and Toulmin (1953) have some important ideas to contribute:

> One of the factors which makes graphic organisation so powerful is that it can draw simultaneously on a number of different codes and so achieve great economy of expression . . . . some codes are more obvious than others. Some are so little obvious as to be invisible (Meredith, 1961, p. 149).

> In geometric optics one learns to draw inferences, not in verbal terms, but by drawing *lines*. . . . this [kind of] diagram plays a logically indispensible part in the physicist's explanation.

> The heart of all major discoveries in the physical sciences is the discovery of novel methods of representation, and so of fresh techniques by which inferences can be drawn—and drawn in ways which fit the phenomena under investigation (Toulmin, 1953, p. xxx).

Toulmin's second, rather daring, thesis can be understood if "methods of representation" is interpreted in a suitably broad way to include mathematical systems as well as graphic devices. Some well-known examples would be the use of calculus in Newtonian dynamics, the role played by Riemannian geometry in the general theory of relativity, and the role played by chemical equations and the periodic table in 19th-century chemistry.

Experimental studies on scientific diagrams are few and far between (see the survey by Holliday, 1973). Dwyer (1972) has conducted a series of experiments on diagrams of the human heart, but unfortunately this work is weakened by poor-quality stimulus material and by a terminal test of uncertain validity. These illustrations were originally part of a linear programmed text written by Dwyer for the purpose of testing some of the principles of programmed learning. Dwyer adopted Gibson's "realism continuum" (a direct descendant of Morris's sign theory). This outlook emphasizes one aspect of biological diagrams (representing form and labeling parts) and undervalues other aspects (providing visual explanations and providing aids to operational action). The terminal test therefore consists of rote recall and low-level comprehension items—though learning names is just one aspect of biology. Even if Dwyer's test items are accepted at face value, the diagrams he used are (to put it mildly) not up to the best standards of biological illustration. Perhaps, as one reasonable idea, the quality of a graphic device is more important than the choice of format, providing the task items are within the domain of the alternative formats. If so, Dwyer's results cannot be generalized.

Experiments on technical or operational diagrams have been rather more successful, largely because the rules for constructing the diagrams and the criteria for their effectiveness are so much clearer. Also, their military and industrial importance has attracted more research interest.

764197435602451

Systems diagrams are good examples; they are used as job aids to help workers set up, operate, maintain, and repair complex equipment. The content and purpose of the diagrams are decided by task analysis, and the typical end product has less "nice-to-know" information and less prose and uses diagrams to carry the burden of the job-relevant instruction. Typical tasks are:

Assembling a machine-gun.

Repairing a television set.

Repairing a tank in the field.

Troubleshooting electronic equipment at sea.

Examples of diagram formats used in job-support documentation are:

Photographs or drawings of equipment.

Functional block diagrams of the system.

Maintenance dependency charts.

Algorithms.

For further details of this specialized but important work, consult Baker (1958), Glaser (1962), Shriver (1960), Shriver and Fink (1964), and Ware, Miller, and Constantinides (1968, 1969). One general caution is in order: these systems depend on task and systems analysis, which is a highly skilled activity. The U.S. Armed Forces were fortunate to have the services of some outstanding researchers in their institutes during and after World War II. Other organizations have since copied the *form* of the graphics without achieving the quality of *analysis* that made the graphic aids effective. Organizations that use job-support documentation should realize that the documentation rests absolutely on the quality of prior analysis; it is no use expecting a technical document department to produce effective material if it is not supported by top-class analysts.

Another, older type of operational diagram is the engineering drawing. The history of engineering drawing is told by Booker (1963), and the rediscovery of Leonardo da Vinci's Madrid codex (Reti, 1974) should also be noted. This is one of the few areas of graphic communication which has a standardised training and examination system. This formalization has good and bad consequences: it makes for widespread usability and standardization (which is absolutely essential in the mechanical engineering industry), but it also helps to perpetuate outmoded and dysfunctional conventions. Researchers can play a useful role as change agents in questioning and testing established practice. Some recent experiments on the effectiveness of different projections and labels are perhaps a start to this process of critical improvement (Spencer, 1973; Cheney & Spencer, 1974).

ALGORITHMS

An algorithm is a visual instrument of telling.
Lewis

The term *algorithm* is used in two different but related senses: the ordinary language (OL) algorithm, and the computer algorithm. OL algorithms show rules, regulations, procedures, and instructions in noncontinuous prose—usually as flowcharts, sometimes in list format (see Figure 5). The source is

Flow chart for Capital Gains Tax

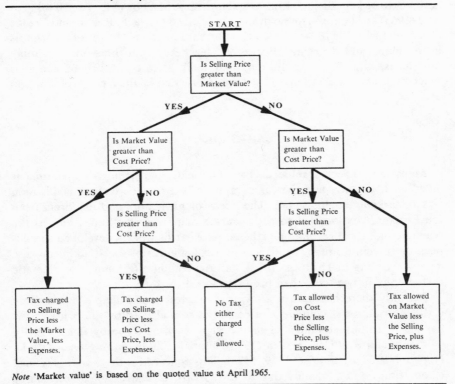

Note 'Market value' is based on the quoted value at April 1965.

Figure 5. An ordinary language algorithm. (From B. N. Lewis, I. S. Horabin, and C. P. Gane, *Flow Chart, Logical Trees, and Algorithms for Rules and Regulations* [London: HMSO, CAS Occasioned Papers No. 2, 1967].)

usually a rule or regulation in prose linked by the words *if, then, unless.* This leads to complex nested subclauses that are extremely difficult—often impossible—to retain and sort out in the mind. The object of an OL algorithm is to break up this prose into its constituent parts and arrange it on the page so that the reader has to deal with only one thing at a time. If the reader is asked one question at a time in simple, active voice, the language can be understood by a much larger target population. Lewis and Wason are the co-originators of OL algorithms, and their papers are well worth reading (Jones & Wason, 1965; Lewis 1970; Lewis & Cook, 1969; Lewis, Horabin, & Gane, 1967; Wason, 1968; Wason & Johnson-Laird, 1972).

In mathematics and computer science an algorithm is a procedure which produces correct results (in contrast with a *heuristic*). This is a usage which deserves to be kept distinct from OL algorithms. Markov (1961) and Trakhenbrot (1963) spell out the foundational theory, and Gerlach, Reiser, and Brecke (1975) and Merrill (1974) are two good recent reviews of the use of algorithms in teaching and learning. For most teachers algorithms mean simply flowcharts, and since the format does lend itself to classroom activities maybe the next generation will get some practice in their construction and use.

CARTOGRAPHY

Maps are ancient graphic devices. One clay map from Mesopotamia is dated at 2,500 B.C.; and the cartography of the Graeco-Roman civilization was remarkably sophisticated. The needs of navigators and explorers from the European nations led to the accurate maps we now know, and as the scientific-industrial revolution gathered pace cartographers developed special-purpose (thematic) maps to display particular kinds of social and economic data. According to Thrower (1972), "all the common techniques of thematic cartography in use today had been developed by 1865."

Recently there has been a growing awareness that a map succeeds only if the information it contains can be extracted and used by the reader. This has led to empirical studies of map design, such as those by Bartz (1970), Christner and Ray (1961), Cuff (1973), Ekman, Lindman, & Olsson (1961), Hopkin (1973), Meihoefer (1969, 1973). This concern for the reader is typical of our times and is mainly due to the growth of instructional technology during and after World War II. The standard of these empirical studies in cartography is quite admirable, perhaps because the experiments were designed by researchers who were familiar with the subtleties of the stimulus material. Cartography is one discipline where graphic communicators can occupy regular university posts.

NOTATIONS

The concept of position puts our arithmetic in the front rank of useful
inventions.   *Laplace*

Notations and codes are invented because of the limitations of ordinary
language: notations to say things that can hardly be expressed in ordinary
language, and codes to hide messages that would otherwise be all too clear.
Notations are certainly important for the growth and expression of ideas
and hence are of interest to us. But few philosophers have paid them much
attention. Leibniz (c. 1966) has some interesting ideas (see Ishiguro, 1972,
and Tymieniecka, 1964), and Frege (1879) and Goodman (1969) are two
important essays on notations by modern philosophers.

Mathematical and logical notations are of great importance, the standard
sources being Cajori (1928), Neugebauer (1951), and Smith (1958). Formal
experiments on the effectiveness of notations are almost never done; mathematics proceeds by trial and experience of new notations, as happens with
the evolution of diagrams. There are dozens—perhaps hundreds—of other
kinds of notations which have never been classified and analysed, though
they must play an indispensable role in thought and communication.

COMIC STRIPS

Comic strips are in their element when used to show the irony of life,
the vagaries of human nature, and the complexities of personal interaction.
The work of Schultz (1952) and Feiffer (1958) provides perfect examples;
in their hands a comic strip has eye-opening qualities. But what are we to
make of comic strips used to "add interest" to subjects like golf, investment,
and military tasks? On the one hand readers may find the format attractive,
and that can help motivate them to read further. On the other hand, there
is the distinct possibility that the illustrations may not help the reader understand the substance of the message. There have been some informal trials,
and one recent handbook for editors of army manuals (Kern, Sticht, Welty,
& Hauke, 1975) does include comic strips as a device for graphic communication. Green and Courtis (1966) give an interesting discussion of the relevance
of Shannon's information theory to the perception of cartoon figures.

TYPOGRAPHY

Die Typographie ist ein Instrument der Mitteilung.
Moholy-Nagy

Typography is the art of arranging print on the page. The new technology
of printing has freed the typographer from most of the mechanical limitations

imposed by hot metal; now any marks on paper can be reproduced. This freedom marks a permanent change in the typographer's art. Once he was a skilled interpreter of mechanical constraints; now he can become a communicator—that is the sense of Moholy-Nagy's manifesto for the new typography.

Surely the arrangement of type is a cut-and-dried issue which was sorted out centuries ago? Surely type cannot affect the quality of educational materials? These are natural reactions of many untrained people, for it takes a trained eye to spot the troubles caused by poor typography. The untrained reader may realize that some books tend to be "easygoing" and others do not, but he is not equipped to diagnose the source of any difficulties. Since the causes of reading difficulty may lie in the subject matter, the author's prose style, the typography, or the reader's skill or prior knowledge (or any combination thereof), the business of diagnosis is indeed complex.

The first kind of typographic problem is the maintenance of basic standards. The setting of continuous prose has long been mastered, but violations of well-founded principles abound. Recently in a small survey I found:

Ragged *left* edge. This disrupts the eye-movement routine.

Illegible second color. Yellow or orange can hardly be seen under household lights.

Lack of contrast between print and paper; print too grey; background screen too dark.

6-point type size in book setting.

Uneven and excessive word spacing (very common).

Large slabs of text set in uppercase and italic.

Often in paperback editions three or four suboptimal conditions occur together. This is quite serious for the reader; as Tinker (1963) showed, these suboptimal features have a cumulative effect. Such mistakes are not theoretically interesting, but they are important to the reader. Commonsense, training, and quality control should dispose of all such cases; but the fact is that errors of this type do occur quite often in educational books.

Educational materials also introduce problems for the typographer, for the only task which has been truly mastered by the craft of typography is the setting of continuous prose. Diagrams and photographs, captions, in-text questions and answers, instructions, and formulas all break up the text and provide novel problems for the typographer. Moreover, many educational texts are designed by people who have no training at all in typography. They do not know which problems are new and which are not, and this reduces their chance of success almost to zero. Several surveys look at the special typographic problems of educational material (Hartley & Burnhill, 1976, 1977; Hartley, Fraser, & Burnhill, 1973; Macdonald-Ross & Waller, 1975b; Watts & Nisbet, 1974). There is no sign that these problems can be solved easily, though they are now being dissected and sorted out for the first time.

There has been a great deal of research on the basic elements of text setting. Tinker's famous summary (1963) is still indispensable, but there is some doubt as to whether the problems he investigated were well formulated. If we take this research at face value (as Rehe, 1974, does), then we are bound to conclude that a great deal of useful work has been done, and what we need is more of the same. If, however, we take a more skeptical look at the experimental design, then maybe (as Macdonald-Ross & Waller, 1975a, suggest) some of the effort put into empirical testing has been wasted. Is it appropriate to do single-variable tests on simplified stimulus material? How does such stimulus material relate to the real design problems of the typographer? The trouble is that most of the variables do interact strongly; for example, justified setting, line length, and word spacing cannot be treated as independent, for they are not. It is worth reading Fisher's (1935) account of the single-factor experiment:

In expositions of the scientific use of experimentation it is frequent to find an excessive stress laid on the importance of varying the essential conditions *one at a time* . . . . in the state of knowledge or ignorance in which genuine research, intended to advance knowledge, has to be carried on, this simple formula is not very helpful. We are usually ignorant which, out of innumerable possible factors, may prove ultimately to be the most important, though we may have strong presuppositions that some few of them are particularly worthy of study (p. xxx).

Despite this clear-cut warning in an important methodological text, most typographical research has used single-variable design (see Tinker, 1963). This makes the results difficult to use in real typographic situations, though there is some broad consensus on such variables as type size, print and paper contrast, and the illegibility of upper-case text.

Tinker's work on the cumulative effect of suboptimal arrangements and his ideas about the "hygenic reading situation" are both relevant and practical. Imagine a text full of conceptual muddle, unclear expression, visual confusion, and suboptimal setting being read by someone who is tired and disinterested, sitting in poor light, with the text not at right angles to the line of sight, and in a noisy room full of interruptions and distractions. This gives you some idea of a real-life reading situation (we might get fewer no-difference results in conditions like these). Suboptimal settings may not produce large effects when tested one by one in clinically perfect reading conditions, but they do produce most significant effects when several occur together and the text is read under poor conditions.

The special problems of newspaper typography are described by Arnold (1969), Evans (1973), Frayman, Griffiths, and Chippindale (1975), Hutt (1967,

1973), and Sellers (1968). Though meant for trainee journalists, these books contain many ideas which could be used by instructional technologists. Some key issues (such as allowing the reader to make the choices that suit him) are well solved by newspapers and magazines. Also worth noting are Chaundy (1970) and Swanson (1971) on the typography of mathematics, and Wright (1975), Wright and Barnard (1975), and Civil Service (1972) on the design of forms.

The design of letterforms is still a live issue. With the introduction of cold composition, calligraphy is now a practical notion, and the creation of suitable typefaces for non-Roman languages is very important indeed. It is extraordinary that Chinese, Japanese, and Arabic still do not have really satisfactory character sets, though (at last) work is going on to meet these needs. It seems that the mainland Chinese government has decided to shelve the alphabetic notion and simplify the basic 5,000 characters instead. This is a sensible decision, since the many dialects of Chinese (some of which are virtually distinct languages) prevent any simple phonetic basis for their language. The mechanical problems of composition will be much simplified by electronic setting, so the chief argument against the idiographic character has less force now.

Typography is a specialized skill, and instructional technologists working with text materials should develop their understanding of it before embarking on experimental work. Good places to start are Dowding (1966), Gill (1931), Morison (1946), Spencer (1952), Tschichold (1967), Williamson (1956), and Twyman (1970).

CONCLUSION

The practitioner who designs a graphic device is acting, as we all do, with imperfect knowledge. A graphic device is an artifact, intended to get across a particular idea to some particular readers. There is no way a science of instruction could lay down minutely detailed prescriptions for all conceivable situations. This is simple realism. However, it is possible to put together the knowledge we already have, to improve it, and to make it more easily available. Reliable knowledge applied intelligently will improve the effectiveness of graphic communication. That is what this review has tried to do.

The knowledge we have about the use of graphic devices is derived from two sources: the expert practitioner and the formal scientific experiment. These are two quite separate traditions, and yet it is necessary to bring them together for their mutual benefit. First of all, let it be said that there are master performers: they are not a fiction of my imagination. Their expertise is real enough, for they can repeatedly produce effective solutions to problems that defeat less skilled practitioners. The knowledge of a master practitioner is mainly tacit (i.e., not articulated). It is the product of practice, experience, and careful thought, but usually the master does not explain his methods. Even where a master has put his thoughts onto paper, they provide only a sketchy outline, insufficient for the purpose of instruction and experimental testing.

By displaying publicly the rationale of the master performer, certain crucial benefits can be obtained. The knowledge can be examined, criticized, tested, and improved. And the knowledge can be communicated to others; younger designers can be trained; minimum standards can be set and maintained. These are absolutely vital benefits which can be gained only by the intervention of researchers willing to open themselves to the possibility of learning some of the basic elements of the master's craft. It does not seem possible to design fruitful experiments in graphic communication if the researcher is entirely ignorant of the object of his research, or, worst of all, if he is not just ignorant but ignorant of his ignorance. There is no doubt that master performers can be improved upon. I do not imagine that their way is better than the way of experiment, but externalizing this knowledge can be a great step toward genuine scientific understanding and reliable prescriptions for the designer.

The experimental work must not be taken for granted. It is a proven way to deepen our understanding, but it is not easy to do experimental work which will stand up to rigorous cross-examination. As many readers will know, it is not possible to lay down hard-and-fast rules for how scientific work shall be conducted—at any rate, all such attempts have failed so far. But it *is* possible to notice occasions when researchers have taken a wrong turn. These mistakes are interesting, and we can learn from them. Moreover, it is absolutely essential for mistaken results and erroneous techniques to be weeded out, else neither researchers nor practitioners can know whether they build on solid ground or on quicksand. I am well aware that I have trained a fairly skeptical eye on the research literature, not because I lack faith in the scientific method (far from it), but because I believe that skepticism is a necessary and useful part of the scientific method. I have been just as demanding in my behind-the-scene search for master practitioners, though this cannot be demonstrated in a written paper.

Despite this skeptical outlook, there turns out to be a surprising stock of knowledge available, and this chapter lists some of the most important sources. I believe that the gulf between researcher and graphic designer ought to be bridged, and that bridge should most likely be embodied in a skilled professional communicator. Such a role-player does exist in other media—for example, a television producer acts as the key coordinator of all the contributing specialties. There is no equivalent role in text production, though there should be. Sometimes instructional technologists do play this role, but more often the coordinating function is just omitted. Consequently a good deal of substandard textual material is used for education and instruction.

If we can build up our knowledge and our personal expertise, and if we can apply this expertise in the right way, then it will be possible to raise the effectiveness of texts.

REFERENCES

Abercrombie, M. L. J. *The anatomy of judgement: An investigation into the processes of perception and reasoning.* London: Hutchinson, 1960.

Allcock, H. J., & Jones, J. R. *The nomogram: The theory and practical construction of computation charts.* London: Pitman, 1932.

Allweis, C. Control systems in physiology, biology and medicine. *Israel Journal of Medical Sciences,* 1971, *7* (Supplement).

Arnold, E. C. *Modern newspaper design.* New York: Harper, 1969.

Baker, C. A., & Grether, W. A. *Visual presentation of information* (Tech. Rep. 54-160). Wright Air Development Center, 1954.

Baker, R. A. *The determination of job requirements for tank crew members* (Tech. Rep. 47). Alexandria, Va., 1958.

Bartlett, R. C., & Mackworth, N. H. *Planned seeing: Some psychological experiments.* HMSO Air Ministry Air Publications 3139B. London, 1950.

Bartz, B. S. An analysis of the typographical legibility literature: Assessment of its applicability to cartography. *Cartographic Journal,* 1970, *7,* 10-16.

Beardsley, A. *The birth, life and acts of King Arthur embellished with designs by Aubrey Beardsley.* London: Dent, 1893.

Beeby, A. W., & Taylor, H. P. J. How well can we use graphs? *Communicator of Scientific and Technical Information,* 1973, *17,* 7-11.

Bland, D. *A history of book illustration: The illuminated manuscript and the printed book.* London: Faber, 1958.

Bobrow, D. G., & Collins, A. (Eds.). *Representation and understanding.* New York: Academic Press, 1975.

Booker, P. J. *A history of engineering drawing.* London: Chatto & Windus, 1963.

Bruner, J. S. *Toward a theory of instruction.* Cambridge, Mass.: Belknap Press, 1966.

Cajori, F. *A history of mathematical notations.* LaSalle, Ill.: Open Court, 1928.

Chapanis, A. *Research techniques in human engineering.* Baltimore: Johns Hopkins Press, 1959.

Chapanis, A. *Man-machine engineering.* London: Tavistock, 1966.

Chapanis, A., Garner, W. R., & Morgan, C. T. *Applied experimental psychology: Human factors in engineering design.* New York: Wiley, 1949.

Chaundy, T. W. *Printing for mathematics: Aids for authors and rules for compositors and readers at the University Press, Oxford.* London: Oxford University Press, 1970.

Cheney, R. L., & Spencer, J. Dimensional information on engineering drawing. *Ergonomics,* 1974, *17,* 343-363.

Christner, C. A., & Ray, H. W. An evaluation of the effect of selected combinations of target and background coding on map-reading performance. *Human Factors,* 1961, *3,* 131-146.

Civil Service, Management Services Division. *Design of forms in government departments.* London: HMSO, 1972.

Croxton, F. E., & Stein, H. Graphic comparison by bars, squares, circles and cubes. *Journal of American Statistical Association,* 1932, *27,* 54-60.

Cuff, D. J. Colour on temperature maps. *Cartographic Journal,* 1973, *10,* 17-21.

Culbertson, H. M., & Powers, R. D. A study of graph comprehension difficulties. *Audio Visual Communication Review,* 1959, *7,* 97-100.

DeGroot, A. *Thought and choice in chess.* Gravenhage, Netherlands: Mouton, 1965.

DeGroot, A. Perception and memory versus thinking. In B. Kleinmutz (Ed.), *Problem solving.* New York: Wiley, 1966.

D'Ocagne, M. *Traite de nomographie.* Paris: Gauthier-Villars, 1899.

Douglass, R. D. Nomograph. *Encyclopedia of science and technology.* New York: McGraw-Hill, 1970.

Dowding, G. *Finer points in the spacing and arrangement of type.* London: Wace, 1966.

Dwyer, F. M. *A guide for improving visualized instruction.* State College, Pa.: State College Learning Services, 1972.

Ehrenberg, A. S. C. Rudiments of numeracy. *Journal of Royal Statistical Society* (Series A, vol. 40), in press.

Ekman, G., Lindman, R., & William, O. W. A psychological study of cartographic symbols. *Perceptual and Motor Skills,* 1961, *13,* 355-368.

Evans, H. *Editing and design: A five-volume manual of English, typography and layout.* London: Heinemann, 1973.

Feiffer, J. *Sick, sick, sick.* New York: McGraw-Hill, 1958.

Feliciano, G. D., Powers, R. D., & Kearl, B. E. The presentation of statistical information. *Audio Visual Communication Review,* 1963, *11,* 32-39.

Fisher, R. A. *The design of experiments.* Edinburgh: Oliver & Boyd, 1935.

Fleming, M. L. *Perceptual principles for the design of instructional materials* (ED–03 7093). Indiana University: Bloomington AV Center, 1970.

Ford, L. R. Nomography. *Encyclopaedia Britannica,* Chicago, 1969.

Frayman, H., Griffiths, D., & Chippindale, C. *Into print: A guide to publishing non-commercial newspapers and magazines.* London: English Universities Press, 1975.

Frege, G. *Conceptual notation and related articles.* London: Oxford University Press, 1879.

Funkhouser, H. G. Historical development of the graphical representation of statistical data. *Osiris,* 1937, *3,* 269-404.

Gerbner, G. Toward a general model of communication. *Audio Visual Communication Review,* 1956, *4,* 171-199.

Gerlach, V. S., Reiser, R. A., & Brecke, F. H. *Algorithms in learning, teaching and instructional design* (Tech. Rep. 51201). Tempe: Arizona State University, Educational Technology, 1975.

Gibson, J. J. A theory of pictorial perception. *Audio Visual Communication Review,* 1954, *2,* 3-23.

Gill, E. *An essay on typography.* London: Sheed & Ward, 1931.

Glaser, R. *Training research and education.* Pittsburgh: University of Pittsburgh Press, 1962.

Gombrich, E. H. The visual image. *Scientific American,* 1972, *227,* 82-96.

Goodman, N. *Languages of art: An approach to a theory of symbols.* London: Oxford University Press, 1969.

Green, R. T., & Courtis, M. C. Information theory and figure perception: The metaphor that failed. *Acta Psychologica,* 1966, *25,* 12-36.

Griffin, H. D. How to construct a nomogram. *Journal of Educational Psychology,* 1932, *23,* 561-577.

Gropper, G. L. Why is a picture worth a thousand words? *Audio Visual Communication Review,* 1963, *11,* 75-95.

Hartley, J., & Burnhill, P. *Textbook design: A practical guide.* Paris: Unesco Division of Materials and Techniques, 1976.

Hartley, J., & Burnhill, P. Fifty guidelines for improving instructional text. *Programmed Learning and Educational Technology,* 1977, *14,* 65-73.

Hartley, J., Fraser, S., & Burnhill, P. A selected bibliography of typographical research relevant to the production of instrumental materials. *Audio Visual Communication Review,* 1973, *22,* 181-190.

Hogben, L. T. *From cave painting to comic strip: A kaleidoscope of human communication.* London: Parrish, 1949.

Hogben, L. T. *Mathematics in the making.* London: Macdonald, 1960.

Holliday, W. G. Critical analysis of pictorial research related to science education. *Science Education,* 1973, *57,* 201-204.

Hopkin, V. D. Human factors in the design of maps. In *Visual presentation of technical data.* Ergonomics Research Society and the Society of Industrial Artists and Designers. Reading, England: University of Reading, Typography Unit, 1973.

Hutt, A. *Newspaper design.* London: Oxford University Press, 1967.

Hutt, A. *The changing newspaper: Typographic trends in Britain and America 1622-1972.* London: Gordon Fraser Gallery, 1973.

Ishiguro, H. *Leibniz's philosophy of logic and language.* London: Duckworth, 1972.

Johnson, F. C., & Klare, G. R. General models of communication research: A survey of the developments of a decade. *Journal of Communication,* 1961, *11,* 13-26, 45.

Jones, S., & Wason, P. C. *The logical tree project.* University College, London: Department of Psychology, 1965.

Kennedy, J. M. *A psychology of picture perception.* San Francisco: Jossey-Bass, 1974.

Kern, R. R., Sticht, T. G., Welty, D., & Hauke, R. N. *Guidebook for the development of army training literature.* Alexandria, Va.: Human Resources Research Organization, 1975.

Kleinmutz, B. (Ed.) *Problem solving: Research, method and theory.* New York: Wiley, 1966.

Knowlton, J. Q. On the definition of "picture." *Audio Visual Communication Review,* 1966, *14,* 158-183.

Koberstein, H. *Statistik in bildern.* Stuttgart: C. E. Poeschal, 1973.

Koffka, K. *Principles of Gestalt psychology.* London: Kegan Paul, 1935.

Lewis, B. N. *Decision logic tables for algorithm and logical trees.* London: HMSO, 1970.

Lewis, B. N., & Cook, J. A. Toward a theory of telling. *International Journal of Man-Machine Studies,* 1969, *1,* 129-176.

Lewis, B. N., Horabin, I. S., & Gane, C. P. *Flow charts, logical trees and algorithms for rules and regulations.* CAS Occasional Papers no. 2. London: HMSO, 1967.

Lindsay, P. H., & Norman, D. A. *Human information processing: An introduction to psychology* (2nd ed.). New York: Academic Press, 1977.

Macdonald-Ross, M. How numbers are shown: A review of research on the presentation of quantitative data in texts. *Audio Visual Communication Review,* in press.

Macdonald-Ross, M., & Smith, E. *Graphics in text: A bibliography.* Milton Keynes, England: Open University, Institute of Educational Technology, 1977.

Macdonald-Ross, M., & Waller, R. Criticisms, alternatives and tests: A conceptual framework for improving typography. *Programmed Learning and Educational Technology,* 1975, *12,* 75-83. (a)

Macdonald-Ross, M., & Waller, R. *Open University texts: Criticisms and alternatives.* Milton Keynes, England: Open University, Institute of Educational Technology, 1975 (b).

Macdonald-Ross, M., & Waller, R. The transformer. *Penrose Annual,* 1976, *69,* 141-152.

Markov, A. A. *Theory of algorithms.* Washington: National Science Foundation, 1961.

Meihoefer, H. J. The utility of the circle as an effective cartographic symbol. *Canadian Cartographer,* 1969, *6,* 105-117.

Meihoefer, H. J. The visual perception of the circle in thematic maps: Experimental results. *Canadian Cartographer,* 1973, *10,* 63-84.

Meredith, P. *Learning, remembering and knowing.* London: English Universities Press, 1961.

Merrill, P. F. *Algorithmic organization in teaching and learning: The literature and research in the USA.* Tallahassee: Florida State University, Center for Educational Design, 1974.

Minsky, M. & Papert, S. *Perceptions.* Cambridge, Mass.: MIT Press, 1969.

Minsky, M., & Papert, S. *Progress report.* Cambridge, Mass.: Massachusetts Institute of Technology, Artificial Intelligence Laboratory, 1972.

Modley, R. *How to use pictorial statistics.* New York: Harper, 1937.

Morison, S. *First principles of typography.* London: Cambridge University Press, 1946.

Morris, C. W. *Foundations of the theory of signs.* Chicago: University of Chicago Press, 1938.

Morris, C. W. *Signs, language and behavior.* New York: Prentice-Hall, 1946.

Morris, C. W. *Signification and significance: A study of the relation of signs and values.* Cambridge, Mass.: MIT Press, 1964.

Neugebauer, O. *The exact sciences in antiquity.* Copenhagen: Munksgaard, 1951.

Neurath, M. Isotype. *Instructional Science,* 1974, *3,* 127-50.

Neurath, O. *Gesellschaft und wirtschaft.* Leipzig: Bibliographisches Institut, 1930.

Neurath, O. *International picture language.* London: Kegan Paul, 1936.

Neurath, O. *Modern man in the making.* New York: Knopf, 1939.

Newell, A., & Simon, H. A. *Human problem solving.* Englewood Cliffs, N.J.: Prentice-Hall, 1972.

Polya, G. *How to solve it: A new aspect of mathematical method.* Princeton, N.J.: Princeton University Press, 1945.

Pylyshyn, Z. W. What the mind's eye tells the mind's brain: A critique of mental imagery. *Psychological Bulletin,* 1973, *80,* 1-24.

Rackham, A. *Illustrations to Wagner's Ring of the Niebelung* (2 vols.). London: Heinemann, 1911.

Rehe, R. F. *Typography: How to make it most legible.* Indianapolis: Design Research Publications, 1974.

Reti, L. (Ed.). *The unknown Leonardo.* London: Hutchinson, 1974.

Schulz, C. *Peanuts.* New York: Holt, Rinehart, 1952.

Sellers, L. *The simple subs book.* Oxford: Pergamon, 1968.

Shannon, C. E., & Weaver, W. *The mathematical theory of communication.* Urbana, Ill.: University of Illinois Press, 1949.

Shriver, E. L. *Determining training requirements for electronic system maintenance.* (HumRRO Res. Rep. 63.) Alexandria, Va.: Human Resources Research Office, 1960.

Shriver, E. L., & Fink, C. D. *FORECAST systems analyses and training methods for electronic maintenance training* (HumRRO Res. R. 13). Alexandria, Va.: Human Resources Research Office, 1964.

Simon, H. A. *The sciences of the artificial.* Cambridge, Mass.: MIT Press, 1970.

Smith, D. E. *History of mathematics.* London: Constable, 1958.

Spencer, H. *Design in business printing.* London: Sylvan Press, 1952.

Spencer, J. Presentation of information on engineering drawings. In *Visual presentation of technical data*. Ergonomics Research Society and the Society of Industrial Artists and Designers. Reading, England: University of Reading, Typography Unit, 1973.

Swanson, E. *Mathematics into type*. Providence, R. I.: American Mathematical Society, 1971.

Thrower, N. J. W. *Maps and man: An examination of cartography in relation to culture and civilization*. Englewood Cliffs, N.J.: Prentice-Hall, 1972.

Tinker, M. A. *Legibility of print*. Ames: Iowa State University, 1963.

Toulmin, S. E. *The philosophy of science: An introduction*. London: Cambridge University Press, 1953.

Trakhenbrot, B. A. *Algorithms and automatic computing machines*. Boston: D. C. Heath, 1963.

Travers, R. M. W. *Man's information system: A primer for media specialists and educational technologists*. Scranton, Pa.: Chandler, 1970.

Tschichold, J. *Asymmetric typography*. New York: Reinhold, 1967.

Twyman, M. *Printing 1770-1970: An illustrated history of its development and uses in England*. London: Eyre & Spottiswood, 1970.

Tymieniecka, A. T. *Leibniz' cosmological synthesis*. Assen, Holland: Van Gorcum, 1964.

Vernon, M. D. Learning from graphical material. *British Journal of Psychology*, 1946, *36*, 145-58.

Vernon, M. D. The visual presentation of factual material. *British Journal of Educational Psychology*, 1950, *20*, 174-185.

Vernon, M. D. A further study of visual perception. London: Cambridge University Press, 1952.

Vernon, M. D. Presenting information in diagrams. *Audio Visual Communication Review*, 1953, *1*, 147-158.

Vernon, M. D. *The psychology of perception*. Baltimore: Penguin, 1962.

Ware, J. R., Miller, E. E., & Constantinides, J. L. *Pictorial methods of instruction for the M73 machine gun and the caliber .45 automatic pistol*. (HumRRO Cons. Rep.) Alexandria, Va.: Human Resources Research Office, 1968.

Ware, J. R., Miller, E. E., & Constantinides, J. L. *Project PIMO (Presentation of Information for Maintenance and Operation)*. (TR 69-155). Washington: Serendipity Inc., 1969.

Washburne, J. N. An experimental study of various graphic, tabular and textual methods of presenting quantitative material. *Journal of Educational Psychology*, 1927, *18*, 361-376, 465-476.

Wason, P. C. The drafting of rules. *New Law Journal*, 1968, *118*, 548-549.

Wason, P. C., & Johnson-Laird, P. N. *Psychology of reasoning: Structure and content*. London: Batsford, 1972.

Watts, L., & Nisbet, J. *Legibility in children's books: A review of research*. Windsor, Berks., England: National Foundation for Educational Research, 1974.

Wertheimer, M. *Productive thinking*. New York: Harper, 1945.

Williamson, H. A. F. *Methods of book design: The practice of an industrial craft*. London: Oxford University Press, 1956.

Winston, P. H. *Learning structural descriptions from examples*. (Project Mac, MAC TR-76). Cambridge, Mass.: Massachusetts Institute of Technology, 1970.

Wittgenstein, L. *Tractatus logico-philosophicus*. London: Routledge & Kegan Paul, Ltd., 1922.

Wittgenstein, L. *Philosophical investigations*. Oxford: Blackwell, 1953.

Wright, P. Forms of complaint. *New Behaviour,* 1975, *1,* 206-209.

Wright, P. Presenting technical information: A survey of research findings. *Instructional Science,* 1977, *6,* 93-134.

Wright, P., & Barnard, P. 'Just fill in this form': A review for designers. *Applied Ergonomics,* 1975, *6,* 213-220.

II

STUDIES IN TEACHING

3

Instruction in Classrooms

REBECCA BARR and ROBERT DREEBEN
University of Chicago

There are two traditions of research on school effects that have developed and remain in almost complete isolation from each other. First, there is a classroom instruction tradition consisting of a large and inconclusive literature on the impact of instruction upon learning. Long before anyone misinterpreted the Coleman Report of 1966 as showing that schools have no effect on achievement, there was ample evidence that the research on classrooms has little to say about the connection between what teachers do and what students learn. Second, a more recent tradition dating to the Coleman Report examines school effects using a quasi–production function formulation to examine the connections between school resources and achievement.

We will argue not only that the two traditions have a connection but that the agenda addressed by one is integral to the agenda addressed by the other. Whatever the inadequacies of past work, the study of the impact of classroom instruction on learning (or achievement) is directly relevant to the application of production function models to schooling. In the production function literature the sources of within-school variation have either been ignored or handled improperly. Moreover, the more complete understanding of the macrosocial aspects of schools and school systems will surely contribute to better understanding of how classrooms work and students learn.

THE PRODUCTION FUNCTION MODEL

The year 1966, in which the Coleman Report appeared, marks a watershed of research on school effects; in retrospect, there was a new turn of the

IAN WESTBURY, University of Illinois, Urbana, served as editorial consultant for this chapter.

We wish to thank C. Arnold Anderson, Charles E. Bidwell, Philip Foster, and Douglas M. Windham, our colleagues at the University of Chicago, for their helpful comments.

research tradition concerned with the influence of school characteristics on achievement. *Equality of Educational Opportunity* (Coleman, Campbell, Hobson, McPartland, Mood, Weinfeld, & York, 1966; hereafter EEO) provided the stimulus for the rapid expansion, particularly among sociologists and economists, of analyses of school effects premised upon a production-function model.

When the concept of production function, taken from economics, is applied to the study of school effects, the school is treated as a firm which transforms inputs (such as books, teachers' time, activities, physical plant, and equipment) into outputs (such as increments of knowledge, change in attitude, or gains in achievement). Thomas (1971) provides a general discussion of educational production functions (pp. 13-21). He notes:

> The economist sees education as contributing individuals with acquired competences to the economic system. In return, the economy contributes resources for the operation of schools. . . . In this production function, outputs are the additional earnings which result from an increment of schooling, while inputs comprise the cost of that increment (p. 22).

Educators and sociologists, however, are primarily concerned not with the economists' interest in incremental earnings and their monetary costs but with the impact of various aspects of schools and schooling, primarily resources, on levels of achievement (though rarely with increments of achievement). That is, they are concerned with the organizational effectiveness of schools as formulated in input-output terms.

Perhaps the term *production function* is more a metaphor than the rigorously developed conceptual scheme employed by economists. The work on school effects simply does not meet the assumptions of the production function model. The model, moreover, presupposes a goal of either achieving maximum output at a given cost or of minimizing cost for a given output. Such a goal is difficult to attain in schools because they are public utilities whose costs are met by taxpayers in a nonmarket situation, and because their technologies are so casually related to outputs that the costs of substitutable technological alternatives are impossible to calculate. The assumption that resources have additive effects, moreover, is inconsistent with the multiplicative premise underlying production functions. Finally, schools are multiple-output firms (e.g., they are expected to achieve both behavioral and cognitive goals), and this cannot be reconciled with the single-output premise (e.g., profit maximization) of economic production functions. A metaphoric use of the formulation appears to be appropriate because we must consider how inputs are transformed into outputs, and while no one has been able to treat schooling within the conceptual constraints imposed by the economists' production function, an unrefined employment of the scheme is appropriate.

There is little reason to review the major substantive contributions of production-function approaches to school effects. The task has been done many times (Averch, Carroll, Donaldson, Kiesling, & Pincus, 1972; Spady, 1973), and Alexander and McDill's recent assessment (1976) serves our interests well enough:

Despite the severely critical initial response to the Equality of Educational Opportunity Report . . . its general conclusions have proven remarkably robust. In particular, the finding that educational outcomes are largely independent of all school-to-school differences has been borne out both in thorough re-analyses of the EEO data themselves . . . and in a substantial body of subsequent research. . . . These results now have been reproduced over a wide range of school outcomes, on numerous samples of students, and with various analytic strategies (pp. 963-964).

While the early critiques and reanalyses are primarily methodological, more recently both substantive and conceptual concerns have been increasing in frequency and importance. In particular, questions are being raised pertaining to the nature of inputs, the flow and character of the productive (schooling) process, and the properties of the firm (the school) itself. We will consider primarily what the firm is and what it does to transform inputs into outputs. To that end, we will turn first to the production function model upon which EEO is predicated, and we will illustrate it with one detailed example.

In outline, the model treats teacher characteristics, school resources, and the environmental characteristics of students at the level of schools; and individual student characteristics within several grade levels and within racial groups (further subdivided by region of residence). The page numbers below refer to the pages on which the variables are discussed in Coleman et al. (1966).

Teacher variables (pp. 316-317)
Average educational level of teachers' families.
Average years of experience in teaching.
Localism of teachers in the school.
Average level of teachers' education.
Average score on vocabulary test.
Teachers' preference for teaching middle-class, white-collar students.
Proportion of teachers in school who are white.

School variables (p. 309)
Per-pupil expenditure on staff (measured at the district level).
Volumes per student in school library.
Science laboratory facilities.
Number of extracurricular activities.
Presence of accelerated curriculum.

Strictness in promotion of slow learners.
Use of grouping or tracking.
Movement between tracks.
School size.
Number of guidance counselors.
Urbanism of school's location.

Student environment variables (p. 309)
Proportion of students whose families own encyclopedias.
Number of student transfers.
Attendance.
Proportion of students planning to attend college.
Teachers' perception of student body quality.
Average hours of homework.

Individual student background variables (p. 301)
Urbanism of background or migration.
Parents' education.
Structural integrity of the home.
Smallness of family.
Items in the home.
Reading material in the home.

The EEO production function model organizes these variables as follows:

● Among students partitioned by race (Puerto Rican, Indian American, Mexican American, Negro, Oriental American, and White; with Negroes and Whites further distinguished by region, north and south), and

● With individual student background characteristics held constant;

● Teacher characteristics aggregated to the school level (summed across grades 9-12 for grade 12 students, across grades 7-12 for grade 9 students, and across grades 1-6 for grade 6 students),

● School characteristics, and

● Student environment characteristics aggregated to the school level, account for some percentage of the variance in student verbal achievement, as shown in Table 1. Note, moreover, that student ability and sex are excluded from the analysis, and race is not free to vary because the analysis is done within racial groups, while other individual characteristics pertaining to rural-urban residence and socioeconomic status are controlled.

In this example, the model treats both school inputs (teacher characteristics aggregated to the school level and school characteristics similarly aggregated) and student inputs as school characteristics. What the school acts upon with these resources, however, is not entirely clear, unless we regard these student

TABLE 1

Percent of Variance in Verbal Achievement Accounted for by Teacher Variables (T), Plus School Variables (S), Plus Student Environment Variables (E), for grades 12, 9, and 6 (six background variables controlled)

	Grade 12			Grade 9			Grade 6		
	T	T+S	T+S+E	T	T+S	T+S+E	T	T+S	T+S+E
Puerto Rican	18.38	20.00	26.39	9.70	11.37	16.26	8.11	10.81	13.97
Indian Americans	15.75	19.56	26.33	7.25	10.17	14.04	17.95	19.41	20.95
Mexican Americans	14.63	16.94	19.16	11.71	14.12	15.04	12.59	13.57	16.52
Negro, South	9.97	11.68	13.90	7.72	11.24	13.33	5.29	7.76	9.02
Negro, North	4.35	6.68	8.97	1.58	3.32	5.36	2.19	2.66	4.93
Oriental Americans	1.77	6.63	—[a]	3.18	—[a]	—[a]	4.19	11.99	14.54
White, South	2.07	3.60	4.80	2.49	3.36	3.83	1.12	1.56	2.94
White, North	1.89	3.16	3.82	1.02	2.06	3.07	1.67	2.02	4.84
Negro total	9.53	10.70	13.78	6.67	8.70	11.22	3.52	4.42	6.52
White total	1.82	3.42	4.18	1.03	2.41	3.18	1.23	1.77	4.13

[a] The regression had insufficient data for estimation.

Source: Coleman et al., *Equality of Educational Opportunity* (Washington, D.C.: U.S. Government Printing Office, 1966), p. 319.

characteristics not as resources but as "raw materials" to be transformed. In this case, however, they should not be aggregated to the school level. Individual student background characteristics do not vary; they are controlled. Other individual characteristics, such as sex and ability, are not considered. Accordingly, school resources treated within racial, regional, and school-grade groupings affect all individuals equally (i.e., on the average) with respect to their levels of achievement. The formulation does not consider events within the school that could affect the learning of individual students, which is to say that it is really a model of school resource availability, not resource use. Consideration of how resources are used entails acknowledging that events may differ from student to student and from class to class, and that different students respond differently to the same events. In the language of the production function, EEO considers inputs and outputs, but not what the firm is and what it does to transform one into the other.

In their general review of the school effects literature, Averch and his colleagues (1972) comment as follows: "Research in this approach views the school as a black box containing students. . . . Resources are applied to the students in the box and from this application some output flows" (p. 4). Is the school in fact a black box in the EEO production function formulation? Are the nature of the firm and its productive activities omitted from the formulation? The answer depends on how the inputs are construed. If per-pupil expenditure and teacher verbal ability, for example, are both treated as inputs, how do they transform students in terms of level of achievement? The formulation does not say. Even if per-pupil expenditure is treated as an input and teacher verbal ability is regarded as part of the transformational process, we still would not know how the transformation occurs. What do teachers do with their verbal ability? Lecture? Hold discussions? Assign worksheets to be completed in silence? Even this minor reformulation does not address the question about the nature of the firm adequately. That is to say, the production function formulation characteristically fails to distinguish inputs to the firm from the firm itself from the raw materials. The firm is characterized by its inputs but not by anything it does to transform raw materials into outputs.

In reaction to the rather unsettling findings that school characteristics have minor effects on achievement, several observers (to whom we will refer) have recognized the need to rethink the elements of the production function model. Others are primarily concerned with matters of statistical analysis and interpretation (problems of collinearity, unique and shared variance, sampling, and the like) which do not entail rethinking the model itself (Armor, 1972; Bowles & Levin, 1968; Mood, 1970; Smith, 1972). We are concerned with several attempts to rethink the model in ways that bear upon the nature of the school as a firm, rather than with efforts to refine the model methodologically or statistically.

Brown and Saks (1975) argue that the failure of production function research to reveal the productivity of school inputs lies in the treatment of outputs. Given that every student's performance is of concern, multiproduct firms such as schools must allocate resources in some rational way among students. In such a formulation mean performance of students may not be sensitive to resource allocation, while its distribution (variance and kurtosis) might be.

In simplest form, the purpose of schools is to maximize some welfare function. This assumes that schools test the things they teach. Student scores depend on two conditions: the nature of existing inputs and endowments, and the allocation of these resources. Inputs include the physical plant, textbooks, teachers' skills, and equipment, all relatively fixed in the short run; endowments refer to student characteristics such as entering skills, socioeconomic status, and the characteristics of other students in the class or school. These are, in fact, the conditions examined for their influence on achievement in EEO. The allocation of a particular resource to a student might result in that amount being unavailable to others. For students taught in classes, however, allocation decisions are more complex, because the resources applied to one student do not necessarily reduce those available to others by an equal amount. Brown and Saks (1975) specify three conditions upon which decisions regarding the distribution of resources depend:

. . . the marginal products of the available inputs when applied to particular students, the marginal utility of particular students' performances as evaluated by the school authorities, and the amount of any input exhausted when that input is applied to a particular student under the existing conditions of production (p. 575).

Biases of distribution originate from two sources: consumption and production. School boards, administrators, or teachers, for example, may be elitists who value the achievement of the select few, or they may be levelers who believe that schools should provide all students with basic skills. The deployment of resources by elitists or levelers takes different forms with regard to individual students, and though the consequence of the bias might not influence average achievement, it could affect achievement variance. Nevertheless, Brown and Saks suggest that consumption bias might be offset by production bias. For example, the leveling goals of school board members might be ineffective where curricular materials or teaching practices aim to maximize individual differences, an elitist goal.

To test a general economic model of school resource allocation, Brown and Saks examine the covariation of the mean and variance of achievement of third- and seventh-graders from 38 city school districts, 116 suburban districts, and 365 town and rural districts with selected inputs (average teacher experience, number with master's degree, number of students, pupil-teacher ratio). They take as given certain student endowments (mean level and standard deviation of socioeconomic status and percentage of white students). Student and teacher inputs are aggregated by districts, as is student achievement described in terms of variance as well as mean level. When a positive coefficient in mean-achievement regressions is taken as the criterion of input productivity, the conclusion is that inputs are not effective, since only three of nine coefficients are significant. When, however, a coefficient, with regard to either mean level *or* variance of achievement, indicates a positive marginal product, then the input is regarded as significantly productive (in seven of nine cases).

Brown and Saks question the proposition that school effects can be understood by comparing mean levels of achievement across schools or districts, but they argue that where variance as well as means is related to inputs, there is presumptive evidence that schools affect individuals in measurable ways that mean comparisons do not reveal. In addition, they show that "regressions [based on means] cannot in principle tell us anything about the size of the marginal products or an input's relative productivity with high- and low-endowment students" (Brown & Saks, 1975, p. 592).

Brown and Saks contribute to our understanding of the school as a firm by distinguishing prevailing conditions (to which EEO limits its perspective) from allocative decisions. In the short run, outputs can be changed by reallocating inputs, but the extent to which short-run input reallocations affect output will be limited by the nature of prevailing resources. More substantial output changes can occur through long-term input reallocations, in all likelihood reflecting new goals or biases sufficient in magnitude to change the nature of resources, and by implication to reduce their constraining impact.

We can carry the problem one step further by considering the Bidwell and Kasarda (1975) study concerning the impact of school-district resources on districtwide levels of achievement. That study concerns ". . . whether and how attributes of school district organization affect the transformation of environmental inputs into students' aggregate levels of academic achievement" (pp. 55-56). It employs a production function formulation that explicitly takes into account the transformational activities of the firm (in this case, the school district). Bidwell and Kasarda argue that it is appropriate to consider variations in achievement (aggregated by district and compared across districts) attributable to the organization's (the district's) management of its environmental conditions, such as size, financial resources, economically disadvantaged students, parental education, and proportion of nonwhite students. The district's organizational characteristics that pertain to the management of these conditions are pupil/teacher ratio, administrative intensity, teacher qualifications, and professional support. They say, "The short-run problem for school districts is to transform such inputs as students, fiscal resources, staff, technology and community preferences into such outputs as student achievement, operating within limits set by law and public policy" (p. 57).

The Bidwell and Kasarda analysis, based on data drawn from 104 K–12 Colorado school districts, must show that certain environmental conditions are related to organizational properties that in turn are related to levels of achievement. Further, environmental conditions must be shown as indirectly related to achievement, mediated through organizational properties. The data provide reasonably convincing support for these contentions. To illustrate: The greater the financial resources available to a district, the larger the ratio of professional support staff to teachers, the lower the number of students per teacher, and the higher the average level of teacher qualifications. The larger the district, the smaller the ratio of administrators to teachers. With respect to achievement, the fewer students per teacher, the fewer administrators per teacher; and the higher the qualifications of teachers, the higher the level of achievement. The greater the financial resources, the higher the level of achievement *when* these resources are used to lower the ratio of students to teachers. Environmental conditions such as resources, district size, and educational level of parents have rather small direct relationships to achievement, but their indirect relationships, all mediated through organizational properties of the districts, are much more substantial. Conceptually, these properties must stand as proxies for input-transforming organizational activities.

Except for the fact that the school, as a firm, is conceptualized as an active transformer of inputs into outputs, this study takes us little farther empirically in understanding the process by which schools transform inputs into outputs. How after all are pupil/teacher ratios, teacher qualifications, and professional support translated into achievement? Conceptually, however, this study does go beyond others in plausibly speculating about what might be going on in classrooms. According to Bidwell and Kasarda (1975), schools transform input into student output (achievement) at the level of the classroom through "instructional technology":

The technology of instruction is primitive, uncodified, and labor intensive, with the classroom teacher at the focal point of the work process. Whatever the variation in the size or quantity of student input to a school district, there are few "non-human" substitutes for, or supplements to, the interaction of teacher and students . . . the teacher, working alone in a classroom, must use his own judgment and fund of experience to evaluate and respond to feedback from students (p. 58).

This statement does not say much about what instructional technology amounts to or about what teachers do. Its importance is that it is there; it completes the logical progression of an argument which states that organizations draw upon and use environmental resources and transform them into outputs through events internal to schools. It also suggests that these events are instructional and that they occur among students and teachers in classrooms.

In his assessment of EEO, Jencks (1972) comments with respect to curriculum that "even when the reported data appear plausible and consistent, moreover, they seldom tell us much about what actually happens in different classrooms" (p. 96). The comment is equally apt in reference to things other than curriculum, but then, in studies where the data are aggregated at the district or school level, classroom events have to be ignored empirically.

In effect, Jencks raises the level-of-aggregation question which is pursued by a number of other investigators, most thoroughly by Summers and Wolfe (1974, 1975). They argue that equity in the allocation of school resources cannot be discussed unless inputs are properly conceptualized and aggregated:

It may be, then—and this is what we conclude—that the reason educational studies have failed to find that the things schools do are effective, is that there are few things which are consistently effective for all students. Many of these studies have been hampered by the limited amount of data which are specifically tied to the pupil. . . . Perhaps, therefore, the reason so many nihilistic results emerged on the effectiveness of school resources was that their averages disguised the true impact (Summers & Wolfe, 1975, p. 15).

Summers and Wolfe's treatment of resource allocation contrasts sharply with most production function analyses, especially that of EEO. Unlike most studies that use level of achievement to measure output, Summers and Wolfe use a value-added measure appropriate to production function formulations: achievement gain. This dependent variable has great sensitivity to educational inputs and also can be used in reference to a limited time period within which change occurs, thus only certain inputs are relevant, the most important of which may be the particular teachers of a student.

In production function studies, teacher and individual characteristics are often aggregated to the school and district levels; EEO is a prime example. While such aggregated measures identify the properties of social environments which arise from the collection of persons within them, they also mask variations from teacher to teacher and student to student.

The Summers and Wolfe analysis has two strengths. First, they disaggregate teacher characteristics. Achievement gains are related to the characteristics of the students' actual teachers rather than to those of all teachers from one or several grades in a school or district, as in EEO. Second, they fundamentally reconceptualize the role of individual student characteristics in production function analysis, such as income, race, and ability, as well as the role of composite indexes for whole schools. In this way they can estimate the relative productivity of an input among students of differing individual traits by examining interaction effects. While EEO controls individual background characteristics to rule out their effects on achievement, Summers and Wolfe treat them as variables at the classroom level. Thus the characteristics of individual teachers interact with student characteristics to influence their achievement. In short, the formulation of Summers and Wolfe considers teachers and students at the point where one influences the other.[1]

Summers and Wolfe analyze data from over 600 sixth-grade students in 103 schools, from over 500 eighth-grade students in 42 schools, and from over 700 twelfth-grade students in five high schools in Philadelphia. They examine in detail the schooling history of each student to determine achievement gain, race, and income, and to match this information with data pertaining to his or her particular school and teacher resources. Thus they treat many variables in a student-specific way.

While these data are far too extensive and complex to summarize here, the nature of the propositions they suggest shows how they try to identify the nature of school effectiveness. For example, they find that high-ability students in elementary schools make the greatest achievement gains with more experienced teachers, but low-ability students decline in achievement with experienced teachers and make modestly positive gains with inexperienced ones. At the junior high school level, very able students make large gains with highly experienced English teachers. Math teachers with three to nine years of experience are generally effective; those with more than ten years are generally ineffective (Summers & Wolfe, 1975, p. 19).

Summers and Wolfe's formulation goes some way in addressing Coleman's and Jencks's contention that most school effects occur within rather than between schools. It is not so much that the data are disaggregated to the classroom and individual levels but rather that they are appropriately aggregated to reflect the impact of specific resources on individual students in the place where it occurs. The formulation is also important because the way individual characteristics of students are treated represents the way the school deals with them. They are not in the form of characteristics related, say, to social or biological origins which are prior and external to schools, whose impact must be ruled out. A teacher may deal with white and black children, boys and girls, differently, and their achievements may vary according to the way they are treated. This is different from saying that race or sex are social characteristics related to achievement, and their likely impact must be controlled to avoid bias in the measure of achievement level or gain (see also Bidwell & Kassarda, 1976).

While appropriately aggregating data will remedy the erroneous assumption that mean school characteristics affect all students equally, this by itself cannot address the question of how school effects come about. That requires knowledge, not just about who the relevant "actors" are (districts, schools, classrooms, tracks, teachers, students) but about how each works. Consider, in the light of Summers and Wolfe's interpretation, how mathematics teaching experience affects gains in achievement. To account for students learning more with teachers having three to nine years of experience than with those having ten or more, Summers and Wolfe (1975) argue as follows: "This latter effect arises, most likely, because these [highly experienced] teachers received pre-Sputnik training. They are teaching the New Math, though they were not originally trained to teach it" (p. 19). The explanation presumes that teachers' effectiveness is based on what they know, and perhaps also on how confident they feel about what they know, which is plausible. The achievement gains of students, however, are more likely to be affected by how well teachers instruct, which in turn may be related to how much they know (as well as to other things). In the Summers and Wolfe explanation, years of training serves as a proxy for what teachers know and for how well they instruct, as well as for other unspecified things.

The lesson to be drawn from Summers and Wolfe is to move downward from the school in level of aggregation so as not to be constrained by the unacceptable assumption that a school is internally homogeneous. But understanding school effects is not simply a matter of disaggregating, no matter how important that is. Bidwell and Kasarda and Brown and Saks consider the district level of aggregation, at the same time they deliberately raise questions about matters of internal school process such as resource allocation and instructional technology.

While there are few production function studies at the classroom level, studies of within-school variations at the track (or curriculum) level are more numerous. The primary focus in studies of tracking has been to explain the placement of students in tracks, a problem that concerns us less than understanding the impact of tracking on achievement and on other kinds of outcomes, such as aspirations and college admission. Two rather well-known investigations have shown that track placement affects college aspirations (Heyns, 1974) and mathematics achievement and class rank (Alexander & McDill, 1976). Even though these investigations analyze within-school events, however, they indicate no more about how the firm (the school) works than do those studies that compare schools.

Rosenbaum, however, made a case study of a single school that was homogeneous in racial and status background of households and finds that track placement explains 16% of the variance in college placement among boys and 34% of variance among girls, not of ability and effort (Rosenbaum, 1976, pp. 87-89). He also finds that track placement accounts for rather substantial changes in IQ scores as students advance from grade 8 to grade 10, with gains occurring to a greater extent in upper tracks than in lower ones and declines occurring to a greater extent in lower ones (p. 130).[2]

While Rosenbaum's statistical analysis may raise doubts, his description of how tracking works is persuasive. In grade 7 of junior high school, students are channeled by guidance counselors into or away from foreign language courses, on the basis of their ability, interest, and performance. While these courses are not explicitly identified with tracks, the foreign language decision strongly influences later high school track assignments. Such assignments tend to be highly stable across subjects and from year to year, with most of the small proportion of changes leading downward rather than upward.[3] According to Rosenbaum, the stability of track membership for individual students is established and maintained by the counselors' use of misinformation, partial information, innuendo, and coercion to keep students in the tracks into which their junior high school language choices have led them.

The importance of this work is that it describes not the instructional activities at the classroom level but rather the advisory and channeling activities at the track level. It indicates what happens within the school to transform inputs into outputs, and to that extent it identifies the productive activities a production function formulation is supposed to conceptualize.

While discussion of the production function model has pointed to the classroom as the likely place where school effects are produced, to claim that school effects are really classroom effects misconstrues the argument. Our critique of EEO indicates first that the characteristics of the school as a firm must be distinguished from inputs to it; second, individual student characteristics must be treated as the raw material; they must be built into the formulation, not ruled out of consideration. These assertions do not contend that consideration of school characteristics in their own right as part of the production process is inappropriate. The difficulty with EEO is not that it fastens on school characteristics but that it does not identify where school characteristics belong in the process of schooling.

At issue is the productive nature of schooling, and to pursue the matter we need to look at productive events wherever they occur. Bidwell and Kasarda (1975) contend that these productive events occur at the school-system level and should be treated at that level. District-level events are not necessarily proxies for lower-level ones.[4] Hiring policies, resource acquisition, creation of a supervisory hierarchy, delineation of district boundaries, purchase of real estate, and allocation of funds to schools by school boards and central office administrators all bear on different forms of school productivity, such as achievement gains, teacher morale and turnover, expansion or retrenchment of the school system, or peaceful school integration.

The contention that school events should be observed where they occur holds, *mutatis mutandis,* at other levels: school, track, classroom, or wherever. Although classroom instruction, for example, may affect student learning, it should not be concluded that because such gains occur at the point where teachers come into direct contact with students the real business of schooling occurs only in classrooms. Indeed, such gains may be more or less likely to occur with a given form of instruction, depending upon school and school-system conditions, community conditions, short- and long-term allocative decisions by administrators, the state of the job market, the cost of going to college, the nature of administrative supervision, and the like. Accordingly, while our understanding of events and conditions is advanced at each distinct level of the schooling process, identification of the connections across levels has the same result. A complete formulation of school effects must treat the full range of organizational levels and their interconnections. In this chapter we pull up considerably short of developing a complete formulation, for our primary concern is to establish the mutual relevance of production function research and classroom research. We do not say that the classroom is *the* important place to look, but we do say that the connection between the two research traditions is not satisfactorily drawn, as it should be.

MODELS OF CLASSROOM INSTRUCTION

Our concern with *formulations* of instructional activities in classrooms led us to treat intensively a small number of important works about instruction, rather than reviewing the whole literature extensively. We selected studies according to three general criteria: they must treat whole classrooms, they must deal with ordinary instructional activities, and they must explicitly formulate some problem of classroom instruction or management in conceptual terms.

We found two broad classes of investigation in our reading, one based on empirical examinations of classroom activities and the other on the imposition of a conceptual scheme taken from outside classroom settings. At issue in this distinction is identification of the properties of classrooms and of instruction. We found it makes a difference if investigators begin with observations or with a commitment to a conceptual framework, an ideology, or a reform. The description of classrooms and instruction—the nature of the phenomena themselves—and the determination of what is problematic about them vary according to the approach of the researchers.

It also became apparent that patterns of instructional activity could be understood as the responses of teachers to issues arising in their work due to the properties of their classrooms. Accordingly, we concerned ourselves with how such issues become problematic. The properties that appeared most central in this respect were availability and distribution of classroom time, diversity of student membership, character of instructional activities, and collective character of classroom membership. The investigations we will discuss are not explicitly organized around these properties or the problems they generate. We will argue, however, that they all have implicit conceptions of what classrooms are like and what instruction consists of, and these conceptions are traceable to how the properties and problematics are treated or ignored.

With these considerations in mind, we identified six well-known and important formulations of classroom instruction, each associated with one or a small number of investigators.

Three of the formulations are based on imposed conceptual schemes:

1. The work by Flanders (1965) on teaching as leadership, based on the notion that instruction should be understood as social interaction.
2. The work by Bellack, Kliebard, Hyman, & Smith (1966), based on the premise that instruction should be seen as a language game.
3. The mastery learning formulation (Bloom, 1968; Block, 1971), based on the idea that classroom instruction should proceed according to a tutorial model.

We also discuss three formulations based on observation of classroom events:

4. Kounin's (1970) work on classroom management.
5. Bennett's (1976) study of teaching style as an example of how multiple dimensions of teaching can be combined.
6. Dahllöf's (1971) frame theory based upon observations of grouping and pacing.

None of the issues related to time, diversity, task, or collectivity is the province of any one investigation; all the investigations deal explicitly or implicitly with a range of issues. Moreover, while the reviewed work includes empirical studies, secondary analyses, reports on innovation, and theoretical statements, we have selected these investigations for the formulation of issues, not for the forms in which they appear.

Teaching as Classroom Leadership

One of the most durable traditions in classroom research stems from the conceptual formulations of Lewin and his colleagues (Lewin, Lippitt, & White, 1939; White & Lippitt, 1960) and of H. H. Anderson and his colleagues (Anderson, 1939; Anderson & Brewer, 1945; Anderson & Brewer, 1946; Anderson, Brewer, & Reed, 1946) on leadership style and group climate. The familiar distinctions in leadership style—integrative or dominative; authoritarian, laissez-faire, or democratic; preclusive or inclusive; and teacher centered or student centered—are based upon work done in the late 1930s and early 1940s and pertain to the nature of the group climate created by the activities of a leader. Investigators in this tradition typically characterize the behavior of students and group members in terms of dependency on a leader, or proclivity to initiate independent action. This behavior is treated as a function of the leader-created climate. They also concentrate on these particular dimensions of leadership, to the neglect of others, and abstract them from existing situations (such as classrooms) or create them experimentally. In all cases, teachers and leaders who run things, give orders and directives, and make and enforce rules, so that they create dependency among followers, are consistently contrasted with those who devolve responsibility, respect feelings, clarify goals, and encourage the initiatives of others, and as a result foster free action.

Flanders' (1965) formulation belongs in this tradition. His distinction between direct and indirect teaching is similarly bipolar; it refers to the same substantive distinction and is abstracted from all other forms of leadership:

Our system of interaction analysis provides an explicit procedure for quantifying direct and indirect influence that is closely related to the teacher behaviors identified by research on classroom climate. Direct influence consists of those verbal statements of the teacher that restrict freedom of action, by focusing attention on a problem, interjecting teacher authority, or both. These statements include lecturing, giving directions, criticizing, and justifying his own use of authority. Indirect influence consists of those verbal statements of the teacher that expand a student's freedom of action by encouraging his verbal participation and initiative. These include asking questions, accepting and clarifying ideas or feelings of students, and praising or encouraging students' responses (Flanders, 1965, p. 9).

Flanders' conception of instruction pertains directly to the activities of teachers responsible for the achievement of learning goals manifested in the content and organization of the curriculum, to be brought about through the learning of skills, facts, and understandings by children (Flanders, 1965, p. 12). In managing a classroom a teacher engages with students so that they learn something; managing does not mean keeping order. Teaching is a process by which teachers influence students by interacting with them, and it is characterized by the form the interaction takes.

While it may appear from this introduction that Flanders was concerned with the relationship between patterns of interaction and levels of achievement, that is not quite the case. According to Flanders (1965), "Our basic purpose is greater understanding of the teacher's role, the control he provides while teaching, and the patterns of influence he uses in classroom management" (p. 2). To what end, then, shall teacher influence (instruction) be used? Flanders says, "One way to describe the process of instruction is to say that the teacher strives to change the response pattern of a student from mere compliance to independent action, determined by the student's own analysis of the problems confronting him" (Flanders, 1965, p. 10). The teacher's task is to free students up, to help them find problems on their own and to work out independent solutions. The alternative is for them to become overly dependent on teachers through repeated compliance with what they ask and expect.

Does this formulation have any connection with more conventional notions that instruction pertains to achievement? Not explicitly, except as Flanders assumes that free, independent problem-solving activity contributes more to achievement than does learning based on compliance, which produces dependency on the teacher. And his direct concern with achievement as an outcome of instruction is manifested in his empirical work.

Before discussing Flanders's empirical findings we must look more closely at his formulation and its derivation. He studies classroom instruction solely in terms of verbal interaction and sees the classroom as the setting in which this interaction occurs. Flanders acknowledges that verbal interaction does not represent the totality of all classroom events, but he maintains it "constitutes an adequate sample of the teacher's total influence pattern" (Flanders, 1965, p. 7). The difficulty with this contention is that we do not know what the "total influence pattern" is from which a "sample" has been taken, or whether everything about teaching, instruction, and classroom life is exclusively part of an influence pattern or also part of something else. For example, are seating arrangements, patterns of ability grouping, or types of learning materials aspects of a total influence pattern? Flanders's exposition does not say, nor does it indicate what a classroom's properties are. By default, then, it is simply the location in which the interactions take place.

If there is neither a description of classroom characteristics nor a general formulation of instruction, how does Flanders justify the importance of direct and indirect teaching? The only justification he provides is the fact that there is a research tradition in which the classroom climate produced by leadership style is believed to influence the likelihood that group members will act freely. Flanders does find empirically that the distribution of his ten interaction categories is quite stable from study to study and within subpopulations of the same group, although he does not comment on these distributions or interpret them as data. He presents his distributions essentially to illustrate the prevalence of direct and indirect teaching and ignores the possibility that the same data describe stable classroom interaction patterns. While his findings provide evidence suggesting characteristically problematic properties of classrooms, he ignores it in pursuing a predetermined conceptual distinction.

Flanders's most interesting data come from a study of 16 social studies and 16 mathematics junior high school teachers. Units unfamiliar to the students were presented over a two-week instructional period, and observers present in all classrooms coded interactions in three-second intervals, using the categories listed in Table 2.[5] In summarizing the data, he first partitions his math and social studies classes according to i/d (indirect/direct teaching) ratio, with high ratios being called indirect and low ratios direct, and then presents the frequency of each interaction category.[6]

Table 2 indicates several things. First, teachers do most of the talking, about 65% of it, and students do less than 25%, a finding many other investigators have also observed. Slightly more than 37% of all interaction consists of the teacher lecturing, by far the most prevalent form of interaction. The

TABLE 2

Percentage Distribution of Interactions

Types of Teacher Behavior		Types of Classrooms				
		Math Indirect	Math Direct	Social Studies Indirect	Social Studies Direct	Total
Indirect	1. Accepts feeling	.23	.11	.11	.03	.12
	2. Praises, encourages	1.69	1.06	1.25	1.14	1.28
	3. Uses pupil ideas	8.11	2.63	8.28	3.03	5.51
	Indirect subtotal	10.03	3.80	9.64	4.20	6.91
	4. Asks questions	12.52	9.53	10.75	10.80	10.90
	5. Lectures	46.72	40.83	37.45	25.67	37.67
Direct	6. Gives directions	3.38	8.64	4.29	9.86	6.54
	7. Criticizes, justifies authority	.94	4.66	1.69	5.32	3.15
	Direct subtotal	4.32	13.30	5.98	15.18	9.69
	8. Pupil talk, response	10.73	13.02	17.54	21.49	15.70
	9. Pupil talk, initiate	6.12	6.74	9.48	8.70	7.76
	10. Silence, confusion	9.56	12.79	9.16	13.94	11.36
No. of classrooms		7	9	7	8	31
No. of interactions observed		26,083	32,726	28,194	23,641	110,644

Source: Flanders, *Teacher Influence, Pupil Attitudes, and Achievement* (Washington, D.C.: U.S. Department of Health, Education, and Welfare, 1965), pp. 75-76.

teacher, in effect, controls the flow of substantive information, and nothing else of a talking nature happens nearly as frequently. Second, although patterns of interaction vary with subject matter, the frequencies of each category across subjects are very similar, and the general pattern appearing in the Total column is repeated in each type of classroom (save for minor variations in the rank order of frequencies). The overall pattern of teacher talk is very similar for both math and social studies and for classrooms characterized both as direct and indirect. Finally, the sum of direct and indirect forms of teaching in both types of classrooms amounts to less than 17% of all interaction, a point we will return to later.

An empirical confirmation of Flanders's argument depends, at a minimum, on his ability to demonstrate positive relationships between teacher style and (1) academic achievement and (2) student dependency. With respect to achievement, he treats the social studies and mathematics classes separately, and within each he compares the achievement scores of students (adjusted for IQ) in the predominantly indirect classes with those in the direct classes. He finds that in each subject matter, and for all three IQ groups into which the classes are partitioned, students in indirect classes achieve at a higher level than those in direct classes.[7]

These findings constitute a straightforward test of the argument but nevertheless pose questions. While Flanders showed that about 17% of all classroom interaction is either direct or indirect, obviously the students experienced all the interactions, not just the direct and indirect ones. Flanders, however, attributes mean differences in achievement only to the 17% of interactive events, while ignoring the other 83%. Moreover, while in indirect classrooms there is about 5-6% more indirect teaching compared to direct classrooms, there is close to 9% more *lecturing*. Accordingly, an equally plausible interpretation of the achievement findings—in fact, a slightly more plausible one— is that the superior achievement in the indirect classrooms is attributable to lecturing, a rather direct form of instruction (whether or not associated with subject matter). This is because the difference in lecturing is quite large, and lecturing takes up far more classroom time than the combination of direct and indirect teaching. This conclusion contradicts Flanders's argument, although there is not much force behind either interpretation because most of what occurs in the classroom does not figure in the empirical test. There is, in short, substantial reason to doubt the salutary impact of indirect teaching on achievement.

With respect to student dependence, Flanders argues that direct teaching fosters dependency on teachers at the expense of freedom of action. By implication, levels of achievement should be higher when students are free to inquire into problems and solve them than when they are not. He employs a dependence-proneness test to characterize students according to the extent to which they "solicit teacher support, approval, and direction" (Flanders, 1965, p.

46). (Why a generalized student trait, as he refers to what the test measures, should provide evidence on the influence of teaching style on dependency rather than on the dependency that students bring with them to the classroom is not clear.) Within each math and social studies class, Flanders finds the dependency score unrelated to teaching style (direct and indirect). Thus dependency proneness introduced as the third variable to account for the relationship between teaching style and achievement has no bearing on that relationship (Flanders, 1965, p. 101).

Flanders's data and his analysis of it fail to support his formulation and it is reasonable to ask how things came to such a pass. As indicated earlier, his formulation originates in an ongoing tradition of research on leadership and group climate. It does not, however, grow from any description of classroom events or from any analysis of what is problematic about classrooms and teaching. Except as a teacher is in some sense a classroom leader, there is no necessary resemblance between teachers and other kinds of leaders, between classrooms and other kinds of groups, or between instructional (or class management) activities and other kinds of activities. Thus the treatment of teachers in classrooms as similar in character to other leader-group phenomena is unjustified. There is no prior attempt to characterize the kind of group a classroom is, or to characterize the events that make classroom activities problematic, as guides to developing a formulation; the formulation, in short, is imposed. The nonsubstantive character of Flanders's study appears clearly in his later work, which is concerned with the methodological refinement of his interaction analysis: "The concept of *classroom interaction* refers to the chain of events which occur one after the other, each occupying only a small segment of time. *Teaching behavior* has been defined as acts by the teacher which occur in the context of classroom interaction" (Flanders, 1970, pp. 3-4). What is noteworthy about these definitions is their remoteness from substantive concern. For example, what is it about the interaction that makes it classroom interaction? What is the sequence of events which, when chained together, characterizes classrooms? Flanders does not address himself to these questions and so the classroom appears to be a location for studying instruction as interaction rather than a setting with peculiar properties in which instruction occurs.

Although this work shows no deliberate, substantive concern with classrooms, an empirical picture of a classroom interaction pattern does emerge. As we noted earlier, that pattern is consistent (with small variations) within subgroups of Flanders's sample; it also resembles one found by Bellack et al. (1966) which shows classroom activities dominated by teachers' talk. While Flanders finds that lecturing predominates, Bellack et al. and Hoetker and Ahlbrand (1969) find that recitation predominates. In both forms of instruction, the teacher runs things. Teacher domination violates what many people believe to be good pedagogical practice—predicated on free, active, and full participation by students. While far less than full empirical documentation of the pattern of teacher dominance has been made, the phenomenon has been discovered often enough to require an explanation. The upshot of Flanders's work is to pose the questions:

What classroom characteristics make lecturing and recitation adaptive responses?

What instructional alternatives are foregone when learning and recitation are selected?

What are the gains and the costs of selecting such activities?

Classroom Language

Whether for good or for ill, the main burden of instructional research has been carried by psychologists. The idea that a psychology of learning might serve as the proper conceptual basis to formulate teaching (or instruction) has drawn fire—well deserved, we believe. But what of the alternatives? Smith and Meux (1962) argue that achievement, in particular students' development of critical thinking, is related to the "logical demands" of instruction. If instruction displays logical rigor, if it contains the activities that comprise logical thought—defining, explaining, proving, justifying, and the like—students will be able to solve problems using these intellectual skills and as a consequence will learn to think critically. Different subject matters, with minor variations, embody these elements of logic. This perspective leads to an exploration of the logic of teaching, to the discovery of the logical operations entailed in instruction. The logical structure of teaching can thus be sought in the didactic discourse occurring in classrooms (Smith & Meux, 1962).

With some variations in theme, the study of instruction as the analysis of discourse and the impact of discourse on achievement constitutes the research agenda of Bellack et al. (1966). They say, "We focused on language as the main instrument of communication in teaching. Our major task was to describe the patterned processes of verbal interaction that characterize classrooms in action" (p. 1). To that end, 345 high school students and their 15 teachers were studied as they covered the material in a pamphlet on international trade interpolated for research purposes into the curriculum over a span of four class lessons. Teachers were asked to teach as they customarily do and not in any special way for the unit.

Bellack et al. see instruction as a language game played by teachers and students. Exactly what *games* are remains unclear, except that they have *rules* to be learned and followed. Playing according to the rules entails making *moves*, that is, verbal statements which have pedagogical significance, presumably because they occur in classrooms. Bellack et al. give this example of their procedure:

In analyzing the utterance of a teacher or students at a given point in class discussion, we were first of all concerned with the pedagogical significance of what the speaker was saying—whether, for example, he was structuring the class discussion by launching or focusing attention on a topic or problem, eliciting a response from a member of the class, answering a question posed by a previous speaker, or reacting to a comment previously made (p. 3).

The content of communication is also a matter of interest: the topic, the facts called for, the explanations offered, the assignment made. Presumably what holds the enterprise together, what constitutes it as a game, is that the players have reciprocal roles, and certain kinds of verbal statements presume responsive utterances in return. Thus, Bellack et al. say, "Questions are asked to be answered; assignments are made to be carried out; explanations are made to be understood" (p. 2). Winning and losing are judged in terms of gains accruing to the reciprocal partner; that is, if teachers move (instruct) well, students win (gain in achievement). How the teacher wins, presumably as a consequence of student moves, is not clear. If teacher winning means instructing well, we are back to the definition of student winning; if it means that the teacher becomes happy, that is conceptually trivial. The game metaphor, in short, evaporates rather quickly and in fact is irrelevant to the empirical study.

The nature of pedagogical moves is the heart of the matter, and Bellack et al. find that "the examination of the transcripts of classroom discourse [generated by the discussion of the pamphlet on international trade, and duly tape recorded] suggested that the verbal actions of students and teachers could be classified in four major categories . . . in terms of the pedagogical functions they perform in classroom discourse" (p. 4). These functions are: (1) structuring, or setting the context for subsequent conduct by starting or stopping interaction; (2) soliciting, or eliciting verbal responses or attention; (3) responding, or answering solicitations; and (4) reacting, acting with respect to or on the occasion of one of the other three moves, but not in direct response (as, for example, commenting upon). It is important to understand pedagogical moves in terms of their functions *for classroom discourse,* and also that classroom discourse has in effect been equated with instruction. We will consider whether we indeed should treat the two as the same later.

These four moves appear, according to Bellack et al., not in isolation but in cycles:

A teaching cycle begins either with a structuring or with a soliciting move, both of which are *initiating* maneuvers; they serve the function of getting a cycle under way. In contrast, responding and reacting moves are *reflexive* in nature; they are either solicited or occasioned by a preceding move and therefore cannot begin a cycle (p. 5).

It is not clear whether the contention that cycles begin with structuring or soliciting moves is empirical, definitional, or normative, nor is it clear where the four categories of moves come from. Only one answer is proffered by Bellack et al.: they were suggested by the transcripts themselves (p. 4).

Starting with the concepts of moves and cycles, Bellack et al. expand their formulation to include discourse pertaining to subject matter (i.e., international trade), to instructional management (i.e., classroom activities and assignments), and to the logical and extralogical operations entailed in both these areas (i.e., use of definitions, explanations, statements of fact, opinions, justifications, and evaluations). They treat instruction as embodied in classroom discourse in terms of what it says about subject matter, classroom management, and the elements of discourse. From the transcripts of tape-recorded classroom proceedings, Bellack et al. code and summarize their data as follows: The question, "Why do industrialized countries trade the most?" is presented symbolically as T/SOL/TWH/XPL/1/-/-/-. This means that the teacher (T) solicits (SOL) a response pertaining to the substantive area "who trades with whom" (TWH), which involves the logical process of explaining (XPL) in one (1) line of transcript, and the statement has no management function (-/-/-).

The major findings of Bellack et al. (1966) are presented in Table 3 as frequency distributions of both moves and lines of typed transcript. The distributions displayed according to each measure differ, but not by much, and the reasons for the differences are obscure. Teachers talk (measured in lines) three times as much as students; they make three moves for every two made by students; and while there is some variation in these proportions, they remain stable across the 15 classrooms and across all four class sessions

TABLE 3
Distribution of Pedagogical Moves

Pedagogical Move	Frequency of Moves 100%	Percent of All Moves By Teachers	By Pupils	Percent of Pupil Moves	Percent of Pupil Lines	Percent of Teacher Moves	Percent of Teacher Lines
Soliciting	5,135	86.0%	14.0%	11.3%	8.7%	46.6%	28.0%
Responding	4,385	12.0	88.0	65.4	57.5	5.5	6.8
Structuring	854[a]	86.0	12.0	1.8	11.1	7.7	20.1
Reacting	4,649	81.0	19.0	15.1	19.1	39.2	44.7
Not codable				6.4	3.6	1.0	0.4
				100%	100%	100%	100%
Frequency of moves and lines				5,910	11,659	9,565	30,897

[a] 2 percent of moves structured by audiovisual devices.
Source: Adapted from Bellack et al., *The Language of the Classroom* (New York: Teachers College Press, 1966), pp. 46-48.

(pp. 42-46). Teachers account for better than 80% of all soliciting, structuring, and reacting; students account for almost 90% of all responding; over half the student talk is responding. Soliciting and reacting constitute the lion's share of teacher talk. Within this array of categories, these patterns of discourse suggest that instruction is primarily recitational in character.

The data on cycles (as distinct from moves) provide stronger evidence for the predominance of the recitational pattern. Among 18 different cycle patterns, the soliciting-responding and soliciting-responding-reacting patterns account for about 50%; the remaining 50% is finely scattered among the other 16 types of cycles, in no case reaching 10% (pp. 196, 202-203). Bellack et al. summarize the findings as follows:

The pedagogical roles of the classroom are clearly delineated for teachers and pupils. Teachers are responsible for structuring the lesson, soliciting responses from pupils, reacting to pupils' responses, and, to some extent, summarizing aspects of the discourse. The pupil's primary task is to respond to the teacher's solicitations. Occasionally pupils react to preceding statements, but these reactions are rarely evaluative. Pupils do not overtly rate teachers' statements, and they rate other pupils' responses only when the teacher asks them to do so (pp. 84-85).

The use of *role* and *responsibility* in this statement, both implying a normative framework prior to the events, might be objected to, but in any case Bellack et al. do observe patterns of talk.

At least 70% of classroom discourse in the Bellack et al. study pertains directly to the subject matter, though classes vary according to which aspects of the material are emphasized (pp.70-71). The findings, however, cannot be interpreted because there is no way to determine whether this is a lot of subject-related talk or a little, and whether it is discourse in general or in response to the fact that teachers are asked to teach international trade (about which they and their students are probably not knowledgeable) for four class sessions set aside from their usual curriculum. Nearly half (47%) of the moves serve a managerial function, and about half of these are of the kind "that's correct" and "repeat that, please." Nearly 10% pertain to matters of procedure, materials, and assignment. About 63% of the substantive moves involve logical operations, and about 80% of these constitute statements of fact and explanations, with analytic and evaluative operations making up the remainder (pp. 74-75). These results are difficult to interpret save for the reasonable conjecture that when unfamiliar subject matter is covered in a short time (four sessions), much time will be spent simply describing what the material is about.

Bellack et al. summarize their general findings about the frequencies of different kinds of discourse classified in terms of moves, meaning, and logic. They do not, however, interpret them. Accordingly, nothing is contributed to our understanding of why discourse is classified in these particular ways and why discourse and nothing else is the subject of analysis. They do determine whether pedagogical moves relate to changing attitudes toward economics as a subject. No change in mean classroom attitude toward the study of economics occurs between a pretest and a posttest, nor is it clear that any should be expected.

With respect to gains in knowledge about economics, Bellack et al. identify two groups of classrooms, one showing higher information levels than expected according to verbal ability, the other showing lower levels.[8] Then they examine the distributions of teacher moves, cycles, and their logical concomitants to determine whether the high and low groups of classrooms differ with respect to discourse. This *post hoc* analysis shows, for example, that teachers of the high-information-level classrooms are somewhat less active than those in the low-information-level classrooms. High-level classes fall in the average range for structuring moves, length of cycles, and proportion of teacher-initiated cycles; low-level classes fall at the extremes. Most of the comparisons show no differences, but why expect differences? Nothing in the move-cycle formulation leads to a conceptual connection between these particular linguistic forms and gains in knowledge.

Furthermore, there is every reason to believe that the students read the pamphlet on international trade, though whether they actually did so is not made clear. What they learned might have more to do with what they read, and perhaps with their interest in the subject, than with subtle variations in pedagogical moves. However, to take students' reading and the information gleaned from it into account is to unravel Bellack's formulation and his categories, for it acknowledges that more happens in a classroom than can be formulated as talk. And if reading occurs in classrooms (or as homework), what else might occur that may not be encompassed by the analysis of moves and cycles? Lots of things.

As we indicated earlier, it is important to determine whether classroom discourse should be regarded as the same thing as instruction.[9] While it is true that much classroom activity consists of discourse, surely everything of instructional significance cannot be so considered. When students read or do math problems they are not engaged in discourse, nor are teachers when they write comments on students' work. When teachers arrange students in groups and assign materials to them, they are not primarily engaged in discourse. Similarly, both teachers and students engage in discourse that has no instructional intention or effect. This work contains no rationale for treating discourse as the only source of data, and, if there is a rationale, it is not based upon a prior analysis of observed classroom characteristics or events, or upon a reasoned justification that discourse, among all classroom events, is critical to understanding the nature and impact of instruction. For teachers to talk about the assignment of work, for example, is not the same thing instructionally as to assign work. For teachers and students to discuss international trade is not the same as to read about it. Reading and discussing are both forms of instruction, but learning cannot be attributed simply to discussing when the subject matter has also been read.

Central to Bellack's et al.'s formulation is the concept of rules derived from the game metaphor:

Within the theoretical framework of this research, the results reported . . . may be summarized in terms of the rules of the classroom game of teaching. Even though teachers rarely state the rules explicitly, and although classes differ somewhat in details, the results indicate that common elements underlie much of the teaching game: pupils and teachers follow a set of implicit rules with few deviations. These rules define the teaching game (p. 237).

A summary description of common elements *cannot* provide evidence of rule-governed conduct; if it did, we should be able to identify the rules of the road by observing how people actually drive, a specious argument at best. Surely a connection exists between how people drive and the rules of the road, but is driving not better understood if we have some knowledge of traffic signals, driving conditions, and the contingencies that arise in traffic? All sorts of stable patterns of conduct exist that do not constitute rule-following. Perhaps the closest Bellack et al. come to identifying a rule is their contention that asking a question indicates the expectation of an answer. This contention is a statement about a rule for conversations in general and does not illuminate anything special about classroom discourse. The classroom question is why teachers, when engaged in instruction, ask questions, of what kinds, at what rate, and under what circumstances.

What Bellack et al. do show is that when new subject matter is introduced, the informational content of which is to be tested after a short period of discussion following reading, teachers will present it through recitation when they ordinarily teach this way, and indifferent attitudinal changes and gains in subject-related knowledge will be achieved. They do not show this to be a general proposition beyond the particularities of the circumstances because there are no contrasting cases. Nor do they show anything about the rules of discourse or of classroom instruction, because both the data and the formulation underlying them are inappropriate to these purposes.

Bellack et al. indicate by prior assertion what instruction is—a language game. Rather than test the viability of the assertion, they improperly claim that the mere existence of certain patterns of behavior constitutes evidence that the patterns are normatively determined and are manifestations of rules of the language game. Aside from this argument by fiat, their findings show two things. First, there is presumptive evidence that instructional activity takes a recitational form, but that evidence is not deemed problematic. Second, though teachers choose among different instructional tasks—in this case, between reading and discussing written material—the preoccupation of Bellack et al. with language games prevents them from considering that instruction entails a selection among tasks and the allocation of resources to them under prevailing conditions.

Mastery Learning

Mastery learning is an instructional strategy designed to remedy the problems of low and dispersed achievement among class members. It aims to enable all (or nearly all) students to master a particular school task at a very high level of proficiency.[10] In broad outline, mastery learning is an instructional scheme in which each student takes the time he or she needs to reach an absolute criterion of mastery. It purports to offer an alternative to the usual pattern of classroom learning, in which individual differences in student aptitude are manifested in widely distributed levels of achievement, under the constraints of equal school time available to all students. While mastery conditions cannot eliminate differences in aptitude, they are designed to provide experiences that permit even the slowest learners to reach mastery within the time allotments that formal schooling makes available.

To understand mastery learning, its instructional principles must be distinguished from its instructional arrangements. The principles are based upon several propositions about the psychological conditions of learning and a conception of instruction believed to create those conditions. The fundamental premise is that a student's likelihood of learning a task depends on (1) aptitudes, which in turn are related to the amount of prior learning or to genetic origins; (2) ability to understand instruction, presumably a function of general intelligence and verbal ability; and (3) perseverance, the amount of time the student is willing to spend learning the task (Carroll, 1963, pp. 726-728).[11] Aptitude is defined as the amount of time needed to learn a specific task (Carroll, 1963, pp. 725-726).

According to Carroll (1963), success in learning also depends on the quality of instruction:

The learner must be told, in words he can understand, what he is to learn and how he is to learn it. . . [He must also] be put into adequate sensory contact with the material to be learned. . . The various aspects of the learning task must be presented in such an order and with such detail that, as far as possible, every step of the learning is adequately prepared for by a previous step. It may also mean that the instruction must be adapted for the special needs and characteristics of the learner, including his stage of learning (p. 726).

Success depends as well on the time allowed by the teacher for learning. The amount of time is characteristically managed by schools and teachers by means of tracking and by varying the pace of instruction, and it is usually constrained by the length of school periods, days, terms, or years. Accordingly, mastery learning strategies are based on pedagogical principles that pertain to three conditions at the level of the individual student: aptitude, ability to understand instruction, and perseverance; and two conditions at the classroom or school level: quality of instruction, and time allowed for learning.

Based upon Carroll's analysis, Bloom (1968) draws a fundamental implication for the design of instruction in mastery learning:

If the students are normally distributed with respect to aptitude [the time needed for learning] but the kind and quality of instruction and the amount of time available for learning are made appropriate to the characteristics of *each* student, the majority of students may be expected to achieve mastery of the subject (p. 3).[12]

Employing Carroll's psychological principles of instruction and learning, Bloom contends, can make it possible to individualize instruction over time to the extent that all students will learn to the same level of mastery as the ablest, and the variation in time required to achieve that end will be minimized.

The principles of mastery learning instruction are based on the model of a tutorial. Bloom states: "One approach to determining the specific aspects of quality of instruction may be derived from observing a very good tutor attempting to teach something to one student. What is the interaction that appears to promote the learning of this one student?" (Bloom, 1971, p. 11). This does not mean that schools should provide a tutor for each student, but rather that what teachers do in classrooms should be based on the principles governing the practices of tutors with individual students: They provide appropriate cues, gain the student's active participation, assure the availability of rewards, and provide feedback and correction (Bloom, 1976, pp. 112-115). At the core of this formulation is the injunction to attend to the particulars of *each* student's learning and to so govern *classroom* instruction. By this means the teacher can bring all or most students to a high level of achievement, whatever their individual starting places and the diversity of their routes along the way.

The arrangement of mastery learning instruction consists of two phases, one devoted to the initial learning of tasks and the second to the remediation of difficulties experienced by students in encountering the tasks. Most striking about the initial-learning arrangements is a reliance on materials arranged in sequence of difficulty or complexity. Programmed and sequenced materials, worked upon by all members of a class, are by definition highly standardized. All students perform the same activities, and the order of materials is established according to an abstraction such as complexity rather than to the particular problems of individual students. This phase of mastery learning does not deal with individualized instruction, at least as far as the nature of tasks and materials are concerned.

It is in the remedial phase that the principles of the tutorial are incorporated. First, remedial instruction is individualized through the device of formative testing: evaluating, diagnostically and nonevaluatively, the particular difficulties that students confront, as well as their strengths and weaknesses in approaching the materials. Second, it is individualized through the provision of feedback as governed by the results of the formative testing: actual tutoring, discussing the work in small groups, reading and working with alternative materials, participating in learning games. Each of these activities is designed to remedy the particular problems faced by the individual student. Third, it is individualized in pace; each student proceeds through the materials at his own rate. Finally, and most significantly, it is individualized in the total amount of time allowed; each student is permitted the time he or she needs to achieve mastery. In short, the principles of individualized instruction based on the tutorial apply clearly to the remedial stage of the mastery learning strategy, and only to that stage.

Other instructional innovations (Suppes, 1968; Talmage, 1975) involve the application of principles of individualized instruction within the classroom, but with one important difference: instruction is not individualized in the total amount of time allowed each student. Rather, students work for similar periods of time, and the consequence is highly dispersed achievement results. This outcome is at odds with the mastery learning goal of high and similar achievement among class members. Individualization of the total time allowed each student is a condition that is *necessary* for the mastery learning strategy to achieve its goal of bringing all class members to a high level of achievement. But while individualized total time makes a great deal of sense applied to one student at a time in tutorial instruction, it is at odds with the collective constraints of classrooms in which many students possess diverse individual characteristics, and with administrative constraints on the total time available in the school day. Time use in individual tutorials is largely unconstrained in its duration and flexibility, but to propose principles of instruction based upon that kind of time availability is to ignore the real constraints imposed by schools. Not only does individualized remediation require a time investment beyond that spent in group instruction, but it enters the instructional picture after students have shown that they need different amounts of time to learn and accordingly contributes to the *differential* utilization of time within classrooms.

We must consider mastery learning, both in conception and in instructional arrangement, as a strategy for using class time and instructional activities to remedy the problem presumably created by initial, standardized group learning: the need to instruct slow students who have not mastered the task at a sufficiently high level. The difficulty with the mastery learning formulation is that it is conceptualized to deal with individuals as if they were receiving tutorial instruction (at least during remediation), when in fact they are members of classrooms receiving group instruction. This means that time and instructional resources must be invested to deal with the problems that collectivities create, in addition to those that individual differences create. In our attempt to discover what sort of solution mastery learning proposes to the problems of low and dispersed achievement, we consider particularly the way in which it treats the properties of classrooms. The classroom represents the arena in which both the individual and collective aspects of instruction are worked out.

In general, the classroom in this formulation is a place where there are students, tasks to be learned, group instruction, feedback and correction procedures, tutors, and teachers. It is difficult, however, to get a sense of the kind of collective enterprise it is from conceptual statements in the literature, because most of its properties are defined in individual and not in aggregate terms (e.g., Carroll's statement of learning principles and Bloom's translation of them into the tutorial model). Matters of classroom size and composition, for example, do not receive the kind of attention one might expect if these considerations were central to the formulation; neither do such topics as the ratio of teachers to students, appropriate duration of instructional sessions, patterns of interaction, grouping, and the like.

What light does the empirical work on mastery learning shed on the collective aspects of instruction? The formulation, expressed at the level of individuals, obviously bears on the collective character of classrooms, and we will consider it with respect to (1) class composition, (2) classroom instruction, and (3) the management of time.

Class Composition.   Mastery learning does not explicitly consider the student composition of classrooms in terms of variation in aptitude, interest, motivation, perseverance, cognitive style, and the like. Although there is direct concern with the cognitive and affective inputs and outcomes of instruction, classroom composition is not treated as an instructional condition. Some of the important empirical efforts to test the mastery strategy provide only the scantest information about classroom composition, and none addresses the composition question directly.

Block (1970), in his study of eighth-graders, indicates that his subjects were middle- and lower-middle-class students "who perform at the national norms on most standardized tests and in other ways are typical of eighth graders across the country" (p. 60), hardly a generous description. From his initial sample of 109 subjects, he eliminated 18 of the brightest to serve as tutors during the implementation of the strategy and another 10 whose performance consistently exceeded or failed to reach mastery criteria or who were unwilling to participate. While Block correctly acknowledges the error that might have resulted from these exclusions, they must also be understood as something different. The impact of the exclusions is to create homogeneous classrooms which constitute the compositional context for the mastery strategy. Class composition is an instructional condition not addressed by the mastery formulation, but it should be. Block, then, is an experimental study whose independent variable is manipulated but not measured and is treated as an instructional condition without being conceptualized as one.

Although L. W. Anderson's (1973) work does not involve similar wholesale exclusions, his subjects possess an above-average verbal IQ (111), with a standard deviation of 8 (p. 116). A similarly composed sample, with IQs distributed between 90 and 130 and clustering in the 110 to 120 range, is employed by Arlin (1973, p. 25). It is surprising that these studies do not contain detailed descriptions of the cognitive characteristics of the subjects, simply to test the conditions under which a mastery strategy works.

Aside from the vagaries of sampling that have led to the creation of relatively homogeneous classes, Block's (1971) review of past mastery research on elementary, secondary, and university students shows that "mastery approaches have produced best results in subjects possessing . . . either minimal prior learning or previous learning which most learners already possessed" (pp. 65-66). Similarly, Anderson (1973, pp. 106-107) and Arlin (1973, p. 24) stress the importance of cognitive prerequisites. In essence, they state that mastery strategies are most effective when students, whatever their intelligence, *already* possess the requisite skills to perform the task in question at the stated criterion of mastery. In all likelihood, however, those who possess the prerequisite skills also possess the necessary intelligence. Whether such methods would work with cognitively heterogeneous samples of students remains an open question, since most of the empirical efforts to date investigate relatively homogeneous groups. The most intractable problems of instruction, however, arise in classrooms where wide disparities of skills and cognitive abilities prevail. The utility of both the formulation and the strategy will depend on what is learned about classrooms of similar levels of mean achievement but varying dispersion, and classrooms of similar dispersion of achievement but varying in mean level. These are the basic arrangements of instructional grouping.

Classroom Instruction. One striking aspect of the mastery learning formulation is the implicit replacement, during the remediation phase, of the teacher as part of classroom organization by diagnostic-feedback-corrective activities carried out largely by tutors. Teachers are present in mastery classrooms, but what they do is not clear, and the activities of tutors are only slightly more clear. As Bloom (1968) states: "Our approach has been to supplement regular group instruction by using diagnostic procedures and alternative instructional methods and materials in such a way as to bring a large proportion of the students to a predetermined standard of achievement" (p. 8). While the diagnostic procedures and alternative instructional methods and materials

are indeed described, regular group instruction is not. There is also no description of how the old and the new instructional methods are combined into
a newly organized classroom or other group arrangement. The mastery formulation clearly does not mean conventional lecturing, question and answer
recitation, or discussion; in fact, these instructional forms are generally viewed
as the sorts of time-restricted strategies that perpetuate undesirable differences
in student achievement. Conventional instruction is the foil against which
mastery strategies are set.

Instead of a view of collective instruction, a set of psychological propositions about learning stimuli contained in the concept *quality of instruction*
is provided. As we indicated earlier, good quality is manifest in "the teacher
(or any person who prepares the materials of instruction)" (Carroll, 1963,
p. 726) presenting subject matter clearly, visibly, audibly, and understandably,
as well as in appropriate order and detail, so that it is suitable for the needs
of all students. Bloom accepts this formulation but puts particular stress
on the last point: *"the degree to which the presentation, explanation, and
ordering of a task to be learned approach the optimum for a given learner"*
(Bloom, 1968, p. 4). "Quality of instruction," one of the main determinants
of achievement, is treated conceptually at the same level of abstraction as
"cognitive entry behavior" (e.g., intelligence, verbal ability, and other stable
attributes of personality) and "affective entry behavior" (e.g., interest, motivation), both of which represent conditions influencing the time needed to
achieve (Bloom, 1971, pp. 11-12; L. W. Anderson, 1973, pp. 34-35).

The pedagogical procedures are designed to realize these principles in
practice. Tutoring, primarily for those students who learn slowly, represents
the basic model. It is justified as a social arrangement that affords the instructor the best opportunities to provide the most appropriate kinds of feedback
and guidance to remedy individual learning difficulties. The principle of the
tutorial is that one instructor responsible for each student's learning is in
the best position to design and present appropriate materials, diagnose the
nature of the difficulties they pose, and provide appropriate remedies. Short
of sustained tutorial arrangements, the mastery learning strategy provides
alternatives that fit more comfortably within the time and budgetary constraints under which schools operate: small-group discussions, the use of audiovisual aids and academic games, having students rework the learning task
with similar or different materials.

As far as we can tell, instruction in mastery learning refers to the presentation of learning materials by teachers or tutors to *individual* students, to
the tutorial review and diagnostic evaluation of individuals' work, and to
the capacity of the materials themselves to impart the pertinent knowledge
required for students to complete the learning task. This conception of instruction does not say how tutors should tutor, how teachers should group (or
not group) in a classroom, how they should discipline, keep order, gain atten-

tion, motivate, ask and answer questions; in short, the formulation of instruction does not refer to the collective aspects of classroom life.

From this view of instruction emerges an implicit model of the classroom as consisting of isolated individuals working alone with materials, and a congeries of dyadic short-term relationships between teacher-tutors and students. Beyond these dyads, save for small-group discussions governed by remedial appropriateness, classrooms have no social properties. Presumably, then, whether students work exclusively in isolated cubicles or on nailed-to-the-floor desks, whether they can come and go, and so on, are matters of indifference to this *formulation* (though not necessarily to its designers).

Preoccupation with the individual learner appears most clearly in Bloom's (1976, pp. 112-115) distinction between the management of learning and the management of learners, a distinction based upon the description of a one-to-one tutorial arrangement. Bloom treats the management of learners (in particular, the securing of their attention) as a *distraction* pertaining more to administrative expectations and the need for control than to instruction and learning. But it is not a distraction; it is an integral part of classroom teaching precisely because classes are social aggregates whose members have diverse individual characteristics and whose conduct must be managed *en masse*, in groups, and individually. Classroom instruction cannot be understood in terms of a model based on a congeries of dyads, and while the management of learners does not usually appear as a problem in tutorial instruction, it does in classroom instruction. The mastery strategy itself requires teachers to tutor, supervise small groups, provide alternative materials, change activities, and carry on whole-class instruction, all at the same time. This poses inescapable problems in the managing of learners. (The problematics of these activities are discussed by Kounin, 1970.)

Management of Time. Time is of the essence for the mastery learning formulation, since all or most students are to achieve high levels of task mastery, and their differences in aptitude are expressed in how long it takes them to learn. The time actually taken by students to achieve mastery must be reasonably manageable and must fall within the time spans that schools can realistically allot to the task, and in reconciling the time differences between faster and slower students, enough time must be allowed for slower students to reach the same level of mastery as faster ones. Of course, schools always deal with time in one way or another: students repeat grades (a practice dropped by most American schools but still used widely in other countries), are assigned to different tracks distinguished by how fast they proceed or how difficult the work they undertake is, attend summer schools, receive remedial help during and after school, and so forth. Mastery learning is not unique in proposing a solution to the time problem; its uniqueness lies in attempting to reduce the *combined* instructional time of initial *and* remedial learning in the context of high mastery standards. As Arlin (1973) correctly argues, the viability of mastery learning depends on its success in both increasing mean learning rate and decreasing learning rate variance (Chap. 2). Its viability also depends on keeping the mastery level high among the slower students (it would be easy to reach mastery criteria if they were set very low) and on keeping the amount of time required within limits manageable in ordinary school environments. We are, after all, talking about *school* learning.

The time problem posed by mastery learning is graphically described by Bloom (1971), who considers its application in a course in a particular subject which is divided into ten subunits organized in a transitive, sequential order: "Let us assume that 90 percent of the students learn Unit 1 adequately (or at a level of mastery) while 10 percent do not. . . . These 10 percent are then helped (outside of class time) until at least 5 percent or more have achieved mastery. The proportion who achieve mastery of Unit 1 will now reach 95 percent . . . before they enter Unit 2" [and so on through all successive units] . . . Using the same summative examination as [in the case of ordinary classroom learning] we should find that over 90 percent of the students under [mastery conditions] reach about the same level of achievement as the top 10 percent under [ordinary nonmastery conditions] (pp. 7-8). The question, then, is whether the time spent out of class in remediation is manageable under school conditions. A correlative question is what happens to those students who achieve the level of mastery on the first try (without remediation) while the minority needing help receive it. The real-time considerations must be kept in mind because studies by several investigators show that time variations between fast and slow learners under ordinary (nonmastery) conditions range from 1:3 to 1:6.

Block's (1970) study provides important evidence on time utilization in a conventional (nonmastery) classroom compared with four experimental (mastery) classrooms. Each of the latter worked at achieving different mastery criteria (65%, 75%, 85%, and 95%) over three successive, cumulative instructional units concerned with matrix algebra computation. Table 4 shows that the four mastery classes spent very similar amounts of original learning time, without review and correction (columns 2, 3, and 4), and that three of the four spent very similar amounts on review (Column 1). All the experimental groups spent more time in original learning than the control group. Showing that time expenditures decline is very important for the mastery model, because review time constitutes an *increment* over what is spent on conventional (nonmastery) instruction. This time must eventually be saved if instructional time used in mastery learning procedures is to fit reasonably within the time constraints of school days, weeks, or terms.

With Block's data, the only way to estimate level of performance as a function of total time used is to divide the mean percent correct on Unit III (Column 7) by total time used in original learning and review (Column

TABLE 4
Expenditure of Time on Original Learning and Review in Mastery Classes under Four Mastery Criteria and in a Nonmastery Class

Mastery Criterion of Class	(1) Total Mean Time Spent in Review	Mean Time Spent in Original Learning, by Unit[a]				(6 = 1 ÷ 5) Total	(7) Mean Percent Correct[b]	(8 = 7/4) Mean Percent Correct/Time[c]	(9 = 7/6) Mean Percent Correct/Time[d]
		(2) Unit I	(3) Unit II	(4) Unit III	(5 = 2 ÷ 3 ÷ 4) Total				
95%	31.5	11.4	14.2	25.8	51.4	82.9	74.4	2.9	.89
85%	28.6	11.4	15.0	29.4	55.8	84.4	63.4	2.1	.75
75%	28.3	11.2	15.2	29.1	55.5	83.8	56.5	1.9	.67
65%	13.6	11.1	14.3	27.1	52.4	66.0	63.7	2.3	.96
Control[e]	—	11.1	12.7	25.3	49.1	49.1	54.2	2.1	1.10

[a] Block (1970), p. 73.
[b] Block (1970), p. 74. Based on Unit III formative test before correction and review.
[c] Block (1970), p. 75. Based on mean percent correct on Unit III divided by time spent on Unit III before correction and review.
[d] Based on mean percent correct on Unit III before correction and review, divided by total time over all units and correction and review.
[e] Block (1970), p. 72. The control group by definition spends no time in review.

Source: Block, The Effects of Various Levels of Performance on Selected Cognitive, Affective, and Time Variables (unpublished doctoral dissertation, University of Chicago, 1970).

6), as we show in Column 9. This shows clearly that the control group learned the most per unit of total time. It is plain from Block's analysis, as far as it goes, that the advantage (over the control group) in performance achieved through the mastery strategy comes from the additional investment in time spent in review, and then only for the 95% mastery group (Column 8). That finding, however, is restricted only to Unit III performance, based upon Unit III original learning time. Learning per unit of *total* time (Column 9) indicates that the investment in total time for review is ill spent. The importance of considering total time expended pertains to the question of how the mastery level strategy fits in with the overall time economy of schooling, a basic issue of administrative policy.

Block's student subjects were a homogeneous lot. Moreover, compared with more or less standard time units of schooling—weeks, months, semesters—this study uses a very brief period of time: less than an hour and a half of learning and review. And although it would not be appropriate to transform this period of instruction into larger school units (that would not be the same as studying mastery learning over, say, one month), it nevertheless appears that the remedial procedures consume a substantial amount of time, in relation to the length of conventional school days, and the questionable achievement gains derived from the additional time expenditure.

As Arlin (1973) states, the question of variance in learning time is critical for mastery learning strategies: it must be possible to reduce the spread in time between the fastest and slowest students in a class. Arlin compares a mastery and a nonmastery group over seven preliminary chapters of a science curriculum, prior to an eighth mastery criterion chapter. He finds that variance in the amount of time taken to reach an 85% mastery level on Chapter 8 is nine times greater in the nonmastery than in the mastery group. Variance in learning rate—time spent/units of material learned over Chapters 1-7—appears to diverge in the expected way, but the statistical test is equivocal. Time taken to master Chapter 8 is less in the mastery group, and learning level over Chapters 1-7 is greater. Time needed for review and correction, however, remains about constant over Chapters 1-7 for the mastery group (the nonmastery group, obviously, gets no review time) and the number of students needing review also remains about the same (Arlin, 1973, pp. 108-111). Arlin summarizes the results as follows:

The results confirmed the hypothesis that mastery students would learn new material at a faster, more efficient rate. However, this increased efficiency was not achieved without cost; the cost was a continual requirement of extra time and help to master previous material prior to learning new material at this faster rate. The failure of the results to confirm the hypothesis of diminishing review time presents a difficulty for mastery strategies (p. 111).

Regrettably, Arlin does not present his raw data (as Block does), showing actual amounts of time at each step of the eight-stage learning process; only statistical summaries are given.

The phenomenon of variance decline is most clearly described in schematic form by Bloom (1971):

On Unit 1 we are likely to find that some of the students reach mastery in 1X amount of time and help, while other students reach this same level of achievement only after as much as 10X amounts of time and help. Perhaps, by the 6th task, the variation may be from 1X to 4X. By the tenth unit, if all has gone well, the variation in time and help required may only be from 1X to 2X (Bloom, 1971, p. 8).

Aside from the importance of variance decline to an understanding of the pattern of learning over time, is this phenomenon of great importance for *school* learning and classroom organization? While the decrease in time needed (from 10X to 2X) by the slower compared to the faster students (1X), is dramatic, still, according to these hypothetical numbers, one class segment requires twice as much as another to complete the same task. In terms of the operation of schools, that is a very large difference.

Variance in time elapsed or in learning rate, moreover, has one very important implication for the operation of classrooms which appears to be unaddressed in the mastery literature but is of enormous importance to teachers. What do the students who reach mastery level without remediation do with their time while the others receive feedback, correction, tutoring, and the like? Bloom speaks of time spent after school,[13] but the studies cited here apparently entail remediation in the classroom, with all students mixed together. The matter does not come up in the research reports. If a handful of students in a class complete their work at the criterion level of mastery in 20 minutes, while others take as much as 40, does the first group sit quietly doing nothing, read, doodle, create a disturbance, tutor the others? Students with time on their hands are a perennial classroom problem, a problem in the management of learners, and teachers must prepare for it. There must be a way to keep a classroom full of students occupied, if for no other reason than that they are an aggregation of young people cooped up in a room, and the problems of managing such groups do not vanish when instruction is treated as a phenomenon existing only at the individual level of aggregation.

Summary. The difficulties with the mastery learning formulation are that it cannot indicate why managing learners is as important as managing learning, nor why teachers must plan time as well as the sequence of learning materials and tests. One reason for these difficulties is that the formulation fails to identify the classroom's collective properties which give rise both to management and time allocation problems. It also fails to acknowledge that classroom properties are instructional conditions equal in importance to individual student characteristics, and classrooms are part of a larger school environment which imposes constraints of its own. The tutorial model narrows attention to the learning of individual students and is unlikely to consider the instructional activities of teachers as being concerned with alternative allocations of time, materials, and tasks and dependent on the composition of a diverse collectivity and the constraints of time and administrative policy within which they operate. Tutors need not cope with diverse interests and capacities or the problems that diversity generates, and it is difficult to understand how classrooms can work with a model designed to fit a radically different case.

The great virtue of the formulation is that it brings the issues out with such clarity—although not by design. The management of learners is viewed as an aberration from the vantage point of the tutorial, but it nevertheless remains a kind of teaching activity in which teachers must invest relative to the management of learning—instruction. Block's evidence can be interpreted as showing the distribution of time investments in remedial and testing activities in terms of amount learned, although he prefers to treat it as showing the superiority of a prescribed conception of what instruction ought to be. A more adequate formulation of instruction must identify the classroom conditions and the individual characteristics that give rise to problems requiring one allocation of resources or another for their solution.

We assume that instruction is a technology, a set of activities involving the alternative uses of time, material, and people under prevailing constraints and opportunities to achieve some end. Of the three formulations reviewed so far, two (Flanders and Bellack et al.) are based upon prior commitments to a conceptual scheme, and the third (mastery learning) upon a commitment to reform. We have tried to show in each case the nature of the commitment (to interaction analysis, language games, and the tutorial model of individualized instruction), and demonstrate how it obscures other aspects of instruction and classroom setting. At the same time, our analysis shows how the presentation of each formulation contains within it useful evidence about how the understanding of instruction can be pursued, more dramatically so with mastery learning than with the others.

Classroom Management

In contrast to the investigations reviewed above, Kounin's work on group management is based on empirical observation of the consequences of a teacher reprimanding a student, on the student himself and on others observing the reprimand (a "ripple effect," as he calls it). The initial concern with ripple effects presumes that classrooms possess collective properties. According to Kounin (1970), "A classroom teacher is not a tutor working with one child at a time. Even though she may work with a single child at times, her main job is to work with a group of children in one room at one time" (p. 109). This statement is so obvious that it is difficult to understand why its implications have been so consistently ignored through decades of classroom research. It makes no sense to investigate ripple effects if classrooms are not collective entities, or if students are treated one at a time or aggregated in terms of a single characteristic. The idea of a ripple effect means that the conduct of students is considered differently, according to their situations in a classroom. In the case of a reprimand, the difference is whether they receive or observe it.

Kounin finds that, "The techniques of dealing with misbehavior, as such, are not significant determinants of how well or poorly children behave in classrooms, or with how successful a teacher is in preventing one child's misbehavior from contaging [sic] others" (p. 70). Whether teachers' reprimands are clear, firm, intense, or designed to steer students toward what they should be doing does not affect whether their reprimands stop the deviant acts. Observing that classrooms vary according to students' involvement in their work or misbehavior, Kounin questions what accounts for classroom variations in work involvement and deviance, if not reprimands and their impact on the audience.

When Kounin abandons the formulation of discipline as types of reprimands and ripple effects he alternatively considers how teachers manage student behavior in collective settings. This change in formulation represents a shift in attention from isolated classroom events (reprimands) and their effects to the regulation of continuing activities. The focus on reprimands, though it explicitly acknowledges the collective quality of classrooms, resembles the conventional model of classroom research, which treats one thing at a time.

In attempting to account for classroom variations in student work involvement and deviancy, Kounin fastens upon several aspects of teacher conduct that are tied to the collective properties of classrooms. The first is whether a teacher knows what is going on and communicates that fact to the students (*withitness,* in Kounin's language).[14] Does she reprimand the right child—the culprit—for misbehaving, or the wrong one—an onlooker or a victim? Does she punish serious misbehavior and let trivial misconduct go by? Does she catch the misbehavior of one student before it spreads to others or becomes more serious? Note that Kounin does not jettison reprimands as objects of investigation. Instead he removes them from the context of ripple effects and compliance and treats them as part of the more general classroom problems of maintaining credibility, being fair, and keeping order.

The second aspect of teacher conduct concerns attending to two issues at the same time (Kounin calls the capacity to do so *overlapping*).[15] Does the teacher deal with both issues or become preoccupied with one at the expense of the other? If a student misbehaves while she is occupied with a recitation, does she deal with the misbehavior and at the same time continue with the recitation? Or, if she is working with one child and another appears with a legitimate problem, does she deal with both children without sacrificing the interests of one of them? (No misbehavior is entailed in the latter case, just ordinary claims on the teacher's attention.)

Knowing what is going on and being able to cope with more than one issue simultaneously are manifestly similar; one probably cannot do the second without being able to do the first. Both concepts pertain directly to the fact that in classrooms spontaneous events arise from collective circumstances that are at moments impossible to predict; managing these events over time to maintain the classroom as a working environment is the teacher's responsibility.

While disruption represents one chronic problem a teacher confronts, she must also start, maintain, and change the flow of ongoing events. Does she, for example, successfully manage the physical movement entailed in changing from whole-class to group activities and in changing one set of work materials for another? Does she time the beginnings and endings of activities poorly (before all students are ready), change an activity and then change back, or fasten her attention on some unrelated matter and lose the continuity of the main activity? All these matters pertain to the smooth continuation and change of activities (in Kounin's language, *smoothness*).[16]

Another concept related to the continuity of classroom activities is *momentum:* maintaining recitation at a steady rate. Momentum is upset by slowdowns caused by teachers dwelling too long on issues already well understood or by breaking an activity or a group into parts when each would have served better as a whole.[17] The effect of breaking momentum is either to slow the work of a whole class unnecessarily or to cause some students to wait and do nothing until the rest catch up.

All four of these concepts pertain to a similar problem: maintaining the continued flow of activities over time in a collective setting. The first two differ from the second two primarily in terms of where the break in continuity originates: from the students or the teacher.

Kounin also considers a fifth concept, concerning the way teachers run recitations. If a teacher asks a question without first identifying who shall respond, she keeps each student in suspense about which one will be called upon. Over time, should this strategem work, students should be better prepared and more attentive than if the teacher identified the responder first and allowed the others to ignore the question. While Kounin claims that this form of classroom management (which he calls *group alerting*)[18] keeps students on their toes and holds their attention, he does not explain why keeping their attention is an important managerial activity.

Kounin also discusses how teachers discover what students know individually by asking them to present their work, to demonstrate their knowledge.

This teaching activity (called *accountability*) represents a conceptual departure from the others, which pertain to some group property, in identifying how teachers gauge individual student conduct in collective setttings.[19] The teacher holds a dual responsibility, for the class as a whole and for each individual in it.

Kounin gathered his data by videotape in 49 first- and second-grade classrooms in Detroit and in one middle-class suburb of that city. Two cameras were employed, one focused on the whole class, the other mainly on the teacher. He selected eight students, two each from four geographical quadrants of the class, and observed their conduct in detail. This sample of eight from each class varied in composition, for when a class activity necessitated the spatial redistribution of students, previously sampled students may have been moved out of their quadrant to be replaced by two others from another quadrant. The design distinguishes between recitation and seatwork activities and calls for the observation of teacher and student conduct under both conditions. Kounin's descriptions refer to grouped and whole-class activities which at times overlap the recitation and seatwork arrangements, but the group whole-class distinction does not form part of the design.[20]

Kounin identifies relationships between teachers' classroom management activities and the involvement of students in their work and students' freedom from deviancy. Note that these are indications not of achievement but of two major aspects of teaching: engaging students steadily in work and maintaining order. Classrooms are classified according to their rates of work involvement and of deviancy. Only in such academic activities as reading, arithmetic, social studies, and science is the behavior of all eight students per classroom coded for evidence of being "definitely and completely involved in work" or "definitely not involved in work" for ten-second intervals over the duration of the activity. Deviancy is coded in terms of the number of ten-second intervals in which the eight students were "engaged in nontask related deviancy" (Kounin, 1970, p. 64).[21] Involvement and deviancy rates differ in the seatwork and recitational arrangements; however, Kounin does not report the differences but rather analyzes the results separately within each classroom arrangement.

Kounin's description of statistical techniques is less than generous. It appears that he derives an involvement score, a deviancy score, and a score for each type of classroom management, and then calculates correlations and partial correlations of classroom scores between the independent and dependent variables. In recitation settings, he finds that withitness, overlapping, smoothness, momentum, group alerting, and accountability correlate with work involvement, with coefficients ranging from .46 to .66; and correlate with freedom from deviancy, with correlations ranging from .36 to .64. In seatwork settings, the correlations vary from .20 to .38 and from .29 to .51 for involvement and freedom from deviancy, respectively.[22] The correlations for each type of classroom management decrease when the other types are partialled out one by one. In most cases, the partials remain substantial; in others, the original relationship declines a great deal or vanishes.

There is strong overall support for Kounin's major argument that forms of classroom management are related to student work involvement and freedom from deviancy; and it is most important to recognize that his argument pertains not to the consequences of managerial activities for individual students but rather to classes as social units. Substantively, all types of management, with the exception of accountability, in one way or another pertain to the efforts of teachers to maintain the ongoing flow of events in the face of disruptions created either by students or by the teachers themselves. Accountability, on its face, appears to concern a different classroom issue: assessing the work of individuals within a collective context.

Kounin also examines the introduction by teachers of a variety of activities in seatwork, in order to prevent student boredom. Providing variety through such techniques as group or whole-class activities, using different kinds of materials, and calling for oral or silent reading is unrelated to the other forms of classroom management. Apparently, it constitutes a very different kind of management, which we will not examine in detail.

Kounin's work represents a marked departure from most studies of classroom process in several ways. First, his selection of independent variables shifts attention away from specific, isolated teacher actions (such as reprimanding) and their consequence for some particular outcome for individuals without regard to the collective and temporal properties of classes. Three of the independent variables—withitness, overlapping, and group alerting—tacitly indicate that classrooms include students who do different things at the same time (pay attention, intrude, cause trouble, recite, observe), and the teacher must deal with the variety of these activities when they occur together. In the same way, two of the independent variables—smoothness and momentum—indicate that classroom activities occur over time and that teachers must maintain the continuity of events. A sixth independent variable—accountability—indicates that despite the collective character of the class, teachers must attend to what the individuals in it are doing. It is this fundamental concern with the collective properties of the classroom that distinguishes Kounin's work.

Second, one dependent variable—work involvement—implicitly takes into account the fact that classroom activities extend over time. Involvement is not considered when activities begin and end very quickly. Freedom from deviancy, the second dependent variable, does not necessarily possess the same temporal quality; it can be understood either as more or less instantaneous compliance or as a matter of longer term maintenance of order.

A conspicuous omission in the formulation is failure to treat the relationship between the two dependent variables, because work involvement may have a major impact on freedom from deviancy. That is, the more students engage continuously in their work, the less likely are they to misbehave or to get involved in activities remote from the main task. It is unlikely that freedom from deviancy will foster work involvement.

As we noted earlier, it is difficult to interpret the high levels of intercorrelation among most of the independent variables and to interpret the pattern of partial correlations; and while Kounin's work is characterized by a massive plausibility, we do not know where his teacher categories come from or the reasons for their conceptual or statistical interrelationship. Of course classrooms are collective in character, and of course teachers must manage the collectivity. But what are the characteristics of the collectivity that make these particular categories of management germane? We can speculate about the answers. If students gathered in a public arena like a classroom differ individually in their interests, attentiveness, and distractibility, and as a consequence one of them misbehaves, the teacher must do something about it to discourage future misbehavior among the others. The action she takes must be appropriate to the magnitude of the offense and must accord with punishments meted out for similar infractions and different from those meted out for greater or lesser ones. Dealing equitably with infractions is an issue posed by the collective character of classrooms, and catching the right culprit (an aspect of withitness) is one response to an issue of equity that arises because classrooms are public places comprised of individuals in similar circumstances (Dreeben, 1968). This line of speculation links the characteristics of classrooms to the activities of teachers; and whether it is right or wrong, it provides a conceptual linkage between Kounin's independent and dependent variables, not just in this particular case but more generally.

We believe that Kounin's intuition serves him well. Others independently observe the importance of keeping students engaged in their work, not simply to improve their achievement but to keep the instructional enterprise moving. As Jackson (1968) comments:

The strategies of keeping students engrossed in their work include actions of two different sorts. One has to do with the maintenance of appropriate working conditions, with the prevention or elimination of extraneous disruptions. The other pertains to the appropriateness of course content, with the 'fit,' as it were, between the students and the material being studied (p. 103).

A theoretical argument, however, that describes class properties and identifies the problematic character of classroom events and the ways teachers deal with them is missing from Kounin's formulation.

The Multiple-Dimension Problem

Teaching in general and instruction in particular are forms of practice, and knowledge about their practice is useful to practitioners if it informs them about their situation and how to act in it. It is important to identify the dimensions of situations and actions in order to know what their parts are, but neither situations nor actions can be adequately understood in terms of simple, abstract dimensions. Knowledge gathered for scientific purposes, to test and develop theories, is not necessarily useful to practitioners because theories are highly general abstractions made from concrete situations. While identifying the abstract dimensions of teaching might well contribute to some theoretical purpose, practitioners (teachers) need to know how these dimensions are combined to characterize the specifics of their situation.

Though the multidimensional conceptions of Bellack et al. and Kounin represent advances over Flanders's dichotomous one-dimensional formulation, such conceptions of teaching pose their own problems: how to recombine the abstracted dimensions to represent a unified conception of teaching. Both Bellack et al. and Kounin (and most others who study teaching) do not resynthesize dimensions but rather examine each one separately for its influence on some aspect of student behavior.[23] Kounin shows, for example, that withitness and smoothness relate to student work involvement, but not how several combined dimensions manifest themselves.

One reason a composite picture might be useful is that each kind of management may not operate as a discrete force, as is assumed by separate analysis, but rather may be tied up with other kinds in conditional, concomitant, and incompatible relationships. Moreover, abstracting one dimension at a time does not permit a comprehension of actual teaching activities as they occur in classrooms.

Brophy and Evertson's (1974) study of teaching third-grade classes represents an extreme case of single-dimension analysis. They measure separately about 1,000 dimensions of teacher background and teaching style to determine their influence on achievement gain. There is no way so many dimensions can be considered one by one, and still provide a conception of teaching as a coherent activity. Two forms of combination of dimensions appear with some frequency. In one, dimensions are combined statistically, using, for example, factor analysis (Soar & Soar, 1972). Statistical combinations, however, are as abstract as single dimensions, and there is no necessary connection between them and reality. In a second, dimensions are combined on the basis of the empirical co-occurrence of events in time, as seen in the work of Gump (1967) and Grannis and Jackson (1973).[24] Bennett's (1976) solution to the multiple-dimension problem takes a statistical form as we shall discuss in detail later.

His work is explicitly polemical; he proposes to discover whether open schooling has the salutary impact on achievement and creativity that its proponents claim and whether formal teaching is instructionally superior to informal. He places himself in the "teaching style" tradition by comparing formal and informal instructional styles for their effect on achievement. This comes as something of a surprise, since his book begins with a critique of this tradition. Despite his use of the teaching-style rhetoric, Bennett's work is vastly different from that of, say, Flanders, and in fact does not concern style at all in the usual sense of group leadership. Bennett investigates the problem in two stages: first, he conceptualizes and operationalizes teaching style; second, he discovers whether relationships exist between teaching style and teacher characteristics, pupil personality, selection through eleven-plus exams, pupil classroom behavior, and pupil achievement.

From interviews with primary school teachers, Bennett extracted a list of teaching methods characteristic of progressive and traditional teachers. Using this material, he devised a questionnaire designed to discover what teachers do in classrooms. This instrument was completed by 1,258 third- and fourth-year primary grade teachers from the 871 grade schools in Lancashire and Cumbria administrative counties in England.

Bennett's work differs from that of others who study teaching style in that he gathers specific information about events occurring in classrooms: methods adopted, classroom organization, curriculum organization, testing, and discipline. He does not employ general categories of social interaction presumably applicable to a range of social situations, but not necessarily descriptive of any—a research strategy characteristic of many observational schemes.[25] He describes the nature of instructional and management activities in their own setting rather than patterns of interaction that just happen to occur in classrooms and whose relevance to instruction and management remains theoretically unclear. Bennett's questionnaire asks in very specific terms what teachers do (or say they do) when they instruct, keep order, test, assign homework, give grades, arrange students spatially, and set them to work. It also yields information about the activities of students as they engage in instructional activities.

While the use of teachers as informants might be questioned, Bennett takes pains to address the validity question raised by his procedures. However, we are mainly interested in his conceptualization of teacher style; the procedures, while alluded to in his book, are more completely described in an earlier paper (Bennett & Jordan, 1975). The issue, of course, is how observations of classroom teaching are combined into indices that represent differences and similarities among teachers. Bennett opts for the statistical device of cluster analysis.

The questionnaire responses for third-, mixed third and fourth, and fourth-year teachers were analyzed separately and with similar results. Bennett bases his discussion on the data gathered from 468 fourth-year teachers. First he does a principal components analysis that yields seven relatively independent factors but no single major dimension.

Factor I is clearly an assessment factor, including frequency of tests and homework.

Factor II concerns teaching mode, particularly with respect to group work.

Factor III relates to the physical control of the classroom.

Factor IV distinguishes between subject centered and integrated curriculum organization.

Factor V appears to be a teacher control factor, relating to restriction of movement and talk, smacking for disruptive behavior and teacher talk.

Factor VI again concerns teaching mode, but here with respect to pupil choice and work.

Factor VII relates to extrinsic motivation. (Bennett & Jordan, 1975, pp. 22-23)

In cluster analysis, not only must the relative independence of factors be established, but they must be about equally represented by items. Thus Bennett next computes a varimax rotation of 28 items which yields the 19 items selected as input for the cluster analysis.

The responses of fourth-year teachers to 19 items loading highly on the seven factors are then subjected to a cluster analysis to identify types of teaching style. Solutions ranging from 3 to 22 clusters are examined; 12 clusters maximize between-cluster distances in relation to within-cluster error. Table 5 shows the percentage of teachers within each teaching style responding positively to the 19 items, and Bennett's description of the 12 clusters derives directly from these response frequencies. For example, Bennett (1976) describes Types 1 and 12 as follows:

Type 1. These teachers favour integration of subject matter and, unlike most other groups, allow pupil choice of work whether undertaken individually or in groups. Most teachers in this cluster allow pupils choice of seating; less than half curb movement and talk. Assessment in all its forms, tests, grading, and homework appears to be discouraged while intrinsic motivation is favoured (p. 45).

Type 12. This is an extreme group in a number of respects. None favours an integrated approach. Subjects are taught separately by class teaching and individual work. None of the teachers allows pupils choice of seating and every teacher curbs movement and talk. These teachers are above average on the use of all assessment procedures and extrinsic motivation predominates (p. 47).

It can be seen that the 12 clusters are ordered along an informality-formality continuum. Bennett explains the criteria used to order the clusters:

The types have been subjectively ordered, for descriptive purposes, in order of distance from the most 'informal' cluster (type 1). This suggests that they can be represented by points on a continuum of 'informal-formal,' but this would be an over-simplification. The extreme types could be adequately described in these terms, but the remaining types all contain both informal and formal elements (Bennett, 1976, p. 47).

Why does Bennett use a unidimensional continuum to organize types of teaching style when a multidimensional scheme follows appropriately from the cluster analysis? We conjecture that his polemical concern diverted him from a conceptualization of teaching in multidimensional terms toward one that easily fits the formal-informal distinction. The methodology, then, does not increase understanding of the qualitative difference among teaching styles, but it enables him to distinguish mixed from extreme types. We note that he composes three groupings of teaching style by selecting from the 12 clusters: informal (Types 1 and 2), formal (Types 11 and 12), and mixed (Types 3, 4, and 7). The implicit basis for ordering types by degree of deviation from the most informal cluster serves as the criterion for selecting the two extreme groupings, but he provides no adequate rationale for selecting the mixed types.

To understand the qualitative differences that distinguish the 12 clusters, we will examine the evidence provided in Table 5. With the exception of Types 1, 2, and 12, the qualitative differences among types do not permit easy ranking. It is difficult to see, for example, why Type 3 is rated more informal than Types 6 and 7 unless integrated curriculum is a more important indication of informality than little formal assessment. The importance of the integrated vs. subject-centered curriculum is also suggested by ranking Type 8 more informal than Types 9, 10, and 11. It is also difficult to see why Type 11 is ranked more formal than Types 9 or 10. The analysis demonstrates the difficulty of ranking all but the most extreme clusters in unidimensional terms when multidimensional criteria are used to establish the clusters.

Problems inherent in ranking types occur within the three major groups—informal, mixed, and formal. For example, the mixed type is composed of a combination of clusters, each distinguished by a different mixture of formal elements. Aggregation in this manner makes it virtually impossible for the investigator to identify which dimensions defining clusters bear on achievement or involvement in work. Though the informal group appears to be most defensibly composed, Type 1 teachers differ from Type 2 teachers in two potentially important respects: dominant pattern of classroom organization (individual and group vs. primarily individual instruction) and assignment of tasks by the teacher or selection by pupils. Finally, within the formal types, Types 11 and 12 differ with respect to seating control, grading work, and perhaps homework. The extreme types contrast along certain dimensions (classroom organization, assessment, teacher control of talk and movement, and integrated vs. subject-centered curriculum) but not always along others (seating control, teacher vs. pupil selected tasks, and grading). The unidimensional conception masks the multidimensional information on which it is based, and testing the contribution of single dimensions, or combinations thereof, is impossible.

Bennett provides a useful solution to the problem of how to combine the dimensions of teaching style. Indeed, the multidimensional characterization of teaching styles and the identification of 12 clusters (at the third-

TABLE 5
Teaching Styles in Primary Schools

Item	Type of Teaching Style											
	1	2	3	4	5	6	7	8	9	10	11	12
1. Pupils have choice in where to sit	63	66	17	46	50	18	7	17	3	7	77	0
2. Pupils allocated to seating by ability	14	16	25	0	12	45	20	7	81	58	3	50
3. Pupils not allowed freedom of movement in the classroom	49	38	83	76	100	84	87	100	86	97	97	100
4. Teacher expects pupils to be quiet	31	34	92	61	23	55	56	90	81	74	90	100
5. Pupils taken out of school regularly as normal teaching activity	51	50	83	49	81	45	17	47	31	19	26	42
6. Pupils given homework regularly	9	22	8	27	65	3	13	43	36	29	21	56
Teaching emphasis 7. *a.* Teacher talks to whole class	29	16	79	58	30	74	83	73	33	94	85	70
8. *b.* Pupils work in groups on teacher tasks	46	13	83	12	77	92	3	3	22	68	10	8
9. *c.* Pupils work in groups on work of own choice	89	3	29	94	19	32	13	3	0	23	0	0
10. *d.* Pupils work individually on teacher tasks	9	97	0	3	42	0	73	83	100	0	72	92
11. *e.* Pupils work individually on work of own choice	94	9	42	85	42	18	57	57	8	3	8	28
12. Pupils' work marked and graded	3	3	13	15	31	16	33	33	8	32	31	97
13. Stars given to pupils who produce best work	9	31	38	55	8	18	17	73	17	87	69	75

14. Arithmetic tests given at least once a week	9	9	71	88	100	8	10	70	50	94	56	81
15. Spelling tests given at least once a week	23	19	67	94	92	18	7	73	92	94	87	92
16. Teacher smacks for persistent disruptive behavior	34	34	96	24	31	45	80	93	42	68	64	58
17. Teacher sends pupil out of room for persistent disruptive behavior	11	25	13	6	8	3	7	10	25	0	33	11
Emphasis in allocation of teaching time												
18. *a.* Separate subject teaching	20	31	4	82	81	95	100	47	81	100	100	92
19. *b.* Integrated subject teaching	97	91	100	24	65	8	10	93	14	7	0	0
(N in cluster)	(35)	(32)	(24)	(33)	(26)	(38)	(30)	(30)	(36)	(31)	(39)	(36)

Source: Bennett and Jordan, "A Typology of Teaching Styles in Primary Schools," *British Journal of Educational Psychology,* 1975, *45,* 4.

and fourth-grade levels) represents a substantial contribution. However, he fails to make good use of the solution. His characterization of teaching styles as formal, mixed, and informal is only slightly better than the dichotomies he eschews; he does recognize mixed types and extreme types.

While Bennett is concerned mainly with the relationship between teaching style and student achievement, he examines many other sets of relationships: the influence of (1) teacher aims and opinions on teacher style, (2) teacher style on writing skill, (3) the eleven-plus examination on pupil achievement, (4) teacher style on pupil classroom behavior, (5) pupil personality on achievement gain directly and as mediated by teacher style, and (6) pupil personality on pupil classroom behavior. We will not report all findings but rather will explore some relationships in detail.

Bennett's central issue is whether teaching style results in differential student progress, where student progress refers to "average gain or loss over the school year above or below [the score] predicted from initial achievement" (Bennett, 1976, pp. 84, 86). Initial achievement score is taken into account by analysis of covariance. He selects 12 informal teachers (half each from Types 1 and 2), 12 formal teachers (half each from Types 11 and 12), 12 mixed teachers (four each from Types 3, 4, and 7), and an additional informal class (13 in all) because of the small size of one informal class. Classes that closely match the group profile of their parent type are selected, but Bennett provides no evidence concerning the actual practices of the 37 teachers.

In general, Bennett finds student achievement gains are higher in reading, mathematics, and English in formal than in informal classrooms. Achievement gains in mixed classrooms show no consistent pattern across subjects, sometimes (in reading) resembling those in formal classrooms and sometimes (in mathematics and English) those in informal classrooms. While he notes that "these analyses may have been unfair to mixed teaching since this includes a more heterogeneous set of teaching approaches" (p. 157), it should not be forgotten that formal and informal styles also each include two distinct patterns of style.

While findings are reported in detail for the three teaching styles, Bennett also examines the achievement results for the seven types that he combines into the three groups. Unfortunately, he reports from this further analysis only that "three of the seven styles are associated with progress above that expected from initial achievement. These are the two formal styles and the mixed style which conjoined a form of integrated day with strict teacher control of content and pupils" (p. 157). We can infer from the description that he refers to teacher style Type 3.

Types 3, 11, and 12 share the following dimensional characteristics: class instruction, assessment (strict control of content), teacher control of talk and movement, and teacher-selected tasks (see Table 5). Seating control (lacked by Type 11), subject-centered curriculum (lacked by Type 3), and extrinsic motivation (lacked by Types 3 and 11) appear not to be *necessary* conditions for high achievement. This analysis (and the small number of classes involved) makes it difficult to know if the four shared dimensions are necessary for achievement, or if some other combinations would do as well.

Bennett undertakes a second type of analysis that also illuminates the rather barren contrast[26] between extreme groups: the interpretation of the deviant case of a single informal classroom in which achievement gain was high. According to the teacher's responses (substantiated by observation) the class is properly designated as Type 2 (integrated curriculum, little pupil control, little formal assessment, and work performed mainly by individual pupils working on teacher-selected tasks). What distinguishes this teacher's teaching from that of the other informal teachers are: (1) amount of time spent on subjects (mathematics and English) is equal to or greater than that of many formal classes, (2) materials are structured, (3) assessment is accomplished not through tests but through a system of records pertaining to individual and group work, and (4) teacher approval is used as an incentive. Bennett summarizes the findings and proposes an important distinction:

> Although the classroom was evidently oriented towards informal practices the content of the curriculum was clearly organized and well structured. This would seem to highlight a distinction between how the learning environment is structured, on the one hand, and the emphasis and structure of curriculum content, on the other. (p. 98)

Although the questionnaire contains items concerning the allocation of teaching time, this information is either not used in the cluster analysis or does not reveal consistent differences. No items pertaining to the structure and organization of instructional materials are included in the questionnaire. Analysis of the deviant case, in the light of additional interview evidence, reveals plausibly significant dimensions not tapped adequately by the questionnaire. It also shows that while teachers may strongly emphasize carefully planned and evaluated activities designed to affect cognitive outcomes, they may also allow students freedom of movement around the classroom. Further, the analysis suggests that the former, not the latter, affects achievement.

The influence of the eleven-plus examination on the relationship between style and achievement, and the influence of teaching style on the relationship between pupil classroom behavior and achievement are two particularly interesting relationships. Concerning the first, Bennett takes advantage of the fact that some schools are subject to eleven-plus procedures and others not. Teachers teach more formally in schools subject to eleven-plus examination (5 formal vs. 3 informal) than in schools not subject to them (7 formal vs. 10 informal). In addition to this direct influence of the eleven-plus examination on style, Bennett finds a mediated effect: Achievement gains in eleven-plus schools exceed those in other schools, and, with minor fluctuations, this pattern holds among teachers characterized by formal and mixed styles.[27] Most interesting is the fact that gains in achievement in *informal* classrooms, compared with gains in formal and mixed classrooms, are substantially greater in eleven-plus than in non-eleven-plus schools.

These results suggest that an external examination constitutes a constraint on teachers to employ activities designed to foster learning in the cognitive domain (the impact of the eleven-plus in informal schools is by far the greatest in reading). Further, this cognitive emphasis produces high achievement in informally run classrooms, in fact, greater achievement gain than that found in formal classrooms. The evidence for the impact of activities is indirect but nevertheless suggestive. The Bennett scheme, however, has no way to deal with this (if in fact it is a real finding, given the small number of cases).

After demonstrating a modest relationship between teaching style and achievement, Bennett attempts to find out why it is so, and the nature of his earlier results leads him to consider the nature of pupil behavior which presumably characterizes formal and informal classrooms. About 100 students in formal and informal classrooms (roughly 50 students in each) were observed for ten five-minute periods, their behavior being tallied every five seconds. Observations were precoded to yield tallies of work-related activity (e.g., computation, reading, writing, making things, queuing to see the teacher), interaction with peers (e.g., asking questions, cooperating, attracting attention), interaction with teacher (same categories but directed toward teacher), and non-work-related activities (e.g., fidgeting, moving around classroom, avoiding work, watching other people).[28] Then, for high, average, and low achievement-gain students, Bennett presents the median frequency (tallies for five-second intervals) of the four types of student activities in formal and informal classrooms.

He finds that actual involvement in work activities occurs more frequently in formal than in informal classrooms at each ability level, and to a lesser extent, so do student-teacher interaction and fidgeting. And although the average-ability students are out of line, work-related interaction and social interaction among students occur more frequently in informal classrooms, as does moving around the classroom.

These findings generally support the contention that students taught in formal classrooms are kept on the job and interact with the teacher more than their counterparts in informal ones. All forms of pupil interaction occur more frequently in informal classrooms. In both types of classrooms students mostly do their work; the frequencies of the various kinds of interaction remain much lower than the frequency of work-related activities. In a separate analysis, Bennett shows that staying on the job is related to high gains in achievement, but not that students engaged in their work show greater gains in achievement in formal than in informal classrooms. If students of comparable initial achievement and comparable work time make higher achievement gains in formal than in informal classes, this would suggest that teaching style influences achievement not only through the quantity of work but also through the nature of the work. If achievement gains were similar for students of comparable initial achievement and work time in both types of classes, this would suggest that the mechanism through which teaching style influences achievement is quantity of work.

Bennett's underlying argument is that differences in achievement gains can be explained by the nature of pupils' classroom activities, which are influenced by teacher style. To judge from his summary, he would like to have shown that (1) the more students are directly engaged in working on tasks that provide opportunities for the development of cognitive skills, the more they develop those skills (as measured by achievement tests); (2) to the extent that teachers control classroom activities by designing appropriate tasks and keeping students at work on them, the achievement gains are greater, and (3) correlatively, if the school and the teacher respond to external influences (such as the eleven-plus examination) which stress the learning of cognitive skills, achievement gains will be greater than when such constraints are absent.[29]

Bennett's empirical work is consistent with the argument but neither confirms nor disconfirms it, for several reasons. Concerning the first conclusion, we find that high achievers in mathematics are described similarly to those in reading and in writing, simply because they appear to be the same group of high achievers. The proportion of time a student spends working may reflect the operation of a general ability factor that influences achievement, regardless of the amount of work on mathematics, reading, and writing respectively. A more sensitive test of the proposition would measure work activity in mathematics, reading, and writing separately to see if each is associated with achievement gains.

The second conclusion does not follow directly from the investigation of formal, mixed, and informal teaching. From a unidimensional conception of teaching style, it is difficult to know what accounts for achievement gains. Indeed, the deviant case analysis suggests that dimensions of teaching style as operationalized by Bennett may be insensitive to temporal emphasis of subject matter and to forms of assessment other than testing, and may fail to tap the degree to which tasks are structured.

Finally, though there is clear evidence that external influences such as the eleven-plus examination affect teaching, the manner in which Bennett operationalizes teaching style does not reveal how the influence occurs. We cannot explain why reading achievement in informal classes was four times that in formal classes within schools subject to the eleven-plus examinations.

Despite its weaknesses, Bennett's study makes an important contribution to the study of instruction by virtue of its emphasis on student engagement in classroom activities as the explanation of variations in student achievement. When looked at closely, in terms of both its formulations and its conclusions (whatever their relationship to the data), it turns out to be not simply a study of how teaching style affects achievement, but also of the impact of student activities on achievement. Teaching pertains to allocating activities and deciding what kinds of things students will do to acquire cognitive skills; it entails different responsibilities from the tutor in the mastery learning formulation and from the monitor in Dahllöf's formulation (to be considered below). Teaching is conceptualized as setting the conditions for student activity in terms of organizational structure, responsibility for task selection, form of student control, sanctions, and assessment; within this context, the student becomes involved in various activities, some of them related to learning. Although Bennett's conclusions gratuitously draw attention to the importance of instructional tasks as influences upon achievement, the flaws in his attempt to measure teaching style reveal the importance of these tasks.

Frame Theory

Dahllöf's examination of teaching, our final example of an empirically derived formulation, is influenced by the question: What price has to be paid for the high standard achieved by a few? (Dahllöf, 1971, p. 6). He considers this in terms of the advantages and disadvantages of ability grouping. The research literature, partly because of inconsistent findings and partly because of the noncomparability of studies, suggests that neither advantage nor cost derive from any particular grouping scheme (Borg, 1965; Goldberg, Passow, & Justman, 1966).

Based on findings from three grouping studies (Svensson, 1962; Carlsson, 1963; Borg, 1965) and his own investigation of the relationship between the coverage of curricular content and achievement-test item composition, Dahllöf argues that the composition of a class formed by a particular grouping plan is linked to the teaching process. He contends that the teacher in a traditionally instructed class monitors the progress of a small group of students at the lower end of the aptitude distribution to determine when to proceed from one unit to the next. He calls this group, which he tentatively defines as including students from the 10th to the 25th percentile in the aptitude distribution, the *criterion steering group*. Dahllöf contends that grouping students affects the ability composition of classes, and this, through the influence of the steering group, affects the number of units covered (instructional pace) and class level of achievement and variation.

Dahllöf locates the grouping decision within the administrative hierarchy of schools. Grouping (and other decisions not discussed here) are viewed as forming the *frame* for the teaching process. While many teacher characteristic and teaching process studies view the teacher's behavior independently of contextual events and as the main determinant of classroom events, and while most input-output investigations examine frame conditions for direct impact on learning without considering teaching process, Dahllöf believes that frame conditions limit and guide teacher behavior. By focusing on the physical and administrative frame conditions that form the context of teaching, the model formulates influences arising at the district and school levels that bear on classroom practice and thus affect learning.

With regard to Dahllöf's formulation we raise three questions:

1. Is the formulation logically derived, empirically based, or both, and what evidence exists to support it?
2. What is the nature of the teaching process envisioned and the role of the steering group within it?
3. What are the frame conditions, and what are their nature and focus of influence on teaching?

Empirical Basis for Frame Theory. Although Dahllöf's marshaling of evidence prior to a systematic development of the criterion steering group hypothesis and frame theory is impressive, the evidence provides only meager support for the formulation. He presents compelling evidence that results from one grouping investigation (Svensson, 1962) should not be trusted because the criterion achievement test is insensitive to curricular unit coverage. In particular, he finds that higher ability grouped classes cover substantially more advanced units than heterogeneous classes, but since the achievement test items pertain almost exclusively to basic units, any advantage deriving from more advanced units could not be revealed by the tests. He argues that because achievement tests possess little validity in terms of content covered, they are inappropriate for measuring instructional effects.

If we accept Dahllöf's argument that the results from grouping studies are suspect because of the insensitivity of the criterion instrument, this leads to a general distrust of existing evidence which relates instruction to achievement. Despite insensitive criterion measures, Svensson (1962) reports achievement differences among fifth- and sixth-grade students during the two years in which ability grouping was in effect in selected areas of Stockholm: students in heterogeneous classes achieve significantly lower than high-ability-grouped students, but not differently from low-ability-grouped students. A similar pattern appears among students from the Carlsson (1963) study in Växjö: 13 of 14 test mean comparisons among seventh-grade students and 9 of 9 comparisons among eighth-grade students in common subjects favored the grouped high-ability students over heterogeneously grouped ones.[30] The latter performed better than the low-ability-grouped students on 10 of 14 tests among seventh-graders but on only 3 of 9 tests among eighth-graders. In both the Svensson and Carlsson studies, the heterogeneous (ungrouped) classes are compared as an aggregate to the high- and low-ability-grouped classes separately (i.e., heterogeneous classes compared to high-ability-grouped classes and then again to low-ability-grouped classes). If the total numbers of students drawn separately into homogeneous (grouped) and heterogeneous (ungrouped) classes are comparable in ability in the first place, the mean ability of the high-ability homogeneous classes would exceed that of the heterogeneous classes, which in turn would exceed that of the low-ability homogeneous classes. The initial condition of comparability, however, is not met in the Svensson study; it is in the Carlsson study.

The third grouping study conducted by Borg (1965) in Utah uses a different set of comparisons. High-, average-, and low-ability students were identified (but not grouped) in the heterogeneous classes and then compared to those in high-, average-, and low-homogeneously grouped classes. Borg followed the progress of five cohorts (fourth-, sixth-, seventh-, eighth-, and ninth-graders) over a four-year period. Dahllöf's argument, however, is based mainly on findings from the fourth- and sixth-grade samples during the first year of the study. The trends indicate higher achievement for average- and high-ability-grouped students than for their heterogeneously grouped counterparts, but similar achievement for the respective low-ability groups. Dahllöf fails to consider that this pattern is not stable during subsequent years of the study.

In a study of his own, Dahllöf finds that able students grouped by ability prior to seventh grade spend considerably less time on elementary arithmetic and more time on advanced units than do able students who were not grouped by ability in preceding years. From this analysis, Dahllöf suggests a correlation between the prior ability composition of a class and subsequent teaching time for the elementary curriculum, and he infers that students cover less in prior years in heterogeneous than in ability-grouped classes.

The inferred relationship between ability composition and teaching time of elementary units provides the basis for Dahllöf's interpretation of the Carlsson and Borg grouping studies.[31] He asks why low-ability-grouped classes and heterogeneous classes do not differ in level of achievement and proposes the following explanation: Traditional instruction assumes that pupils are treated as a class when new curriculum units are introduced. Teachers must have a criterion to determine the appropriate time to proceed to the next unit; further, they need a majority of students with them before proceeding. Low-ability-grouped classes and heterogeneous classes include pupils of similar ability at the lower end of the class distribution. If teachers consider the learning of pupils from that end as the signal to proceed to the next unit, rather than the learning of students in the middle or upper end, then low-ability-grouped classes and heterogeneously composed classes should proceed through the curricular materials at about the same rate, because both have similar distributions of low-ability students.

Dahllöf supports his choice of the criterion steering group by comparing the achievement results from the first year of the Borg (1965) study for high-, average-, and low-ability students with the distribution statistics of

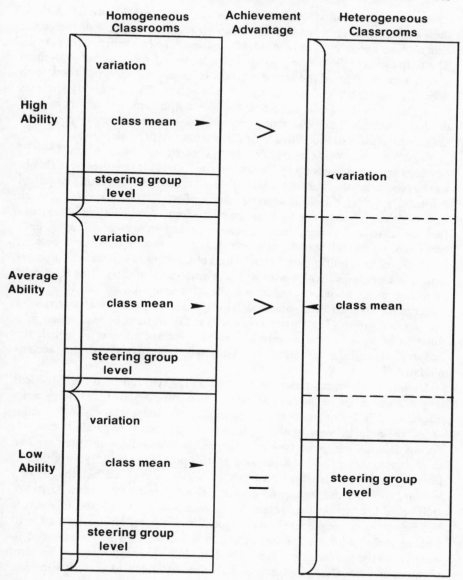

Figure 1. Distributional characteristics of ability-grouped and heterogeneous classes: Mean, variation, and ability level represented in the steering group.

classes: mean, variation, and steering group level (see Figure 1). Among these statistics, the only one that covaries with achievement for ability-grouped and heterogeneously grouped students is the criterion-steering-group level. The ability level of the steering groups in the high- and average-ability-grouped classes exceeds that of the steering-group level in heterogeneous classes; so does achievement of students comparable in ability. For low-ability students from the respective grouping plans, the steering groups are similar in level of ability, and their achievement is comparable. Neither mean level of class ability nor class variation covary in this manner with achievement.

Conception of the Teaching Process. Though we can see how Dahllöf develops the steering-group hypothesis in the form of frame theory, it should not be concluded that the formulation follows directly from existing empirical evidence;[32] rather, the skillful juxtaposition of selected evidence is the work of a sensitive clinician. The formulation stems from a combination of evidence (not all of it convincing), logical treatment, and insight based upon first-hand experience with the phenomenon. It is an attractive hypothesis because it is dynamic and, unlike most formulations of teaching, it explains the progression of curricular activities within the instructional process. The teacher is conceived as a responsive coordinator of instruction who adjusts its content (determined by curricular materials and objectives) to the learning rate of the steering group. The theory accounts for the content of instruction as a function of instructional materials, and also for the manner in which the learning capabilities of students instructed collectively can be accommodated.[33]

Unlike most formulations of teaching that view the student at the individual level of aggregation or the class as only a mean value of individual characteristics, Dahllöf's formulation explicitly recognizes that a class is a collection of individuals who vary in ability, interest, and motivation, and all students do not provide the same type of information relevant for instruction. The formulation also provides a solution to the problem posed by variation in learning ability: Instruction proceeds so that it allows all but the slowest learners to learn the instructed content. Dahllöf provides a formulation of *traditional* instruction that resembles the *innovative* formulation of mastery learning in its consequence: homogeneous learning at a level consistent with teacher goals. Whereas Dahllöf describes collective instruction extended in duration to the learning time needed by low-ability students, mastery learning proposes individualized instruction with time extended to accord with time needed for mastery. This comes to very much the same thing, because the slow students require remedial attention.

The pacing of instruction, however, is undertaken in quite different ways: steering-group monitoring by a perceptive teacher in frame theory, rather than individual monitoring by formative tests in mastery learning. The formative tests provide specific information that may focus further instruction and thereby decrease time needed; however, if the specific aspects of instruction needing review differ from individual to individual, this makes collective review inefficient. Evaluation by steering-group monitoring appears to take less time than formative testing, but the assessment is limited (in student and concept focus) and therefore less comprehensive than in mastery learning. As a consequence, the review following the evaluation may be less well directed.

In any case, within the constraints of class time, the two approaches share many characteristics. These result in common problems: for example, in both approaches students who master material quickly must overlearn, waste time, or engage in some alternative activity. The common characteristics may also result in similar advantages; for example, if mastery of prior concepts decreases learning time needed on subsequent tasks (as the mastery learning position asserts), this benefit should also accrue to traditional instruction.

Having acknowledged the value of the formulation, we must view it with a critical eye to test its adequacy to deal with the complexities of classroom life. Dahllöf identifies the special group of students who provide information about the rate at which instruction should proceed in terms of aptitude test scores. This description might be accepted as a rough manner of speaking rather than as an operational definition were it not for the fact that this is precisely the manner in which Lundgren (1972), one of Dahllöf's students, identifies the steering group. Most teachers do not rank their students in terms of prior aptitude test results to determine what group of students they should watch during class discussion. By defining the steering group in this manner, Dahllöf avoids dealing with several issues, most important of which is how steering-group members are identified by the teacher.

His description of steering-group influence on pacing represents the most carefully worked out aspect of the formulation. Yet, in regard to teacher monitoring, we know neither what is monitored nor exactly what use is made of the observed behavior. For example, it is possible that a teacher asks specific questions about curricular concepts and directs these questions to steering-group members; if comprehension is indicated by the response, the teacher proceeds to the next unit, and if the concept is not mastered the teacher continues with the same unit. This view of monitoring assumes that the teacher has in mind certain important concepts from each unit and periodically directs key questions to steering-group members in order to determine whether or not the class should proceed. Further, the effectiveness of this monitoring seems to depend on the teacher's ability to identify important concepts within each unit, to pose questions that tap the learning of students, and, in the case of student failure, to respond appropriately by providing diagnostic information that will direct further work on the same unit. This conception links learning directly to the teacher's abilities to select important concepts and to monitor effectively.

However, this calls for a highly rational teacher who thoughtfully poses questions and evaluates student responses during the give and take of discussion, a reality not supported by such students of classroom life as Jackson (1968). Jackson portrays the teacher as one who keeps a complex social system functioning by enforcing rules, praising and punishing, distributing supplies, keeping the class on schedule, and overseeing class discussion. One major responsibility of the teacher, according to Jackson, is to keep students involved, and consistent with this portrayal of classroom life, the teacher may monitor involvement. Progression to a new topic, unit, or activity may occur when the teacher senses boredom with the present activity. The point is that one cannot take for granted that learning is the teacher's main concern.

On a related point, Dahllöf's development of the steering-group hypothesis fails to account for what we know about learning in traditional classes, where learning activities are closely tied to class discussion and the textbook. His formulation is based on the assumption that steering-group monitoring bears on the assignment of texts to be read either as homework or during class time and assumes that "homework has the same relation to school work in all grouping systems . . . Thus, curriculum units with a low number of lessons during the school year are also supposed to have a low total time for homework" (Dahllöf, 1971, p. 81).

This isomorphism between class work (discussion) and homework (reading, and often answering questions) eliminates from consideration the relation between classwork and homework. For example, it is possible that measures of learning reflect mainly how much reading students do; text reading, in turn, may depend on student skill and teacher incentives. Conceivably, the main purpose of class discussion is to provide a spot check of class members who have completed the reading and to create a degree of anxiety or incentive so that future reading assignments will be completed. Given this view, one might expect learning to be a function not of the content of class discussion but of the degree and manner in which students complete assigned reading, in class or out. Progress from unit to unit would occur arbitrarily: given a textbook to be covered during a semester or year, and an estimate of how many pages students can and will read per week, homework assignments would be determined accordingly. Perhaps some adjustment may be made on the basis of queries during class discussion or quality of written homework, but this would only temporarily modify the rate of progress through the text.[34] The point is that to identify the linkages between what a teacher does and what students learn, the length and difficulty of assigned reading cannot be ignored (as, for example, Bellack et al. and Flanders do), nor can it be assumed to be isomorphic to class discussion.

Nature of Frame Conditions. Dahllöf's formulation represents a unique solution to the problem of how contextual conditions influence teaching. Whereas most researchers tend to treat a single contextual dimension of teaching, he proposes that certain conditions—instructional materials and goals, the temporal duration of instruction, and the size and composition of the class—shape but do not determine the form of the teaching process. This conception of constraints on instruction resembles the point made by Brown and Saks that resources, relatively fixed in the short run, influence allocation decisions. He refers to these relatively fixed conditions as *frame factors*.

Dahllöf specifies frame factors by example rather than by a comprehensive analysis of source, type, and function. Frame conditions fall into two categories based on their stability, but both form the temporal and spatial context of instruction. Physical frame factors, such as school location and building structure, represent fixed constraints. Administrative frame factors—such as grouping, class size, structure and objectives of the syllabus, length of the school year, and number of lessons per week—are subject to change (at least in the long run); hence their practical as well as theoretical interest. Dahllöf, however, does not treat administration in anywhere near the same detail that he treats teaching.

What does the theory say about the effects of frame conditions on teaching? The explanation that frame conditions "influence the teaching process by promoting or inhibiting it" (Dahllöf, 1971, p. 75) or that "they set certain time and space limits for that part of the educational process that takes place in school" (pp. 75-76) simply replaces the term *frame* with *promote, inhibit* and *limit,* which in turn require clarification. This explanation tells us little about their influence.[35]

Only with regard to grouping do we find a thorough examination of how a frame condition influences instruction: *curricular pace* is the aspect of teaching affected by class composition and *steering-group monitoring* is the mechanism. Though Dahllöf suggests that other conditions, such as level at which teachers expect material to be mastered, may also influence instructional pace, he fails to formulate how the impact occurs.[36]

Dahllöf suggests that frame conditions are not controlled by a single teacher (p. 75). Perhaps he means that frame conditions do not arise from individual differences among teachers (e.g., from their experience, attitudes, or goals). Rather, they are conditions that apply to all teachers, regardless of their idiosyncracies. This is not to say that individual differences among teachers do not affect aspects of teaching, but rather that the source of this influence is unsystematic. But is it true that individual teachers control no frame conditions? To the extent that they are stable over time, the activity structure identified by Gump (1967) and the grouping patterns described by Barr (1975) should be considered frame factors, if this refers to conditions that systematically constrain the behavior of teacher and pupils.

We suspect that the setting in which Dahllöf studied instruction, departmentalized classes meeting for about 50 minutes daily, may not require the establishment of a schedule of events. In fact, the sequence of activities within 50-minute periods may vary from day to day, depending on curricular objectives and the like. This may be the basis for his assertion that individual teachers do not establish frame conditions.[37] Whatever the reason, we suggest that whether a class is departmentalized or self-contained throughout each school day is an important distinguishing characteristic, a frame condition, if you will. Because of this characteristic, the formulation of teaching that arises from a study of departmentalized (usually secondary) classes (Flanders, 1965; Bellack et al., 1966; Dahllöf, 1971; Lundgren, 1972) may differ in important respects from those arising from self-contained (full-day) classes (Kounin, 1970; Gump, 1967; Bennett, 1976).

The formulations of Kounin, Bennett, and Dahllöf clearly do not speak to each other in any explicit and direct way. The diverse phenomena they do address, however, suggest the existence of a central and fundamental set of instructional concerns: keeping students at work, determining the pace of instruction, maintaining order, forming appropriate social aggregations within classes, selecting appropriate learning tasks. The work of these investigators, and of others studying classroom interaction, in short, suggests some useful categories of teachers' instructional and managerial activities and how these activities vary with the properties of school organization and school levels.

CONCLUSION

The juxtaposition of production function research and classroom research brings into relief the focus, the questions, the formulations, and the methodologies of each. We argue not only that the two traditions have a connection, but that the agenda addressed by one is integrally important for the agenda addressed by the other. Levels of organizations can be investigated as autonomous units, as is the case with most classroom studies; but other levels, too—schools and districts—can be the exclusive focus of investigation. A major contribution of the production function formulation is to shift concern away from the productiveness of any single level within an organization and toward the interrelationships among levels by enquiring about *organizational* productivity. From this more inclusive conceptualization, investigations directed mainly or exclusively toward the functioning of levels within the organization can be directed.

An examination of the production function literature reveals that although economists and sociologists have investigated the transformation of school resources into outputs (usually rates of achievement), they have in fact been considering "organizational effectiveness" in terms of the application of school resources to student populations, without strict regard to premises of maximization and appropriate mathematical functions. There does not seem to be any alternative on the horizon to such rather loose-jointed sociological models of organizational effectiveness, because the transformational technology by which inputs are turned into outputs is largely unknown, let alone translatable into statements about cost. We know too little about the activities and events occurring within organizational levels, and even less about how their interrelationships bear on the transformational process. In effect, one of the primary reasons for looking at the problem of school effects is to identify and conceptualize the technology. Without such a conceptualization, the study of school productivity amounts to little more than contemplating black boxes and spinning fantasies about what happens inside them.

A major contribution of production function analysis to understanding school effects is its general concern with the properties of school districts and school organization and their impact upon learning. Despite the limitations of this approach, it locates the process of schooling in a broad social setting and pays particular attention to those financial, human, and material resources and their allocation that bear upon the schooling process. This general concern of production function analysis with organizational properties and resources, however, contributes little to our understanding of how the productive process in schools and school districts occurs. While patterns of resource availability are amply identified, patterns of resource usage are not; and while the formulation identifies organizational levels, it has little to say about how they are tied together to form a productive process. The approach, moreover, remains to be applied to the complete range of organizational levels; most attention has been paid so far to schools and districts, and less to tracks and classrooms.

The paucity of work on the nature of the productive work occurring in classrooms is most conspicuous in production function studies. Questions pertaining to the characteristics of classrooms, the nature of teaching activities, and how teaching affects learning largely fall outside their scope. Without a formulation of what constitutes resources at the classroom level and how they are used to facilitate learning, there is little basis for determining ways in which school events and classroom events bear upon each other.

Examination of the classroom literature proves to be of little value in understanding the events and activities within classrooms which transform resources into products, or how these events relate to activities within other levels of the school organization. Two characteristics of classroom research limit its usefulness: the tendency to examine only a portion of the events occurring within classes, ignoring others which may bear on the productive process, and the tendency to ignore the contextual properties of classrooms. For example, with a few exceptions, there is no attempt to describe and formulate the social characteristics of classrooms except as they are defined in terms of teacher conduct in relation to an aggregate of pupils. Rarely are the characteristics of individual pupils (ability, race, sex), as they may affect the instructional and noninstructional transactions within classes, considered. In addition to social properties, classes have temporal, spatial, and technological characteristics which are largely ignored, though in all likelihood they affect the nature and effectiveness of instruction.

Classroom research characteristically examines one independent variable at a time. There are very few satisfactory attempts to deal with the co-occurrence of more than one instructional activity and its stability over time, or with the prevalence of instructional activities under certain classroom conditions but not under others. Attempts to combine more than one independent variable usually end up with the creation of ostensibly single dimensions which in fact are composed of relatively independent multiple dimensions.

These limitations in the formulation of classroom processes are attributable in part to conceptualizations of instruction and other aspects of teaching which are based primarily on formulations imported from other areas of investigation. Examples are studies of cognitive psychology and learning theory, group climate, verbal communication, the logical structure of language, behavior in small groups, leadership, and so on. All of these have some plausible bearing on instruction, but they are erroneously assumed to be either instruction itself or to provide the most appropriate categories for conceptualizing it.

The production function and classroom instruction research traditions have had little to say to each other, despite their common preoccupation with the effects of schooling. Classroom instruction consists in good part of the allocation of resources to student learning, but to understand the allocative process we need to know what classrooms are like, how they work, and what situations affecting the allocation of resources arise in them. Without knowing the problems teachers encounter and the patterned set of instructional activities that reflect their responses to these problems, it is not possible to establish connections between the two traditions.

Our analysis of selected classroom studies reveals the form classroom investigations should take to investigate the allocation of resources to students in classrooms. First, classrooms must be described in their own right. We find that classrooms are crowded, collective places, and they will not yield to formulations which deny this fact or fail to consider it. They are diverse in their human composition, and the activities occurring in them must be viewed in terms of how they pertain to that diversity. Classroom events occur over time, and attention must be paid to the prevailing sorts of time units—lessons, days, terms, and the like—and the utilization of time within those units. Classrooms are also characterized by nature and variety of instructional materials, and by the fact that teachers take responsibility for the central goal of schooling—the creation of individual student learning—and direct the events designed to achieve it.

Second, the existence of all these classroom properties poses problematic issues for teachers, and their activities can be understood as responses to these issues. For example, a teacher wanting to achieve a learning goal assigns one task to a whole class. If the task is appropriate to the goal, if all the students are equally capable of doing it and are equally happy about doing it, if they can complete it in the same reasonable amount of time and learn it to the same criterion of achievement, the teacher can proceed to the next task to reach the next goal, and the process will repeat itself. This is pure fantasy, we admit, but still a useful way to begin thinking about classroom instruction.

More realistically, we can expect that some of these conditions will not prevail. The task is not appropriate to the goal, for example, and an alternative must be sought. The task is apparently appropriate to some students but not to others. Should the teacher use two or more tasks simultaneously, appropriate to different segments of the class? If so, a decision must be made either to group the class by task or to run all tasks at the same time. Can a teacher do whole-class instruction with different tasks? Only if all students work at their seats. If oral instruction, discussion, or recitation are necessary, whole-class instruction with multiple tasks is impossible. This means group instruction must be used. Does the teacher know how to keep the majority of the class productively occupied doing seatwork while she is orally instructing a small segment of the class? A teacher cannot manage small-group instruction unless the more general problem of order has been solved. The majority of students must at least remain quiet, if not actively engaged in work, while a small group receives instruction.

If a teacher uses more than one task, there is no guarantee that each one will take the same amount of time overall or that all students working on each task will finish in the same amount of time. The teacher, then, must plan for different kinds of time use in the same classroom, through varying materials, grouping, differentially pacing instruction—all depending on how diverse the class is and the characteristics in which the diversity appears (ability, interest, attentiveness, and so on). In addition to providing for different learning rates within the time required for students to complete a task, the teacher must also decide when to proceed to the next task, a problem multiplied in difficulty when two or more tasks with different time conditions are going on simultaneously. The problem of moving on entails deciding how many shall proceed before learning satisfactorily, or how many groups working on different things at different rates can be accommodated, or how large a claim can be made on students' out-of-school time and resources. The alternative to these limited solutions, all of which increase the labor intensiveness of the teacher's job, is to hire more teachers, hire paraprofessionals, or enlist parents, all of which are costly alternatives.

It is of utmost importance to recognize that these instructional alternatives to the problems that emerge from the task-time-diversity-collectivity properties of classrooms all have implications for classroom management. Students bring to school not only individual differences in ability, but differences in desire, interest, attentiveness, patience, and impulsiveness. These noncognitive characteristics and their dispersion will determine how much time, energy, and ingenuity a teacher must expend to keep a class coherent, orderly, and peaceful. But there are derivative management problems as well. Some students are easy to manage under the surveillance of whole-class instruction. When they are engaged in unsupervised seatwork or group work, it is another story. Accordingly, the teacher's decision to group, initially for instructional reasons, may have consequences for classroom management. Teachers, to put it crudely, have to teach students how to learn and also how to behave.

The management of classrooms, the maintenance of a coherent set of activities over time, is not simply a matter of good behavior; it is also a matter of establishing and maintaining student interest and engagement in tasks. While we began with the assumption that the teacher assigns the activity, there is no guarantee that what the teacher assigns, however appropriate to the learning goals, will sustain interest and engagement. Teachers, accordingly, vary activities, but they also devolve responsibility to students for deciding what to do.

We have tried in this chapter to argue a very simple case: that schools are productive organizations in which resources are applied to raw materials in a particular organizational context whose social properties are problematic to the members. The general formulation is familiar enough, but for the most part has been applied partially (as in the production function literature) and unwittingly (as in the classroom instruction literature). The most troubling issue has been the identification of social properties, typically confused with resources (in the former) and with teaching activities (in the latter). The social properties are an issue in their own right: They represent the settings in which resources are allocated and in which instruction and administrative activities take place. They are also the origin of emergent problems for teachers and administrators, whose conduct can be conceptualized as the allocation of resources to alternative patterns of activity. Hiring experienced teachers and grouping classes for instruction are activities of precisely this nature, at the administrative and classroom levels, respectively. To regard schools as productive organizations means describing all their productive levels and establishing the connections among them, and identifying how events at each level constitute constraints and opportunities for what occurs at other levels. Our discussion has drawn attention to some of the social properties, some of the allocative choices, some of the tasks, some of the resources, some of the problematic issues facing teachers and administrators. To that extent this chapter can represent the beginning of a conceptual agenda.

NOTES

1. Our colleague, Charles Bidwell, has observed that the effects of teacher activities on students may not be limited to the production of value added in the form of

student achievement, but, by virtue of the nature of classroom transactions, may include increments to the talents of teachers themselves. These may properly be regarded as additions to resources at the classroom or school levels.

2. As indicated by Rehberg (1976) in his review of Rosenbaum, caution is appropriate in interpreting the statistical findings. The school's dropout rate is high, and the IQ increases and decreases between grades 8 and 10 are rather small and are not clearly attributable to tracking.

3. Rosenbaum argues, in contrast to Turner's (1960) well-known work on sponsored and contest mobility, that "contest mobility" characterizes high school selection less well than "tournament mobility," by which any failure means dropping out of the competition. The predominance of downward rather than upward shifts in tracks provides indirect support for the tournament metaphor.

4. Note, for example, that the EEO use of a district-level measure of per-pupil expenditure on staff is a proxy for the more appropriate school-level measure. If it had been available, it would have been used.

5. Flanders's quantitative analysis of classroom interaction is based on a ten-category classification of teacher and student talk by which an observer codes what is said every three seconds. The observations are presented in 10 X 10 matrices showing paired sequences of three-second observations and, in the rows and columns, the distribution of each coded activity over the instructional unit. Flanders develops two measures of direct and indirect teaching. One measure (I/D) is the sum of items 1, 2, 3, and 4 divided by items 5, 6, and 7, a measure that he believes to be influenced by the nature of subject content (Flanders, 1965, p. 35). In the empirical work, he concerns himself mainly with the second measure (i/d), presumably free of content influence: $i/d = 1 + 2 + 3/6 + 7$. For detailed descriptions of observation and coding procedures, see Flanders (1965, 1970).

6. We identify the direct and indirect categories on the y-axis. Naturally, higher indirect frequencies in the indirect classrooms and higher direct frequencies in the direct classrooms are to be expected.

7. Flanders (1965) compares the means of the direct and indirect groups which differ by three points in social studies and slightly more than two points in mathematics. Both mean differences are statistically significant, though rather small (pp. 96-97).

8. Bellack et al. (1966) obtain individual knowledge scores, correct them according to level of knowledge predicted from verbal ability scores, and sum the scores of individual knowledge for each classroom (pp. 223-224).

9. Note that Bellack uses the term *instruction* in a special sense, to refer to discourse that pertains to classroom management as distinguished from substance; hence his distinction between substantive and instructional moves. We are using instruction more generally and conventionally, to refer to pedagogy.

10. We do not treat the Personalized System of Instruction as a form of mastery learning, as does Block (1974).

11. Carroll (1963) contends that some of these individual characteristics influence the amount of time needed to learn, while others influence time spent in learning; but since there is no independent definition of *time needed* (except in terms of

Carroll's argumentation in explaining his model), we have treated all such characteristics together.

12. Bloom (1968) is unpaginated. We have taken the liberty of supplying page numbers
1 to 12 and using them in our citations.

13. Out-of-school learning becomes problematic if it takes as long as in-school learning.
Furthermore, it does not deal with the within-classroom problem created when
some students finish their work earlier than others. (See also Bloom, 1974, p.
683.)

14. To measure withitness, Kounin (1970) divides the total number of reprimands
by the number of error-free reprimands over a given period of time, yielding a
teacher score for the classroom (p. 82).

15. To measure overlapping, Kounin codes the number of acts, however brief, indicating attention to both events, divided by the number of situations in which the
teacher is confronted by dual issues for a given period of time. Our description
is derived from Kounin's report (Kounin, 1970, p. 87).

16. Smoothness is measured in terms of the number of teacher-initiated breaks in
the flow of activities per six-second observational unit over the total time for
observation: for example, stimulus-bound preoccupation with an extraneous event
intruding on an ongoing activity in which students are engaged, returning to
an activity just ended, and so on. Our description is derived from Kounin's
report (Kounin, 1970, p. 101).

17. Slowdowns, or breaks in momentum, are measured in terms of the number of
six-second slowdowns occurring during recitations, divided by the total number
of six-second time units coded (Kounin, 1970, p. 106).

18. Group alerting is measured by counting, during 30-second intervals, the number
of times the teacher uses positive alerting cues, such as doing something to create
suspense, and the number of times she uses negative cues, such as continuing
to question one student while the others remain uninvolved. Many positive acts
and few negative ones produce a high score (Kounin, 1970, pp. 118-119).

19. The measurement of accountability is based on the number of times, during
30-second intervals, the teacher asks for evidence of work or knowledge from all
students, individually, from half, and from fewer than half the students. Note
that evidence from all in unison is regarded as inadequate. The better the individual
evidence from more students, the higher the accountability score (Kounin, 1970,
p. 120).

20. One of the anomalies is that certain teacher activities are defined in terms of
recitation, for example, group alerting. In the statistical presentation, however,
we find correlations between group alerting and the dependent variables under
seatwork conditions. It is not clear how this came to pass, nor is it clear how
Kounin uses the recitation-seatwork distinction to organize his data (Kounin,
1970, p. 63).

21. The index of involvement is the ratio of involved/not involved per ten-second
interval, not the ratio of involved/involved + not involved. The index of deviancy
is simply the number of deviant acts per ten-second interval. It is not clear how
or whether these different measures affect the results (Kounin, 1970, pp. 77-79).

22. Only in the case of accountability and freedom from deviancy in seatwork settings does the correlation fall to —.35 (Kounin, 1970, p. 169).

23. For example, Dunkin and Biddle (1974) describe various approaches to the study of teaching: those concerned with classroom climate, management and control, the classroom as a social system, sequential patterns of classroom behavior, and discourse. Most striking about their review is the fact that investigations of teaching proceed dimension by dimension. That is, several aspects of teacher behavior may be measured (e.g., use of praise, acceptance of pupils' ideas, criticism); they are neither conceptually nor empirically interrelated, but rather each aspect is examined for its influence on some aspect of pupil behavior or its association with teacher background characteristics or contextual dimensions.

24. Gump (1967), using specimen records dictated by observers and time-lapse photographs, examines the activities in six third-grade classes for two full days. Five dimensions characterizing the structure of classroom activities are interrelated: *concern* (whether the activity focused, for example, on reading, music, milk-story, mixed academic work, and the like), *teacher leadership* (whether or not the teacher participates in a particular activity, and if so, in what capacity), *pupil activity* (what pupils are expected to do; e.g., seatwork, attend to class discussion), *action sequencing* (whether or not pupils pace their own work, and the form of their activity) and *grouping arrangements* (whether private work, engagement with other students or neither are involved within class, group, or individual structures). For a description of how activities are commonly structured within third-grade classes, see Tables 3.0 and 3.1 in Gump (pp. 48-50).

    Grannis and Jackson (1973) analyze the recorded reports from behavior-stream observation of two children from each of ten second-grade classrooms over the course of a single school day. The main organizing concept of the study is that aspects of activities in which pupils are engaged can be judged in terms of whether the teacher, the pupil, or the teacher and pupil jointly exercise control over that aspect of an activity. Four dimensions are considered in combination to characterize the activities in first-priority (reading, arithmetic) and second-priority (science, social studies, art, music, games) curricular areas. These are *pacing* (teacher, joint, or pupil regulation), *interaction among learners* (low, moderate, high), *task options* (teacher, joint, or pupil determination), and *feedback opportunities* from instructional materials (none, restricted, and unrestricted). Grannis and Jackson contend that consistency among dimensions of activities with regard to source of control facilitates higher pupil work engagement than incongruence among conditions, and they present some evidence (for first-priority activities) to support the hypothesis.

25. See, for example, Rosenshine and Furst (1973) for a discussion of classroom observational schemes.

26. Barren in terms of understanding instruction, not in terms of accomplishing Bennett's polemical purposes.

27. We note that Bennett, in discussing the effects of the eleven-plus, refers to formal, informal, and mixed *schools.* We assume that this actually means formal, informal, and mixed classrooms in schools subject and not subject to eleven-plus procedures.

We make this assumption because nowhere else in the book does he describe teaching styles at the school level of aggregation.

28. For a more complete, though not a satisfyingly complete, description of behavior categories, see Bennett (1976), pp. 103-108.

29. Bennett is also concerned with the question of whether students of different personality types show similar gains in different kinds of classrooms. To that end he identifies eight personality profiles (albeit with some of the same difficulties present in the identification of teacher types). While he finds that achievement gain varies with personality type, students of all types show greater gains in formal than in informal classrooms; those in mixed classrooms vary inconsistently. This analysis, though interesting in its own right, pertains less to our concerns than it does to his polemical ones. One cannot conclude from his results that all kinds of students will flourish comparably, irrespective of their personalities, nor does he claim that they will. Even though all types of students do better with formal instruction, there are no clear guidelines for coping with personality variation in classrooms.

30. These comparisons seem to involve mean score differences rather than statistically significant differences.

31. The form of Borg's data does not lend itself directly to this interpretation, but Dahllöf fails to note this difficulty. Dahllöf eliminates the findings from the Stockholm (Svensson) grouping study from consideration because the two original samples are not comparable; as a result the high-ability grouped pupils are significantly more able than the heterogeneous pupils, but no ability difference is found between the latter and the low ability grouped pupils. Thus, the observed achievement differences could easily reflect initial aptitude differences. Dahllöf's investigation of unit coverage seems also to include Stockholm students; since Dahllöf fails to report evidence concerning the comparability of the high-ability students who had been grouped previously and those who had not, it is possible that the coverage differences are, in part, also a reflection of aptitude differences. But this possibility is not inconsistent with the point he is trying to make.

32. Note that the Växjö trends (Carlsson, 1963) may not be statistically significant and that the second and third years of the Utah investigation (Borg, 1966) are not consistent with the first.

33. Though our concern is primarily with the conceptual form of the theory, Dahllöf's analysis and subsequent research (Lundgren, 1972; Barr, 1973-74, 1975) suggest that three conditions may need to be met before the steering-group effect can be demonstrated: (1) the criterion measure must be sensitive to instructional content, (2) material coverage must be allowed to vary, and (3) the ability of the criterion steering groups must differ significantly among compared groups.

    For example, Lundgren (1972), in his dissertation under Dahllöf's direction, finds that the steering-group level for 46 sophomore classes in five subject areas, studied for the duration of a school year, has little relation to instructional pace: "[We] calculated the time spent on the units which the teachers had marked as being elementary. Totally, there is a weak connection between the mean value for pupils in P 10/25 [the steering group] and time spent" (p. 184). However, since the teachers were constrained by the same syllabus, material coverage may not have been allowed to vary. In addition, whereas class groups that result from an ability-grouping decision vary widely in steering-group level, this is not the case when all classes are heterogeneously composed *within* student tracks, as is true in the Lundgren investigation. As a consequence, steering-group differences reflect differences in the student groups attending the different schools in Lundgren's study, rather than systematic differences brought about by grouping.

Recent investigations of instructional groups, established by administrative decision (teacher and administrator), where material coverage is allowed to vary from group to group, and where the criterion measure is sensitive to instructional content, demonstrate a strong relationship between group ability level and rate of progress through the text during first-grade reading instruction, and suggest the plausibility of the steering-group hypothesis (Barr, 1973-74, 1975).

34. Some evidence on the role of the textbook in influencing instruction can be found in the descriptive account of Smith and Geoffrey (1968). One is struck by the influence of the text on class discussion and the additional burden that a text, inappropriate in content and readability, places on the ingenuity of the teacher to keep students involved in school work. In an extensive investigation of 46 sophomore classes in five subject areas over the duration of a school year, Lundgren (1972) concludes that "the textbook, by its sequence of units and massive content, governs the planning of the teaching and the way it is carried out and to what extent. For these two aspects, the textbooks show marked variations between each other" (p. 175).

35. We examined Lundgren's dissertation for clarification of frame conditions and their influence. Lundgren accepts the theory described by Dahllöf with the following exceptions: First, he specifies three sets of frame factors as influencing the form of the teaching process: curricular content and goals, time available for instruction, and class composition (p. 12), but he provides neither empirical support nor theoretical justification for these particular conditions. Second, though Lundgren examines aspects of the teaching process other than curricular pace (e.g., sequence of curricular topics and verbal interaction), he fails to formulate how the three sets of frame conditions interact to influence these aspects of the teaching process; as a consequence, his investigation consists of a series of *post hoc* analyses.

36. This failure to formulate how teacher objectives may influence teaching is similar to Bennett's failure to formulate how the eleven-plus examination might influence achievement.

37. An alternative explanation is simply that Dahllöf chooses to limit the definition of frame factors to conditions outside teacher control, but, if so, he fails to discuss the advantage of this limitation.

REFERENCES

Alexander, K. L., & McDill, E. L. Selection and allocation within schools: Some causes and consequences of curriculum placement. *American Sociological Review,* 1976, *41,* 963-980.

Anderson, H. H. The measurement of domination and of socially integrative behavior in teachers' contacts with children. *Child Development,* 1939, *10,* 73-89.

Anderson, H. H., & Brewer, H. M. Studies of teachers' classroom personalities, I: Dominative and integrative behavior of kindergarten teachers. *Applied Psychology Monographs,* 1945, 6.

Anderson, H. H., & Brewer, J. E. Studies of teachers' classroom personalities, II: Effects of teachers' dominative and integrative contacts on children's classroom behavior. *Applied Psychology Monographs,* 1946, 8.

Anderson, H. H., Brewer, J. E., & Reed, M. F. Studies of teachers' classroom personalities, III: Follow-up studies of the effects of dominative and integrative contacts on children's behavior. *Applied Psychology Monographs,* 1946, 11.

Anderson, L. W. *Time and school learning.* Unpublished doctoral dissertation, University of Chicago, 1973.

Arlin, M. N. *Learning rate and learning rate variance under mastery learning conditions.* Unpublished doctoral dissertation, University of Chicago, 1973.

Armor, D. J. School and family effects on black and white achievement: A reexamination of the USOE data. In F. Mosteller & D. P. Moynihan (Eds.), *On equality of educational opportunity.* New York: Vintage Books, 1972.

Averch, H. A., Carroll, S. J., Donaldson, T. S., Kiesling, H. J. & Pincus, J. *How effective is schooling: A critical review and synthesis of research findings.* Santa Monica, Cal.: Rand, 1972.

Barr, R. Instructional pace differences and their effect on reading acquisition. *Reading Research Quarterly,* 1973-74, *9,* 526-554.

Barr, R. How children are taught to read: Grouping and pacing. *School Review,* 1975, *83,* 479-498.

Bellack, A. A., Kliebard, H. N., Hyman, R. T. & Smith, F. L. *The language of the classroom.* New York: Teachers College Press, 1966.

Bennett, N. *Teaching styles and pupil progress.* London: Open Books, 1976.

Bennett, S. N., & Jordan, J. A typology of teaching styles in primary schools. *British Journal of Educational Psychology,* 1975, *45,* 20-28.

Bidwell, C. E., & Kasarda, J. D. School district organization and student achievement. *American Sociological Review,* 1975, *40,* 55-70.

Bidwell, C. E., & Kasarda, J. D. Reply to Hannan, Freeman and Meyer, and Alexander and Griffin. *American Sociological Review,* 1976, *41,* 152-160.

Block, J. H. *The effects of various levels of performance on selected cognitive, affective, and time variables.* Unpublished doctoral dissertation, University of Chicago, 1970.

Block, J. H. (Ed.). *Mastery learning: Theory and practice.* New York: Holt, Rinehart & Winston, 1971.

Block, J. H. (Ed.). *Schools, society, and mastery learning.* New York: Holt, Rinehart & Winston, 1974.

Bloom, B. S. Learning for mastery. *Evaluation Comment.* UCLA–CSEIP, 1968, *1,* n.p.

Bloom, B. S. Individual differences in school achievement: A vanishing point? *Education at Chicago,* 1971, *1,* 4-14.

Bloom, B. S. Time and learning. *American Psychologist,* 1974, *29,* 682-688.

Bloom, B. S. *Human characteristics and school learning.* New York: McGraw-Hill, 1976.

Borg, W. R. Ability grouping in the public schools. *Journal of Experimental Education,* 1965, *34,* 1-97.

Bowles, S., & Levin, H. M. The determinants of scholastic achievement—An appraisal of some recent evidence. *Journal of Human Resources,* 1968, *3,* 3-24.

Brophy, J. E., & Evertson, C. M. *The Texas Teacher Project: Presentation of non-*

linear relationships and summary observations (Rep. 74-6). University of Texas at Austin, 1974.

Brown, B. W., & Saks, D. H. The production and distribution of cognitive skills within schools. *Journal of Political Economy,* 1975, *83,* 571-593.

Carlsson, B. *[The effect of school differentiation on students' scores on achievement tests: An experimental investigation.]* Licentiate paper. Uppsula; Institute for Education, Uppsula University, 1963 (mimeo).

Carroll, J. B. A model of school learning. *Teachers College Record,* 1963, *64,* 723-733.

Coleman, J. S., Campbell, E. Q., Hobson, C. J., McPartland, J., Mood, A. M., Weinfeld, F. D. & York, R. L. *Equality of educational opportunity.* Washington, D.C.: U.S. Government Printing Office, 1966.

Dahllöf, U.S. *Ability grouping, content validity, and curriculum process analysis.* New York: Teachers College Press, 1971.

Dreeben, R. *On what is learned in school.* Reading, Mass.: Addison-Wesley, 1968.

Dunkin, M. J., & Biddle, B. J. *The study of teaching.* New York: Holt, Rinehart & Winston, 1974.

Flanders, N. A. *Teacher influence, pupil attitudes, and achievement.* Washington, D.C.: U.S. Department of Health, Education, and Welfare, 1965.

Flanders, N. A. *Analyzing teaching behavior.* Reading, Mass.: Addison-Wesley, 1970.

Goldberg, M. L., Passow, A. H. & Justman, J. *The effects of ability grouping.* New York: Teachers College Press, 1966.

Grannis, J. C., & Jackson, D. E. Analysis and interpretation of the Spring, 1971, behavior stream observations of children: Toward a political pedagogy. In J. C. Grannis (Ed.), *Columbia Classroom Environments Project Final Report* (OEC-0-71-0593). New York: Institute for Pedagogical Studies, Columbia University, 1973 (mimeo).

Gump, P. V. The classroom behavior setting: Its nature and relation to student behavior (Final Rep., Project No. 2453). Lawrence, Kan.: Midwest Psychological Field Station, University of Kansas, 1967.

Heyns, B. Social selection and stratification within schools. *American Journal of Sociology,* 1974, *79,* 1434-1451.

Hoetker, J., & Ahlbrand, W. P. The persistence of the recitation. *American Educational Research Journal,* 1969, *6,* 145-169.

Jackson, P. W. *Life in classrooms.* New York: Holt, Rinehart, & Winston, 1968.

Jencks, C. S. The Coleman Report and the conventional wisdom. In F. Mosteller & D. P. Moynihan (Eds.), *On equality of educational opportunity.* New York: Vintage Books, 1972.

Kounin, J. S. *Discipline and group management in classrooms.* New York: Holt, Rinehart, & Winston, 1970.

Lewin, K., Lippitt, R., & White, R. K. Patterns of aggressive behavior in experimentally created social climates. *Journal of Social Psychology,* 1939, *10,* 271-279.

Lundgren, U. P. *Frame factors and the teaching process.* Stockholm: Almqvist & Wiksell, 1972.

Mood, A. M. Do teachers make a difference? In *Do teachers make a difference?* Washington, D.C.: U.S. Office of Education, 1970.

Rehberg, R. A. Review of Rosenbaum, *Making inequality. American Educational Research Journal,* 1976, *13,* 227–232.

Rosenbaum, J. E. *Making inequality: The hidden curriculum of high school tracking.* New York: Wiley, 1976.

Rosenshine, B., & Furst, N. F. The use of direct observation to study teaching. In

R. M. W. Travers (Ed.), *Second handbook of research on teaching.* Chicago: Rand McNally, 1973.

Smith, B. O., & Meux, M. O. *A study of the logic of teaching.* Urbana, Ill.: University of Illinois Press, 1962.

Smith, L. M., & Geoffrey, W. *The complexities of an urban classroom: An analysis toward a general theory of teaching.* New York: Holt, Rinehart, & Winston, 1968.

Smith, M. S. *Equality of educational opportunity:* The basic findings reconsidered. In F. Mosteller & D. P. Moynihan (Eds.), *On equality of educational opportunity.* New York: Vintage Books, 1972.

Soar, R. S., & Soar, R. M. An empirical analysis of selected follow through programs: An example of a process approach to evaluation. In I. J. Gordon (Ed.), *Early childhood education.* 71st Yearbook of the National Society for the Study of Education. Chicago: University of Chicago Press, 1972.

Spady, W. G. The impact of school resources on students. In F. N. Kerlinger (Ed.), *Review of research in education 1.* Itasca, Ill.: F. E. Peacock, 1973.

Summers, A. A., & Wolfe, B. L. *Equality of educational opportunity quantified: A production function approach.* Unpublished manuscript, Federal Reserve Bank of Philadelphia, 1974.

Summers, A. A., & Wolfe, B. L. *Disaggregation in analyzing educational equity issues: Methods and results.* Unpublished manuscript, ETS–NBER Workshop on the Economics of Education, Princeton, N.J., October 2–4, 1975.

Suppes, P., Jerman, M., & Brain, D. *Computer-assisted instruction: Stanford's 1965-66 arithmetic program.* New York: Academic Press, 1968.

Svensson, N. E. *Ability grouping and scholastic achievement: Report on a five-year follow-up study in Stockholm.* Stockholm: Almqvist & Wiksell, 1962.

Talmage, H. (Ed.). *Systems of individualized education.* Berkeley, Cal.: McCutchan, 1975.

Thomas, J. A. *The productive school.* New York: Wiley, 1971.

Turner, R. H. Sponsored and contest mobility and the school system. *American Sociological Review,* 1960, *25,* 855-867.

White, R. K., & Lippitt, R. *Autocracy and democracy: An experimental inquiry.* New York: Harper, 1960.

4

Paradigms for Research on Teacher Effectiveness

WALTER DOYLE
North Texas State University

> The formulation of a problem is often more essential than its solution, which
> may be merely a matter of mathematical or experimental skill.
>
> Einstein and Infeld (1938), p. 92.

Teacher effectiveness research has occupied a conspicuous place within
the spectrum of scientific inquiry in education. Interest in the question of
what distinguishes superior from inferior teachers has flourished since the
early 1920s and by midcentury had stimulated an impressive number of studies
(Domas & Tiedeman, 1950). The quest was rejuvenated in the 1950s with
the formation of the AERA Committee on Criteria of Teacher Effectiveness
(American Educational Research Association, 1952, 1953), whose work cul-
minated in the publication of the *Handbook of Research on Teaching* (Gage,
1963a). This developmental path underscores the axial role of the teacher
effectiveness question within the broader field of research on teaching. Even
a cursory inspection of recent literature suggests that effectiveness inquiry

JERE E. BROPHY, Michigan State University, and BARAK ROSENSHINE, University of Illinois,
Urbana, were editorial consultants for this chapter.

Note: A version of this review was presented at the meeting of the American Educational
Research Association, Washington, D.C., April 1975. The chapter was improved substantially
by discussions during a conference at the Institute for Research on Teaching, Michigan State
University, November 17–19, 1976, and by meetings with the staff of the Research and Develop-
ment Center for Teacher Education, University of Texas at Austin. I am indebted to Lee S.
Shulman and Carolyn M. Evertson for arranging for me to participate in these sessions. Revision
of the manuscript was supported in part by grants from the North Texas State University
Organized Research Funds and the National Institute of Education, Department of Health,
Education, and Welfare. However, the opinions expressed herein do not necessarily reflect the
position or policy of North Texas State University or the National Institute of Education,
and no official endorsement by either institution should be inferred.

continues to attract the resources of researchers, funding agencies, and professional organizations.

Throughout its history, research on teacher effectiveness has faced problems of productivity, methodology, and theory (for general discussions, see AERA, 1952, 1953; Barr, 1939; Berliner, 1976; Gage, 1972). Reviewers have concluded, with remarkable regularity, that few consistent relationships between teacher variables and effectiveness criteria can be established (Barr, 1961; Dunkin & Biddle, 1974; Getzels & Jackson, 1963; McKeachie & Kulik, 1975; Medley & Mitzel, 1959; Morsh & Wilder, 1954; Rosenshine, 1971; Rosenshine & Furst, 1973; Stephens, 1967). Although optimism is more apparent in recent writings (Flanders & Simon, 1969; Gage, 1977; Good, Biddle, & Brophy, 1975; Rosenshine, 1976a, 1976b), a general perception of low productivity would seem to prevail. The productivity issue is associated in part with several basic, largely unresolved, methodological problems that have impeded attempts to compare studies, integrate findings, or apply results to teacher education (Borich, 1977; Flanders, 1973; Glass, 1974; Heath & Nielson, 1974; Shavelson & Dempsey-Atwood, 1976). There has also been a continuing concern for the adequacy of theoretical foundations in the field (Dunkin & Biddle, 1974; Gage, 1963b, 1964; Guba & Getzels, 1955; Rabinowitz & Travers, 1953; Turner & Fattu, 1960). Researchers have shown considerable ingenuity in generating variables that might possibly relate to effectiveness indicators. There are, however, few theoretical grounds for selecting variables or for interpreting available findings.

This chapter is based on the premise that many of the persistent questions of productivity, methodology, and theory are related to the underlying assumptions which shape inquiry. The discussion can be characterized, therefore, as an analytical review of the conceptual foundations of research on teacher effectiveness. It is focused on alternate ways of thinking about teaching and their implications for asking questions and interpreting answers about effective teachers. Of necessity, methodological issues are considered only as they illustrate the structure or assumptions of teacher effectiveness research. No attempt has been made to compile an up-to-date list of current findings. The review emphasizes common features among investigations, an approach that does not do justice to the diversity of work in this field. Despite these limitations, there is reason to expect, on the basis of previous attempts to examine the form of the teacher effectiveness question (Gump, 1964; Olson, 1972; Stephens, 1967), that an analysis of conceptual issues is a fruitful direction for inquiry.

Kuhn's (1970) concept of *paradigm* provides a useful tool for inquiry into the way researchers think about their work. A paradigm is, according to Kuhn, an implicit framework that defines legitimate problems, methods, and solutions for a research community. It is, in other words, a *shared perception of adequacy,* part of the taken-for-granted reality of research practice, which researchers use tacitly to make judgments about work in their domain. As an implicit outlook, a paradigm shapes the general character of studies generated within a research tradition, that is, it "determines much about the research that will be done" (Gage, 1963b, p. 96). In addition, a paradigm serves as a screen for interpreting research findings. These interpretive functions have far-reaching consequences for the accumulation and utilization of knowledge in a field (on this point, see Gilbert, 1976).

The discussion is organized around three paradigms. The first is the *process-product paradigm,* which defines legitimate inquiry in terms of relations between teacher behavior and student learning outcomes. The primary focus of the first section is on the structure of the paradigm and the implicit model of teaching that guides inquiry within this framework. These considerations are helpful in understanding some of the premises operating within the teacher effectiveness field. The effectiveness question is then examined from the perspective of two other frameworks, a *mediating process paradigm* derived mainly from prose learning research, and a *classroom ecology paradigm* constructed from naturalistic studies of school life. These two paradigms make explicit certain processes that presumably intervene in relationships between teacher variables and student learning outcomes. As mediational paradigms, these frameworks provide useful alternatives for conceptualizing how teaching works which are especially suited to present directions in effectiveness inquiry.

THE PROCESS-PRODUCT PARADIGM

Despite some diversity in emphasis among investigators, the process-product paradigm functions as an organizing framework for most contemporary research on effective teaching (see, especially, Gage, 1972; Rosenshine, 1971, 1976a). An analysis of this paradigm, therefore, provides access to the main lines of current thinking about teacher effectiveness.

The Structure of Process-Product Research

Within the process-product paradigm the effectiveness question is formulated in terms of relationships between measures of teacher classroom behaviors (processes) and measures of student learning outcomes (products). This approach is based on a two-factor criterion-of-effectiveness structure that relates teacher variables directly to effectiveness indicators (Gage, 1963b). The structure of the paradigm corresponds in essence, therefore, to a prediction formula: Define the criterion and find its predictors. Such a structure has the advantages of simplicity and generality. Any number of process and criterion variables can be inserted into the formula, and the empirical associations can then be calculated. As a result, the paradigm can be used by investigators who differ markedly in their definitions of appropriate variables.

Rosenshine (1971) has described the basic stages of a process-product study in the following manner:

(1) the development of an instrument which can be used systematically to record the frequency of certain specified teaching behaviors; (2) use of the instrument to record classroom behaviors of teachers and their pupils; (3) a ranking of the classrooms according to a measure of pupil achievement adjusted for initial difference among the classes; and (4) a determination of the behaviors whose frequency of occurrence is related to adjusted class achievement scores. (p. 18)

In a further elaboration of the paradigm, Rosenshine and Furst (1973) recommended a research strategy in which findings from correlational studies in natural classroom settings are used as the source of variables for experimental investigations (for an example of this strategy, see Program on Teaching Effectiveness, SCRDT, 1976). Within this framework, answers to the teacher effectiveness question take the form of process-product laws that specify causal relationships between teacher classroom behaviors and student learning outcomes at the completion of an instructional sequence.

It is important to note that process-product investigators are, in Gage's (1966) terms, "improvers," not merely "describers" of the teaching process. Effectiveness is not seen as solely a research question. The results of process-product inquiry are expected to have direct practical application as sources of content for teacher education and as tools individual teachers can use to improve their instruction (Berliner, 1976; Brophy & Evertson, 1976b; Flanders, 1974; Gage, 1972; Good, Biddle, & Brophy, 1975; McDonald, 1974; Rosenshine & Furst, 1971). Although the degree of influence is not easily determined, these practical considerations have played a part in directing choices about which process dimensions to measure, which variables to manipulate, and how to interpret findings. In this sense, expectations concerning the use of process-product laws are an inherent component of the paradigm itself.

Explanatory Assumptions

At a conceptual level, the process-product paradigm contains few explicit explanatory principles to guide the selection of variables or the interpretation of results. Nor does the two-factor structure of the paradigm incorporate variables linking teacher behaviors to student learning outcomes, which might contribute to an explanation of how teacher effects occur. In practice, selection decisions appear most often to have been based on either personal preferences—what Dunkin & Biddle (1974) call "commitments"—or on strictly empirical criteria, such as the magnitude of correlation coefficients. With few exceptions (e.g., Brophy & Evertson, 1974a, 1974b), generalizations in process-product research have tended to be descriptive summaries of results of statistical analyses. On the strength of correlation coefficients, Rosenshine and Furst (1971), for example, concluded that variables such as clarity, enthusiasm, variability, and task orientation appeared "promising." On similar grounds, Rosenshine (1976a) asserted more recently that "direct instruction," a pattern which includes dominant teacher leadership, clear goals, systematic procedures, and an accepting climate, warranted further attention. Although useful, such summaries do not explain why these variables should be expected to relate to achievement. In the absence of formal explanatory propositions, it is difficult to interpret contradictory findings or select other potentially fruitful avenues for investigation.

Despite the lack of formal explanatory principles, process-product research has evolved a set of implicit assumptions about teaching. These tacit premises have, in a general sense at least, guided thinking about the effectiveness question. The following short review is designed to explicate the content of this informal explanatory model. For a more complete discussion of the methodological issues raised in this section, see Berliner (1976), Brophy and Evertson (1976b), and Dunkin and Biddle (1974).

Stimulus vs. Response Variables. By its very nature, the effectiveness question is a question about teachers. This concentration on the teacher has often led to the assumption that the teacher is the single most important influence on student achievement. The assumption of teacher primacy has, in turn, shaped research decisions. In process-product research, process dimensions have typically meant *teacher* behaviors, even though this set of variables represents only a small portion of the classroom variables that have been codified (e.g., Ryans, 1963; Smith, 1960; Snow, 1968). The focus, in other words, has been on *stimulus* rather than *response* categories in formulating hypotheses and selecting dimensions for investigation (on this distinction, see Levie & Dickie, 1973, and Salomon, 1970). Information about students is confined primarily to scores on pretest and posttest achievement measures. Even when data about student classroom behaviors are available, the tendency in the past has been to deemphasize this evidence in interpreting findings (e.g., Rosenshine, 1971).

Researchers stressing teacher variables have also tended to focus on discrete classroom events, with little attention to antecedent or subsequent class meetings or to other instructional resources (such as library books, films, television, etc.) that potentially affect student learning outcomes (McClellan, 1971). Similarly, there have been few attempts until recently to integrate curriculum effectiveness studies, such as those reviewed by Walker and Schaffarzick (1974), into teacher effectiveness formulations or to structure analyses in terms of the comparative magnitude of teacher effects (e.g., Anderson & Kaplan, 1974; Walberg, 1971).

Direction of Causality. The structure of the effectiveness question predisposes investigators to assume that teacher behaviors have a direct causal impact on student outcomes, in spite of the fact—acknowledged by these same investigators—that the correlational nature of most studies does not warrant such conclusions (Mitchell, 1969). Greater teacher enthusiasm or more complex teacher questions, for instance, are implicitly thought to cause increased student achievement, even though the opposite interpretation—that teachers ask complex questions and are more enthusiastic with higher achieving students—is equally permissible from the type of evidence available in most studies. Isolating teacher variables would seem, however, to oversimplify the picture of causality in classrooms. Several investigators have reported evidence to support the proposition that student behavior is a cause of observed teacher behavior (Emmer, Oakland, & Good, 1974; Fiedler, 1975; Haller, 1967; Jenkins & Deno, 1969; Klein, 1971; Noble & Nolan, 1976; Sherman & Cormier, 1974). A similar effect has been observed in other helping relationships (Loeber & Weisman, 1975). Students apparently play a role in creating classroom conditions and therefore in directing the course of their own learning. Such findings have important implications for interpreting research on effective teachers. If classroom relationships are reciprocal, assigning meaning to process-product relationships requires a more thorough understanding of classroom conditions.

Dimensions of Teacher Behavior. In addition to emphasizing teacher variables, investigators have also concentrated on selected dimensions of teacher behavior. Two of these dimensions—frequency and stability—will be discussed briefly here for illustrative purposes. For a more thorough treatment of several issues related to these dimensions, see Borich (1977).

Process-product researchers have generally preferred low-inference observation systems (i.e., techniques that record discrete instances of specific behaviors), on the grounds that results based on such instruments are more readily converted into prescriptions for teaching practice or skill training programs (e.g., Rosenshine & Furst, 1971; Soar & Soar, 1972). A low-inference approach to measurement, however, isolates *frequency* as the most salient dimension of teacher behavior. The implication is that the number of times a behavior occurs determines its effects. It would often seem, in other words, that more is better. The assumption that frequency determines effects would appear to have little support on empirical or conceptual grounds, however. Recent analyses of process-product data indicate that many nonlinear relationships occur, suggesting that for some behaviors optimum level rather than absolute quantity determines effects on student learning (Brophy & Evertson, 1974b; Soar, 1972).

Conceptually, it can be argued that dimensions other than frequency are of equal if not greater importance for studying effectiveness. Research on contingency management techniques indicates that for variables such as teacher praise the dimension of *timing* is a key factor in determining effects on learning (e.g., Resnick, 1971). We might also speculate that infrequent behaviors, that is, events which are exceptions to the general pattern, are especially informative to students and therefore have the greatest effects on outcomes. Finally, it is possible that qualitative dimensions of teacher behavior and instructional materials, such as the appropriateness of a textbook to the reading level of the student, are of significance in studying teaching effects (Berliner, 1976). Regardless of the accuracy of these proposals, it is clear that a simple frequency model of teaching behavior does not capture the complexity of process-product relationships in classrooms.

A similar case can be made for *stability* as a dimension of teacher behavior. Emphasis on stability follows from a number of practical and methodological considerations in effectiveness research. Teacher educators prepare personnel in a number of different fields and for a variety of still-to-be-encountered settings. Such a task requires process-product laws that are stable and broadly applicable across setting, learner, and task conditions. If the same teacher variable has markedly different effects at different times, then the variable has little practical utility for training decisions. A related set of problems concerns the stability of teacher behavior. Investigators frequently observe teachers for a relatively short period and then attempt to relate this observational data to outcomes measured at the end of a semester or an academic year. Such a practice presupposes a high degree of teacher stability. If there is wide variability in either the behavior of teachers or the instruments used to measure that behavior, then estimates of process-product relationships are precarious at best (see Borich, 1977). Parenthetically, recent analyses have suggested that stability coefficients, especially for narrowly defined units of teacher behavior, are generally lower than expected (Brophy, 1973; Good & Grouws, 1975; Rosenshine, 1970b; Shavelson & Dempsey-Atwood, 1976).

In terms of a model of teaching, however, stability may not determine how teacher effects occur. Variations resulting from adaptations to momentary classroom conditions may be the most important teacher behaviors from the perspective of the student. There is little reason to presume on a priori grounds that behaviors which are either stable or generalizable across settings are necessarily those that are the most powerful correlates of achievement in a given classroom situation.

Taken to an extreme, the search for answers to the teacher effectiveness question becomes a search for instructional variables that are least susceptible to modification by conditions existing in individual classroom environments. The ideal, in other words, takes the form of a set of process-product laws that are context-proof, teacher-proof, and even student-proof. Although few have explicitly adopted such a radical position, this ideal has been implicit in many of the discussions of effective teaching.

Recent Directions

Recent process-product investigations (Brophy & Evertson, 1974a, 1974b; Evertson & Brophy, 1974; McDonald, 1975, 1976; Program on Teaching

Effectiveness, SCRDT, 1976; Stallings, 1975; Tikunoff, Berliner, & Rist, 1975) have generally reflected an increased sensitivity to underlying assumptions and a greater sophistication in design, measurement, and data analysis. Two general features would seem to characterize this current work. First, considerably more attention is being given to a wider range of process variables, including materials, activities, pace, time allocations, and classroom management practices (for summaries, see Rosenshine, 1976a, 1976b). Second, more emphasis is being placed on a variety of "context" variables, such as grade level, content, and student characteristics, which appear to influence relationships between process and product dimensions in classrooms (see Berliner, 1976; Brophy & Evertson, 1976a). The teacher effectiveness question, in other words, is now being asked more often in terms of who is learning, who is teaching, and what is being taught.

The complex interactions among setting, learner, and instructional characteristics discussed above suggest the limitations of the two-factor structure of the process-product paradigm as a framework for considering teacher effectiveness. The contributions to effectiveness inquiry of a mediating process paradigm and a classroom ecology paradigm as structures for integrating and interpreting information are discussed in the sections to follow.

THE MEDIATING PROCESS PARADIGM

Mediating process research is focused directly on "the implicit human processes that mediate instructional stimuli and learning outcomes" (Levie & Dickie, 1973, p. 877). This response-oriented approach has been especially prominent in research on programmed instruction and instructional media (Anderson, 1970; Glaser, 1972, 1976; Glaser & Cooley, 1973; Levie & Dickie, 1973; Lumsdaine, 1961, 1963; Olson & Bruner, 1974; Salomon, 1970, 1974; Snow, 1970, 1974). Interest in student responses has also been evident in studies in special education (Cobb, 1972; Spaulding, 1970, 1973, Spivak, 1973). It is not possible, or even desirable, to review the bulk of this literature on student variables. For our purposes it is sufficient to outline the essential features of the mediating process paradigm and delineate the implications of this framework for thinking about teacher effectiveness.

Components of the Mediating Process Paradigm

The mediating process paradigm is perhaps most clearly represented in the context of prose learning research (for useful reviews, see Anderson & Biddle, 1975; Bransford & Franks, 1976; Frase, 1975; Montague, 1972; Paivio, 1971). One distinctive contribution of the prose learning field is Rothkopf's (1965, 1970, 1976) mathemagenic hypothesis, which posits a set of mediational responses learners use to process instructional stimuli (see Faw & Waller 1976, for a recent review). Mathemagenic responses—literally, behaviors that give birth to learning—encompass a number of human information-processing operations, such as attending, translating, segmenting, and rehearsing, which enable learners to extract instructional content from complex displays and process this information for memory storage.

The structure of the paradigm is readily apparent in Rohwer's (1972, 1973) research on the mediating effects of elaboration. Rohwer found that mastery of noun-pair lists (*bat-cup, chain-bowl,* etc.) depended upon the extent to which students elaborated the items during the acquisition process. Elaboration here refers primarily to a sentence construction process by which some conceptual link is established between the two items, as in the sentence "The bat is in the cup." Rohwer's data further indicated that the elaboration effect was not dependent upon such traditional differentiators as IQ, SES, or age. If elaboration occurred, mastery was achieved. Learners differed, however, on the magnitude of the prompts required to activate elaboration, with younger learners in general requiring more explicit prompt conditions. A 3-year-old, for instance, required a maximal prompt (an actual demonstration of a bat being placed into a cup) to activate elaboration, whereas an 18-year-old could achieve mastery with only a minimal prompt (instructions to learn the list).

Although limited to noun-pair learning tasks, these studies nevertheless illustrate the basic components of the mediating process paradigm as used in this analysis. According to this paradigm, variations in student learning outcomes are a function of the mediating activities employed by students during the learning process. In turn, the mediating processes that students use are influenced in part at least by instructional conditions.

This three-factor model represents a fundamentally different approach to the question of how teacher effects occur. In particular, the direct link between instructional conditions and student learning outcomes which is inherent in the structure of the process-product paradigm is recast within the mediating process framework to incorporate information-processing responses made by students during exposure to instructional stimuli. From this perspective, teacher behaviors and instructional materials, rather than "causing" student learning, influence outcomes only to the extent that they activate information-processing responses (such as elaboration) which determine what a student learns.

On an even more basic level, the mediating process paradigm redefines the nature of the relationship between instructional stimuli and student response variables. Students do not simply stand between process and product variables as passive recipients of stimuli. Rather, their responses play an active mediational role in determining "*what* is processed, *how* it is processed, and therefore *what* is remembered" (Rothkopf, 1976, p. 116). Central to this view is the distinction between "nominal" and "effective" stimuli in instruction (Rothkopf, 1965, 1976). *Nominal* stimuli are the objectively defined features of an instructional display; *effective* stimuli are those that a learner actually processes on a given occasion. The selective transformation of nominal stimuli into effective stimuli is done by the learner. From this perspective, process-product connections are "caused" not by the teacher but by the student.

Rothkopf further argues that the direction of this transformation is determined by the student's perception of both the demands of the learning task and the relevance of available stimuli to that task. Attending and processing, in other words, depend not on the discrete dimensions of an instructional treatment but on the task structure defined by that treatment. This premise shifts the analysis from the surface attributes of single stimuli to the function of stimuli in activating student responses under different task conditions (see Levie & Dickie, 1973; Salomon, 1970). A functional analysis of stimuli suggests that teaching strategies differing in a number of surface characteristics may, from the students' perspective, offer nearly identical learning tasks (see Bloom, 1963; Olson & Bruner, 1974). Similarly, substantially different learning outcomes can be achieved by individual students under the same instructional conditions (Salomon, 1974).

An interesting example of the relationship between instructional conditions and mediating responses is contained in Shimron's (1976) study of an Individually Prescribed Instruction classroom. He found that students who finished instructional units fastest spent twice as much classroom time attending to task as did students who completed the fewest number of units. It seems reasonable to argue that students who worked at a faster rate experienced a greater amount of variety, a condition that would seem to help maintain attention and information-processing efficiency. By their own activity, in other words, students generated an environment that sustained their work involvement in a manner independent of the characteristics of teacher behavior or instructional materials, to a degree at least.

Uses of the Mediating Process Paradigm

Given the recent emphasis on instructional materials in teacher effectiveness research (Rosenshine, 1976a, 1976b), the mediating process paradigm, based largely on studies of prose passages and media, would seem to have immediate applicability. But the utility of the paradigm is not limited to this common interest in materials. At a conceptual level, the mediating process paradigm, as a more complex model of how teaching works, provides a structure for interpreting existing teacher effectiveness studies. From a mediating process viewpoint, information about relationships between instructional conditions and learning outcomes (process-product associations) is of interest primarily as a basis for reasoning about the kinds of student mediating responses that make such relationships possible. Glaser (1971) demonstrated this approach in his analysis of a series of teacher lecturing studies conducted by Gage and his associates (Gage, Belgard, Rosenshine, Unruh, Dell, & Hiller, 1971). In the lecturing studies, teacher variables such as clarity of presentation, gestures and movements, and use of explanatory links characterized the more effective presentations. Glaser, noting that the amount of student attention was significantly related to learning outcomes, suggested that clarity was a signal to students that the teacher knew what he/she was doing and hence that it was important to pay attention. Gestures and movements were interpreted as variables that aroused and sustained student attention. Explanatory links were viewed as organizing cues that facilitated student information processing. Interpretations such as this one establish a basis for generating hypotheses about teacher effects.

In addition to its interpretive functions, the mediating process paradigm serves as a framework for combining results from several different traditions in research on teaching. Process-*process* studies, for example, have demonstrated with reasonable consistency that teacher classroom behaviors have an impact on overt student behavior, including the amount of attention and task involvement (Cogan, 1956, 1958; Gallagher, 1970; Kounin, 1970; Kounin & Doyle, 1975; Kounin & Gump, 1974; Ryans, 1961a, 1961b). Several other studies have shown that, in turn, measures of student classroom behavior are positively associated with learning outcomes (Cobb, 1972; Lahaderne, 1968; McKinney, Mason, Perkerson, & Clifford, 1975; Morsh, 1956; Perkins, 1965; Spaulding, 1970; Spaulding & Papageorgiou, 1972; Spivak, Swift, & Prewitt, 1971; Swift & Spivak, 1973). Intervention studies have indicated that student classroom behavior can be modified, with corresponding improvement in learning outcomes, and that teachers can be trained in skills that increase the frequency of student behaviors related to achievement (Cobb & Hops, 1973; Spaulding & Showers, 1974). Wang (1976), in particular, has examined systematic arrangements for influencing such student behaviors as time utilization and task completion rates in ways that maximize achievement.

Although these results are not conclusive (see Brophy & Evertson, 1974b; Dunkin & Biddle, 1974, pp. 135–145), this selective review illustrates the value of a mediational model for enriching the conceptual and empirical foundations of effectiveness inquiry. In particular, the paradigm provides a framework for integrating descriptive studies—that is, studies which do not include an achievement criterion—with more conventional process-product research and for interpreting this process-process work in ways that are relevant to the teacher effectiveness question.

The mediating process paradigm would also seem to be useful to teachers because it generates propositions in a form compatible with the decision-making demands of classroom teaching (Brophy & Evertson, 1976b; Shulman & Elstein, 1975). Using results from the lecturing studies reviewed above, a teacher would be guided to plan a presentation containing clarity, gestures and movements, and explanatory links. In the event that the presentation did not accomplish its objective, the process-product formulations would offer no further guidance. Just knowing the relation of a technique to terminal performance fails to supply sufficient information about immediate contingencies in the classroom. A mediating process interpretation, however, directs a teacher to experiment with other procedures which are potentially related to activating student attention. The response focus of the mediating process paradigm, in other words, enables a teacher to practice what Cronbach (1975) has called "short-run empiricism," in which "one monitors responses to the treatment and adjusts it, instead of prescribing a fixed treatment on the basis of a generalization from prior experience with other persons or in other locales" (p. 126). In this view of the practitioner's task, information concerning *effects* assumes greater importance than information concerning *effectiveness*.

The mediational perspective suggests a need to reformulate the general strategy of research on effective teachers. If the question is truly one of improving student achievement, then it is necessary to look first at what students do in order to learn. In other words, research that traces different patterns of student behavior and the relationships of these patterns to achievement (Soli & Devine, 1976; Stodolsky, 1975) is the starting point for effectiveness inquiry. With a more thorough picture of student response variables, it would be possible to formulate meaningful questions and interpret answers about the effectiveness of instructional conditions.

Current Status

Interest in the general form of the mediating process paradigm has been apparent in teacher effectiveness research in recent years. Rosenshine (1970a), for instance, invoked student attention to explain the effects of teacher enthusiasm on learning outcomes. Berliner (1976) has recommended specifically that a mediating process paradigm be used to formulate research. Contemporary teacher effectiveness studies have more consistently and explicitly incorporated measures of student behaviors, such as attention, task persistence, and time utilization, and have related composite indices of these behaviors to general instructional conditions and to terminal outcomes (Brophy & Evertson, 1974a, 1974b; Stallings, 1975).

One of the most elaborate uses of a mediating process structure is the Harnischfeger and Wiley (1976) model relating quantity of schooling (time) to achievement. The key proposition of the model is that a student's total active learning time determines the amount of content comprehended. Total active learning time, in turn, is related to pupil background, teacher activities, and various curricular and institutional systems that affect time allocation and utilization. In this model, teacher competencies, such as planning (i.e., time allocation), monitoring, and motivation, which increase active learning time for different pupils are of central importance.

The Harnischfeger and Wiley model and the other approaches reviewed in this section represent an important first step in adapting a mediating process paradigm to research on teacher effectiveness. If the full potential of the paradigm is to be realized, however, several significant extensions of this work are necessary. Two of these are of special importance in the present discussion.

The first issue concerns the conceptualization of student mediating responses. Most current work in this regard, by emphasizing such variables as attention, time utilization, and task completion rates, reflects a preference for overt manifestations of student mediating responses. Although perhaps useful proxies for initial work, such overt variables are relatively gross measures of information-processing responses which, by their very nature, are inferred rather than directly observable operations (Rothkopf, 1976). It is necessary, therefore, to define more precisely the covert information-processing responses that operate during "active learning time." In this connection, Bloom's (1953) early work on student thought processes during different instructional procedures is especially relevant.

Shimron's (1976) findings provide a useful perspective on attention as a mediating response. He reported that fast students spent twice as much time on task but completed three times more units of work than slow students. Fast students, in other words, spent more time on task each class period but less time on task per unit of work. The relationship between attention per unit and learning was therefore negative in this study. Such results suggest that efficiency of processing is an important dimension in accounting for differences in student achievement.

The second issue concerns the contrast in setting and task features between the laboratory conditions of mediating process research and the natural classroom environment. Studies of learning from prose provide a useful illustration of the structure of the mediating process paradigm, as well as a basis for identifying certain types of mediating responses. Nevertheless, the reliance in these studies on a restricted range of learning tasks and on heavily controlled instructional conditions is simply not representative of most classroom environments. The basic issue here is that of task validity (Shulman, 1970), that is, the extent to which task dimensions in the laboratory are congruent with the complex task demands operating in classrooms. On such grounds McKeachie (1974) and Cronbach (1975) have questioned the generalizability of laboratory-based findings to "natural educational settings."

In sum, the mediating process paradigm serves as a useful way of studying how teaching works and integrating and interpreting evidence related to teacher effectiveness. A fundamental question, however, remains: What mediates instructional effects in classrooms? To address this question, we consider an ecology paradigm which extends the mediating process approach to teaching as it occurs in classroom environments.

A CLASSROOM ECOLOGY PARADIGM

The classroom ecology paradigm outlined in this chapter focuses on mutual relations among environmental demands and human responses in natural classroom settings. Using naturalistic data, "the repetitive demands work makes on people and the ways in which they come to adjust, in myriad ways, to those demands" (Lortie, 1973, p. 485) are described. The analysis is restricted to *student* strategies fostered by classroom environments (for a parallel analysis applied to teachers, see Doyle, 1977b). By concentrating on the flow and texture of classroom events, part of what Sarason (1971) has called the "culture of the school," it is possible to enlarge the mediating process paradigm to encompass student response variables operating in settings that are more representative of school learning conditions.

The ecological model integrates and interprets the descriptive material from naturalistic studies of classrooms. It is difficult to reflect in this review the rich array of data and insight found in the naturalistic literature (see Burnett, 1974; Goetz, Rice, & Bailey, 1976; Wax, Diamond, & Gearing, 1971; Wolcott, 1975). Therefore the review is restricted to a brief and highly selective summary of the essential features of a classroom ecology paradigm. This version of the paradigm brings together two main sources: (1) recent ethnographic studies of classrooms in England and America (Barnes, 1971; Cusick, 1973; Jackson, 1968; Mehan, 1974; Nash, 1973; Rist, 1973; Smith & Geoffrey, 1968), and (2) a general ecological framework for interpreting relationships between behavior and environment (Barker, 1968; Gump, 1964, 1969; Kounin, 1970; Willems, 1973a, 1973b). These major resources are supplemented, where necessary, by material from more traditional classroom process studies. In its present state of development, the paradigm consists primarily of a set of tentative propositions derived from a two-stage process: identifying environmental demands, and speculating about the mediational strategies necessary to meet these demands successfully.

The Nature of Classroom Tasks

From an ecological perspective, a classroom can be described in terms of a set of overlapping task structures, each consisting of a goal and operations to achieve that goal and each specifying a behavior ecology. In this review, the formal task structure of a classroom is defined as *an exchange of performance for grades*. Becker, Geer, and Hughes (1968) contend, on the basis of naturalistic data, that this "exchange of performance for grades is, formally and institutionally, what the class is about" (p. 79). In a related fashion, Schellenberg (1965) describes the task structure of classrooms as an exchange of performance for status. There are certainly other classroom tasks as well as several motivational and ability variables that influence both the extent to which a given student will choose to engage in this performance-grade task and the probability of a favorable exchange.

It is not possible in this review to account for all of these contingencies. Rather, we posit the somewhat specialized case of a student who desires to achieve a favorable performance-grade exchange. Then we examine the kinds of competencies necessary to reach this goal with some measure of consistency. Although admittedly idealized, this situation is especially useful for isolating student mediating processes that explain differences in achievement.

Environmental Demands

Although the structure of the formal classroom task itself is relatively simple, the task is enacted within a setting which contributes substantially to the complexity of securing a successful exchange. These environmental dimensions are basic to the structure of the classroom ecology paradigm.

From a naturalistic standpoint, classrooms at both the elementary (Jackson, 1968) and secondary (Cusick, 1973) levels contain a large and complex set of environmental features. In a single classroom there are typically 20 to 30 students, one or perhaps more adults, and a range of assorted books, pictures, and pieces of equipment, all of which potentially carry instructional significance. Such factors contribute to the sheer amount of information impinging upon students (Cicourel, 1974). As Barnes (1971) has observed, "An enormous amount of talk washes over pupils in lessons" (p. 37). In addition, classroom groups convene on a regular basis over a fairly long period of time, usually five days per week for one or more semesters of approximately 16 weeks. As a result there are sequential and cumulative effects in classroom contexts, as well as variations in structure and processes over time. From the perspective of classroom tasks, a wide range of responses ultimately enters into the performance-grade exchange.

In addition to these quantitative dimensions, the quality of communication complicates classroom tasks for students. Advocates of behavioral objectives have charged that performance expectations in classrooms are seldom defined with adequate specificity. Recent naturalistic studies (Barnes, 1971; Cicourel, 1974; Mehan, 1974) have confirmed that teachers tend to leave performance expectations unstated. Further, they show that teachers are highly inconsistent in reacting to student responses. In observing a first-grade classroom, for example, Mehan (1974) found that teacher instructions were incomplete; that is, they did not delineate fully the requirements for acceptable performance. Moreover, teacher reactions to incorrect responses did not always contain useful corrective information. Significantly, there also was considerable variability in the teacher's practice of labeling responses as correct or incorrect; that is, the same student response received opposite teacher reactions at different points in the same lesson. Acceptability would seem to depend, then, on factors other than "correctness" as defined by the teacher's own rules.

A similar pattern of ambiguity and inconsistency can be gleaned from more traditional examples of classroom process research. Smith and Meux (1962), in a study of logical processes in classrooms, found that teachers were in general poor models of appropriate logical operations. In a study of teacher reaction patterns, Zahorik (1968) found that teacher feedback during class discussion was not very informative and that feedback practices appeared to depend upon a number of factors other than the quality of student responses. Along similar lines, Bellack, Kliebard, Hyman, and Smith (1966) found that teacher reaction to student responses, whether correct or incorrect, was surprisingly uniform. Teacher reactions rarely supplied additional information, even when a response was incorrect. Moreover, 19.8 percent of the correct responses received negative teacher ratings and 78.8 percent of the incorrect responses received positive teacher ratings (Bellack et al., 1966, p. 185), an outcome Turner (1971) considers "distinctly bizarre" if not "irrational." These data suggest that, from a student perspective, all teacher verbal behavior is not a reliable source of information concerning the acceptability of responses in the performance-grade exchange.

From an ecological stance, the pattern of inconsistency and ambiguity described here does not result primarily from "bad" teaching. These communication practices are shaped, rather, by the quantitative dimensions (e.g., number of people, amount of material, duration of meetings) that are intrinsic features of classroom life. The patterns result, in other words, from teachers' attempts to cope with demands of a classroom environment (Doyle, 1977a, 1977b). Inconsistency, in particular, would seem to be directly related to the continuing need for teachers to shift attention in order to manage simultaneous events (Kounin, 1970; Mehan, 1974; Smith & Geoffrey, 1968).

The effects of ambiguity are intensified for students by the generally unpredictable and uncontrollable nature of classrooms. Naturalistic observers such as Adams (1972) and Jackson (1968) have pointed out that a classroom is susceptible to a large number of disruptions in the flow of events, disruptions coming from internal (e.g., student misbehavior) and external (e.g., public address announcement) sources. Such unplanned disruptions would certainly seem to produce further discontinuity and incompleteness in classroom communication. Moreover, a classroom can be characterized as a selective rather than an adaptive educational environment (Glaser, 1972). That is, a classroom is a mass processing system which is not always responsive to individual requirements and over which the individual student has only limited control (Cusick, 1973). As a result, a student has little opportunity to stop the system in order to clarify ambiguity or to resolve inconsistencies concerning performance expectations.

To this point we have considered complexities within a single classroom environment. From the earliest years, however, students change classroom settings on at least a yearly basis, and by the time they reach the secondary level, they commonly encounter from four to six different classrooms each day. This feature of school life provides, at regular intervals, a new and possibly different set of environmental contingencies. Although there is apparently stability in the general interpersonal structure of classrooms (Glidewell, Kantor, Smith, & Stringer, 1966), available evidence indicates that there are also localized differences across classrooms and even within a single classroom over time (Withall, 1952). Students at least seem capable of perceiving differences in classroom environments across subject matter areas (Steele, Walberg, & House, 1974) and even within a broad content field such as science (Lawrenz, 1976). Differences across classrooms stem in part from the fact that "every class has a culture of its own," a culture that defines such matters as "who should talk, how much they should talk, what kinds of things they should say, how they should say them, and what the consequences are of behaving appropriately or otherwise" (Becker et al., 1968, p. 75). Meanings, in other words, are negotiated within a continuous process of classroom interaction and are therefore context specific (Cicourel, 1974; Keddie, 1971; West, 1975).

In this regard, ethnographers have noted that teachers spend a good deal of time in early class meetings establishing routines that, in effect, assign meaning to subsequent moment-to-moment behaviors (Rist, 1973; Smith & Geoffrey, 1968). There is, in other words, a cumulative effect in classrooms: The meaning of events and processes at any one point in time depends upon knowledge about what has gone before and predictions about what will happen in the future. This negotiated quality of classroom knowledge limits the transferability of performance capabilities across environments. Procedures and even answers learned in one setting may not apply in another.

Dimensions of Student Competence

This brief review suggests that classroom tasks are enacted in an environment of considerable complexity. Two points are in order concerning this picture of classroom life. First, to say that classrooms contain inconsistency and ambiguity does not mean that all students experience these environments as continually confusing. Any language, for example, is an extremely complex entity for which no complete set of rules can be written. It does not follow that a proficient user of the language is necessarily conscious of this complexity, except on very special occasions. Similarly, there is little reason to expect that proficient students would necessarily describe classrooms as complex or confusing. Second, the basic issue in this ecological analysis is not simply the "quality" of teaching. As indicated earlier, complexity is for the most part an inherent feature of the classroom environment. Moreover, students apparently spend a good deal of time in classrooms that are not ideal. The central question here is the effects on students of this long-term experience in coping with classroom environments, regardless of their "quality." The analysis is focused, that is, on defining the set of strategies that enable students to adjust to environmental complexity and learn from classrooms (for related discussions, see Dweck, Hill, Redd, Steinman, & Parke, 1976; Salomon, 1974; Silvers, 1975).

Evidence reviewed earlier indicated that student attention is related to learning outcomes. In a classroom, however, mere frequency of attention would not appear to be a sufficient condition for success. The sheer magnitude and unreliability of information sources suggest that the ability to accomplish classroom tasks must also include selectivity and timing, a strategy Barnes (1974) calls "differential attentiveness" (p. 62). The student who is unable to distinguish between significant and insignificant information or who fails to attend when relevant information is being communicated would presumably operate at a disadvantage in the performance-grade exchange. There is even evidence that the student must learn to recognize when performance appraisal is taking place. Activities that, from the student's viewpoint, are conducted simply to fill available time can, from the teacher's position, have considerable significance in estimating performance capability (Leiter, 1974).

The degree of differentiation a successful student must exercise can be illustrated by a brief look at feedback practices in classrooms. As noted earlier, teacher praise sometimes appears to be administered without regard for the accuracy of a student's response. There is evidence, however, that teacher criticism is more accurate than praise and therefore communicates more information about performance standards (Paris & Cairns, 1972; Parke, 1976; Redd, 1976). To interpret teacher feedback, then, a student must learn to differentiate between positive and negative forms of that behavior. Hill (1976) reported that students even become skilled in interpreting nonreaction as a mode of feedback. The interpretive problem is further complicated by the fact that teachers differentiate in their reactions to students (Brophy & Good, 1974; Nash, 1973; Rist, 1973). Rowe (1974a, 1974b) found, for instance, that higher achieving students tended to receive more accurate feedback than lower achieving students. It would seem, therefore, that a student must also learn to account for the target of praise to interpret teacher feedback. This state of affairs certainly would complicate learning from classrooms, especially for those students whose academic skills are least highly developed.

A successful student must not only attend selectively but also must monitor a wide band of information sources, from the responses of fellow students to test questions and teacher comments on written assignments. This situation results in part from the fact that teachers regularly employ other instructional instruments, such as textbooks, workbooks, and films (Wallen & Travers, 1963). But this is not the only reason students must learn to use multiple resources. Given the incompleteness of teacher communications, a student who relies exclusively on the teacher will seldom have access to adequate information to determine performance adequacy (Cicourel, 1974). A student must become skilled in "paying attention to much more than the teacher's presentation of stimulus items in order to answer questions" (Mehan, 1974, p. 124), regardless of whether the teacher specifically assigns supplementary materials.

In monitoring alternative information sources, the student must, however, keep in mind the relevance of these sources to performance requirements as defined by the classroom task structure. Naturalistic studies indicate that classroom knowledge is to some degree always context specific and arbitrary (Barnes, 1971; Keddie, 1971; Nash, 1973). All potentially "correct" answers are not necessarily acceptable to a given teacher on a given occasion. Even when more than one answer is clearly possible, teachers tend to designate one as the "most correct." The student must learn, therefore, to identify which answer is appropriate in a particular situation at a particular time. Consistent success in the performance-grade exchange would seem to require continuous attention to situational indicators of response expectations.

The exercise of differential attentiveness, a difficult enough task in an interfering environment, is made even more arduous by the duration of class meetings and the delays that permeate class routine, apparently even in individualized classrooms (Shimron, 1976). Jackson (1968) maintains that, in view of the repetitiveness and delays in the flow of classroom life, patience is one of the most salient skills required for student success. Patience might possibly account, in part, at least, for differential student ability in attending to classroom events (Lahaderne, 1968).

In addition to monitoring multiple information resources, successful students apparently adopt, or at least capitalize on, strategies that delimit and concretize performance expectations. At a collective level, Schellenberg (1965) has argued that students minimize performance requirements by attempting to establish "standards of democratic justice" and "fairness" that standardize and simplify performance expectations (e.g., "How long should the term paper be?"). The significance of these standardizing and routinizing strategies for coping with ambiguity in teacher instructions may explain why Cusick (1973) found that high school students were obsessed with procedures. A successful student has several options which enable him or her to meet performance expectations. Mehan (1974), in a naturalistic study of first-grade lessons, observed students using three strategies to compensate for incomplete instructions. The first was that of "searching," which consisted of eliciting a teacher reaction to a provisional response (e.g., "Under the table?"). The second involved "imitating" responses previously emitted by the teacher or by classmates. The third was labeled "cohort production," a process whereby a student, by hesitating during responding, was able to get the teacher or classmates to contribute the answer. The latter two strategies, imitating and cohort production, allow a student to achieve a favorable in-class exchange, at least in terms of positive teacher sentiment, even when performance expectations are not fully understood prior to the response occasion. In addition to these strategies for getting the "right" answer, Noble and Nolan (1976) found that students were capable of controlling the number of response occasions they received in classrooms.

This brief analysis of the interaction among environmental demands and student strategies defines the general features of a classroom ecology model. We will now consider the contributions of this model to research on teacher effectiveness.

Applications to Teacher Effectiveness

In contrast to much of the work in the process-product and the mediating process traditions, the ecological approach emphasizes the richness and complexity of classroom settings. This emphasis on complexity results in part from the naturalistic methodology upon which the ecological paradigm is based (for views on this methodology, see Bronfenbrenner, 1976; Overholt & Stallings, 1976; Tinbergen, 1972). In naturalistic research, a high priority is placed on detailed, long-term observations of behavior in natural settings. In addition, few decisions concerning what behaviors to record are made prior to conducting observations. Indeed, a self-conscious effort is made to minimize preconceived notions about the meaning and interrelationships of behavior in a particular situation. Such a stance understandably generates a complex picture of classroom life.

Simplification does occur in naturalistic research, but it is done after rather than before observing, and it is considered to be primarily a conceptual rather than a methodological process. The simplification is not done by constructing category systems to code only selected aspects of behavior or by constructing artificial laboratory settings, although these techniques are sometimes useful in later stages of a research program. Rather, parsimony is achieved by a continual process of fashioning interpretive propositions to account specifically for the intrinsic patterns of events and processes in the setting being observed. Through such a process, it is eventually possible to formulate precise hypotheses about environment-behavior relationships in a particular setting. The value of this naturalistic approach lies in the potential for capturing aspects of behavior that are not accessible through standard correlational or experimental studies (Willems & Raush, 1969). Kounin's (1970) "withitness" and Smith and Geoffrey's (1968) "ringmaster," emerging from naturalistic work, are good examples of classroom dimensions that are not easily derived from standard psychological formulations.

This methodological perspective has important implications for the application of the classroom ecology paradigm to research on teacher effectiveness. The purpose of the ecological paradigm is not simply to generate a new set of variables for correlational studies to discover new process-product relationships. Rather, it is to build and verify a coherent explanatory model of how classrooms work, a model that can be used to ask questions and interpret answers about teacher effectiveness. The paradigm is designed, in other words, to be most useful as a framework for thinking about interrelationships among classroom variables and the connection between such variables and student achievement. Clearly, such an approach is less directly related to the design of a specific teacher effectiveness study than either the process-product or the mediating process paradigm. It can serve, nevertheless, as a useful guide for formulating research questions. Needless to say, considerably more conceptual and empirical work is necessary before the full interpretive potential of the ecological model can be realized.

At its present stage of development, the classroom ecology paradigm should contribute to research on teacher effectiveness in two general ways: by defining a new set of student mediators, and by offering a framework for interpreting how instructional effects occur in classrooms. The final sections of this review clarify and illustrate these two contributions.

Classroom Mediators

The classroom ecology paradigm supplements the mediating process approach by offering a more complete understanding of the student competencies necessary in order to learn from classrooms. The probability of a long-term favorable exchange of performance for grades depends upon the extent to which a student can consistently exhibit approved responses. Success at this task requires a student to have the competence to *acquire* performance capabilities. The skills necessary to acquire subject matter competence are the special province of laboratory research on mediating responses. From an ecological position, however, skill in subject matter acquisition would not be a sufficient condition for learning from classrooms. Because of the complexity that characterizes the context in which school learning takes place, successful students must master strategies that enable them to *identify* from among possible responses those performances for which they will be held accountable, as well as to *adjust* definitions of performance expectations to account for variability over time. In a general sense, that is, they develop an *interpretive competence* to navigate classroom demands (Cicourel, 1974).

Brunswik's "probabilistic functionalism" (Brunswik, 1952, 1955; Snow, 1968) and the inference models which have been built on this foundation (e.g., Sarbin, Taft, & Bailey, 1960) provide a useful way of conceptualizing the impact of classroom demands on students. Probabilistic functionalism postulates that experience with the events and objects in an environment produces knowledge about the cue value of recurring stimuli, which enables the person to predict the consequences of various responses. Functional achievement depends on the person's ability to select and utilize cues that are especially salient in defining the requirements of the environment. It is also proposed that long-term experience in a particular setting establishes a systematic bias toward certain cues because of their consistent functional value in predicting outcomes.

Brunswik's model focuses attention on the processes involved in learning to utilize classroom cues that have ecological validity in the sense of signaling performance expectations (for a similar approach, see Dweck et al., 1976). A competent student is one who is able to recognize, from among the range of available cues, those that communicate the greatest amount of information about the acceptability of responses in a given classroom environment. Consistent success in achieving a favorable exchange of performance for grades would depend on this basic cue utilization skill. The model is also useful for understanding the biasing effects of long-term classroom experience. Given the duration of class meetings, a successful student would presumably learn to prefer certain cues that have high functional value in predicting performance expectations (e.g., teacher tests over teacher praise for classroom responses). Such cue utilization preferences would seem essential to ensure learner efficiency in a complex classroom environment.

Evidence for the development of cue preferences is contained in recent studies of the comparative effects of different curricula. Tamir (1975) found, for instance, that students who had long-term experience with a BSCS curriculum exhibited a preference for inquiry tasks in contrast to recall tasks. Walker and Schaffarzick (1974), in reviewing curriculum effectiveness research, observed that for those studies in which the posttest content favored the experimental curriculum, students in the experimental groups scored higher than those in the traditional curriculum groups. A similar trend was present for students in the traditional groups when test content favored the traditional curriculum. This evidence suggests in a very general way that continuous classroom experience produces bias in the cue utilization strategies students employ to navigate a particular type of learning task (for related material, see Mayer & Greeno, 1972; Olson & Bruner, 1974).

In addition to skill in identifying functional cues, learning from classrooms also seems to require the ability to *compensate* for the unreliability and inconsistency of classroom cue resources such as teacher instructions. In essence, this compensatory ability consists of such dimensions as (1) searching beyond immediate contingencies for functional cues, (2) recalling cues available on previous occasions, and (3) restructuring available cues to increase their functional value. Evidence for this ability to compensate for irregularities in classroom environments is found in Gagné's (1973) recent review of learning and instructional sequence. He concluded that variations in the sequence of instructional presentations have little differential effect on the retention of verbal information. Students, at least in the upper grades and in college, appear capable of supplementing stimulus presentations by imposing a structure necessary to acquire information, in spite of the character of immediately available cue resources. A student, in other words, is an active agent in his own learning, capable of responding independently of moment-to-moment stimuli in order to navigate classroom conditions.

This ecological perspective on classroom mediators has important implications for analyzing differences in student achievement. Mediating process research focuses on variations in abilities to process subject matter as a source of differences in student learning outcomes. The classroom ecology approach calls attention to skills necessary to interpret classroom tasks. It is conceivable that a student would fail to learn from a particular instructional setting, regardless of its "quality," because of an inability to recognize and interpret cues that signal which performances are being taught. The student's model of a classroom may be simply inadequate or erroneous (see Keddie, 1971), so that treatment effects do not occur. In this connection, recent efforts to investigate student perceptions of treatment variables in effectiveness studies (e.g., Peterson, 1976; Stayrook & Corno, 1976) seem to be a promising direction. At a conceptual level, Walberg (1976) has provided a comprehensive framework for studying the role of student perceptions in teaching. Stodolsky's (1972, 1974, 1975) work on how individual students use different environments is an especially useful example of research on how classroom mediators affect achievement.

Explaining Instructional Effects

In addition to expanding the general concept of student mediating responses, the classroom ecology paradigm can contribute to a redefinition of how instructional effects occur. The basic features of this outlook for interpreting instructional effects are outlined in this section.

Classroom Effects.   The key to understanding how the classroom ecology paradigm contributes to teacher effectiveness formulations lies in the connection between classroom tasks and student learning outcomes as measured by standardized achievement tests. From an ecological perspective, a variety of skills is learned through the continuous experience of classroom life. Two of these learning outcomes are of particular importance in this discussion. First, a student learns how to locate and interpret cue resources for navigating classroom tasks. Second, a student learns a set of responses which are useful in the performance-grade exchange. The capabilities a student ultimately acquires, in other words, are a function of the operations used in identifying and acquiring acceptable performances to be exchanged for grades. To the extent that the interpretive and academic skills acquired in a classroom are congruent with skills required for a standardized achievement test, a student will score high on a conventional indicator of effectiveness.

Relationships among Instructional Variables.   Given this ecological interpretation of classroom effects, any attempt to define the effect of an instructional variable on achievement must focus on the structure of classroom tasks, especially the performance-grade exchange that integrates the formal properties of classroom environments. Within the ecology of the classroom, the treatment value of a specific variable is defined not simply by the stimulus properties of that variable but rather by its position in the hierarchy of interacting cue resources in the situation. The position of the variable on a given occasion—indeed, the character of the cue hierarchy itself—is defined in turn by the nature of the performance-grade exchange. This means that such factors as the frequency of a teacher behavior or the appropriateness of a prose passage to a student's reading level may not determine how that variable influences student learning. The manner in which a student attends to and processes an instructional resource is shaped by the student's perception of how the resource relates to the identification and acquisition of capabilities congruent with performance expectations operating in a particular environment.

This ecological approach to defining classroom treatments offers some basis for interpreting the effects of changes in classroom procedure. As suggested above, a student presumably learns, over time, the relative position of instructional resources in the cue hierarchy of a given classroom. Since variability is a common feature of daily classroom life, a student would also learn to compensate for moderate changes in cue values. The nature of classroom experience would seem, therefore, to reduce the significance of small changes in instructional conditions, unless these changes have a clear relationship to the definition of performance expectations. Modifying a particular teacher behavior or certain instructional material without modifying the position of that resource in the cue hierarchy would be expected to have little impact on student learning outcomes.

This perspective on variability in classrooms suggests that classroom effects operate at a molar rather than a molecular level. Students apparently monitor relatively large units of difference in instructional conditions to navigate performance-grade exchanges. Along these lines, Walker and Schaffarzick (1974) have presented a compelling argument for "inclusion" and "emphasis" as molar variables which influence student learning to a greater extent than more molecular units of classroom processes.

From a similar molar perspective, it is possible to interpret process-product evidence concerning the effects of such variables as clarity, enthusiasm, variability, and task orientation (Rosenshine & Furst, 1971). Clarity and task orientation, for example, would function to reduce the complexity of identifying performance expectations; variability and enthusiasm would encourage attention by creating an attractive stimulus display. Such teacher behaviors would therefore increase the total number of students who are able to locate performance expectations and, in turn, would raise class mean achievement. A similar explanation could presumably be applied to recent findings concerning "direct instruction" (Rosenshine, 1976a), a framework which includes many of these same teacher variables.

How Teachers Affect Achievement. The ecological paradigm also offers a new perspective on how teachers affect achievement in classrooms. Given the range of instructional resources available to students and the possible unreliability of many teacher behaviors as cues for the performance-grade exchange, there is little reason to expect large effects on student achievement of many types of teacher variables. Consistent with this proposition, analysis of the comparative effects of factors influencing achievement have indicated that teacher behaviors, at least as conventionally measured, seldom account for more than 10 percent of the variance in learning outcomes (Anderson & Kaplan, 1974; Heath & Nielson, 1974; Walberg, 1971). It even appears that students rank teachers low as a perceived source of influence on their achievement (Perry, 1975).

This evidence does not mean, however, that teachers have no impact on outcomes. From an ecological perspective, teacher influence operates indirectly through the manner in which a teacher defines and manages the performance-grade exchange. This point is similar to Gump's (1964) argument that teacher effects occur primarily through the activity structures teachers establish in classrooms. By creating classroom tasks, in other words, a teacher activates a particular set of student responses which result in achievement. At a behavioral level, teacher cues that define or signal potential changes in performance requirements would be especially relevant to outcomes.

Of the cue resources teachers manage, tests seem to be especially salient in defining performance expectations (Becker et al., 1968). Bloom (1963) has reviewed evidence that "the type of mental process the student *expects* to be tested will determine his method of study and preparation" (p. 392). McLeish (1976) observed that preparation for examinations produces an "equalization effect" that overrides differences in instructional procedures. Because of their role in defining performance expectations, tests, in fact, seem to determine the patterns of differential attentiveness in classrooms. If, for example, a teacher consistently asked higher order questions in the classroom but tested only for recall of answers given to those questions, it is reasonable to expect that students would eventually pay more attention to the answers the teacher accepts than to the cognitive demands of the higher order questions. Similarly, if a teacher measures primarily for recall of the names of historical figures in the textbook, then the reading level of the test is irrelevant to the use of the material as an instructional resource in that situation.

It is important to note, however, that tests do not define the performance-grade exchange in its entirety. Performance appraisal is a continuous process in classrooms and depends in part on the subjective reaction of teachers. Students must therefore be able to exhibit at appropriate times approved responses in the classroom setting, even if those responses are not part of the content of formal examinations. For example, even though a teacher's tests do not measure higher order thought processes, a student might increase the likelihood of getting a better grade by answering higher order questions in class discussions. In this circumstance, a teacher's expectations for classroom performance would also affect achievement.

The ecological view of interconnections among instructional resources in classrooms has implications concerning the value of laboratory investigations in research on teacher effectiveness. Under experimental conditions, it is possible to restrict student access to the kinds of resources that typically exist in classrooms (e.g., textbooks and teacher feedback on test performance) and thus to increase dependence upon the teacher as a cue resource. The final outcome should be to inflate the effects of teacher variables on student learning outcomes. Such findings would not, however, be transferable to classroom settings in which other environmental cues are readily available.

CONCLUSION

This review has concentrated on conceptual alternatives in the teacher effectiveness field. The most obvious conclusion is that this interpretive work needs further elaboration and refinement. Little attempt has been made here, for instance, to analyze the role of affective mediators in learning from classroom environments. Furthermore, additional data are certainly needed to substantiate many of the tentative interpretations about learning from classrooms.

The analysis does suggest, however, that the space between instructional conditions and student learning outcomes is indeed crowded. From this perspective, attempts to attribute differences in student achievement to a few generalizable dimensions of teacher behavior or instructional materials may well be futile. The implication is that teacher effectiveness formulations should include both contextual variables and the meanings teachers and students assign to the events and processes that occur in classrooms. One is even inclined to speculate, on the basis of an ecological analysis, that the teacher effectiveness question itself might best be changed from "Which instructional conditions are most effective?" to "How do instructional effects occur?" Knowledge of how effects occur might be especially useful to teachers in interpreting classroom conditions and designing classroom tasks that enhance student learning.

REFERENCES

Adams, R. S. Observational studies of teacher role. *International Review of Education,* 1972, *18,* 440-458.

Adams, R. S., & Biddle, B. J. *Realities of teaching: Exploration with video tape.* New York: Holt, Rinehart & Winston, 1970.

American Educational Research Association. Report of the committee on the criteria of teacher effectiveness. *Review of Educational Research,* 1952, *22,* 238-263.

American Educational Research Association. Second report of the committee on criteria of teacher effectiveness. *Journal of Educational Research,* 1953, *46,* 641-658.

Anderson, B. D., & Kaplan, J. *Toward a model of teacher behavior and student achievement.* Paper presented at the meeting of the American Educational Research Association, Chicago, April 1974.

Anderson, R. C. Control of student mediating processes during verbal learning and instruction. *Review of Educational Research,* 1970, *40,* 349-369.

Anderson, R. C., & Biddle, W. B. On asking people questions about what they are reading. In G. H. Bower (Ed.), *The psychology of learning and motivation* (Vol. 9). New York: Academic Press, 1975.

Ausubel, D. P. *Educational psychology: A cognitive view.* New York: Holt, Rinehart & Winston, 1968.

Barker, R. G. *Ecological psychology.* Stanford, Cal.: Stanford University Press, 1968.

Barnes, D. Language in the secondary classroom. In London Association for the Teaching of English, *Language, the learner and the school* (Rev. ed.). Baltimore, Md.: Penguin Books, 1971.

Barr, A. S. The systematic study of teaching and teaching efficiency. *Journal of Educational Research,* 1939, *32,* 641-648.

Barr, A. S. Teacher effectiveness and its correlates. In A. S. Barr, D. A. Worcester, A. Abel, C. Beecher, L. E. Jensen, A. L. Peronto, T. A. Ringness, & J. Schmid, Jr., *Wisconsin studies of the measurement and prediction of teacher effectiveness: A summary of investigation.* Madison, Wis.: Dembar Publications, 1961.

Becker, H. S., Geer, B., & Hughes, E. *Making the grade: The academic side of college life.* New York: Wiley, 1968.

Bellack, A. A., Kliebard, H. M., Hyman, R. T., & Smith, F. L. *The language of the classroom.* New York: Teachers College Press, 1966.

Berliner, D. C. Impediments to the study of teacher effectiveness. *Journal of Teacher Education,* 1976, *27,* 5-13.

Bloom, B. S. Thought processes in lectures and discussions. *Journal of General Education,* 1953, *7,* 160-169.

Bloom, B. S. Testing cognitive ability and achievement. In N. L. Gage (Ed.), *Handbook of research on teaching.* Chicago: Rand McNally, 1963.

Borich, G. D. Sources of invalidity in measuring classroom behavior. *Instructional Science,* 1977, *6,* 283-318.

Bransford, J. D., & Franks, J. J. Toward a framework for understanding learning. In G. H. Bower (Ed.), *The psychology of learning and motivation* (Vol. 10). New York: Academic Press, 1976.

Bronfenbrenner, U. The experimental ecology of education. *Educational Researcher,* 1976, *5*(9), 5-15.

Brophy, J. E. Stability of teacher effectiveness. *American Educational Research Journal,* 1973, *10,* 245-252.

Brophy, J. E., & Evertson, C. M. *Process-product correlations in the Texas teacher effectiveness study: Final report.* Austin: University of Texas, Research and Development Center for Teacher Education, 1974. (ERIC Document Reproduction Service No. ED 091 394) (a)

Brophy, J. E., & Evertson, C. M. *The Texas teacher effectiveness project: Presentation of non-linear relationships and summary discussion* (Res. Rep. 74-6). Austin: University of Texas, Research and Development Center for Teacher Education, 1974. (ERIC Document Reproduction Service No. ED 099 345) (b)

Brophy, J. E., & Evertson, C. M. *Context effects on classroom process variables* (Res. Rep. 76-10). Austin: University of Texas, Research and Development Center for Teacher Education, 1976. (a)

Brophy, J. E., & Evertson, C. M. *Learning from teaching: A developmental perspective.* Boston: Allyn & Bacon, 1976. (b)

Brophy, J. E., & Good, T. L. *Teacher-student relationships: Causes and consequences.* New York: Holt, Rinehart & Winston, 1974.

Brunswik, E. *The conceptual framework of psychology.* Chicago: University of Chicago Press, 1952.

Brunswik, E. Representative design and probabilistic theory in a functional psychology. *Psychological Review,* 1955, *62,* 193-217.

Burnett, J. H. *Anthropology and education: An annotated bibliographic guide.* New Haven, Conn.: Human Relations Area Files, 1974.

Cicourel, A. V. Some basic theoretical issues in the assessment of the child's performance in testing and classroom settings. In A. V. Cicourel, K. H. Jennings, S. H. M. Jennings, K. C. W. Leiter, R. MacKay, H. Mehan, & D. Roth (Eds.), *Language use and school performance.* New York: Academic Press, 1974.

Cobb, J. A. Relationship of discrete classroom behaviors to fourth-grade academic achievement. *Journal of Educational Psychology,* 1972, *63,* 74-80.

Cobb, J. A., & Hops, H. Effects of academic survival skill training on low achieving first graders. *Journal of Educational Research,* 1973, *67,* 108-113.

Cogan, M. L. Theory and design of a study of teacher-pupil interaction. *Harvard Educational Review,* 1956, *26,* 315-342.

Cogan, M. L. The behavior of teachers and the productive behavior of their pupils: I. "Perception" analysis. *Journal of Experimental Education,* 1958, *27,* 89-105.

Coxe, W. W. Minority report. *Review of Educational Research,* 1952, *22,* 263.

Cronbach, L. J. Beyond the two disciplines of scientific psychology. *American Psychologist,* 1975, *30,* 116-127.

Cusick, P. A. *Inside high school: The student's world.* New York: Holt, Rinehart & Winston, 1973.

Domas, S., & Tiedeman, D. V. Teacher competence: An annotated bibliography. *Journal of Experimental Education,* 1950, *19,* 101-218.

Doyle, W. *Learning the classroom environment: An ecological analysis of induction into teaching.* Paper presented at the meeting of the American Educational Research Association, New York, April 1977. (a)

Doyle, W. The uses of nonverbal behaviors: Toward an ecological model of classrooms. *Merrill-Palmer Quarterly,* 1977, *23,* 179-192. (b)

Dunkin, M., & Biddle, B. *The study of teaching.* New York: Holt, Rinehart & Winston, 1974.

Dweck, C. S., Hill, K. T., Redd, W. H., Steinman, W. M., & Parke, R. D. The impact of social cues on children's behavior. *Merrill-Palmer Quarterly,* 1976, *22,* 83-123.

Einstein, A., & Infeld, L. *The evolution of physics: From early concepts to relativity and quanta.* New York: Simon & Schuster, 1938.

Emmer, E. T., Oakland, T. D., & Good, T. L. Do pupils affect teachers' styles of instruction? *Educational Leadership,* 1974, *31,* 700-704.

Evertson, C. M., & Brophy, J. E. *The Texas teacher effectiveness project: Questionnaire and interview data* (Res. Rep. 74-5). Austin: University of Texas, Research and Development Center for Teacher Education, 1974. (ERIC Document Reproduction Service No. ED 099 346)

Faw, H. W., & Waller, T. G. Mathemagenic behaviors and efficiency in learning from prose materials: Review, critique and recommendations. *Review of Educational Research,* 1976, *46,* 691-720.

Fiedler, M. L. Bidirectionality of influence in classroom interaction. *Journal of Educational Psychology,* 1975, *67,* 735–744.

Flanders, N. A. *Knowledge about teacher effectiveness.* Paper presented at the meeting of the American Educational Research Association, New Orleans, February 1973. (ERIC Document Reproduction Service No. ED 088 875)

Flanders, N. A. The changing base of performance-based teaching. *Phi Delta Kappan,* 1974, *55,* 312-315.

Flanders, N. A., & Simon, A. Teacher effectiveness. In R. L. Ebel (Ed.), *Encyclopedia of educational research.* New York: Macmillan, 1969.

Frase, L. T. Prose processing. In G. H. Bower (Ed.), *The psychology of learning and motivation* (Vol. 9). New York: Academic Press, 1975.

Gage, N. L. (Ed.) *Handbook of research on teaching.* Chicago: Rand McNally, 1963. (a)

Gage, N. L. Paradigms for research on teaching. In N. L. Gage (Ed.), *Handbook of research on teaching.* Chicago: Rand McNally, 1963. (b)

Gage, N. L. Theories of teaching. In E. R. Hilgard (Ed.), *Theories of learning and instruction.* 66th Yearbook of the National Society for the Study of Education, Pt. 1. Chicago: University of Chicago Press, 1964.

Gage, N. L. Research on cognitive aspects of teaching. In *The way teaching is.* Washington, D.C.: Association for Supervision and Curriculum Development and NEA Center for the Study of Instruction, 1966.

Gage, N. L. *Teacher effectiveness and teacher education: The search for a scientific basis.* Palo Alto, Cal.: Pacific Books, 1972.

Gage, N. L. *The scientific basis of the art of teaching.* New York: Teachers College Press, 1977.

Gage, N. L., Belgard, M., Rosenshine, B., Unruh, W. R., Dell, D., & Hiller, J. H. Explorations of the teacher's effectiveness in lecturing. In I. Westbury & A. A. Bellack (Eds.), *Research into classroom processes: Recent developments and next steps.* New York: Teachers College Press, 1971.

Gagné, R. M. Learning and instructional sequence. In F. N. Kerlinger (Ed.), *Review of research in education, 1.* Itasca, Ill.: F. E. Peacock, 1973.

Gallagher, J. J. Three studies of the classroom. In *Classroom observation.* AERA Monograph Series on Curriculum Evaluation, No. 6. Chicago: Rand McNally, 1970.

Getzels, J. W., & Jackson, P. W. The teacher's personality and characteristics. In N. L. Gage (Ed.), *Handbook of research on teaching.* Chicago: Rand McNally, 1963.

Gilbert, G. N. The transformation of research findings into scientific knowledge. *Social Studies of Science,* 1976, *6,* 281-306.

Glaser, R. Comments. In I. Westbury & A. A. Bellack (Eds.), *Research into classroom processes: Recent developments and next steps.* New York: Teachers College Press, 1971.

Glaser, R. Individuals and learning: The new aptitudes. *Educational Researcher,* 1972, *1*(6), 5-13.

Glaser, R. Components of a psychology of instruction: Toward a science of design. *Review of Educational Research,* 1976, *46,* 1-24.

Glaser, R., & Cooley, W. W. Instrumentation for teaching and instructional management. In R. M. W. Travers (Ed.), *Second handbook of research on teaching.* Chicago: Rand McNally, 1973.

Glass, G. V. Teacher effectiveness. In H. J. Walberg (Ed.), *Evaluating educational performance.* Berkeley, Cal.: McCutchan, 1974.

Glidewell, J. C., Kantor, M. B., Smith, L. M., & Stringer, L. A. Socialization and social structure in the classroom. In L. W. Hoffman & M. L. Hoffman (Eds.), *Review of child development research* (Vol. 2). New York: Russell Sage Foundation, 1966.

Goetz, J. P., Rice, M. J., & Bailey, W. C. Anthropology and education. *Journal of Research and Development in Education, 1976, 9* (4, entire issue).

Good, T. L., Biddle, B. J., & Brophy, J. E. *Teachers make a difference.* New York: Holt, Rinehart & Winston, 1975.

Good, T. L., & Grouws, D. A. Teacher rapport: Some stability data. *Journal of Educational Psychology, 1975, 67,* 179-182.

Guba, E. G., & Getzels, J. W. Personality and teacher effectiveness: A problem in theoretical research. *Journal of Educational Psychology, 1955, 46,* 330-344.

Gump, P. V. Environmental guidance of the classroom behavioral system. In B. J. Biddle & W. J. Ellena (Eds.), *Contemporary research on teacher effectiveness.* New York: Holt, Rinehart & Winston, 1964.

Gump, P. V. Intra-setting analysis: The third grade classroom as a special but instructive case. In E. P. Willems & H. L. Raush (Eds.), *Naturalistic viewpoints in psychological research.* New York: Holt, Rinehart & Winston, 1969.

Haller, E. J. Pupil influence in teacher socialization: A sociolinguistic study. *Sociology of Education, 1967, 40,* 316-333.

Harnischfeger, A., & Wiley, D. E. The teaching-learning process in elementary schools: A synoptic view. *Curriculum Inquiry, 1976, 6,* 5-43.

Heath, R. W., & Nielson, M. A. The research basis for performance-based teacher education. *Review of Educational Research, 1974, 44,* 463-484.

Hill, K. T. Individual differences in children's response to adult presence and evaluative reactions. *Merrill-Palmer Quarterly, 1976, 22,* 99-104.

Jackson, P. W. *Life in classrooms.* New York: Holt, Rinehart & Winston, 1968.

Jenkins, J. R., & Deno, S. L. Influence of student behavior on teacher's self-evaluations. *Journal of Educational Psychology, 1969, 60,* 439-442.

Keddie, N. Classroom knowledge. In M. F. D. Young (Ed.), *Knowledge and control: New directions for the sociology of education.* London: Collier-Macmillan, 1971.

Klein, S. S. Student influence on teacher behavior. *American Educational Research Journal, 1971, 8,* 403-421.

Kounin, J. S. *Discipline and group management in classrooms.* New York: Holt, Rinehart & Winston, 1970.

Kounin, J. S., & Doyle, P. H. Degree of continuity of a lesson's signal system and the task involvement of children. *Journal of Educational Psychology, 1975, 67,* 159-164.

Kounin, J. S., & Gump, P. V. Signal systems of lesson settings and the task related behavior of preschool children. *Journal of Educational Psychology, 1974, 66,* 554-562.

Kuhn, T. S. *The structure of scientific revolutions* (2nd ed., enlarged). Chicago: University of Chicago Press, 1970.

Lahaderne, H. M. Attitudinal and intellectual correlates of attention: A study of four sixth-grade classrooms. *Journal of Educational Psychology, 1968, 59,* 320-324.

Lawrenz, F. Student perception of the classroom learning environment in biology, chemistry, and physics courses. *Journal of Research in Science Teaching, 1976, 13,* 315-323.

Leiter, K. C. W. Ad hocing in the schools: A study of placement practices in the kindergartens of two schools. In A. V. Cicourel, K. H. Jennings, S. H. M. Jennings, K. C. W. Leiter, R. MacKay, H. Mehan, & D. Roth (Eds.), *Language use and school performance.* New York: Academic Press, 1974.

Levie, W. H., & Dickie, K. E. The analysis and application of media. In R. M. W. Travers (Ed.), *Second handbook of research on teaching.* Chicago: Rand McNally, 1973.

Loeber, R., & Weisman, R. G. Contingencies of therapist and trainer performance: A review. *Psychological Bulletin,* 1975, *82,* 660-688.

Lortie, D. C. Observations on teaching as work. In R. M. W. Travers (Ed.), *Second handbook of research on teaching.* Chicago: Rand McNally, 1973.

Lumsdaine, A. A. (Ed.) *Student response in programmed instruction: A symposium.* Washington, D.C.: National Academy of Sciences, National Research Council, 1961.

Lumsdaine, A. A. Instruments and media of instruction. In N. L. Gage (Ed.), *Handbook of research on teaching.* Chicago: Rand McNally, 1963.

Mayer, R. E., & Greeno, J. G. Structural differences between learning outcomes produced by different instructional methods. *Journal of Educational Psychology,* 1972, *63,* 165-173.

McClellan, J. E. Classroom-teaching research: A philosophical critique. In I. Westbury & A. A. Bellack (Eds.), *Research into classroom processes: Recent developments and next steps.* New York: Teachers College Press, 1971.

McDonald, F. J. The national commission on performance-based education. *Phi Delta Kappan,* 1974, *55,* 296-298.

McDonald, F. J. *Research on teaching and its implications for policy making: Report on phase II of the beginning teacher evaluation study.* Paper presented at the Conference on Research on Teacher Effects at the University of Texas, Austin, November 1975.

McDonald, F. J. *Beginning teacher evaluation study: Phase II summary.* Washington, D.C.: National Institute of Education, 1976.

McKeachie, W. J. The decline and fall of the laws of learning. *Educational Researcher,* 1974, *3*(3), 7-11.

McKeachie, W. J., & Kulik, J. A. Effective college teaching. In F. N. Kerlinger (Ed.), *Review of research in education 3.* Itasca, Ill.: F. E. Peacock, 1975.

McKinney, J. D., Mason, J., Perkerson, K., & Clifford, M. Relationship between classroom behavior and academic achievement. *Journal of Educational Psychology,* 1975, *67,* 198-203.

McLeish, J. The lecture method. In N. L. Gage (Ed.), *The psychology of teaching methods,* 75th Yearbook of the National Society for the Study of Education, Pt. 1. Chicago: University of Chicago Press, 1976.

Medley, D. M., & Mitzel, H. E. Some behavioral correlates of teacher effectiveness. *Journal of Educational Psychology,* 1959, *50,* 239-246.

Mehan, H. Accomplishing classroom lessons. In A. V. Cicourel, K. H. Jennings, S. H. M. Jennings, K. C. W. Leiter, R. MacKay, J. Mehan, & D. Roth (Eds.), *Language use and school performance.* New York: Academic Press, 1974.

Mitchell, J. V. Education's challenge to psychology: The prediction of behavior from person-environment interactions. *Review of Educational Research,* 1969, *39,* 695-721.

Montague, W. E. Elaborative strategies in verbal learning and memory. In G. H. Bower (Ed.), *The psychology of learning and motivation* (Vol. 6). New York: Academic Press, 1972.

Morsh, J. E. *Systematic observation of instructor behavior* (Rep. No. AFPTRC–TN–56–52). Lackland AFB, Texas: Air Force Personnel and Training Research Center, 1956.

Morsh, J. E., & Wilder, E. W. *Identifying the effective instructor: A review of the quantitative studies, 1900-1952* (Rep. No. AFPTRC–TR–54–44). Chanute AFB, Ill.: Air Force Personnel and Training Research Center, 1954. (ERIC Document Reproduction Service No. ED 044 371)

Nash, R. *Classrooms observed: The teacher's perception and the pupil's performance.* London: Routledge & Kegan Paul, 1973.

Noble, C. G., & Nolan, J. D. Effect of student verbal behavior on classroom teacher behavior. *Journal of Educational Psychology,* 1976, *68,* 342-346.

Olson, D. R. Why different forms of instruction result in similar knowledge. *Interchange,* 1972, *3*(1), 9-24.

Olson, D. R., & Bruner, J. S. Learning through experience and learning through media. In D. R. Olson (Ed.), *Media and symbols: The forms of expression, communication, and education.* 73rd Yearbook of the National Society for the Study of Education, Pt. 1. Chicago: University of Chicago Press, 1974.

Overholt, G. E., & Stallings, W. M. Ethnographic and experimental hypotheses in educational research. *Educational Researcher,* 1976, *5*(8), 12-14.

Paivio, A. *Imagery and verbal processes.* New York: Holt, Rinehart & Winston, 1971.

Paris, S. G., & Cairns, R. B. An experimental and ethological analysis of social reinforcement with retarded children. *Child Development,* 1972, *43,* 717-729.

Parke, R. D. Social cues, social control, and ecological validity. *Merrill-Palmer Quarterly,* 1976, *22,* 111-118.

Perkins, H. V. Classroom behavior and underachievement. *American Educational Research Journal,* 1965, *2,* 1-12.

Perry, R. H. *Teachers and students: The effects of some interpersonal movement styles.* Paper presented at the meeting of the American Educational Research Association, Washington, D.C., April 1975.

Peterson, P. L. *Interactive effects of student anxiety, achievement orientation, and teacher behavior on student achievement and attitude.* Stanford, Cal.: School of Education, Stanford University, 1976.

Program on Teaching Effectiveness, SCRDT. *A factorially designed experiment on teacher structuring, soliciting, and reacting* (R & D Memorandum No. 147). Stanford, Cal.: Stanford Center for Research and Development in Teaching, 1976.

Rabinowitz, W., & Travers, R. M. W. Problems of defining and assessing teacher effectiveness. *Educational Theory,* 1953, *3,* 212-219.

Redd, W. H. The effects of adult presence and stated preference on the reinforcement control of children's behavior. *Merrill-Palmer Quarterly,* 1976, *22,* 93–97.

Resnick, L. B. Applying applied reinforcement. In R. Glaser (ed.), *The nature of reinforcement.* New York: Academic Press, 1971.

Rist, R. C. *The urban school: A factory of failure.* Cambridge, Mass.: MIT Press, 1973.

Rohwer, W. D., Jr. Decisive research: A means for answering fundamental questions about instruction. *Educational Researcher,* 1972, *1*(7), 5-11.

Rohwer, W. D., Jr. Elaboration and learning in childhood and adolescence. In H. W. Reese (Ed.), *Advances in child development and behavior* (Vol. 8). New York: Academic Press, 1973.

Rosenshine, B. Enthusiastic teaching: A research review. *School Review,* 1970, *78,* 499–514. (a)

Rosenshine, B. The stability of teacher effects upon student achievement. *Review of Educational Research,* 1970, *40,* 647-662. (b)

Rosenshine, B. *Teaching behaviors and student achievement.* Windsor, Berkshire, England: National Foundation for Educational Research in England and Wales, 1971.

Rosenshine, B. Classroom instruction. In N. L. Gage (Ed.), *The psychology of teaching methods.* 75th Yearbook of the National Society for the Study of Education, Pt. 1. Chicago: University of Chicago Press, 1976. (a)

Rosenshine, B. Recent research on teaching behaviors and student achievement. *Journal of Teacher Education,* 1976, *27,* 61-64. (b)

Rosenshine, B., & Furst, N. Research on teacher performance criteria. In B. O. Smith (Ed.), *Research in teacher education: A symposium.* Englewood Cliffs, N.J.: Prentice-Hall, 1971.

Rosenshine, B., & Furst, N. The use of direct observation to study teaching. In R. M. W. Travers (Ed.), *Second handbook of research on teaching.* Chicago: Rand McNally, 1973.

Rothkopf, E. Z. Some theoretical and experimental approaches to problems in written instruction. In J. D. Krumboltz (Ed.), *Learning and the educational process.* Chicago: Rand McNally, 1965.

Rothkopf, E. Z. The concept of mathemagenic activities. *Review of Educational Research,* 1970, *40,* 325-336.

Rothkopf, E. Z. Writing to teach and reading to learn: A perspective on the psychology of written instruction. In N. L. Gage (Ed.), *The psychology of teaching methods,* 75th Yearbook of the National Society for the Study of Education, Pt. 1. Chicago: University of Chicago Press, 1976.

Rowe, M. B. Relation of wait-time and rewards to the development of language, logic, and fate control: II. Rewards. *Journal of Research in Science Teaching,* 1974, *11,* 291-308. (a)

Rowe, M. B. Wait-time and rewards as instructional variables, their influence on language, logic, and fate control: I. Wait-time. *Journal of Research in Science Teaching,* 1974, *11,* 81-94. (b)

Ryans, D. G. Inventory estimated teacher characteristics as covariants of observer assessed pupil behavior. *Journal of Educational Psychology,* 1961, *52,* 91-97. (a)

Ryans, D. G. Some relationships between pupil behavior and certain teacher characteristics. *Journal of Educational Psychology,* 1961, *52,* 82-90. (b)

Ryans, D. G. Teacher behavior theory and research: Implications for teacher education. *Journal of Teacher Education,* 1963, *14,* 274-293.

Salomon, G. What does it do to Johnny? A cognitive-functionalistic view of research on media. *Viewpoints* (Bulletin of the School of Education, Indiana University), 1970, *46*(5), 33-62.

Salomon, G. What is learned and how it is taught: The interaction between media, message, task, and learner. In D. R. Olson (Ed.), *Media and symbols: The forms of expression, communication, and education.* 73rd Yearbook of the National Society for the Study of Education, Pt. 1. Chicago: University of Chicago Press, 1974.

Sarason, S. B. *The culture of the school and the problem of change.* Boston: Allyn & Bacon, 1971.

Sarbin, R. R., Taft, R., & Bailey, D. E. *Clinical inference and cognitive theory.* New York: Holt, Rinehart & Winston, 1960.

Schellenberg, J. A. The class-hour economy. *Harvard Educational Review,* 1965, *35,* 161-164.

Shavelson, R., & Dempsey-Atwood, N. Generalizability of measures of teaching behavior. *Review of Educational Research,* 1976, *46,* 553–611.

Sherman, T. M., & Cormier, W. H. An investigation of the influence of student behavior on teacher behavior. *Journal of Applied Behavior Analysis,* 1974, *7,* 11-21.

Shimron, J. Learning activities in individually prescribed instruction. *Instructional Science,* 1976, *5,* 391-401.

Shulman, L. S. Reconstruction of educational research. *Review of Educational Research,* 1970, *40,* 371-396.

Shulman, L. S., & Elstein, A. S. Studies of problem solving, judgment, and decision making: Implications for educational research. In F. N. Kerlinger (Ed.), *Review of research in education, 3.* Itasca, Ill.: F. E. Peacock, 1975.

Silvers, R. J. Discovering children's culture. *Interchange,* 1975, *6*(4), 47-52.

Smith, B. O. A concept of teaching. *Teachers College Record,* 1960, *61,* 229-241.

Smith, B. O., & Meux, M. *A study of the logic of teaching.* Urbana, Ill.: University of Illinois, Bureau of Educational Research, 1962.

Smith, L. M., & Geoffrey, W. *The complexities of an urban classroom.* New York: Holt, Rinehart & Winston, 1968.

Snow, R. E. Brunswikian approaches to research on teaching. *American Educational Research Journal,* 1968, *5,* 475-489.

Snow, R. E. Research on media and aptitudes. *Viewpoints* (Bulletin of the School of Education, Indiana University), 1970, *46*(5), 63-89.

Snow, R. E. Representative and quasi-representative designs for research on teaching. *Review of Educational Research,* 1974, *44,* 265-291.

Soar, R. S. Teacher-pupil interaction. In J. R. Squire (Ed.), *A new look at progressive education.* Washington, D.C.: Association for Supervision and Curriculum Development, 1972.

Soar, R. S., & Soar, R. M. An empirical analysis of selected follow-through programs: An example of a process approach to evaluation. In I. J. Gordon (Ed.), *Early childhood education.* 71st Yearbook of the National Society for the Study of Education, Pt. 2. Chicago: University of Chicago Press, 1972.

Soli, S. D., & Devine, V. T. Behavioral correlates of achievements: A look at high and low achievers. *Journal of Educational Psychology,* 1976, *68,* 335-341.

Spaulding, R. L. *Educational intervention in early childhood: A report of a five-year longitudinal study of the effects of early educational intervention in the lives of disadvantaged children in Durham, North Carolina* (Final Rep.; Vol. 1). Durham, N.C.: Duke University, 1970. (ERIC Document Reproduction Service No. ED 050 814)

Spaulding, R. L. *The coping analysis schedule for educational settings (CASES).* Paper presented at the meeting of the American Educational Research Association, New Orleans, February 1973. (ERIC Document Reproduction Service No. ED 076 694)

Spaulding, R. L., & Papageorgiou, M. R. *Effects of early educational intervention in the lives of disadvantaged children* (Final Rep.). Durham, N.C.: North Carolina Educational Intervention Program, 1972. (ERIC Document Reproduction Service No. ED 066 246)

Spaulding, R. L., & Showers, B. *Application of the Spaulding system of classroom behavioral analysis in field settings.* Paper presented at the meeting of the American Educational Research Association, Chicago, April 1974. (ERIC Document Reproduction Service No. ED 091 399)

Spivak, G. *The concept of behavioral effectiveness in the classroom.* Paper presented at the meeting of the American Educational Research Association, New Orleans, February 1973. (ERIC Document Reproduction Service No. ED 080 180)

Spivak, G., Swift, M., & Prewitt, J. Syndromes of disturbed classroom behavior: A behavioral diagnostic system for elementary schools. *Journal of Special Education,* 1971, *5,* 269-292.

Stallings, J. Implementation and child effects of teaching practices in follow through classrooms. *Monographs of the Society for Research in Child Development,* 1975, *40*(7-8, Serial No. 163).

Stayrook, N. G., & Corno, L. *Student perceptions of teacher behavior as related to student achievement.* Paper presented at the meeting of the American Educational Research Association, San Francisco, April 1976.

Steele, J. M., Walberg, H. J., & House, E. R. Subject areas and cognitive press. *Journal of Educational Psychology,* 1974, *66,* 363-366.

Stephens, J. M. *The process of schooling: A psychological examination.* New York: Holt, Rinehart & Winston, 1967.

Stodolsky, S. S. Defining treatment and outcome in early childhood education. In H. J. Walberg & A. T. Kopan (Eds.), *Rethinking urban education.* San Francisco: Jossey-Bass, 1972.

Stodolsky, S. S. How children find something to do in preschools. *Genetic Psychology Monographs,* 1974, *90,* 245-303.

Stodolsky, S. S. *Observational studies of variation in child behavior in classrooms* (Rep. No. NIE–C–74–0030). Chicago: University of Chicago, 1975.

Swift, M. S., & Spivak, G. Academic success and classroom behavior in secondary schools. *Exceptional Children,* 1973, *39,* 392-399.

Tamir, P. The relationship among cognitive preference, school environment, teachers' curricular bias, curriculum, and subject matter. *American Educational Research Journal,* 1975, *12,* 235-264.

Tikunoff, W. J., Berliner, D. C., & Rist, R. C. *An ethnographic study of the forty classrooms of the beginning teacher evaluation study known sample* (Tech. Rep. 75-10-5). San Francisco: Far West Laboratory for Educational Research and Development, 1975.

Tinbergen, N. Functional ethology and the human sciences. *Proceedings of the Royal Society of London, Series B,* 1972, *182,* 385-410.

Turner, R. L. Conceptual foundations of research in teacher education. In B. O. Smith (Ed.), *Research in teacher education: A symposium.* Englewood Cliffs, N.J.: Prentice-Hall, 1971.

Turner, R. L., & Fattu, N. A. Skill in teaching: A reappraisal of the concepts and strategies in teacher effectiveness research. *Bulletin of the School of Education, Indiana University,* 1960, *36*(3), 1-37.

Walberg, H. J. Models for optimizing and individualizing school learning. *Interchange,* 1971, *2*(3), 15-27.

Walberg, H. J. Psychology of learning environments: Behavioral, structural, or perceptual? In L. S. Shulman (Ed.), *Review of research in education 4.* Itasca, Ill.: F. E. Peacock, 1976.

Walker, D. F., & Schaffarzick, J. Comparing curricula. *Review of Educational Research,* 1974, *44,* 83-111.

Wallen, N. E., & Travers, R. M. W. Analysis and investigation of teaching methods. In N. L. Gage (Ed.), *Handbook of research on teaching.* Chicago: Rand McNally, 1963.

Wang, M. C. *Maximizing the effective use of school time by teachers and students.*

Paper presented at the meeting of the American Educational Research Association, San Francisco, April 1976.

Wax, M. L., Diamond, S., & Gearing, F. O. (Eds.). *Anthropological perspectives on education.* New York: Basic Books, 1971.

West, W. G. Participant observation research on the social construction of everyday classroom order. *Interchange,* 1975, *6*(4), 35-43.

Willems, E. P. Behavior-environment systems: An ecological approach. *Man-Environment Systems,* 1973, *3*(2), 79-110. (a)

Willems, E. P. Behavioral ecology and experimental analysis: Courtship is not enough. In J. R. Nesselroade & H. W. Reese (Eds.), *Life-span developmental psychology: Methodological issues.* New York: Academic Press, 1973. (b)

Willems, E. P., & Raush, H. L. (Eds.). *Naturalistic viewpoints in psychological research.* New York: Holt, Rinehart & Winston, 1969.

Withall, J. Assessment of the social-emotional climate experienced by a group of seventh graders as they moved from class to class. *Educational and Psychological Measurement,* 1952, *12*, 440-451.

Wolcott, H. (Ed.). Ethnography of schooling. *Human Organizations,* 1975, *34*(2, entire issue).

Zahorik, J. A. Classroom feedback behavior of teachers. *Journal of Educational Research,* 1968, *62*, 147-150.

III

POLICY STUDIES

5

Does Schooling Matter? A Retrospective Assessment

VINCENT TINTO
Syracuse University

Students of educational inequality would do well to heed the time-tested adage that it is one thing to get a job and another to keep it. In assessing the relationship between education and social attainment, it is one thing to ask about the effect of education on getting a job and another to ask how it affects the ability of a person to do well in the job. The two questions are quite distinct. They differ in the same way that access to jobs differs from performance on the job. Furthermore, they deal with different educational processes.

Regrettably, research on the impact of educational inequality on social attainment has often failed to mark this simple yet important distinction. The two questions have often been confused as being one and the same. The result is that researchers have frequently defined questions and employed methods of research that were not particularly suited to the specific problem at hand. It is undeniable that we have made considerable advances in our understanding of how schooling is related to the system of social stratification (Duncan, Featherman, & Duncan, 1972; Sewell, Hauser, & Featherman, 1976). Yet a number of important questions remain unresolved. The intent of this review is as much to assess what else we need to do in the study of education and social attainment as it is to judge what has been done thus far.

In this review we will first present a brief sociological overview of education as being tied into the wider system of social stratification in society. This

---

RAYMOND BOUDON, University of the Sorbonne, and JAMES S. COLEMAN, University of Chicago, were the editorial consultants for this chapter.

The author is indebted to Professors C. Arnold Anderson, Gerald Grant, Thomas Green, and Emily Haynes for comments on earlier versions of this article.

section will also consider problems in the measurement of social status and in the choice among multiple measures of status in studying the impact of education on social attainment. Then we will examine the current state of knowledge concerning the separate and interactive effects education has on access to jobs and performance on the job. We will try to determine to what degree and in what manner these effects, if any, vary as a function of sex, race, and college origins. Next we will focus on the limits of large-scale survey research as a tool for understanding the educational processes that affect subsequent social attainment. Several alternative methods will be suggested as particularly promising, especially because they may yield insight into unresolved problems in the study of inequality. The chapter concludes with a brief summary of the more important points raised in the review and several comments on the need for future studies designed to increase our understanding of the way education impacts on the complex process of status attainment.

EDUCATION AND SOCIAL STRATIFICATION: AN OVERVIEW

Education's Varying Impact on Status Attainment

Sociologists have generally understood the term *social inequality* to refer to the unequal distribution of valued social goods (property, power, and prestige) among individuals and groups in society. These goods are seen as residing in the complex web of social statuses or positions that make up society and as associated with the multiplicity of roles and related activities that comprise the social system. Individuals and groups acquire property, power, and prestige as they occupy differing social statuses. And they gain (or lose) additional shares of these valued goods, that is, they exhibit upward (or downward) social mobility, as they occupy statuses of increasing (or decreasing) worth.

In this sense, societies are thought of as being socially stratified into hierarchies and clusters of individuals and groups according to their differential possession of valued social goods (i.e., by the unequal distribution of these goods among differing social statuses). Cutting across the stratification system are interlocking networks of statuses or, to borrow White's (1970) term, *chains of opportunity*. These serve as dynamic networks of affiliation that link differing statuses to one another and provide for differing degrees of access to elite statuses. Modern stratification systems thus are seen as resembling old European cities, with some chains of opportunity leading boulevard-like into the center of the status system; others turning in upon themselves and often leading to deadends, where no further movement is possible; and a variety of other chains, like streets, avenues, roadways, and back alleys, providing for a complex pattern of access to the major chains of opportunity and thus to elite statuses in society. Mobility, therefore, occurs not in a random fashion but in discrete patterns that follow the networks of linking statuses. Frequently mobility operates through particular institutions that act as important nexus points in the opportunity structure of society and in the age-graded movement of persons through the stratification system.

In studying social stratification, sociologists have focused both on the changing character of social inequality over time (Blau & Duncan, 1967) and on the dynamic social processes that underlie its development and patterning within a population (Sewell, Hauser & Featherman, 1976). Of central concern are two distinct questions: First, why does social inequality exist? Second, how does it assume particular patterns of distribution among varying populations?[1] In accounting for the patterning of social inequality, sociologists have been particularly interested in how different individuals and groups come to occupy differing social statuses and therefore to possess differing shares of the valued social goods available in society.

Education has been a prime concern to those who study social stratification because it is thought to play a central role in the allocation of persons to social statuses. Though sociologists of differing theoretical leanings may disagree as to the proper explanation for this relationship, most would not dispute the claim that for most persons a high level of educational attainment is an important first step to the attainment of high-status positions in adulthood (Alexander & Eckland, 1975; Blau & Duncan, 1967; Hauser & Featherman, 1976; Jencks, 1968; Sewell, Haller & Ohlendorf, 1970; Spaeth, 1970). A few commentators, most notably Berg (1971), Jencks, Smith, Acland, Bane, Cohen, Gintis, Heyns, and Michelson (1972), and Bowles and Gintis (1976), have questioned the functional importance of education to later social mobility. Closer scrutiny of these studies reveals, however, that differences in results are only partially the outcome of initial disagreements over social theory (e.g., Bowles & Gintis). They reflect as well the differential emphases that researchers give to the varying impacts schooling can have on subsequent social attainment.

It has been suggested that education can have at least two distinct types of impact upon the process of status attainment. On the one hand, education can be viewed as leading to the acquisition of skills appropriate to the performance of a variety of adult roles, especially those roles associated with the occupational world (Trow, 1962). On the other hand, it can be seen as an institutionalized part of the opportunity structure of society which serves as a certifying agency to sponsor selected graduates into the more desirable statuses in society (Kamens, 1974). In order to disentangle the complexity of relationships that tie educational attainment to social status attainment, we must carefully distinguish between those educational processes that provide opportunities for access to different statuses (i.e., jobs in the occupational structure) and those leading to the acquisition of skills and values that influence people's ability to perform well in those statuses (jobs). Though both processes necessarily impact on long-term status attainment, they are clearly distinct in character and in short-term impact, and each must receive separate attention.

Measures of Social Status Attainment

Before we assess past research, several comments are in order regarding the use of different measures of social status in the study of educational and social inequality. Generally speaking, there are three basic methods for determining the rank of an individual in the stratification hierarchy of a society. These are (1) objective measures of attainment as determined by one's property, power, and prestige; (2) subjective measures of self-placement; and (3) measures of placement according to reputation. Of the three, objective measures of attainment associated with an individual's occupation are the most useful in the study of modern systems of social stratification (Abrahamson, Mizruchi, & Hornung, 1976). And of these, the most commonly employed have been income, occupational prestige, and composite measures of income, occupation, and education, generally referred to as indices of socioeconomic status.

The researcher's choice among these indicators is neither methodologically arbitrary nor unrelated to questions of meaning. Knowing the association between education and income, for instance, does not necessarily increase our understanding of the relationship between education and occupational prestige. Income, as commonly measured by earned wages, is more directly a function of on-the-job performance. Occupational prestige, however, tends to reside in the short run more in the character of the position than in the performance of its incumbents.[2] More importantly, the processes governing earnings attainment vary from one occupation to another. They are a function not only of the demand and supply of labor but also of the differences between occupations in the social organization of work and wage-setting (Spaeth, 1976; Stolzenberg, 1975b). And even though there are significant differences among the mean earnings of differing occupations, there is a tremendous variance in earned income among incumbents within the same occupation (Stolzenberg, 1975b).

The central point is that education is not related in either the same degree or the same sense to measures of income (earnings) and measures of occupational prestige. Past research clearly indicates that educational attainment is more closely associated with measures of occupational prestige than it is with measures of income. It also suggests that income and occupational prestige reflect, in the short run, differing facets of the multidimensional impact of schooling on social attainment. Occupational prestige is a better measure of education's impact on access to the first job (i.e., entry into the occupational world) than it is of its subsequent effect upon job performance. Conversely, excluding those instances where strict regulations govern the setting of wage scales (e.g., civil service), earnings appear to be more reflective of the individual's performance on the job entered. As such, income measures seem to be more suited to the assessment of education's impact upon job performance through its presumed effect upon skill acquisition. In the long run, of course, the distinction between income and occupational prestige fades as prior performance on the job influences the prestige of subsequent jobs.

Composite measures of socioeconomic status are admittedly more reflective of the total valued-good basis of social stratification than are income and/ or occupational prestige alone (Featherman, Jones, & Hauser, 1975). But they are less well suited, in this sense, to the study of education's multiple impacts on social attainment. By their very construction such measures tend to reduce two distinct questions to one, combining the effects of education on access to jobs with performance on the job. Thus they fail to distinguish between two very different educational processes and potential educational outcomes. What composite measures may gain through increased statistical accounting of variance in attainment they sacrifice in the way of understanding.

Furthermore, as occupational prestige and income reflect different types of social resources inherent in occupational positions, they may be utilized in differing ways by individuals in the process of status attainment. Moreover, they may be exchanged for one another at varying points in an individual's occupational career (Coleman, Berry, & Blum, 1972). Differential utilization of the prestige and income components of occupational positions may reflect important differences in individuals' utility functions regarding the relative value of primary and secondary educational goods (i.e., skills vs. certificates). It may also reflect the existence of market constraints affecting the ability of individuals to invest in the various elements of status attainment.

SCHOOLING AND STATUS ATTAINMENT: A RESEARCH ASSESSMENT

Education and Occupational Status Attainment

As demonstrated in a number of large-scale survey studies of social attainment, educational attainment is the single most important measurable determinant of the occupational status of a person's first job (Alexander & Eckland, 1975; Alexander, Eckland, & Griffin, 1975; Blau & Duncan, 1967; Duncan, Featherman, & Duncan, 1972; Kelley, 1973; Sewell & Hauser, 1975; Spaeth, 1970). Even relatively simple models of attainment—those employing measures of individual ability, social background (e.g., parents' occupation and education), and educational attainment (number of years)—have been able to account for nearly one-half of the variance in status of the first job entered. Though ability and social background influence social attainment, their impact occurs largely in an indirect manner, through their direct effect on educational attainment.[3] For most persons and most occupations, obtaining a higher educational degree has become a prerequisite for entry into higher status occupational positions.

In this respect, recent evidence suggests that the returns of occupational status to schooling have increased somewhat, relative to social background factors, during the years since 1962 (Featherman & Hauser, 1976b). While during that period the effect of social origins on occupational status has declined somewhat, the overall process of status attainment through education for most groups has remained largely unchanged (Blau & Duncan, 1967; Featherman & Hauser, 1976a, 1976b). During this period there has been a marked increase in the amount of schooling diffused throughout the population and a decrease in its variability (Hauser & Featherman, 1976). Thus education has continued to function as a mechanism for occupational attainment, even though there has been a noticeable decline in inequality of schooling as determined by the amount of schooling people obtain.

All groups, however, do not realize similar occupational status returns for their investment in schooling. While differences between white men and women appear quite small in this regard, among blacks and between blacks and whites there are substantial differences in the effect of educational attainment on occupational status attainment. Although past research has pointed to significant differences in the processes of educational attainment of white men and women (with female attainment being found to be more a function of social background), the overall impact of education on early occupational status appears to be quite similar for men and women (Alexander & Eckland, 1974; Chase, 1975; DeJong, Brawer, & Robin, 1971; McClendon, 1976; Treiman and Terrell, 1975b). Nevertheless, the occupational positions they attain in the hierarchy of jobs are often quite different. While men tend to be clustered at both the high and low ends of the occupational prestige hierarchy, women tend to be concentrated in the middle or white-collar sector of the economy (McClendon). Among black men and women, however, Treiman and Terrell found that occupational prestige returns to schooling are considerably higher for women than for men. Quite possibly, the double-negative effect may be applicable here; being both female and black may work to the advantage of some individuals in getting a job (Epstein, 1973).

Studies of the attainment of blacks and whites reveal differences in their patterns of both educational and early occupational attainment (Jencks et al., 1972; Kerckhoff & Campbell, 1977; Porter, 1974; Portes & Wilson, 1976). Given important variations between urban and rural areas and between different regions of the country (Weiss, 1970), the first-job occupational prestige returns to schooling are, for the most part, significantly greater for whites (in particular for men) than for blacks (Coleman, Blum, Sorensen, & Rossi, 1972; Jencks et al., 1972; Portes & Wilson, 1976; Stolzenberg, 1975a). Nevertheless, comparison of the patterns of early occupational attainment for blacks and whites suggests that the process of occupational attainment among blacks is generally more socially determined and particularly more influenced by educational attainment than it is for whites (Blum, 1972; Porter, 1974). Given observable differences in their patterns of educational attainment, Porter goes on to argue that black mobility can be better characterized as one of "sponsorship," wherein educational institutions, controlled mainly by whites, serve to screen, socialize, and promote (i.e., sponsor) those few blacks destined for relatively high-status occupational positions. Although additional studies may substantiate Porter's argument, it may well be that similar comparison between mainstream whites and rural Appalachian whites, for instance, would yield equivalent findings, without any reference to racial differences. The process involved may be as much enculturation of minority groups into majority culture as it is covert racial discrimination. While few would deny the existence of discrimination against blacks on job entry, we must be careful to distinguish discriminatory behaviors from those that unavoidably reflect processes of cultural differentiation and the social diffusion of opportunities and their utilization throughout a social system (Anderson & Foster, 1964).

Discrimination against blacks still exists, but it is apparent that as a group blacks have somewhat closed the gap between themselves and whites as a group. Specifically, the socioeconomic status returns to educational attainment for black men, though still less than for white men, increased more rapidly during the period 1962-73 than they did for white males (Featherman & Hauser, 1976a). Given recent policies designed to equalize work opportunities, it is not surprising that differences in socioeconomic returns to schooling are smaller for younger blacks than they are for the group as a whole. Despite such gains, however, black patterns of educational and occupational attainment still differ significantly from those of whites. Over the period 1962-73 the overall process of occupational status attainment for most groups remained essentially unchanged in character, but for black men it became somewhat more deterministic, as judged by the total impact of schooling and background on occupational attainment. It seems that in terms of status attainment, the schools have become even more important for blacks than for whites. But whether this leads to the conclusion by Porter (1974) that this is largely the result of the relative paucity of alternative routes to attainment for blacks outside the formal educational system is still unresolved. It is quite possible that such findings also reflect the long-term impact of social policies specifically designed to enhance the educational attainments of blacks. In any event, we should not lose sight of the fact that the substantial gains made by blacks over the recent past have only reduced, not eliminated, the significant racial differences in occupational prestige returns to schooling (Featherman & Hauser, 1976a; Farley, 1977).

Education, Earnings, and On-the-Job Performance

That education helps individuals gain access to desirable occupations is evident, but that it also assists them to do well in those occupations is not. If we accept the notion that earnings are a relatively good indicator of on-the-job performance, then the work of Jencks et al. (1972), Blum (1972), Kelley (1973), Sewell and Hauser (1975), and Alexander, Eckland, and Griffin (1975) shows that educational attainment has only a very limited impact on performance. Using longitudinal models of attainment very much like those employed in the study of early occupational attainment (except that occupational prestige is often included in the analysis), these researchers have been unable to account for more than 13% of the variance in adult earnings, not a very impressive amount. Results are no more encouraging when direct measures of on-the-job performance are obtained. Comparing performance on the job of high school and college graduates in a number of occupations, Berg (1971) found little consistent evidence to support the claim that differences in educational attainment are, in any simple or direct fashion, associated with differences in on-the-job productivity.

Failure to observe a significant relationship between educational attainment and income does not necessarily lead, however, to the conclusion by Jencks et al. (1972) that schooling does not impact upon earnings or on-the-job performance. It can be properly concluded from past analyses, however, that our current models of education and earnings have not been able to ascertain any sizable association between the two. We will return to this point in another section, but it can be pointed out here that the models of education attainment employed thus far have not been very sensitive to the processes of skill acquisition in school that may impact on performance on the job and therefore on earnings. There is little reason to assume, for example, that years of schooling are in and of themselves related in any direct fashion to the varying skills individuals acquire in school.

It may well turn out, upon subsequent analysis, that education, however measured, is indeed unrelated to variations in earnings. But the analyses of Jencks et al. (1972) and Sewell and Hauser (1975) have yet to prove the point convincingly.

Despite the lack of overall explanatory power of the models, comparison of the earnings of differing social groups (men and women, black and white) do reveal significant variations in the income returns to schooling among groups (Blum, 1972; Featherman & Hauser, 1976a, 1976b; Jencks et al., 1972; Stolzenberg, 1975a; Wright & Perrone, 1977). For women relative to men, and blacks relative to whites, it is clear that there are substantial differences not only in their incomes generally but also in the income returns they obtain from given years of schooling. Simply put, education does not pay as well for women and blacks as it does for men and whites.

Whether these differences result from direct discrimination on the job is at present unclear. A number of studies of the wages of blacks and whites within broad categories of occupations have indicated significant differences in their respective earnings (Duncan, Featherman & Duncan, 1972; Siegel, 1965; Thurow, 1967). At the same time, several recent studies involving highly detailed comparisons within and between occupations of differing status and earning levels have suggested a different conclusion (Coleman, Berry, & Blum, 1972; Stolzenberg, 1975a; Wright & Perrone, 1977). Stolzenberg, for instance, argues that race differentials in returns to schooling are produced primarily by race differences in workers' ability to convert their schooling into employment in the better paying occupations, and not by racial differences in the impact of education on wage differences between incumbents of the same occupation. Within broad categories of occupations (e.g., professional, technical), Stolzenberg finds that blacks tend to be concentrated in the lower status positions where wages are generally lower.

The recommended policy of equalization of incomes differs markedly from that of Jencks et al. (1972), who argue that a "reform strategy which equalizes access to jobs would be less valuable than that aimed at equalizing income within jobs." The reverse policy is suggested here. Ensuring access to occupations in the broad sense does not guarantee access to equally rewarding positions within the occupation. For blacks, the latter form of access to jobs appears to account for their lower income returns to schooling.

The infrequently cited work of Coleman, Berry, and Blum (1972) further suggests that long-term career strategies differ for black and white workers. Their analysis of the careers of blacks and whites over a 10-year period (after the completion of full-time education) indicates that whites, more than blacks, tend to direct a greater proportion of their resources to the prestige rather than to the income components of occupations. Among black workers, income is more often the dimension to which resources are directed. This does not mean that whites enter lower paying jobs; quite the reverse is true. Rather, it suggests that in their investment patterns they place greater relative emphasis upon the prestige components of occupations. Also implied is the notion that differences in the educational and occupational attainment patterns of varying social groups may be partly attributable to underlying differences in their utility curves regarding the relative merit of various educational and social goods (Boudon, 1973; Green, 1977). The perhaps unavoidable limitation in the ability of any social policy to affect the attainment patterns of diverse social groups, outside of strict enforcement of desired behavioral norms, is also suggested.

Different investment strategies regarding initial entry into the occupational world may have long-term impact upon subsequent attainment. Coleman, Berry, and Blum point out that the investment strategies of whites (i.e., an early emphasis upon the prestige components of jobs) appear to yield greater long-term benefits in future earnings than do black patterns of investment. The strategy of early emphasis on income appears to result in lower relative gains in earnings over the long run for blacks. They begin by earning less than similarly educated whites, and whether by restrictions to job entry or as a result of career strategy, their earnings fall further behind over time.

Of course, what appears to be a self-initiated strategy may in fact be the outcome of formal and informal social constraints which effectively channel blacks into lower prestige positions within occupations, the future benefits of which are relatively lower (Bowles & Gintis, 1976; Carnoy, 1974). These constraints need not be overt in character, as direct discrimination is. They may also be covert, resulting primarily from the differential socialization experiences of blacks in a white society, which may be self-fulfilling in outcome (Carnoy, 1974). The difficulty is to distinguish forms of socialization that are peculiar to blacks as a racial group from those that are common to persons from lower social status backgrounds. As noted earlier, in any social system there are differential patterns of utility, and therefore of investment in occupations, which are associated with social status background. Thus though blacks as a group exhibit different investment patterns than whites as a group, this need not be prima facie evidence of social discrimination.

Research on the earnings of men and women indicates that women experience different sorts of handicaps, relative to men, than blacks do relative to whites. Though women do not appear to face widespread discrimination in entry to occupational positions (as do blacks), they apparently do experience a significant degree of differential treatment on the job. Women earn less than men, even among persons of equivalent social origins, educational attainments, occupational standing, statistically equivalent work experience, and levels of labor force participation (Featherman & Hauser, 1976b).

Of course, men and women are not similarly distributed among occupations of differing statuses. Thus, though it is true that discrimination on the job appears to be the primary constraint for women, it does not follow that the current move to provide women with equivalent access to the occupational world is unwarranted. Rather it suggests that such access will go only part way to the equalization of earnings among similarly educated men and women. It is noteworthy, in this respect, that while blacks as a group apparently gained in earnings relative to whites over the period 1962-73, there is little consistent evidence to warrant a similar conclusion for women relative to men (Featherman & Hauser, 1976b). Whether this reflects the more deep-rooted intransigency of sexual inequality or the fact that attempts to reduce such inequality have only taken place in a serious manner since 1973 must be determined by future study.

Education, Earnings, and Occupations

Comparisons of earnings between members of varying occupations also reveal important differences in the way educational attainment impacts on income. In addition to the works of Coleman, Berry, and Blum (1972) and Stolzenberg (1975a, 1975b) cited earlier, studies by Thurow (1972), Taubman and Wales (1974), Spaeth (1976), and Wright and Perrone (1977) argue, in differing ways, that education's impact upon wages is a function of the type of occupation entered (e.g., its social organization of work) and not merely of the relative supply and demand of labor. Taubman and Wales, for instance, find that current regression models of education and earnings can account for variance in earnings among professional types of occupations better than among other types. The types of occupations for which the fit between education and earnings is best are generally considered to be of higher status. They also appear to resemble in work characteristics those activities carried on in a school setting (e.g., medicine, academic and scientific work).

More intriguing is Wright and Perrone's (1977) analysis, which is derived from Marxist theory. Using occupational class categories based upon relative control over the means of production (e.g., workers, managers, and employers), they found that employers have higher incomes than either managers or workers, even after differences in education, occupational status, age, and job tenure are taken into account. But within class categories, returns to education for different racial and sexual groups are not very different. Where income differences within classes do exist, they are considerably larger between men and women, both black and white, than between blacks and whites.

Besides supporting the contention made earlier that racial differences in earnings are largely the outcome of differences in access to jobs, Wright and Perrone's work also suggests the relatively simple, though often overlooked, notion that the structure of occupations and work is an important factor in understanding the varying relationships observed between education and occupational status on one hand and education and earnings on the other. Though we need not accept their Marxist analysis as the only plausible interpretation of their data (see Stolzenberg, 1975b, and Spaeth, 1976), their analysis deserves closer inspection, much more than that of Bowles and Gintis (1976). This is especially true given their focus on the structure of social control (power, in our terminology) as the basis for the analysis of educational and social inequality.

Wright and Perrone's analysis further highlights a point made earlier regarding the suitability of the models of income attainment commonly employed in the study of inequality. Although similar models have been effectively utilized in the study of education and access to jobs, there is scant reason to suppose that a priori they should apply equally well to the study of education's impact on earnings. In either case, there is little hard evidence to support the belief that models that can be used to study general processes of occupational status and income attainment are also appropriate to the study of occupation-specific patterns of access to jobs and performance on the job. Indeed, evidence from a recent study of status attainment in differing occupations (Tinto, 1977) suggests that general attainment models can be quite misleading when applied uniformly across different occupational settings. As will be seen in the section on the effects of college origins on status attainment, path models of occupational attainment can be quite different in both explanatory power and meaning when they are derived separately for different types of occupations.

Education, Occupational Status, and Earnings over Time

The distinction between access to jobs and performance on the job helps make sense of the evidence concerning the changing relationships over time among education, occupational status, and earnings. As shown by Blau and Duncan (1967) and Kelley (1973), the direct impact of schooling on occupational status is greatest for the first job and declines thereafter to some stable, considerably lower level. Though status of the first job is the single best predictor of the status of subsequent jobs, its relationship is understandably mediated by on-the-job performance and therefore by income.[4] But while the direct impact of educational attainment on occupational status declines over time, its direct association with income appears to increase over time (Kelley, 1973). At the same time, the percentage of variance in income explained by a relatively simple model of attainment increases from only 10% for the first job to nearly 50% for subsequent jobs (Kelley, 1973, p. 481). Interestingly, Solmon's (1975) study of lifetime earnings of a national sample of males drawn from National Bureau of Economic Research data files yields similar conclusions, even after taking account of differences in individual ability, socioeconomic background, and occupational choice. Suggested then is the relatively simple notion that the various effects of education on occupational status and income are sequenced differently. Schooling's impact upon future on-the-job performance and therefore on income may reflect the tendency of more highly educated persons to invest more heavily in other forms of education after entry into the occupational world. Learning how to learn may be an important part of education's impact upon future attainment. Whether these effects exist and are invariant across occupations and social groups is, however, unclear. In view of the variable structure of occupational careers, comparative analysis of education's short- and long-run impacts on occupational status and earnings would be, in this context, a most welcome addition to the field.

Schooling and Individual and Group Mobility

An assessment of education's impact on social attainment also requires a careful distinction between individual and group mobility. The two are quite distinct. The prevalence of one, individual mobility, does not guarantee the pervasiveness of the other. To determine that education permits a degree of individual mobility is not to say that it also provides for an equivalent amount of group mobility in society. Indeed, although sufficient data exist to support the former contention, there is little evidence that education has served in and of itself to promote widespread group mobility. The joining of these two propositions is associated with the seemingly obvious, though much overlooked, fact noted by Anderson (1961) that schooling generally results in almost as much downward individual mobility as it does in upward mobility. The net effect of education on societal patterns of social stratification is quite limited, even though its impact upon individual careers can be quite marked (Boudon, 1973).

These distinctions also help explain the consistency of observed relationships among family background, educational attainment, and subsequent social status over periods of time marked by significant expansion of the educational system. As pointed out by Blau and Duncan (1967) and more recently by Featherman & Hauser (1976a, 1976b), the data have not permitted observation of any significant alteration since the late 1800s in the correlation between educational attainment and social attainment. Yet this period has been marked by rapid expansion of the educational system, in both the numbers and the proportions of age cohorts entering schools and reaching higher levels of educational attainment.

This phenomenon becomes immensely more understandable when we inquire into the way education is diffused throughout the social system. We discover that education, much like other social resources, tends to be diffused in a manner which follows, in queue-like fashion, the prevailing patterns of social inequality in society. Additional school places which result from educational expansion tend to be occupied first by those who are next on the social queue. Thus the middle class has been most aggressive in its utilization of the educational places provided by the growth of public junior colleges (Jencks, 1968). It does not follow, however, as Jencks et al. (1972) argue, that specific policies designed to aid particular social groups will not help equalize group differences. The recent gains in educational attainments of blacks as a group appear to be one instance where educational policies have had some impact on group differences in educational attainments (Hauser & Featherman, 1976).

QUALITATIVE DIMENSIONS OF EDUCATIONAL IMPACTS ON SOCIAL STATUS ATTAINMENT

As we have said, the models and measures of education employed thus far have not, for the most part, been very sensitive to how the knowledge and skills acquired in schools may affect subsequent social status. Certainly, educational attainment as measured by years of schooling is not related in any direct fashion to the varying skills and resources individuals acquire in schools. We turn now to consider the impact of educational *quality* on subsequent status attainment. Does it in fact make any difference to future social status whether one goes to Harvard University or to the local state university? For many people the choice is indeed significant. Given public impressions about differences between colleges, most parents would prefer to send their children to the prestigious private institution, believing that in so doing they would enhance the likelihood of their children's future success. Yet the evidence for the advisability of that choice is quite mixed.

In differing ways, the work of Hunt (1963), Coleman et al. (1966), Jencks et al. (1972), Sewell and Hauser (1975), Treiman and Terrell (1975b), and Alwin (1974, 1976) argues that differences in the quality of schooling individuals receive have little impact on future social status. However, studies by Johnson and Stafford (1973), Solmon (1975), Solmon and Wachtel (1975), and Wachtel (1975) point to the opposite conclusion. Coleman's study has been extensively reviewed by Mosteller and Moynihan (1972) and requires little comment here. Coleman's contention that differences in secondary school resources are not significantly related to differences in selected student learning outcomes seems entirely warranted. However the more widely publicized contentions by Jencks et al., for instance, that differences in the quality of schools and colleges do little to explain subsequent differences in social status attainment as measured by earned income, require further attention.

Putting aside the possibility that earned income may be a poor measure of the net social status outcomes of differing collegiate institutions, other difficulties remain in Jencks's analysis which affect the interpretability of his findings.[5] The most obvious one, commented upon by Coleman (1973), is the possibility that purely academic measures of college quality, such as employed by Jencks, do not accurately tap the institutional processes of learning and socialization that lead to the acquisition of skills, norms, and value orientations which may influence on-the-job performance and therefore earnings. Nor do they appear to be sensitive to the manner in which differing institutions train and socialize their students for performance in different occupational settings. Solmon's (1975) parallel analysis of earnings, for example, employs reputational indices of college quality (Gourman indices) and does find college quality to be associated with subsequent earnings. More importantly, his careful analysis also shows that differences in college quality affect later incomes more than they influence incomes immediately upon entry into the labor force, where such effects are small. Regrettably, since Jencks's analysis does not employ equivalent lifetime earning streams, we have no direct way of checking these results.

College Destinations and Occupational Placement over Time

Despite the inconclusiveness of past research on the influence of college quality on earnings, there is reason to believe that where one goes to college has been and is becoming an increasingly more important factor in gaining entrance to high-status occupational positions. When the proportion of the age cohort going on to higher education increases beyond the point where over one-half of all similarly aged persons enter college, college attendance per se becomes less of a guarantee of gaining access to an occupation than it was when fewer persons attended. Since more individuals are obtaining college degrees, the simple possession of a degree has less value in future occupational placement, even though it remains valuable in the sense that not having one labels a person as uneducated. If levels of market demand for highly trained manpower are held constant, as more persons enter college others will be more apt to feel inclined to do so. This is so even though they may recognize that the product of their efforts will be increasingly less valuable.

Given the real-world constraints on people's tendencies to accumulate more advanced degrees, it is likely that qualitative distinctions between colleges will increase in importance in differentiating and selecting persons for entrance into high-status occupational positions. It is not that qualitative differences among colleges will become more important for entry to occupations generally. Rather, they will become increasingly more important in gaining access to higher status occupations as opposed, for instance, to middle-class ones. Though studies by Sewell and Hauser (1975) and Alwin (1976) of the postcollegiate experiences of Wisconsin high school graduates have attended to the former possibility, they have ignored the latter. That is, though they have been able to show that differences between colleges in Wisconsin are not significantly related either to overall differences in early occupational prestige attainment or to subsequent earnings, they have not tested whether differences in where one goes to college affect attainment in differing types of occupations (e.g., high vs. low status).

Studies of occupation-specific patterns of status attainment of academics (Crain, 1970; Hargens, 1969), business leaders (Domhoff, 1967; Keller, 1953; Mills, 1956; Pierson, 1969), engineers (Perrucci & Perrucci, 1970), and scientists (Zuckerman, 1970, 1977) support the notion that college origins do influence the likelihood of attaining high-status positions within particular occupations. Perrucci and Perrucci's long-term study of the careers of engineers indicates that college origins remain a factor in high-status attainment even after academic performance and social origins are taken into account. Collins (1971) has taken evidence of this sort to mean that the relationship between college origins and status attainment is more a function of the power resources inherent in the occupation than of its knowledge-based attributes. As power becomes a more dominant element in occupational positions, present incumbents will use education to select recruits who have been socialized into the dominant-status culture (Collins, 1971, p. 1011). Though skill acquisition is a necessary concern, the primary interest of employers lies in preserving control over high-status occupational positions. For that reason, occupational elites, in seeking out prospective employees, look to particular educational institutions which are seen to effectively socialize their graduates into an elite culture. In the process important networks of opportunity may be established between particular collegiate (or postcollegiate) institutions and occupational elites which enhance the ability of institutions to sponsor their graduates to the more desirable statuses in society (Kamens, 1974).

We recently sought to test this proposition by studying the longitudinal impact of college destinations upon the process of early occupational prestige attainment in high- and middle-status occupations separately (Tinto, 1977). Using information on the postcollegiate educational and occupational experiences of a national sample of male and female college graduates drawn from NORC data files, we have been able to show that the impact of college quality upon occupational attainment varies considerably from middle- to high-status occupations. The early results of these analyses are shown in Figures 1 and 2. Whereas among middle-status occupations, college quality has no measurable direct impact upon early occupational prestige attainment (Figure 1), it has both direct and indirect effects upon attainment among high-status occupational positions (Figure 2). College-quality effects are indirect in that they influence grade performance, occupational expectations, and the completion of postcollege degrees. And they remain significant and direct even after account is taken of their indirect impacts and the effects of social background, sex, and type of high school on early occupational attainment.

More importantly, the social processes that characterize attainment among high-status occupational positions are essentially different from those that describe mobility within the middle-status sectors of the economy. While middle-class mobility is only marginally associated with the factors included in the model (less than 14% of the variance in attainments being explained by the model), high-status attainment is determined much more not only by performance but also by social and sexual attributes and by the quality of the college attended. Furthermore, the process of attainment is more determined generally, with nearly 40% of the variance in attainments being explained by the model.

In a number of respects, the process of attainment among high-status occupations appears to resemble the sponsorship mode of mobility described by Turner (1960). Relative to "contest" patterns of mobility, which are largely based on individual performance, sponsorship mobility suggests that occupational elites actively sponsor persons selected primarily on the basis of social attributes to become future elites. In the educational system particular institutions may serve as legitimating sponsoring agencies for these elites by screening, socializing, and promoting selected individuals as future incumbents of elite positions (Collins, 1971, 1975; Kamens, 1974; Turner, 1960). Linkages between institutions and occupational elites developed in this way may be occupation specific in character (Kamens, 1971), or they may apply differentially to members of different racial and sexual groups (Porter, 1974).

The process depicted here, however, does not conform to this description. As seen in the path models (Figures 1 and 2), performance, expectations,

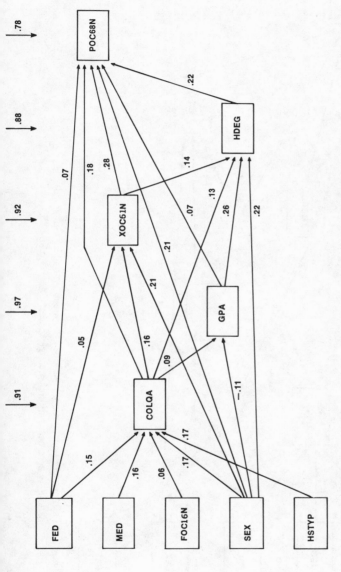

Figure 1. Path model of occupational prestige attainment among middle-prestige occupations, where occupational prestige NORC score is *below* 58.

Key:
FED = Father's educational level.
MED = Mother's educational level.
FOC16N = Father's occupational prestige score (respondent at age 16 years old).
XOC61N = Expected occupational prestige score (in 1961).
POC68N = Occupational prestige score in 1968.
Note: All path coefficients shown are in standardized form.

SEX = Respondent's sex (0 = female, 1 = male).
HSTYP = High school type (0 = public, 1 = private).
GPA = Grade point average in college.
HDEG = Higher degree since graduation.
COLQA = College quality (Astin Selectivity).

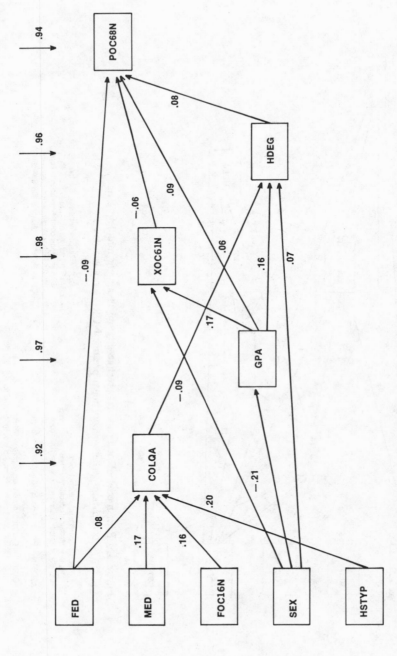

Figure 2. Path model of occupational prestige attainment among high-prestige occupations, where occupational prestige score NORC is *above* 58.

Note: For key, see Figure 1.

and subsequent postcollege degree attainment are also central factors in the attainment of high-status occupational positions. Sponsorship, should it occur, does not apply equally to all persons who gain entrance to high-quality institutions. Rather it appears to be applicable primarily to those whose performance warrants future sponsorship. Indeed, additional evidence strongly suggests that sponsorship is largely a latent capacity of institutions which can be activated by able and ambitious individuals within them. The individual, rather than the institution, seems to be the causal force in the process of attainment. Simply being present at the institution is no guarantee of being sponsored to high-status positions.

The conception of educational stratification suggested falls somewhere between the more strictly Marxist and therefore more deterministic perspective of Bowles and Gintis (1976) and Collins (1971), and the perspective of Jencks et al. (1972), which posits a great deal of coincidence or "luck" in social attainment. Though the latter position may prove, upon subsequent study, to apply to attainment in middle-status occupations, for those of high status it appears to be the case that both performance and institutional location count. It is necessary to be able to demonstrate competence, but this must be done in institutions with the capacity to sponsor graduates into the more prestigious occupational positions in society. While some may seek to redefine this phenomenon as being at the right place at the right time, it is clear from our analyses that being able to be at the right place (i.e., a high quality college) is not a socially random phenomenon. Access to these institutions is a function of both sex and social origins, as well as type of high school attended.

These preliminary results of a more extensive research project point up another intriguing finding regarding the effect of sex on attainment. While an individual's sex is only indirectly related to attainment among middle-status occupations, it is a significant direct factor in access both to high-quality colleges and to higher status occupations, irrespective of the college attended. As a result, these analyses suggest an interpretation of the impact of sex on attainment which is different from that implied by the studies of social attainment cited earlier (e.g., Treiman and Terrell, 1975b). Whereas the earlier studies argue that men and women of equivalent educational attainment are not differentially constrained in attempting to gain entry to the occupational world, the later results support the existence of such constraints, not in any widespread fashion (e.g., among middle-status occupations) but primarily among high-status occupations. Women appear to have a double handicap in attempting to gain access to high-status positions. Not only do constraints operate against them in gaining access to colleges of higher quality, but they also experience significant barriers to entry to high-status occupations even after social background, college origins, college performance, expectations, and post-college educational attainments are taken into account. Certainly, the question of sexual discrimination in entry to the occupational world has yet to be fully resolved.

METHODS AND MEANING IN THE STUDY OF EDUCATIONAL INEQUALITY

In turning to the methodology of research on schooling and social inequality, it is not our intention to critique the application of given methodologies in particular studies. This has been attended to in great detail in a number of instances (e.g., "Perspectives on Inequality," 1973). Nor is it our aim to explore the methodological nuances or statistical variations which may be employed in the solution of problems of data analysis. Such discussions are better left to social statisticians. Rather, we will ask in broad terms how the use of different analytic methods influences our understanding of educational inequality and its impact on subsequent social inequality.

The Dilemma of Scope versus Detail

Educational and social inequality has been most commonly studied through large-scale survey methods. These studies have usually applied various statistical techniques of correlation, factor analysis, and regression analysis to ascertain the broad relationships among various attributes of the sampled population (e.g., ability and social origins) and their level of educational and social attainments (e.g., Blau & Duncan, 1967). The use of large-scale survey research has made it possible to gather a great deal of valuable information on the changing character of social inequality and its relationship, at various levels of analysis, to the distribution of educational attainment among groups and individuals in society. Nevertheless, though large-scale survey methods have done much to paint a relatively representative and broadly based picture of social and educational inequality, they have often served to constrain our view of the details of inequality at the individual and group levels of behavior.

Even at the macro level, the use of large-scale methodologies has often tended to oversimplify and even overlook the complexity of group, community, state, and regional patterns of inequality which are the underpinnings of broadly based "national" patterns of inequality. Studies like those of Anderson, Bowman, and Tinto (1972), Gastil (1972), and Shin (1976), for example, have shown significant and important variations among states and regions in the patterning of relationships between educational inequality and social attainment. In Anderson, Bowman, and Tinto, careful analysis of the patterns of college choice among high school seniors in five states (California, Illinois, Massachusetts, North Carolina, and Wisconsin) revealed significant differences among states in how the availability of public junior colleges influences the likelihood that high school seniors will go on to higher education after graduation. Relative to such state-specific analyses of educational behaviors, national-sample survey studies of the same problem, that is, of the proximity effect of junior colleges, have yielded markedly different and often misleading conclusions (e.g., Medsker & Trent, 1965).[6]

At the group and individual interactional levels of analysis, survey methods are hard pressed to convey the richness of detail found, for example, in Granovetter's (1974) study of job-seekers in the Boston area or in Kohn's (1969) study of status-related family child-rearing patterns as they pertain to the child's ability to move upward in the social system. Granovetter's study is of particular interest, as it points out with great clarity the importance of personal contacts in the process of high-status job acquisition; these personal contacts, it might be added, may have been formed earlier in specific schools and colleges (Crain, 1970; Kamens, 1974). In a similar fashion, it is unlikely that survey methods will ever yield the same sense of the dynamic processes of student-teacher interaction within classrooms which is seen in Rist's (1970) observational study of urban elementary classrooms. As his study suggests, potentially self-fulfilling patterns of interaction can give rise to unequal grade performance among persons of differing social origins.

The inability of survey research methods to ascertain the micro details of social behavior is not simply a reflection of the limitations on time and expense which face most research projects. Rather, it is largely the result of unavoidable social constraints not entirely dissimilar in principle from those observed in quantum physics (i.e., the Heisenberg Uncertainty Principle) which prevent researchers from being able to reliably determine simultaneously both the scope and the detail of human interactions. Attempts to utilize survey methods to develop a truly representative picture of social behavior may necessarily constrain the researchers' ability to probe the underlying processes of interaction which give rise to observable patterns of behavior at the aggregate level. Furthermore, the very act of investigation required at one level may in the process alter the behaviors to be studied at another level. The present resistance of the public to survey research questionnaires may well be one rather limited reflection of this phenomenon at work.

The implication being drawn here is that past studies of inequality, in relying so heavily on large-scale survey methods, have been necessarily limited in what they have been able to indicate about educational inequality in society. Although recent utilization of longitudinal follow-up survey methods (Sewell & Hauser, 1975) and time-sequenced cross-sectional analysis (Hauser & Featherman, 1976) has improved the picture considerably, large-scale survey methodologies are still limited to inferential claims about the time-related association between differing attributes of the population, schools, and educational attainment and social inequality.[7] They are, for the most part, unable to probe effectively the underlying causal roots of micro and macro levels of inequality in society. Clearly, other, if not multiple, modes of analysis are called for in the further study of education and social attainment.

Large-scale survey methods are only one of a number of possible methodological approaches to the study of educational attainment and social inequality. Other methods, both macro and micro, that have been gainfully employed in the past in other fields are only now becoming popular among educational researchers. Several of the more promising of these methods are discussed in the sections to follow.

Simulation Models and the Specification of Social Dynamics

One particularly intriguing method suited to the study of macro-level patterns of inequality is simulation modeling. As applied by the Organization for Economic Cooperation and Development (1973) and Boudon (1973), the utilization of simulation models provides a possible vehicle for the testing of hypotheses specifying the underlying dynamics of inequality in society. Although Boudon's study is subject to a number of methodological criticisms (see Hauser, 1976, and Boudon's, 1976, reply), its conceptual strengths are significant enough to warrant our attention.

Boudon's (1973) use of simulation modeling involves the creation of artificial data derived from a set of explicitly stated hypotheses specifying the effect of individual and group attributes upon educational attainment, and of both upon subsequent social attainment. Given corollary assumptions as to the size of differing student populations, the availability of educational places, and the number of occupational positions open to entry, Boudon is able to create data on the social and timewise patterning of educational and occupational inequality. These data are then compared to "real" data drawn from past survey studies dealing with the same phenomena. The degree of correspondence between the two sets of data is then taken as an indication of the degree to which the stated hypotheses accurately describe the actual world. Where data fit is poor, the initial hypotheses are modified by, for instance, altering the weights assigned to the effect of ability and social class background upon attendance, so as to yield a greater degree of fit between the created data and the real-world data sets.

Despite some limitations (e.g., dependence on the results of other survey studies), the simulation-modeling technique represents an exciting innovation in the study of inequality because of its ability to test, in an explicit manner, the correctness of underlying social theory. Contrasted to Boudon's analysis, most other studies represent at best ex post facto explanations. As is frequently the case in the studies reviewed here, explanation is sought from the models obtained from the application of various forms of linear curve-fitting designed to yield both high degrees of explanation of variance in dependent outcomes and residuals which are uncorrelated with factors included in the model.

There are several difficulties in such procedures. First, they often result in very low levels of explanation of variance. That is, they yield unexciting theory which turns out to have small scope. Sewell and Hauser's (1975) extensive analysis of a model of income attainment which accounts for only

10% of the variance in incomes is such a case, as is Jencks et al.'s attribution to the whims of chance ("luck") the responsibility for the high degree of unexplained variance in their model. Skeptics point out that such levels of unexplained variance reflect the weakness of the model more than they do social reality, and "luck," whatever that may mean, is more likely to be distributed along social class lines than it is to be randomly distributed in society. Second, the ex post facto development of theory may give rise to very different theoretical interpretations of given data sets. Collins's (1971) comparative study of the technical and conflict theories of educational stratification is, in this context, one of the more interesting critiques of ex post facto methods of theoretical explanation. Such modes of explanation often reflect the underlying value positions of the researcher more than the degree of fit between proposed theory and data.

Of course, it can be argued with regard to the simulation method that different sets of initiating hypotheses may well exist which fit data drawn from the actual world equally well. Though it was not Boudon's intention to produce or test the existence of all such competing sets of hypotheses, it would be interesting to determine if such alternative hypotheses do in fact exist. In any event, the particular strength of the simulation-modeling technique lies in its ability to yield immediate tests of theory and therefore tests of the correctness of varying explanations of educational and social inequality.

It is noteworthy that Boudon's analysis results in the confirmation of several findings noted earlier regarding educational and social inequality. First, it is observed that the spread of education, even in highly meritocratic societies, has not significantly altered the pattern of social inequality in society, a finding, parenthetically, that is not as surprising as Boudon makes it (see our earlier discussion of individual and group mobility). Second, Boudon finds that the effect of social origins on educational attainment and occupational status is stronger among highest status groups (in helping to prevent downward mobility) and lowest status groups (in constraining upward mobility) and is least influential among middle-status groups in society.[8] As suggested by Tinto (1977), this also implies a structure of society which is largely meritocratic in the middle and more ascriptive in the upper and lower segments of the stratification system.

Network Analysis and the Study of Opportunity Structure

Stratification systems can be seen as consisting of dynamic networks of interlocking chains of opportunity (White, 1970). Based on established patterns of affiliation between occupants of differing statuses, these chains provide for the essential communication of information and interests and for the social exchange of valued social goods among members of society (Ekeh, 1974). As such they can also serve as the basis for the movement of individuals and groups through the complex system of statuses which make up society.

Access to high social statuses may depend in very specific ways upon the ability of persons to gain entrance to the associated chains of opportunity which link up to those statuses and to move upward within them.

Societal institutions such as the educational system can be seen as providing particularly important opportunities for status advancement through their housing of societally recognized chains of opportunity. These may serve to legitimately sponsor graduates to particular niches in the world of work or provide them with valuable information as to the availability and character of opportunities for job entry (Boorman, 1975; Granovetter, 1974). In studying the impact of college origins on social status attainment, we would therefore seek to determine the character of institution-specific linkages to the occupational world and ascertain the degree to which individuals are able to employ them for status advancement. It is in this context that network analysis can be gainfully employed.

Network analysis has been used primarily in the study of community structure by anthropologists (Mitchell, 1969) and has only recently been applied to the study of social structure and the interlocking character of societal elites (Bernard, 1974; Freitag, 1975; Holland & Leinhardt, 1976; White, Boorman, & Breiger, 1976). Given its power to trace out interstatus and interorganizational patterns of affiliations, network analysis seems particularly well suited to the much-needed study of the patterning of associations which tie in particular educational institutions to each other and to specific segments of the occupational world. Outside of a few observational studies intended for other purposes, we do not have the sorts of data to carry out such analyses. Yet it is precisely this empirical tracing out of linkages that is required to substantiate the proposition that where one goes to college affects subsequent occupational placement.

It should be noted that network analysis is neither empirically uncomplicated nor immune to serious problems of representation sampling (Granovetter, 1976). And though such analysis can ascertain the existence of reoccuring patterns of interstatus affiliations, it cannot in itself determine how such affiliations are formed or how effective they are in assisting individuals to move upward in the stratification system. For that, other methods, including observational study, are required.

Observational and Case Study Analysis and Inequality within Schools

In the light of Coleman's finding that most of the variance in educational performance occurs within rather than between schools, it is surprising that relatively few studies of educational inequality have attempted to relate within-school patterns of behavior to differential educational and social outcomes. Of the major studies noted here, only those of Duncan, Featherman, and Duncan (1972, chap. 7) and Hauser, Sewell, and Alwin (1976) have attended to this question in a thorough manner. Yet, as noted by Duncan, Featherman, and Duncan (p. 204), their attempt to assess within-school effects of peers on individual aspirations gives rise to formidable problems of identification and estimation of parameters, which may reflect the limitations of the methodology as much as the phenomenon itself.

Of the more recent attempts to study within-school patterns of inequality (Alexander and McDill, 1976; Heyns, 1974; Rist, 1970; Rosenbaum, 1975), Rist's observational study of behaviors within classrooms is perhaps the most interesting.[9] The main thrust of Rist's work as it is understood from the perspectives of symbolic interactionism (Berger & Luckmann, 1966) and labeling theory (Schur, 1971) is that the creation of inequality in schools is largely the result of the social as well as academic evaluation of student competence by school officials. Observational analysis of elementary school classrooms showed kindergarten teachers judged the academic competence of their children largely from the behavioral clues exhibited early in the school year. Both the clues and the evaluations leading to judgments of competence were primarily social in nature, reflecting, in this instance, the middle-class origins of the teachers. For the most part, children from lower status backgrounds were judged less competent than children of higher social status origins.

More importantly, teachers and student peers tended to pattern their interactions with one another (in both frequency and quality) to create supportive interactional environments for students who were judged to be competent and inhibiting ones for those who were not. The resulting patterns of performance within the classroom tended to recreate, in academic form, the social evaluations of competence that had been made earlier. Students judged competent early in the school year tended to outperform those judged to be less competent. Strikingly, subsequent IQ testing revealed few differences between the groups which would account for their differential grade performance. This suggests the notion of the creation of inequality within schools through self-fulfilling prophecies (Rist, 1977).[10]

Differences in performance among students in the kindergarten year tended to reappear in subsequent years of schooling (in Rist's study, to the end of the observation period in the third year). Though there were some changes in student rankings at the end of the third school year, the overall pattern of performance established during the first grade tended to maintain itself over the period of observation. Students who were judged to be relatively incompetent during kindergarten (mostly of lower status origins) were, for the most part, also those who exhibited lower grade performance during the second and third years of schooling. The judgments of competence made by teachers in the first year in effect were repeated by teachers in subsequent grades, and the differential performance levels recorded in preceding years served to substantiate and reinforce these judgments in both the formal and informal organization of the school. Thus there is a causal process whereby social status background and educational performance become associated across time.

There are several obvious questions regarding Rist's study which can serve as beginning points for the much-needed link of classroom patterns of inequality to those observed in the school generally and in the wider society. First, how are teachers' perceptions of academic competence formed in the context of the school? Second, how do the school and the teaching profession act to reinforce or induce teachers to structure their interactions with students in ways which favor those perceived to be more academically promising? It is not in the evaluations themselves that unequal performance arises, but in the associated patterns of interaction which teachers and student peers exhibit toward those who are evaluated. Finally, to what degree and in what manner are early patterns of unequal performance (such as those associated with social origins) transmitted through the educational system? Determination of the processes of transmission might make it possible for us to link up early patterns of family socialization, which lead to differential behavioral styles among children of different families, to subsequent patterns of educational and therefore social inequality in society (see Kohn, 1969).

Without attempting to answer these questions, we can point out that each question shares a common element which may serve as a starting point for future research in these areas. This is the central role played by educational organizations as the mediator between micro and macro patterns of inequality in society. A number of different directions of inquiry are suggested. First, we would want to inquire as to the nature of the educational institutions in which teachers were trained and socialized and the character of the teaching profession which serves to establish normative referents for teacher behaviors (Touraine, 1974). Similarly, we would like to ascertain more clearly both the social orientations of teachers and the reward and belief structures of the schools in which they work (Lortie, 1975). These may serve to reinforce teachers' behaviors that tend to favor students judged to be more academically promising (Kamens, 1977). We would also want to consider, as Heyns (1974), Rosenbaum (1975), and Alexander and McDill (1976) have, the manner in which the allocation of individual and educational resources within the school among classes (as seen for instance in academic tracking) impacts on student performance.

Beyond the school, at the district level, we might attend to those social and political processes that result in the differential allocation of educational resources within and among school districts. As Bidwell and Kasarda (1975) have shown, these resource allocations may have significant impact on student performance in schools. And at the societal level, we could turn to the analyses of Weber (1947), Dahrendorf (1959) and Katz (1975) of the conflict between social groups for the control of societal and educational organizations and to Bernstein's (1977) analysis of the social origins of pedagogy as suggesting the possible ways in which societal distributions of resources influence both the organization of education and the knowledge base upon which it is founded (see Young, 1971).

Merged together, these disparate lines of inquiry can serve as one basis, among others, for the linking up of macro patterns of social inequality with school and classroom patterns of educational inequality. Joined with the much-needed studies of the linking networks of opportunity to tie in schools and occupations, these analyses can yield significant increases in our understanding of education's impact on social attainment.

CONCLUDING COMMENTS

This brief review has assessed the current state of knowledge regarding the effect of schooling on social attainment. Beginning with the relatively simple notion that the impacts of education on getting a job are different from those on performance on the job, we have sought to clarify how and to what extent schools affect a person's subsequent status attainment. The available evidence suggests that the acquisition of educational credentials is more closely associated with the ability of a person to gain access to high-status occupations than it is with ability to do well in the occupations that are entered.

Regarding access to jobs, recent research questions the position of the more radical revisionists that particular educational institutions, controlled by existing elites, act as sponsoring agencies to promote selected individuals to high-status (elite) positions. Only among high-status occupations are such institutional effects evident. These effects appear more as latent institutional capacities which able and motivated persons of a variety of social origins can activate for their own personal advancement. Sponsorship does not seem to be an active institutional phenomenon which applies to all members within the institution; simply being at a high-quality college does not guarantee access to high-status occupations. At the same time, the research does not support the position of Jencks et al. that ability and "luck" are the most important factors in status attainment. Though it is true that performance counts, it is also true that college quality matters in the attainment of high-status occupations. Furthermore, it is evident that access to prestigious colleges is not a random phenomenon in the social system or determined solely by past academic performance.

With respect to education's impact on on-the-job performance, it is evident that we have been unable to detect any simple or sizable direct effect of schooling on job performance as it can be measured by earnings. Whether this finding reflects the real world or the shortcomings of current research models is unclear. It is our impression that the latter is the case; our current models have been unable to capture the manner in which education leads to the differential acquisition of skills that impact on subsequent on-the-job performance. Regrettably, researchers continue, for the most part, to rely on models of attainment which emphasize between-school differences, even with mounting evidence that differences within schools are more effective in accounting for differential student outcomes.

In any event, it should not be assumed that we will ever be able to explain, through the application of relatively simple models of attainment, most of the variance in adult occupational status. As currently conceived, our present models of status attainment are based on the assumption that most people evaluate potential outcomes of education in very much the same way, and such evaluations are in some simple manner directly associated with social status background. That is, it is assumed that most persons have the same values regarding different orders of educational and social goods or that these values are a direct function of social status. Although a number of persons have pointed out the inaccuracy of this assumption (e.g., Boudon, 1973), we have yet to see a thorough application of social models of decision theory to the study of education and social attainment. When we do, it is likely that important linkages will appear between the family, the school, and other important socializing contexts and the manner in which educational attainment impacts on social status attainment of differing individuals and groups (Kohn, 1969).

Further increases in the power of research models will also depend on the more extensive application of a variety of methods of social research to the study of educational and social inequality. What is required, in particular, is the merging of methodologies and studies at different levels of analysis (e.g., societal, community, organization and group) so as to lend insight to the complex set of linkages which tie in micro and macro patterns of inequality through the mediating influence of the school. At the same time, there is a clear need for the development of a comparative profile of occupation-specific studies of education and status attainment (e.g. Tinto, 1977). Though a number of such studies now exist (Perrucci and Perrucci, 1970; Zuckerman, 1977), they were not intended, nor can they be used, for a strictly comparative analysis of education's variable influence on social status attainment. Finally, so as not to lose sight of the culture-specific basis of stratification, there should be additional studies of the longitudinal process of attainment in differing countries. A number of such studies are now becoming available (Boudon, 1973; Treiman & Terrell, 1975a; Lin & Yauger, 1975; Garner & Hout, 1976; Hazelrigg and Garnier, 1976; and Currie, 1977), but there is much more that can be done in this area.

Although we have learned much about the impact of education on the process of status attainment, much more remains to be learned. As in most fields of intellectual endeavor, answers to current questions give rise to more questions which serve as the objects for future inquiries.

NOTES

1. With reference to policy, discussions involving the first question often deal with the reduction and/or eradication of inequality in society, while those of the second sort generally focus on the shifting distributions (or burdens) of inequality among differing groups within society as, for instance, in the elimination of inequality on the basis of race. As Coleman (1973, pp. 130-131) has correctly pointed out, Jencks (Jencks et al., 1972) tends to confuse these two questions. While Jencks's analysis generally speaks to the latter question—inequality of opportunity for differing individuals and groups—his policy proposals speak to the former question, that is, the elimination of inequality of income in society. This does not imply that the analyses and the policy recommendations are unwarranted; rather, it suggests that the validity of one does not rest on the other.

2. The distribution of earned income is neither an unbiased estimator of total income nor an accurate indicator of the distribution of social status among individuals and groups in society. In the former instance, earned income tends to underestimate the total income available to persons of high status, and in the latter it tends to distort the actual distribution of status in society by both overestimating and underestimating, at differing points of the social hierarchy, the power and prestige of occupational positions.

3. Measures of ability, social background, and social-psychological orientations (e.g., ambition) generally account for 55 to 60 percent of the variance in the length of schooling (Hauser, 1972; Sewell, Haller, & Ohlendorf, 1970; Sewell, Haller & Portes, 1969).

4. We would reasonably expect significant variations among occupations in the changing long-term impact of education on status and income. In those occupations that exhibit relatively rigid promotion and wage systems (e.g., civil service), a stronger intertemporal association between education and subsequent occupational status attainment would be anticipated.

5. Several review essays were written following publication of the then-controversial study by Jencks and his colleagues in 1972. For a more complete review of that work, see "Perspectives on Inequality," 1973; "Symposium on Jenck's Inequality," 1973; "Symposium Review," 1973.

6. Even if national patterns of educational inequality are worthy of study (and they are for certain purposes), large-scale survey methods have rarely been able to obtain a purely random, representative sample of individuals for their analysis. Unless great expense is taken to include a range of follow-up procedures (e.g., Sewell's use of telephone follow-up to obtain 94% coverage of high school seniors in the state of Wisconsin), most survey studies are frequently content with analyzing data based on sample sizes often no greater than half of the original target population. Though there are a number of devices that can be called upon to

deal with individual (and item) nonresponse bias, no one has seriously suggested that these do much more than protect against obvious aggregate-level biases in the resulting images obtained from subsequent analysis.

7. The application of longitudinal statistical techniques such as path analysis (as employed in many of the studies considered here) requires that the data meet a number of very restrictive conditions infrequently met in social research. One of the more unsatisfactory uses of longitudinal path analysis is, in this respect, the attempt of Jencks et al. (1972) to assess the longitudinal relationship between IQ and achievement. The major difficulty arises in their attempt to merge very different data sources for their longitudinal analysis. Without being able to ensure, among other things, uniformity of variance between samples, such analysis is at best very speculative. At worst it can be extremely misleading, if not entirely incorrect.

8. Given the obvious fact that individuals in the upper status groups are necessarily more prone to downward movement than are other persons (since little further upward movement is possible), the desire to avoid social demotions becomes a central concern among those groups. It is unfortunate, in this respect, that Boudon did not follow up this line of reasoning and deal with the variant value orientations of different social groups and the process of educational differentiation as it pertains to the interests of those groups in society.

9. Case studies of school situations are by no means new. Studies such as those by Waller (1967) and Gordon (1957) have provided important insights into the within-school creation of inequality. Regrettably, modern researchers have tended to overlook these studies in favor of those employing the currently popular regression models.

10. No mention has been made here of Rosenthal and Jacobson's (1968) study of the same phenomenon. For a number of reasons that study has been shown to be seriously defective. From our perspective, the most serious error on their part was to assume that teachers relied primarily on formal reports of students' potential rather than on their own observational evaluations in the classroom. Apparently it is the latter, not the former, that serves as the basis for the evaluation of student competence in the first years of schooling.

REFERENCES

Abrahamson, M., Mizruchi, E. H., and Hornung, C. A. *Stratification and mobility.* New York: Macmillan, 1976.

Alexander, K. L., & Eckland, B. K. Sex differences in the educational attainment process. *American Sociological Review,* 1974, *39,* 668-682.

Alexander, K. L., & Eckland, B. K. Basic attainment processes: A replication and extension. *Sociology of Education,* 1975, *48,* 457-495.

Alexander, K. L., Eckland, B. K., & Griffin, L. J. The Wisconsin model of socioeconomic achievement: A replication. *American Journal of Sociology,* 1975, *81,* 324-342.

Alexander, K. L., & McDill, E. L. Selection and allocation within schools: Some causes and consequences of curriculum placement. *American Sociological Review,* 1976, *41,* 963-980.

Alwin, D. F. College effects on educational and occupational attainments. *American Sociological Review,* 1974, *39,* 210-223.

Alwin, D. F. Socioeconomic background, colleges and post-collegiate achievements. In W. H. Sewell, R. M. Hauser, and D. L. Featherman (Eds.), *Schooling and achievement in American society.* New York: Academic Press, 1976.

Anderson, C. A. A skeptical note on the relation of vertical mobility to education. *American Journal of Sociology,* 1961, *66,* 560-570.

Anderson, C. A., Bowman, M. J., and Tinto, V. *Who goes where to college: Effects of accessibility on college attendance.* New York: McGraw-Hill, 1972.

Anderson, C. A., & Foster, P. J. Discrimination and inequality in education. *Sociology of Education,* 1964, *38,* 1-18.

Ayella, M. E., & Williamson, J. The social mobility of women: A causal model of socioeconomic success. *Sociological Quarterly,* 1976, *17,* 534-554.

Berg. I. *Education and jobs: The great training robbery.* Boston: Beacon Press, 1971.

Berger, P. L., & Luckmann, T. *The social construction of reality: A treatise in the sociology of knowledge.* Garden City, N.Y.: Doubleday, 1966.

Bernard, P. *Association and hierarchy: The social structure of the adolescent society.* Unpublished doctoral dissertation, Harvard University, 1974.

Bernstein, B. Class and pedagogies: Visible and invisible. In J. Karabel and A. H. Halsey (Eds.), *Power and ideology in education.* New York: Oxford University Press, 1977.

Bidwell, C. E., & Kasarda, J. D. School district organization and student achievement. *American Sociological Review,* 1975, *40,* 55-70.

Blau, P. M., & Duncan, O. D. *The American occupational structure.* New York: John Wiley, 1967.

Blum, Z. White and black careers during the first decade of labor force experience. Part II: Income differences. *Social Science Research,* 1972, *1,* 271-292.

Boorman, S. A. A combinatorial optimization model for transmission of job information through contact networks. *Bell Journal of Economics,* 1975, *6,* 216-249.

Boudon, R. *Education, opportunity and social inequality: Changing prospects in Western society.* New York: John Wiley, 1973.

Boudon, R. Comment on Hauser's review of *Education, opportunity, and social inequality. American Journal of Sociology,* 1976, *81,* 1175–1187.

Bowles, S. & Gintis, H. *Schooling in capitalist America: Educational reform and the contradictions of economic life.* New York: Basic Books, 1976.

Carnoy, M. *Education as cultural imperialism.* New York: David McKay, 1974.

Chase, I. D. A comparison of men's and women's intergenerational mobility in the United States. *American Sociological Review,* 1975, *40,* 483-505.

Coleman, J. S. Equality of opportunity and equality of results. *Harvard Educational Review,* 1973, *43,* 129-137.

Coleman, J. S., Berry, C., & Blum, Z. White and black careers during the first decade of labor force experience. Part III: Occupational status and income together. *Social Science Research,* 1972, *1,* 293-304.

Coleman, J. S., Blum, Z., Sorensen, A., & Rossi, P. White and black careers during the first decade of labor force experience. Part I: Occupational status. *Social Science Research,* 1972, *1,* 243-270.

Coleman, J. S., Campbell, E. Q., Hobson, C. J., McPartland, J., Mood, A. M., Weinfeld, F. D., & York, R. L. *Equality of educational opportunity.* Washington, D.C.: U.S. Government Printing Office, 1966.

Collins, R. Functional and conflict theories of educational stratification. *American Sociological Review,* 1971, *36,* 1002-1012.

Collins, R. *Conflict sociology: Toward an explanatory science.* New York: Academic Press, 1975.

Crain, R. L. Social integration and occupational achievement of negroes. *American Journal of Sociology,* 1970, *75,* 593-606.

Currie, J. Family background, academic achievement and occupational status in Uganda. *Comparative Education Review,* 1977, *21,* 14-28.

Dahrendorf, R. *Class and class conflict in industrial society.* Stanford, Cal.: Stanford University Press, 1959.

DeJong, P. Y., Brawer, M. J., & Robin, S. S. Patterns of female intergenerational occupational mobility: A comparison with male patterns of intergenerational occupational mobility. *American Sociological Review,* 1971, *36,* 1033-1042.

Domhoff, G. W. *Who rules America?* Englewood Cliffs, N.J.: Prentice-Hall, 1967.

Duncan, O. D., Featherman, D. L., & Duncan, B. *Socioeconomic background and achievement.* New York: Seminar Press, 1972.

Ekeh, P. *Social exchange theory: The two traditions.* Cambridge, Mass.: Harvard University Press, 1974.

Epstein, C. F. Positive effects of the multiple negative: Explaining the success of black professional women. *American Journal of Sociology,* 1973, *78,* 912-35.

Farley, R. Trends in racial inequalities: Have the gains of the 1960s disappeared in the 1970s? *American Sociological Review,* 1977, *42,* 189-208.

Featherman, D. L., & Hauser, R. M. Changes in the socioeconomic stratification of the races, 1962-1973. *American Journal of Sociology,* 1976, *82,* 621-651. (a)

Featherman, D. L., & Hauser, R. M. Sexual inequalities and socioeconomic achievement in the U.S., 1962-1973. *American Sociological Review,* 1976, *41, 3,* 462-483. (b)

Featherman, D. L., Jones, F. L., & Hauser, R. M. Assumptions of social mobility research in the United States: The case of occupational status. *Social Science Research,* 1975, *4,* 329-360.

Freitag, P. J. The cabinet and big business: A study of interlocks. *Social Problems,* 1975, *23,* 137–152.

Garner, M., & Hout, M. Inequality of educational opportunity in France and the United States. *Social Science Research,* 1976, *5,* 225-246.

Gastil, R. D. The relationship of regional cultures to educational performance. *Sociology of Education,* 1972, *45,* 408-425.

Gordon, C. W. *The social system of the high school: A study in the sociology of adolescence.* Glencoe, Ill.: Free Press, 1957.

Granovetter, M. S. *Getting a job: A study of contacts and careers.* Cambridge, Mass.: Harvard University Press, 1974.

Granovetter, M. S. Network sampling: Some first steps. *American Journal of Sociology,* 1976, *81,* 1287-1303.

Green, T. F. Personal communication, July 1977.

Hargens, L. L. Patterns of mobility of new Ph.D.s among American academic institutions. *Sociology of Education,* 1969, *42,* 18-37.

Hauser, R. M. Disaggregating, a socio-psychological model of educational attainment. *Social Science Research,* 1972, *1,* 159–188.

Hauser, R. M. Review essay: On Boudon's model of social mobility. *American Journal of Sociology,* 1976, *81,* 911-928.

Hauser, R. M., & Featherman, D. L. Equality of schooling: Trends and prospects. *Sociology of Education,* 1976, *49,* 99-120.

Hauser, R. M., Sewell, W. H., & Alwin, D. F. High school effects on achievement.

In W. H. Sewell, R. M. Hauser, & D. L. Featherman (Eds.), *Schooling and achievement in American society.* New York: Academic Press, Inc., 1976.

Hazelrigg, L., & Garnier, M. Occupational mobility in industrial societies: A comparative analysis of differential access to occupational ranks in seventeen countries. *American Sociological Review,* 1976, *41,* 498-511.

Heyns, B. Social selection and stratification within schools. *American Journal of Sociology,* 1974, *79,* 1434-1451.

Holland, P. W., & Leinhardt, S. Local structure in social networks. In D. R. Heise (Ed.), *Sociological methodology.* San Francisco: Jossey-Bass, 1976.

Hunt, S. *Income determination for the college graduate and return to educational investment.* Yale Economic Essays, No. 3. New Haven, Conn.: Yale University Press, 1963.

Jencks, C. Social stratification and higher education. *Harvard Educational Review,* 1968, *38,* 277-316.

Jencks, C., Smith, M., Acland, H., Bane, M. J., Cohen, D., Gintis, H., Heyns, B., & Michelson, S. *Inequality: A reassessment of the effect of family and schooling in America.* New York: Basic Books, 1972.

Johnson, G. E., & Stafford, F. P. Social returns to quantity and quality of schooling. *Journal of Human Resources,* 1973, *9,* 139-155.

Kamens, D. H. The college "charter" and college size: Effects on occupational choice and college attrition. *Sociology of Education,* 1971, *44,* 270–296.

Kamens, D. H. Colleges and elite formation: The case of prestigious American colleges. *Sociology of Education,* 1974, *47,* 354-378.

Kamens, D. H. Legitimating myths and educational organization: The relationship between organizational ideology and formal structure. *American Sociological Review,* 1977, *42,* 208-219.

Katz, M. B. *Class, bureaucracy and schools: The illusion of educational change in America.* New York: Frederick A. Praeger, 1975.

Keller, S. *The social origins and career lines of three generations of American business leaders.* Unpublished doctoral dissertation, Columbia University, 1953.

Kelley, J. Causal chain model for the socioeconomic career. *American Sociological Review,* 1973, *38,* 481-493.

Kerckhoff, A. C., & Campbell, R. T. Black-white differences in the educational attainment process. *Sociology of Education,* 1977, *50,* 15-27.

Kohn, M. L. *Class and conformity: A study in values.* Homewood, Ill.: Dorsey Press, 1969.

Lin, N., & Yauger, D. The process of occupational status achievement: A preliminary cross-national comparison. *American Journal of Sociology,* 1975, *81,* 543-562.

Lortie, D. C. *School teacher: A sociological study.* Chicago: University of Chicago Press, 1975.

McClendon, M. J. The occupational status attainment process of males and females. *American Sociological Review,* 1976, *41,* 52-64.

Medsker, L., & Trent, J. *The influence of different types of public higher education institutions on college attendance from varying socioeconomic and ability levels.* Berkeley: Center for the Study of Higher Education, University of California, 1965.

Mills, C. W. *The power elite.* New York: Oxford University Press, 1956.

Mintz, B. The president's cabinet, 1897-1972: A contribution to the power structure debate. *Insurgent Sociologist,* 1975, *5,* 131-148.

Mitchell, J. C. (Ed.). *Social networks in urban situations: Analyses of personal relation-*

ships in Central African towns. Manchester: Manchester University Press, 1969.

Mosteller, F., & Moynihan, D. P. (Eds.). *On equality of educational opportunity.* New York: Vintage Books, 1972.

Organization for Economic Cooperation and Development. *Mathematical models for the educational sector: A survey.* Paris: OECD, 1973.

Perrucci, C. C., & Perrucci, R. Social origins, educational contexts, and career mobility. *American Sociological Review,* 1970, *35,* 451-462.

Perspectives on inequality: A reassessment of the effect of family and schooling in America. *Harvard Educational Review,* 1973, *43,* 37-164.

Pierson, G. W. *The education of American leaders: Comparative contributions of U.S. colleges and universities.* New York: Frederick A. Praeger, 1969.

Porter, J. N. Race, socialization, and mobility in educational and early occupational attainment. *American Sociological Review,* 1974, *39,* 303-316.

Portes, A., & Wilson, K. L. Black-white differences in educational attainment. *American Sociological Review,* 1976, *41,* 414-431.

Review symposium on *Inequality* by Christopher Jencks et al. *American Journal of Sociology,* 1973, *78,* 1523-1544.

Rist, R. C. Student social class and teacher expectations: The self-fulfilling prophecy in ghetto education. *Harvard Educational Review,* 1970, *40,* 411-451.

Rist, R. C. On understanding the process of schooling: The contributions of labeling theory. In J. Karabel & A. H. Halsey (Eds.), *Power and ideology in education.* New York: Oxford University Press, 1977.

Rosenbaum, J. E. The stratification of socialization processes. *American Sociological Review,* 1975, *40,* 48-54.

Rosenthal, R., & Jacobson, L. *Pygmalion in the classroom: Teacher expectations and pupils' intellectual development.* New York: Holt, Rinehart & Winston, 1968.

Schur, E. M. *Labeling deviant behavior: Its sociological implications.* New York: Harper & Row, 1971.

Sewell, W. H., Haller, A. O., & Ohlendorf, C. W. The educational and early occupational status attainment process: Replication and revision. *American Sociological Review,* 1970, *35,* 1014-1027.

Sewell, W. H., Haller, A. O., & Portes, A. The educational and early occupational attainment process. *American Sociological Review,* 1969, *34,* 82-92.

Sewell, W. H., & Hauser, R. M. *Education, occupation, and earnings: Achievement in the early career.* New York: Academic Press, 1975.

Sewell, W. H., Hauser, R. M., & Featherman, D. L. (Eds.). *Schooling and achievement in American society.* New York: Academic Press, 1976.

Shin, E. H. Earning inequality between black and white males by education, occupation and region. *Sociology and Social Research,* 1976, *60,* 161-172.

Siegel, P. M. On the cost of being a Negro. *Sociological Inquiry,* 1965, *35,* 41-57.

Solmon, L. C. The definition of college quality and its impact on earnings. *Occasional Papers of the National Bureau of Economic Research,* 1975, *2,* 537-587.

Solmon, L. C., & Wachtel, P. The effects on income of type of college attended. *Sociology of Education,* 1975, *48,* 75-90.

Spaeth, J. L. Occupational attainment among male college graduates. *American Journal of Sociology,* 1970, *75,* 632-644. ⋅

Spaeth, J. L. Characteristics of the work setting and the job as determinants of income. In W. H. Sewell, R. M. Hauser, and D. L. Featherman (Eds.), *Schooling and achievement in American society.* New York: Academic Press, 1976.

Stolzenberg, R. M. Education, occupation and wage differences between white and black men. *American Journal of Sociology,* 1975, *81,* 299-323. (a)

Stolzenberg, R. M. Occupations, labor markets, and the process of wage attainment. *American Sociological Review,* 1975, *40,* 645-665. (b)

Symposium Review: *Inequality,* Jencks et al. *Sociology of Education,* 1973, *46,* 427-470.

Taubman, P., & Wales, T. *Higher education and earnings: College as an investment and a screening device.* New York: McGraw-Hill, 1974.

Thurow, L. C. The occupational distribution of a return to education and experience for whites and negroes. In *The Proceedings of the Social Statistics Section of the American Statistical Association.* Washington, D.C.: American Statistical Association, 1967.

Thurow, L. C. Education and economy equality. *Public Interest,* 1972, *28,* 66-81.

Tinto, V. *College origins and attainment among high and middle status occupations.* Unpublished manuscript, Syracuse University, 1977.

Touraine, A. *The academic system in American society.* New York: McGraw-Hill, 1974.

Treiman, D. J., & Terrell, K. The process of status attainment in the United States and Great Britain. *American Journal of Sociology,* 1975, *81,* 563-583. (a)

Treiman, D. J., & Terrell K. Sex and the process of status attainment: A comparison of working men and women. *American Sociological Review,* 1975, *40,* 174-200. (b)

Trow, M. The democratization of higher education in America. *European Journal of Sociology,* 1962, *3,* 231-262.

Turner, R. H. Sponsored and contest mobility and the school system. *American Sociological Review,* 1960, *25,* 855-867.

Wachtel, P. The effect of school quality on achievement, attainment levels, and lifetime earnings. *Occasional Papers of the National Bureau of Economic Research,* 1975, *2,* 502-536.

Waller, W. *The sociology of teaching.* New York: John Wiley, 1967.

Weber, M. *Max Weber: The theory of social and economic organization.* (T. Parsons, Ed.) New York: Free Press, 1947.

Weiss, R. The effect of education on the earnings of blacks and whites. *American Economic Review,* 1970, *52,* 150-159.

White, H. C. *Chains of opportunity: System models of mobility in organizations.* Cambridge, Mass.: Harvard University Press, 1970.

White, H. C., Boorman, S. A., & Breiger, R. L. Social structure from multiple networks. I: Block models of roles and positions. *American Journal of Sociology,* 1976, *81,* 730-780.

Wright, E. O., & Perrone, L. Marxist class categories and income inequality. *American Sociological Review,* 1977, *42,* 32-55.

Young, M. F. D. (Ed.). *Knowledge and control: New directions for the sociology of education.* London: Collier-Macmillan, 1971.

Zuckerman, H. Stratification in American science. *Sociological Inquiry,* 1970, *40,* 235-257.

Zuckerman, H. *Scientific elite: Nobel laureates in the United States.* New York: Macmillan, 1977.

6

Impact of Policy Decisions on Schools

MARTIN BURLINGAME
University of Illinois at Urbana-Champaign

Questions about the impact of policy decisions on schools have been considered in part by political scientists, social psychologists, and evaluators. Political scientists have been interested particularly in the struggles to formulate policies (Grumm, 1975); social psychologists have dwelt on factors which have affected the implementation of programs (Fullan, 1972); and evaluators have sought ways to assay the direction and worth of any changes made (House, 1974). This background enriches the focus of the review in this chapter.

Since the end of World War II, concerned citizens, politicians, educators, federal officials and others have stated the need for developing, implementing, and then assessing various educational policies and attendant programs affecting life in the schools (Spring, 1976). The failure to foresee the consequences of geographic mobility and demographic changes for school enrollments, for example, provides ready evidence of the critical importance of planning in educational policy making. In the early 1970s, a literature also developed which examined the implementation of programs (Kritek, 1976). These studies have illuminated how educational organizations have responded to various efforts to change their goals, technologies, service personnel, or clients. Mechanisms believed to promote change, such as in-service training, new organizational arrangements, or new curricula, and factors expected to hinder fulfillment of these changes, such as old loyalties or unclear objectives, have been scrutinized. Since the mid-1960s, too, evaluations of specific educational programs based on larger policy considerations have become common. These activities have produced not only a bustling enterprise but also a vast, diffuse,

LAURENCE IANNACCONE, University of California, Santa Barbara, was the editorial consultant for this chapter.

uncodified, but excited literature. Evaluation has generally meant study of the achievements and values of programs, with particular emphasis on the success or failure of specific efforts to change the impacts of schools on some or all of their clients.

This review attempts to frame a larger interpretation of the impact of policy decisions on schools by reviewing the literature of the 1960s and 1970s. Our interpretation suggests that two fundamentally different frameworks predominated as ways of policy development and policy impact assessment (Allison, 1971). These views are labeled the rational–systems analysis approach and the negotiations-authority approach. They differ most in their conception of goals. The rational–systems analysis approach contends that goals are capable of clear, unequivocal statements and of being ordered in some ranking or priority fashion. The negotiations-authority approach contends that goals are ambiguous, equivocal, and intangible, and they are difficult if not impossible to order in some ranking or priority fashion (Cohen & March, 1974).

We suggest that during the 1960s the systems analysis approach dominated thinking about development and implementation of policy. By the early 1970s, however, a series of problems, most notably described in the research on implementation, was uncovered, and the systems analysis approach now is being replaced by the authority-negotiations frame. We begin by examining these frameworks in some detail. The second section of the review deals with two issues. The first is the role of the federal government in educational policy during the 1960s and 1970s. Acting through the executive, judicial, legislative, and administrative branches, the federal government was involved intimately in fostering educational change. A second issue was that stability was being sought in a number of characteristics of local school systems. The issues of stability and change, and of frequent tensions between national and local interests, dominate this section. The final section of the review pulls together the general argument made and then suggests some lines of future inquiry.

ALTERNATIVE EXPLANATIONS

At least two major frameworks can lend coherence to the question of the impact of policies on schools. These frameworks provide different ways of describing and analyzing the world of policy. The first is systems analysis, and the second involves a family of slightly different models with common elements, labeled in this review as the negotiations model and the professional authority models.

Systems Analysis

Certainly the best known device for examining the impact of policy on schools is the systems analysis approach. The systems analysis approach suggests that organizations such as schools receive inputs from their environment, convert them into some output, and receive feedback from their environment about success or failure.

Of the many systems analysis efforts in education, the works of James Coleman (Coleman, Campbell, Hobson, McPartland, Mood, Weinfeld, & York, 1966) and Christopher Jencks (Jencks, Smith, Acland, Bane, Cohen, Gentis, Heyns, & Michelson, 1972) have received the most attention. In *Equality of Educational Opportunity,* Coleman and his associates consciously adopted a model which sought to assess multiple factors as they influence school achievement. The use of multiple regression techniques allowed Coleman to manipulate the data in ways that assessed various sources which might contribute to schooling effects, and then to suggest possible remedies. Jencks and his associates used similar techniques to ascertain the effects of schooling on income distributions. The controversy surrounding both of these studies, including the quality of the data, the statistical manipulations, and the assumptions of the model, continues unabated. But Coleman and Jencks brought to the conscious attention of many interested persons a systems model of education, a model which intentionally links inputs, conversion process, outputs, and feedback mechanisms.

By the mid-1960s politicians, managers, and scholars were increasingly finding the systems analysis model appealing. Politicians found in it a way of linking the demands of their constituents to governmental programs. What constituents desired now could be joined with accountable and cost-conscious programs housed in responsible agencies. The oversight function of legislators would be lessened considerably because of the ease of understanding, tractability, and responsiveness of programs based on system models.

For managers, the model provided a rationalistic tool for linking costs and benefits. If selected outputs were not achieved, information could be generated about inputs or conversion processes which would allow their fine-tuning. The creation of feedback mechanisms provided data for necessary organizational corrections. The Defense Department, for example, adopted a Planning-Programming-Budgeting System (PPBS) which compared output to planned objectives. The system seemed to endow those in command with a synoptic view, a view which encouraged continuous readjustment to achieve planned goals and which promised to lessen the burden of reporting failures to legislators.

In a number of academic fields, the systems analysis framework captured the imagination of scholars. For example, in political science David Easton summarized over a decade of activity in *A Systems Analysis of Political Life* (1965). In organizational analysis Katz and Kahn (1966) found in open systems theory a more adequate and dynamic framework for examining complex organizations. The framework seemed a new paradigm, capable of illuminating disparate disciplinary arenas and offering hopes for interdisciplinary integration. Systems analysis became an integral part of a climate of opinion which affected politicians, administrators, and scholars in the 1960s.

The systems analysis model became intimately linked to federal education policies, programs, and expenditures. Policies and programs required active participation of multiple groups ("input"), careful retooling of schoolmen ("conversion process"), intensive measurement of student outcomes through testing ("output"), and systematic analysis of deficiencies or excesses by decision makers ("feedback"). Broad-aimed policies in education and in other social fields led to specific programs based on a systems analysis model. The model suggested that programmatic effects could be scrutinized, and in turn, either improved or dropped. One critical link in this rationalistic process was the development of feedback ("evaluation data") to both local sites and national planners. Such feedback made possible programmatic adjustments. An activist, "can do" mentality in government now had available a powerful tool for manipulating social institutions. The deficiencies which could be found in education, in places such as ghetto schools or in failures of teachers to use newer educational technologies, seemed capable of solution through systems analysis.

This discussion constitutes more of a characterization than a history of this era, but it does indicate the importance of systems analysis as an intellectual and pragmatic framework, the emphasis upon feedback as critical to change, and the importance of computer technology and regression statistical techniques to provide formulas for describing a manipulable system. This perspective and its tools offered policy makers the seeming luxury of understanding the impacts of various inputs on conversion processes and outputs, and systematically manipulating various parts of programs to achieve policy objectives.

These happy images of educational reform often failed to materialize. Systems analysis techniques and manipulations became goals sought by policy makers rather than descriptions of reality. What had seemed such a rational way to proceed, what looked so technologically feasible, what felt so democratically right and just, simply did not come to pass. It is important to review why this was so.

Problems of Systems Analysis. Three problems plague systems analysis as a way of examining the impact of policies on schools. First, policies created by legislative bodies are rarely clear or singular in purpose, or prove sweeping in overturning traditional modes of operation. Second, the conversion process in education is inconsistent. Third, feedback does not seem important to public monopolies in the ways systems analysis suggests.

If policies are viewed as the dependent variable of legislative processes, they are at best multipurposed. For example, Campbell et al. (Campbell, Cunningham, McPhee, & Nystrand, 1970) suggest that large changes in society are eventually filtered by legislative bodies into specific policies. These larger changes rarely strike all groups in society similarly. In this filtering process, then, those who support specific policies must seek the support of others who may seek other, differing policies. Often these demands appear in direct conflict with one another. Bargaining predominates, with conscious efforts made to include something for everyone. A single piece of legislation in the field of education, for example, seeks simultaneously to achieve gains on standardized test scores, to inculcate old or new patriotic virtues, to alter attitudes toward learning and schooling favorably, and to provide employment for well-educated, but currently unemployed, mothers. All of these concerns are wrapped into a single legislative package. In sum, most legislative policies are results of a process which literally ensures their multiple-purpose nature (Cohen, 1975).

This bargaining process also ensures that educational policies offer only "weak" treatments. The multiplicity of interests provides for not only opportunity for change but also conservation of older prerogatives. Bargained policies tamper with the margins of schools and their traditional interests. Teachers are retrained or given special new materials but positions are not eliminated. Schools are reorganized, but children stay in them and off the streets for the same number of hours. Computers assist in instructional tasks, but teachers, chalkboards, and books still overwhelmingly predominate. Policies are usually add-ons to the existing interests of the system. They are not aimed at overturning and creating anew; the treatments are not "strong." Hence, the study of policy impacts in education concerns policies that lack singularity and power.

Such weaknesses might be overcome, at least partially, if we had clear expectations about conversion processes in educational settings. In the systems analysis approach, conversion processes are modeled after technologies in industries. That is, conversion processes are situations in which there are scientific ("theoretical") expectations about what is supposed to occur, vigorous controls on the events occurring ("mechanistic"), and models of the expected impact of the conversion process ("outcomes"). Such mechanistic models of the conversion process are lacking in education (Averch, Carroll, Donaldson, Kiesling, & Pincus, 1972; Cohen, 1975; Reid, 1975). Systems analysts therefore could not be certain if the treatment had been implemented, if the normal set of conversion processes merely had occurred, or if outcomes were what had been expected because of changes in the conversion process.

Lacking robust models of a mechanistic process, system analysts were confounded when they "discovered" that conversion process variance was as great (or greater) within a single school as it was across a number of schools (Coleman et al., 1966). Instead of finding that a single school (teacher) uniformly impacted (processed) its student body (classroom), they now had to explain away a tremendous volume of extraneous within-school variance. Under the systems analysis model, no mechanistic process should produce such a variety of outcomes. Without robust mechanistic models of the conversion process, supporters or detractors of various programs could confront clients, educators, program administrators and legislators with ex post facto explanations—of what may have occurred because someone may have done such-and-so, perhaps.

Observers certainly did go and see what was happening. But, lacking the vigorous model of the conversion process required by systems analysis, their reports pictured different aspects of what they thought had happened. Instead of clear and precise goals linked to specific procedures, these observers often found ambiguous and conflicting goals and highly individualized processes which often had been uniquely tailored to specific clients. Such ambiguity in the conversion process did not permit the peaceful burial of alternative hypotheses about other than mechanistic conversion processes in education. Other models, such as those in the negotiations-authority framework, seemed better suited to description and explanation of the conversion process in education.

Another persistent problem involves disentangling weak and imprecise treatments from environmental influences. It seems clearly inadvisable to use methodological paradigms which suggest that observers should ignore the unintended consequences of shifting environmental factors on the point of policy impact. More acceptable, but much more difficult to use, seem to be methodologies that take societal changes into account. The influences of shifts in the prosperity of the nation, the mobility of populations, or expectations about child bearing and rearing, for example, are of significance to the formulation and impact of educational policies. Hence, program proponents must always expect detractors to claim that changing times offer better explanations for why a policy either achieved or failed to produce its expected outcome than the program treatments do (Timpane, Abramowitz, Bobrow, & Pascal, 1976).

The inconsistency of the conversion process also leads to problems concerning the measurement of outcomes. The multiplicity of purposes of policy and the weakness of most treatments portend that outputs will be incrementally different only after the policy has been implemented and its impact has occurred. Indicators of output may register changes on only a few dimensions, and to restructure the conversion process to these indicators alone may induce several pathologies (Ostrom, 1973). In education, these pathologies may include such things as "teaching only to a specific test." The inconsistent conversion processes thus create major problems about the implementation of treatments, control of alternative hypotheses, impact of environmental changes, and measurement of outcomes.

A final problem with the systems analysis framework is the critical role of feedback. Feedback is viewed as the way that organizational leaders and participants can detect needs for policy changes and then assess their impacts.

Effectiveness can be assessed, gaps between intended and actual results closed, and revisions of means and goals accomplished—*if* organizations would develop and monitor feedback mechanisms. In particular, schools and school districts have been chastised for maintaining records of neither graduates' successes and failures nor of the results of differing curricula on different types of students.

Some have challenged the importance of feedback to organizational operation and success. Rosenthal and Weiss (1966), for example, suggested that factors such as status and power influence the use of sources of feedback. Feedback from sources which are low in power and status may be perceived as irrelevant, while feedback from high status and power sources may be valued too highly. They further note that criticism rarely deflects the truly committed. In the same vein, Michael (1973) discussed "benefits of calculated ignorance" (p. 267), problems of information overload with subsequent withdrawal to familiar ways of acting, and a persistent tendency to use input rather than output measures by organizations and their subunits. Michael goes so far as to claim that many "organizations are structured to attenuate, diffuse, obscure, and otherwise reduce the impact of feedback, usually to the point of impotence" (p. 277). Yet they persist, particularly if they are public-supported monopolies.

In a rare empirical test of this line of reasoning, Grumm (1972) sought to assess the impact of feedback on state legislatures. Grumm used correlational methods to analyze state legislative policies over time. His findings suggest the importance of stability. This stability is gained from the level of the state's economy as the major determinant of solutions proposed by legislators to conflicting demands, the ability of state legislatures to survive in a great deal of tension, the importance of federal programs and grants aimed at social problems, and the mobility of interstate populations. These factors all induced stability in the functioning of state legislatures. On the other hand, the impact of "outputs on the environment are not fed back as information about increased or reduced tensions to the legislatures" (p. 285). For state legislatures, Grumm found feedback "inoperative."

The same phenomena seem to apply in the area of school financial referenda. If school districts are in a period of relative economic prosperity, if boards face only normal conflict about their financial requests, if slack resources are available from federal grants, and if the incoming population is in favor of education, referenda will pass (Piele & Hall, 1973). If referenda fail, the board rarely seeks systematic feedback on all items and instead cuts what it believes to be frills and threatens dire cuts to essential areas. The process becomes one of board-community negotiations, but rarely with systematic attempts to involve all segments of the community or to explore nonconventional options. The transactions occur, but they do not look like feedback as described by systems analysts.

These counterarguments and findings suggest that transactions between public organizations and their environments occur in ways that systems analysts would see as pathological. Some sources of feedback are unduly attended to and other possible information sources are ignored; some subunits are too attentive to their environs, while others ignore them.

Nearly all actors simplify and distort feedback to fit their conceptions of the situation. Some bureaucratic blunders thus seem linked systematically to the notion that where you stand depends on where you sit (Allison, 1971). Feedback of similar data serves different functions in several levels of the organization (Biderman, 1970). At the lowest level, the actual line units, feedback is viewed as "information" which may or may not be brought to bear on particularistic situations. At intermediate levels, in midmanagement operations, feedback is viewed as "intelligence" about the operations of the organization and its various subunits. At the highest organizational levels, in the policy-making chambers, feedback becomes a part of "policy knowledge" about what is happening. Finally, the feedback from one segment of society becomes part of the public domain. This feedback affects the conception of the social world held by publics ("enlightenment").

Many systems analysis models simplistically assume that the same set of statistics will be used in the same ways by various levels, organizational members, and general publics. That the "same" data could be perceived "differently," result in conflict, or produce very "different" behaviors over time seemed incomprehensible to systems analysts. This meant that systems analysis could not cope with problems related to the fact that various organizational participants would react in markedly different ways to the same data (Cyert & March, 1963).

In sum, the explanatory power of systems analysis for developing and examining the impact of policy decisions on schools is flawed in three ways. First, as independent variables, policies are usually multipurposed and weak. Second, the conversion process in the field of education is not mechanistic. Finally, feedback does not seem to play a critical role in the way public institutions operate.

The Negotiations Model

A second explanatory model (the first in the negotiations-authority framework) suggests that the impurity of professional authority may lead to negotiations between professionals and their clients. Freidson (1968) claims that professionals always face the problem of having clients who want something other than what the expert feels is appropriate. To ensure compliance, the professional seeks to deny clients access to alternative forms of service. The professional thus seeks a monopoly for his services by controlling all access to goods and services the client may need. Often this monopoly takes the form of institutionalization. The client is limited by institutionalization to either dealing with the professional or going without the service. The layman submits to the professional less because he values the professional's competence and more because the professional is the only alternative for the service he needs.

The institutionalization of service does not resolve the issue of authority. As Strauss et al. (Strauss, Schatzman, Ehrlich, Bucher, & Sabshin, 1971) found, institutionalization exacerbates tensions surrounding authority. In their study of a psychiatric hospital, they found that a negotiated, not dictated, order prevailed. The order was negotiated, first, because no one knew all the rules of professional practice at any one time. The complexity of the services offered by the hospital made it impossible for any single professional actor to know exactly what was anticipated or expected from himself and others in any particular case. When conflicts between professionals or professionals and clients developed, no single standard could be found. Conflicts were mutually resolved and agreements were made as professionals developed a solution to the immediate problems. These solutions became, in turn, rules which the participants followed but which others did not know existed because they were not present in this particular set of negotiations surrounding a particular conflict.

Second, negotiations occurred in the hospital because different professional groups defined the goals of the hospital differently. Methods of diagnosis and prescription, standards of humaneness of treatment, shared symbols or material rewards, and differing ambitions separated various strata of workers. The training of occupational groups such as nurses or doctors differed sharply on what was to be done. These differences meant that negotiations proceeded apace between and among these groups.

Third, each group offered differing routes of mobility. For those who saw or sought little professional mobility, rules and professional identities provided comfort and security. Others who valued professional mobility sought to use rules and identities to further themselves. The conflicts between these various ambitions are negotiated in ways that facilitate mutual cooperation as much as possible. Yet sources of conflict are close at hand (Turner, 1968).

Clients themselves also are involved in the negotiation process. They differ sharply on what they want done to them, how effective they see their treatment in opposition to professional opinion, and what they feel ought to be done with other patients. The array of differing rules, occupational specialists, and career lines presents multiple opportunities for negotiations for patients.

The range or limit of these negotiations is less than explicit. In general, institutionalized professionals seem to develop, from training and practice, general senses of justice, fair play, and humaneness. Clients also seem to develop senses of what is to happen and what is expected of all parties. Such agreements constitute what Summerfield (1971) labels *cuing*. In general, the cuing argument stresses the development of fundamental frames of congruency between public and institution. With such implicit understandings, psychiatric hospitals, schools, and state legislatures, for example, rarely are confronted by the need for negotiations to resolve conflicts or for elaborate and obvious feedback mechanisms. Administrators and governing boards of public institutions may seem to blithely ignore their publics. But these officials are in constant communication with their constituents and clients because they "represent subconsciously" the demands and solutions typical of the population. They "know" about schools, hospitals, and government because they have "common sense." Pressures for change are slow in developing and are often processed by the ruling bodies as they are sensed rather than explicitly petitioned.

In communities where the leaders and the led are in congruence, problems often are handled before they become part of agendas. Common understandings predominate. If sudden changes occur in the community, such as an influx of in-migrants with different demands, political struggles occur because cuing can no longer take place (Iannaccone & Lutz, 1970). A period of conflict develops, followed by a lengthy process of negotiation and the reestablishment of consensus, often along new dimensions. A new pattern of cues now exists.

In sum, this line of explanation suggests that schools are institutions which seek to impose professional authority on students and parents. Within these institutions, however, professionals negotiate among themselves, with their clients, and with the community at large over what is happening or what ought to happen. The authority of the professional is fragile, and continuous negotiation seeks to enhance control over an ever-changing scenario. Clients themselves become adept at bargaining. Change appears the order of the day, but stability exists because of general congruency in public and professional expectations. Cuing helps, limits, and perpetuates the educational institution.

Professional Authority Model

A third line of explanation suggests that ambiguity of goals permits some latitude of professional discretion and authority. Frank (1958-59) hypothesizes that conflict over the meaning of goals prevents subordinates' behavior from being directed by rules alone. Subordinates thus are able to treat issues individually, without restraint from former precise interpretations. Each subordinate becomes a policy maker, implementing selected aspects of goal statements. Such a process blurs the distinctions drawn between means and ends. Means can be elevated to ends by subordinates. Subordinates are responsive, in some measure, to the environment and to superiors. The environment and superiors are able to enhance control of subordinate behavior by enforcing sanctions and rewards in a selective, not predetermined, fashion. Nonetheless, the subordinates maintain possibilities of unilateral action, particularly if they use due process procedures to devise uniform ways in which sanctions and rewards are dispensed.

Warner and Havens (1968) link goal displacement to the intangibility of organizational goals. As goal displacement increases (as means become ends), the less are goals attained. Such attainment is impossible because intangible goals communicate intended states of affairs but lack the steps necessary to attain these desired states. Intangibility of goals does provide the advantages of incorporating diverse or competing subgoals, facilitating flexibility, permitting action without consensus, and promoting assumptions of effectiveness. The disadvantages of goal displacement are that people may expect intangible goals to be accomplished, frustration and anxiety are ever present, and the assumption of effectiveness prevents evaluation.

Cohen, March, and Olsen (1972) propose that organizations lacking clear, consistent goals could use a "garbage can" model of organizational choice. The model posits a stream of choices, a stream of problems, a rate of flow of solutions, and a stream of energy from participants. Choices, problems, flow of solutions, and energy seem to get unceremoniously dumped and mixed together. Using a computer simulation model, the authors varied the time patterns of the arrivals of problems, choices, solutions, and decision makers under different allocations of energy and different linkage patterns. They found that in organizations characterized by unclear goals, much decision making is either by flight or oversight; the system is sensitive to the load of problems, choices, and solutions; important problems are more likely to be solved than unimportant ones; and unimportant choices resolve problems.

One way to summarize this line of reasoning is that the diffuseness of goals permits individuals wide ranges of latitude in their actions. In such situations, individuals are able to find in their work those rewards they personally desire and can avoid unpleasant experiences. As members of organizations, nonetheless, individuals are accountable to their superiors and clients. Generally, accountability is not pursued vigorously, and individuals are permitted latitude as the organization avoids making decisions (flight and oversight). When decisions are made, consensus dominates where important decisions are made, but unimportant decisions are used by participants to act "as if" crucial problems had been resolved. Participants determine much of their fate as organizational members.

Many of these characteristics concerning goals are found in public schools. As organizations, schools seem characterized by conflicts over ambiguous and often intangible goals. Teachers appear governed as much by ends they determine themselves as by those determined by the administrator, governing boards, or clients (Firestone, 1977). Means often are visibly elevated to ends. Discussions become so interwined with multiple problems and solutions that decisions seem to be avoided. Thus schools appear to offer those conditions that should support some professional authority and discretion.

The line of explanation involving the ambiguity of goals suggests that less negotiation and more unilateral displays of individual authority are available, if the ecology of the organization permits autonomy. Autonomy seems to require a flow of work that necessitates neither close collaboration nor cooperation. The individual actors may be heavily restrained in certain areas, but in many ways these individual actors have latitude in making judgments about their interpretation of which goals will be implemented, which means will become ends, and which goals become even more hazy and intangible. To a large extent these individuals act and determine what will or will not come to pass in their domains. Some of these judgments are predetermined by professional training and competence, some are restrained by environmental pressures, and some are made on the basis of tradition. But many judgments are made by the individual and reflect his sense of taste and professional wisdom (Elboim-Dror, 1970, 1971, 1972).

In contrast to the negotiations model, the authority model clearly preserves an eminent domain of professional autonomy. The argument for negotiations suggests that various professionals within the organization are involved in shifting but mutually constraining negotiations and sets of work rules. The likelihood of unilateral action, either positive or negative, is reduced substantially by the constant process of mutual accommodation. Each participant becomes domesticated, and change is incremental (Hirschman & Lindblom, 1962). In the constant give-and-take of organizational politics, the negotiation of means displaces energy that might have been used to achieve more distant goals (Allison, 1971).

These three lines of reasoning also produce sharply different metaphors of leadership (Cohen & March, 1974). The systems analysis approach views leaders as experts of calculation. They must derive and calibrate priorities, measure and contrast conversion processes, and quantify and weigh outputs. Leadership depends upon various supremely rational modes of descriptive quantification and comparative evaluation. The second model of explanation sees a leader as a master negotiator, always seeking equity, if not an edge, with other negotiators. What develops is a continuous game of bargain hunting, making, and remaking. Heavy emphasis is placed on processes of deliberative reasoning, tactics, and incrementalism. Yesterday's bargain is replaced today by a newer, richer web of rules. The third model of explanation sees the leader as a judicial figure, imposing authority in a manner that is often consistent with principles of self-determination for subordinates. Authority is vested in positions, with clear areas in which that power is supreme, but other authorities carry other zones of authority. Between these secure fortresses are twilight regions ripe with potential for conflict. All parties are wary of trespassing and trespassers. Once one is trespassed upon, however, conflict seems inevitable, and it usually is confined consciously to smaller objectives. If the conflict persists and if it seems clear that all sides are being severely damaged, then they may turn to a third party to mediate the dispute (Bredo & Bredo, 1975).

Summary

This section has explored three different models of explanation for the impact of policy decisions on schools. The first, systems analysis, suggests that policy should be studied as it influences input, conversion, output and feedback processes. Three major problems with this approach were discussed. The second, the negotiations model, suggests that policy should be studied as it influences a negotiating process among professionals, clients, and publics. The background for this process may include a coherent system of assumptions about the limits of what may or may not be negotiated. The third, the authority model, suggests that policy should be studied as it influences common or unique domains of professional autonomy. While there are limits to authority, the ambiguity of organizational goals permits the latitude of professional discretion and authority to vary.

STABILITY AND CHANGE

This section of the chapter is devoted to two aspects of stability and change in school policy. It suggests that the federal government has dealt with education as a system, while localities see it as a negotiated, but generally professional service. It also shows how the factors of stability and change in schools provide a basis for analysis of the impact of policy decision.

The Federal Presence

With the end of World War II, the federal government began to play an increasing role in educational policy (Spring, 1976). Since 1945 there have been elements of national policy making in education: in Congress, where for some time acts were passed with increasing frequency and larger fundings; in the Supreme Court, whose docket had long been free of education cases but which became besieged with them; and in the growing federal administrative bureaucracy, where the coterie of agencies, officials, and regulations increased geometrically. Tied closely to the federal presence have been the efforts of several foundations and private educational corporations (Campbell & Bunnell, 1963).

As might be expected with such a large number of actors, such efforts have often been less than military in precision. In fact, they often have seemed disparate and sometimes downright contradictory. But no observer can ignore efforts such as manpower training programs, the developing interest and funds made available in federal and private agencies for curriculum improvement, the 1954 desegregation decision attacking the equality of racially separate school systems, and the National Defense Education Act with its press for excellence in such fields as science, mathematics, and foreign languages. The Civil Rights Act of 1964, the many titles of the Elementary and Secondary Education Act of 1965, and literally hosts of other federal initiatives, including the creation in 1972 of the National Institute of Education as an agency charged by legislation with improving the quality of schooling in America, have provided other evidence of the federal presence.

In striking fashion, this effort apes an earlier era of reform in American education. The period from 1900 to about 1930, labeled by Callahan (1962) the cult of efficiency, was dominated by a concern for modernizing American education. This modernizing tendency emulates the American business community. Modern education was based on the training of professional managers who would in turn plan their educational systems in such a way that workers (teachers) would efficiently increase their production (students/outcomes). This factory model of schooling claimed to be the offspring of Frederick Taylor's principles of scientific management for businesses and industries such as steel mills. Management devices such as school surveys, platoon schools, and elaborate pupil accountings, including ratios of cost for class size or analysis of supply costs, were in vogue. The 1930s and 1940s witnessed less attention to both these elaborate devices and their assumptions about needed rationality and efficiency in education. But in the late 1950s and in the 1960s and 1970s a new cult of efficiency, now cloaked as systems analysis, reemerged (James, 1969).

While definitive histories of this period do not exist, it seems reasonable that the Cold War played a part in the emergence of interest in education as a national resource (Campbell & Bunnell, 1963). Certainly the events surrounding the Russian Sputnik provide prima facie evidence for such a case. Of importance for this review is the emergence at this time of managerial technologies which could be subsumed under the label of systems analysis. These techniques were interpreted as ways to implement educational policies intended to strengthen vital national resources (Spring, 1976). These efforts began with a view of education as an untidy system with inadequate outputs. By judicious applications of federal funds and initiatives, it was thought the input and conversion processes of education could be reshaped, and then educational outputs would serve national needs better. The development of feedback mechanisms would allow monitoring and maintenance of this educational system.

It fell to a variety of social scientists to develop ways of monitoring social indicators to ascertain trends, to develop specific tools for the evaluation of governmental policies and programs, and to link federal costs precisely to federal benefits (Rossi, 1972). These efforts produced suggestive new terms such as *investment in human capital, teacher-proof materials,* and *dissemination of best practices,* as well as efforts to learn from and model other federal programs such as agriculture or defense. New creations, such as the R & D labs and centers, and old partners, such as state departments of education, received generous federal funding and guidance.

One area of federal presence was sponsorship of a number of ideas. These ideas aimed at assisting managers to run their schools more efficiently and thus make schools serve their clients better. A system which was peddled aggressively was the Planning-Programming-Budgeting-Evaluation System (PPBES) mentioned above. Linked closely to the Department of Defense, the system seemed to offer a powerful range of diagnostic and prescriptive tools to managers. In a study of two school districts, however, van Geel (1973) found little use was being made of PPBES. These districts felt they were using the system, but van Geel discovered that neither one had installed or used it because the conditions for its use could not be met. There were no adequate theories to build cause-effect models, no agreed-upon and unambiguous goals, no time to move through the elaborate procedures, and no managerial analytical know-how or motivation to make the system work. Instead, the district managers operated in a clearly political field of forces, acting as if more resources were always better for students. They dealt only in input rather than output terms and displayed a profound distrust for analytically produced information. Van Geel contended that these school districts and their managers believed themselves responsible for providing equity of input, but they assumed little or no responsibility for outcomes such as increased student reading skills. Kirst (1975) chronicles the PPBES disaster in California.

A second technological innovation was the Management Information System (MIS), an elaborate, often computer-based, feedback mechanism. In a California study, Hanson and Ortiz (1975) examined the use by a school district of MIS to promote educational change. Many of their findings reaffirm van Geel's analysis of the use of PPBES by district managers. What impressed these authors was the lack of sensitivity by educational managers to both information and public demands. Because the school district was not compelled to struggle for existence, being in effect a domesticated creature guaranteed by the state, no good reasons appeared for managers to seek information about the school's fit with its environment. The feedback system was inoperative. Thus the processes of the school directly, and its products indirectly, were not changed by MIS information to meet shifting societal needs.

At the level of technical aid, the federal presence in assisting managers through technological feedback systems such as PPBES and MIS has been less than a smashing success. School managers have deflected federally sponsored systems which sought to aid them in dealing rationally with their constituents and environment. They seem to prefer an intuitive and highly politicized wisdom which permits them to stress equality of inputs within limited ranges and to avoid accountability for outputs. All in all, they seek cues from their localities.

The direct infusion of federal dollars to attend to certain federally derived priorities was a direct attempt to influence schooling. The early NDEA funds and the later, greater ESEA dollars all were targeted on specific programs or clients. Efforts to trace the use of federal dollars as aid to education have been summarized with insight by Porter, Warner, and Porter (1973). Arguing that schools, like other organizations, seek to satisfy their own priorities and actively mobilize funds for these tasks, they found many federal dollars were being applied to local needs. The extensive and often cumbersome legislative and agency controls had only a small impact on how dollars were expended.

Put simply, administrators seek to create a pot of money from various sources, to expend these dollars on the priorities of the district as they perceive them, and then to prepare reports which appease funding agencies but which misrepresent expenditure patterns. In this multipocketed budgeting system the varying strictures on income sources—such as local tax sources, state aid formulas, state title programs, and NDEA and ESEA titles—force administrators to expend the funds with the greatest restrictions first. Those with lesser restrictions become part of a general pool. Overall, budget categories and expenditure guidelines are so imprecise that dollars gravitate toward local priorities, not those intended by state or federal legislation and agencies.

District managers also consciously solicit funds that are at the margins of school operations. Such funds neither upset fundamental agreements already struck nor require managers to negotiate new understandings. These marginal funds become free-floating resources to be applied to local needs, regardless of their source or the limitations supposedly attached to them. Those districts that seek to capture additional funding develop significantly different patterns of relations with professional associations and state and federal agencies (Berke & Kirst, 1972; Murphy, 1971; Pressman & Wildavsky, 1973, chap. 5 and 6).

Perhaps the high point in much of this federal activity was the Alum Rock voucher experiment. The plan introduced the market mechanism as a tool for making schools responsive to diverse and potentially ignored client wants. It depended upon extensive federal dollars and employed elaborate feedback mechanisms. A preliminary review presents a generally gloomy picture of the voucher demonstration (Levinson, 1976). This review of three years of implementation stresses the difficulties of producing even incremental changes in the school system. Coupled tightly to declines in funds were increased centralization and drastic loss of consumer choice. The result seemed to have been less a shift to consumer control and more a way of letting some teachers and principals gain advantages, such as more small-group teaching and a more participatory atmosphere in certain schools. Because the belief in consumer sovereignty was held and sponsored only by district outsiders, their influence waned when dollar amounts decreased, and then district educators reasserted their belief in schools as public monopolies. All in all, the system did change, and in ways it now offers more alternatives for students (and for educators), but the consumer and the market were never allowed to reign supreme.

This line of studies suggests a contradiction between the limited power of the federal dollar and its intent to deflect local priorities. Derthick (1972) concluded that federal government programs that fail to change local behaviors do so because of their limited knowledge and control of events, as well as their idealistic ends. Unless federal programs are based on extensive knowledge of local politics and incentives and can supply enough incentives and direct them to local power figures, federal programs will flounder. In many government programs, time, energy and other resources are not available for such intensive and costly articulation. Federal agents and their universalistic programs usually possess limited knowledge, resources, and discretion in applying aid to localities. Federal initiatives usually are idealistic and progressive, while local preferences often are particular and parochial. Unless the resources necessary for articulation are available, lofty federal program intent will flounder, and federal aims will be turned to local ends. What results from this lack of know-how and failure to meet local concerns is a federal government unfettered from the gritty problems of local conflict and free to espouse bold and imaginative new ideals. Federal officials thus become enamored of a "demonstration strategy" approach, a tactic which sees inspiration, not perspiration, as the key to changing localities.

These processes can be viewed as instances of the politics of scarcity (Weiner, 1962; Wilson, 1967). Wilson claims that in political systems (such as the local school district) with scarce resources, law is repressive rather than restitutive; illegality is an act of disloyalty rather than an act of breaking an abstract rule. Law and custom become complementary and hard to distinguish from each other. Conflict is met by redistributing existing resources or by acts of suppression. Scarcity is associated with centralizing tendencies. This centralized scarcity means that few resources are "free," and rarely will consent for localized innovation be granted.

If the bulk of school districts operate on what they believe to be scarce resources, it should be expected that outside resources would be marshalled and distributed by some centralized decision center (superintendent, central office, or school board). Resources would be dispersed to meet locally perceived needs and to those who were loyal to local priorities. If conflict arose among subunits (such as attendance area schools), resources would be distributed in a manner which halted this conflict, regardless of federal aspirations. If local subunits sought more funds to meet more completely their conception of these federal programs, additional funds would come if and only if additional federal resources became available. Otherwise, these subunit demands would be quashed. In the great bulk of school districts, then, federal dollars would be turned to the satisfaction of local priorities through local mechanisms (Gittell & Hollander, 1968).

In sum, the awesome federal presence in education in the past 25 years or so has induced some change in local American school districts, but much less than anticipated. Often the particularistic interests and political mechanisms of these districts have diverted federal dollars away from idealistic federal intents to locally perceived needs and to workers in the system who are loyal to these perceptions. Federally designed or fostered management systems have been rejected by local districts as not only cumbersome but also as unable to produce the kind of information necessary to meet local political demands. In districts whose leaders saw them as financially poor, the politics of scarcity predominated. Local loyalties overcame federal intentions. In the face of these problems, federal agencies retreated to a demonstration strategy, hoping that some of the bread they cast on the waters would return. In only a few instances did federal programs in education take into account local needs, power brokers, or loyalties. In place of the rapid changes anticipated from the federal presence in education or promised by the systems analysis approach, stability seems to have dominated local school districts.

Stability and Change in Local Schools

The resistance of local school districts to federal efforts suggests a stability which may thwart most, if not all, policy decisions seeking to change schools. This section examines the relations between schools and communities, the continuities in schools, and general findings about the changing of schools. These topics suggest reasons for the stability of schools.

The community provides the contextual field and political climate in which local school districts operate. This is the major source of all inputs to the school. The locality provides clients, most practitioners, resources, and expectations for the operation of the system. The community also is the major recipient of the school's conversion and output processes (Burnett, 1969). The school is linked horizontally to its community. Whatever the inputs to the school from other sources such as state, federal, or professional agencies, these vertical influences are mediated by the local context.

Litt (1963), for instance, demonstrated that although the textbooks used in civic education classes in three communities did not differ in references to the democratic creed, the books did differ in their views of political participation, politics as process, and the functions of political systems. These differences about politics related systematically to social and economic characteristics of these three communities. In the middle-class community, texts emphasized political process, group process, and conflict resolution. In the two working-class communities, texts deemphasized these aspects of political life.

As noted earlier, Summerfield (1971) would describe this fit between the curriculum and the community as "cuing." Cuing suggests a mutual accommodation between the server and the served. Two aspects of this accommodation were found in Peshkin (1977) and Wiggins (1970).

In an anthropological study of the relationship between a village and its small high school, Peshkin recorded the process of selecting a new superintendent. A fascinating account of the final selection meeting notes why the farmer-dominated school board picked candidate Reynolds:

> Both Reynolds and Rogers said they have no hours. They work by the job. Reynolds worked his way through college.
> He (Reynolds) was on the ground floor as far as salary goes.
> And he's country. . . . (p. 188)

The deciding factors form a constellation. The new superintendent embodies not only hard work and frugality, but also an empathetic sense of the community, a sense based upon his background.

In a study of urban districts, Wiggins found that the replacement of principals in urban schools had little or no effect on teachers' perceptions of the school's climate. Instead of becoming more or less authoritarian, schools stayed pretty much the same. Wiggins argues that principals may be interchangeable parts to the extent that they have been socialized by the district, first as teachers, then as principals, "to behave in a rational, predictable, and uniform manner" (p. 176). Wiggins believes research should use as its focus the district's socialization patterns, rather than individual principals.

These studies, and the study by Litt, suggest that both the local community and the school system become sources of cues. Two reinforcing processes occur: first, the community seeks leaders and workers who fit that community, those who are "country" or "city." Second, the school system communicates to employees expectations which maintain these community linkages with minimum disruption. When disagreements do occur, either third-party negotiations or major political conflict of a rancorous nature could be expected. Some studies illustrate these possibilities.

Bredo and Bredo (1975) found that the introduction of two innovations (course choice and modified homeroom) greatly altered patterns of leadership in a junior high school. The principal found that as the innovations failed to fulfill the expectations of the faculty, the collective sense of injustice of faculty members increased. The faculty felt that resolution of this growing conflict involved either more faculty participation, or more directed leadership by the principal, or, sometimes, both of these at the same time. Resolution was reached finally by a third-party evaluation, the results of which were used by both principal and staff to rid themselves of these two innovative changes (Deal, 1975; Fullan, 1972).

Much conflict can be avoided if school and community maintain persistent biases in favor of school personnel and changes in schools which fit the community. Yet as communities change, whether by population shifts, changes in school personnel, or local interest in nationalistic prescriptions about education or other lifestyle matters, political conflicts do develop. Iannaccone and Lutz (1970) have generated a theory stressing that community change leads to changes in the composition of school boards. In turn, these new board members replace the old superintendent and seek a new, outside superintendent embodying their conceptions of education. Some studies suggest that such a process is rancorous, and that newcomers are not always successful.

Steinberg (1972) traced the conflict in a single community between school officials and a community elite. This elite sought the implementaton of what it saw as a modern curriculum. Although the nonelite sections of the community did not become involved in the struggle, school officials resisted the efforts of the elite group. School leaders had definite conceptions of the role of mothers and of the attitudes toward schools that the home should foster in children. These conflicts could be understood as part of a religious factionalism which had a long history in the community. The elites differed from the nonelites and school officials on variables such as length of residency, religious and social background, and views concerning professional autonomy and authority.

In a study of educational change in an economically depressed community, Parelius (1969) found reformers eventually lost. The village old-timers sought to protect vested interest in village schools, while the newcomers sought efficient, politically clean schools. To the newcomers, the schools were part of a corrupt patronage system. Much of the conflict centered on where the power to control the educational system would rest. The reforming newcomers wished control to be in the hands of a professional superintendent, while old-timers sought to maintain their control of the schools. The role of the school district as the largest employer in the village, and by far the richest resource, became critical as the rural, traditional, local, conservative, and patronage-supported villagers successfully resisted the reform efforts of the urban, modern, cosmopolitan, and liberal newcomers.

The fit between school and community involves constant processes of negotiation. There are perennial threats to the balance established in the cuing process. Outsiders in the community are resisted, old cleavages persist, and mechanisms are available which hinder efforts to change. But if newcomers are able to capture the means of political control, shifts do begin occurring as new cues are transmitted.

The life in schools, nonetheless, provides continuities which may well resist efforts at change. The commonplaces of the school provide a sense of stability.

In a longitudinal study of the Gary, Indiana, schools, McKinney and Westbury (1975) found stability enhanced by financing, school plants, and texts. In order for the Gary schools to make curriculum changes, they were forced to marshal new resources. Older funds were exhausted completely in the maintenance of ongoing district activities. These activities were the commonalities of the schools—activities which seemed to be replicated from one school to another. Teachers and students generally met in rooms with desks, chalkboards, and textbooks. At certain times either the subjects of discussion, lecture, or seatwork changed or teachers changed.

Additional funding was necessary to alter these replicative patterns. The luxury of more dollars provided ways to retrain teachers, replace texts, alter building patterns and facilities, and generally to add to these necessary functions some new activities. To this end, external citizen groups became important not only for voicing complaints about what schools were or were not doing but also because they were vehicles for generating new, additional funds. As the district sought these additional dollars, the researchers found that underestimations of costs could be even more fatal to innovations than overestimations of their impact on children. Unless monies existed to alter buildings or change texts, innovations failed.

Texts are important for at least two reasons. They are the chief tool for presenting conventional understandings. As a baseline, Shaver (1965) found that texts in both American government and history failed to discuss significant value conflicts, provided few guidelines for resolving value disputes, and offered no conceptual frameworks students could apply to problems. History texts failed to discuss the methods of historians or the various interpretative schools of historians which see events such as the Civil War in different ways. What Shaver found was a hodgepodge of topics, lacking systematic treatment of procedures for resolving either factual or value conflicts. The plural and contradictory nature of some American values was not displayed to students, nor were mechanisms of adjudication presented.

Texts also diffuse new learnings. Voege (1975) traced the diffusion of Keynesian macroeconomic ideas in American high school texts. In general, he found that while these ideas were influencing governmental actions from the 1930s on, with rare exceptions macroeconomic ideas were almost totally absent from texts. It would have been possible, for example, for an individual to have been a high school senior in 1945 and a teacher of high school seniors in 1967 and to have used various editions of Dodd's *Applied Economics* both as student and teacher. In that 22-year time span, the amount of Keynesian macroeconomics in that text increased from 8 to 12 percent. Topics of Keynesian interest, such as national growth or national fiscal policy, were not discussed in any edition of Dodd's work. Voege also points out that as texts change, they displace or discontinue certain ideas. In the Dodd example, 4 percent of the older text was discontinued. While Voege studies only the adopting of new ideas, he urges future analysis of discontinuance of textbook content.

The physical arrangement of schools also has an impact on what happens in schools. Lortie (1975) believes that the physical facilities of schools prevent communication among teachers. The "egg-crate ecology" of school buildings traps teachers for long periods with only their students. The conventional design of rooms on a corridor hinders linkages among teachers. They must use time other than their "work" time to talk to, observe, and learn from other teachers. Teachers work in isolation from their peers. They are denied opportunities to interact freely with other teachers and to compare themselves and their work with co-workers.

Acting as a participant-observer in a high school, Cusick (1972) observed some ways students overcame classroom-created problems of isolation. Student activities and groups provided opportunities for students to act freely with and to differentiate themselves from other students. The consequences of these student group activities often were at cross-purposes to intended schooling outcomes. Students and teachers shared classrooms but had little interaction. Students did not have to become involved in formal class activities, student learning experiences were fragmented by different classes and never integrated holistically, and students learned how to "do well" (graduate with acceptable grades) by providing only the compliance demanded in individual classroom situations. If the activities of student groups upset teachers, teachers instituted rules intended to deny them the freedom and differentiation offered by group activities. In turn, this increased pressure heightened the social importance of student groups.

These transactions among teachers and pupils are handled often by conventional coin—grades. The ritual of grading has become the relevant solution to a larger cultural problem of how to distribute rewards both in society and in schools (Hiner, 1973). Grades become the currency by which students are paid for their activities. The acts of assessment and payment by school personnel in turn reflect fundamental distribution patterns that can exist in our society. These patterns range from absolute equality regardless of effort, through some admixture of equality and achievement, to complete achievement. Blanket A's, a mix of achieving and trying, and achieved scores are solutions to school and societal distribution problems. The application of these systems of distribution nonetheless varies from school to school and from teacher to teacher. Students are well aware of these discrepancies.

Hence, various series of commonplaces provide stability in schools. Financing, texts, and buildings provide the context for transactions among teachers and students. Increasing abundance makes possible, but does not guarantee, change. The politics of abundance (Wilson, 1967) means that new ideas need not be justified in the short run or related closely to pressing organizational goals. The costs of "messing around" by using resources to plan for a new and better tomorrow are ignored. An excess of resources makes possible wide deviations from standard operating procedures, reduction of conflict, because everybody can be "bought off"; and choice by decentralized units, which may contradict centralized decision makers. These conditions of abundance suggest that necessity may not be the mother of invention, but austerity is the destroyer of change. Strapped by resource scarcity, school systems are prone to adopt a politics of scarcity which emphasizes replication of old and understood ways of operating because their costs are known and their practice displays loyalty to a system and its economy of priorities (House, 1974).

These conventional ways of doing things and their normal physical geography segregate teachers from peers and students. While students are able to develop groups which circumvent some intentions of schools, teachers appear trapped in their work situation (Dreeben, 1973). The sense that teachers have of their effect on future society is often displayed in their philosophy about grading. But grades are coins of two realms—gold for teachers, dross for many students. A conventional, well-understood game develops in which students succeed to the extent that they are passive. Changing the game requires more than minor tinkerings with marginal considerations or incremental funding increases.

These considerations of the relation between school and communities and the commonplaces of schools provide one way of understanding the findings of the literature about implementation of policy decisions.

Using different questions, methodologies, subjects, innovations, and sites, a number of studies have produced a general sense of implementation questions and answers (Fullan & Pomfret, 1975; Gross, Giacquinta, & Bernstein, 1971; House, 1974; Pressman and Wildavsky, 1973). In general, these investigators have usually asked questions such as: Who provided the impetus for change? (Answer: Outsiders.) What are the characteristics of the guidelines for change provided by initiators? (Answer: Vague, equivocal, and emphasizing ease and immediacy of change.) How adequate are administrative plans for supporting and integrating the change of older routines? (Answer: Plans are nonexistent.) How precisely are new behaviors explained and illustrated before participants decide to enter the new program? (Answer: New behaviors are either not presented or are presented in a misleading fashion as easily learned and acquired, or no information is available to anyone.) How much does the "new" replace the "old" way of doing things? (Answer: Because the new is vague, and often both conflict-producing and time-consuming, the "new" is soon replaced by the "old.")

Berkson (1974) has specified that the problems of implementing a policy can be studied using four major questions. They are: (1) Do people comply? (2) Does the policy make a difference? (3) Are there any side effects? (4) Is the problem solved? Berkson's questions depend on assumptions that we are able to study policies over long periods of time, specify treatments precisely, and control for marked environmental changes. In general the cited literature on educational innovation would illustrate that most innovations are not studied over long periods of time, as treatments they are weak and unspecified, and changes in the environment are neither statistically controlled in analysis nor accounted for in assessing the effectiveness or failure of the innovation (Salisbury, 1968).

In sum, the commonplaces of schooling—texts, teachers, buildings, students, grades—provide the context for considering the impact of policy decisions on schools. The larger setting is provided by a politics of scarcity involving schools and their communities. The literature dealing with implementation of innovations suggests that this context generally overwhelms the innovation, while the literature on school-community relations suggests the community shapes the outlines of what schools can do.

POLICY IMPACT ON SCHOOLS

In this section, the explanatory models are used to assess some questions of the impact of policy decisions on schools. We also raise issues about needs for future research.

Policy and the Explanatory Models

Most would agree that the furious pace of the 1960s is gone, and few mourn its passing. The rush to rectify errors in the system of American education with new programs left most breathless. All were intent upon helping, even if the helpers might be inept and those to be helped might be unwilling. Much of this frenetic search for solutions, expenditure of time, energy, and money, and expressions of goodwill came to be called policy. Such a labeling insinuates less a scrambling about for possibilities and more a dispassionate, rational attempt to bend societal problems to the intent of some collective will. In the retelling, the helter-skelter becomes calm, cool, and collected. When policy is recounted it becomes the offspring of reason and data, not the bastard of inspiration and hunch.

Systems analysis as a model for reason came to predominate in the mentality of those who formed policy in the 1960s. The seemingly rational precision of input, conversion process, and output, and the inestimable value of feedback, seemed suited to the purposes of the reformers. Systems analysis suggested that problems were "out there" in a system dominated by its environment, highly stable in its operation, and staffed by reactive professionals (Anton, 1975). Problems could be solved by removing these three obstacles. Removal meant finding which factors in the environment dominated the system ("what inputs counted"), comprehending the regularities of the system ("what conversion processes were manipulable or nonmanipulable"), and alerting administrators to changes that needed to be made ("analysis of output from feedback information"). Thinking about changing education came to be dominated by a model of analysis and explanation which ignored three factors: the complexities of the environment, the instabilities found in many situations, and the capacities of human beings to generate their own sets of goals.

For those who sought to link the school and its environment in the simplistic terms of the systems model, life was hard. The efforts to develop citizen advisory councils, parent advisory groups, or interested applicants for traditional positions, such as school board members, moved forward slowly and painfully. Rather than opening the lines of communication between a simple environment and an even simpler school system, the multiple and complex array of interests and loyalties in schools collided with a tangled web of supports and demands found in the environment. Two highly intricate, often inarticulate, constantly changing, and disaggregated systems had to come to grips with a vexing series of questions. Issues such as the following had to be resolved: Why should professionals and publics share control? When should control be shared, and what should be expected? Who should be involved? How are members selected? What should they do? What are their responsibilities for communication? How should the group be organized? How can professionals assist? (Mann, 1976.) Substantive and procedural issues thrived. In some sense, the complexity of the environment, the schools, and their interactions overwhelmed the systems analysis framework.

Situations seemed much less stable than anticipated. There were commonplaces in schools, communities, and situations. But there were also persistent instabilities which confounded these commonalities. The shifts of population from geographic areas and from cities to suburbs, the rapid changes in birth rates, the changes in economic and political relations, and the rapid transitions from peace to war and back to peace economies—all parodied the stabilities suggested by the systems analysis approach. Time seemed an inherent enemy of the input-output model.

The intentions of the actors as they generated their own sets of individualistic goals further frustrated systems analysis. For example, the uses of evidence became an interesting problem. To the systems model, evidence was to be accumulated as a way of determining what was happening. Evidence served as a baseline, much as in scientific research. Problems of accumulating evidence for systems analysts involved issues such as weakened inference because of measuring difficulties, size of sample, relations found by inferential statistics, and ways of creating propositional inventories (Glass, 1976; Light & Smith, 1971; Piele & Hall, 1973). This function of evidence, however, seemed to play only a limited role in educational policy analysis.

In large measure, educational policies envisioned larger social dreams of a better world based on justice, equality, and truth. What was dreamed often contradicted current evidence. Various groups, convinced of their righteousness, regardless of current data, sought to reshape the world in ways that would permit later evidence to reflect accurately the implementation of their sense of future justice. Under these conditions, the visions of actors, their expectations and aspirations, their happy accidents and self-fulfilling prophecies, are all significant elements. Today's evidence does not illuminate tomorrow's vision. The larger issues involved failures not of the accumulation of evidence but of prescriptive insight. The complexity of the world, the instabilities of situations, and the intentions of the actors all were denigrated by the systems analysis approach.

From the hindsight of the mid–1970s, the limitations of a systems analysis approach seem evident. Yet as an image for policy making it remains potent. Much of this potency rests on the inherent simplifications which the image fosters. Systems analysis assumes that simple questions can be asked about simple processes and that simple evidence results. Once analyzed and reconstituted, the resulting mechanism should operate flawlessly. If flaws do develop, the analytical tools are available for diagnosis. Figures such as average daily membership, pupil/teacher ratio, volumes in the library, and beakers in the lab became critical markers. That these statistics are institutionally generated to serve institutional purposes was overlooked frequently (Cicourel, 1975). Systems analysis measured what schools frequently measured themselves and overlooked the harder tasks of measurement that schools conventionally ignored. The already simplified formulas that schools had developed to display their wares to publics were knighted by systems analysis into precise and scientific notions.

What was lost is any sense of something occurring, of persistent processes which do not fit with institutionally contrived measurement schemata. Images of determinism, stability, and reactive actors feed upon institutionally developed measures. What the pupil/teacher ratio ignored was how often the teacher actually dealt with all pupils in a room at the same time (Dyer, 1972). This allocative process was missed completely by the measure adopted from the schools by the systems analysis approach. Taking complex matters, systems analysis often simplified what actually happened into a few highly contrived measures. A language developed by schoolmen to inform their publics in a simplified way of what schools did became a precise research jargon. This conversion left systems analysts untroubled until they looked at data generated from these measures. They discovered a vast array of extraneous variance which overwhelmed their measures. The amount of within-school variance suggested a need to inspect carefully what actually happened, with new and greatly improved measurement techniques. Their earlier notions of a simple system, easily understood and readily manipulable, evaporated.

The remaining frames of explanation present alternative views of the impact of policy decisions on schools. Their emphasis on processes and decisions provides a more complex sense of the world of education. In these complexities, nonetheless, rest both their strength and their weakness for educational

policy makers. This sense of complexity confounds those who sought to find
simple answers to issues of understanding and reform. Process studies, for
example, suggested that minute inspections of life in school should caution
policy makers against naive use of information schools generated about themselves (Center for Educational Research and Innovation, 1973; March &
Olsen, 1976). Simple indices incorporated wide variances, and suspicion was
in order. For example, persistent differences among schools seem to exist
along three dimensions: grade level, size, and geographical location. Elementary schools are not like junior high and middle schools, and none of these
are like high schools. Very small and very large schools are different from
small, medium, or large schools. Schools located in rural areas are not like
suburban or urban schools; urban schools look unfamiliar to suburban students. A small rural elementary school bears only a family resemblance to
a large urban high school. Certainly there are administrators, teachers, pupils,
books, and classrooms in all. Nonetheless, these categories disguise more
than they reveal. What counts are patterns of interaction.

To come to grips with the complexities of schooling requires major efforts.
In the case of educational policy makers in the 1960s, efforts had to be
made in three areas. First, they had to know much more about what went
on in schools than most cared to. When confronted by the complexity, the
awesome task of disentangling multiple threads, and the long-range consequences of many actions, simplification and ignorance seemed almost virtues.
Second, they had limited prescriptive visions. Most cast their arguments about
the welfare of children in ways that made stereotypical middle-class parents
feel comfortable, or they argued about equality of justice in the language
of Thomas Jefferson and Andrew Jackson. In many ways they sought to
recapture a democracy of opportunity and equality which many saw as dying
in a technocratic and meritocratic society. Simple visions created simple answers. Third, when they sought to link vision and fact, they found an implementation void that few suspected existed. The engineering of changes required immense resources, understandings, patience, fortitude, and cleverness.
In most cases, retreat seemed wiser than futile attempts at change. Policy
lost its meaning as the production of a better society and came instead to
signify inept, sometimes well-funded but generally ineffectual, tampering. The
margins may have been dented, but the middle persisted unchanged because
the costs of knowing seemed higher than the costs of ignorance.

The explanatory models of negotiation and professional authority may
not overcome the exhaustion of the systems analysis approach. They hint
at a model based on complex interrelations among many different groups
with divergent aims. These views suggest that outsiders are easily thwarted,
resources are bent quickly to local needs, and implementation processes are
critical. Both models provide insights into the behavior of those involved
in schooling, insights which stress the indeterminate character of their envi-

ronment, the instability present in many situations in schools and communities, and the goal-generating capacities of many actors (Sieber, 1968).

By the mid–1970s these models had come into their own. They seem better suited to policy making and implementation than the derelict systems analysis approach. They permit visions of local autonomy, collective bargaining, locally developed problem-solving capacities, and dissemination of products to willing locales only. The professional discretion or negotiations that once seemed such a bane to systems functioning now are glorified. Yet the models clearly conflict with each other on the issue of authority. The negotiations model posits authority in the results of mutually binding agreements, while the authority model frames authority in the discretion of professionals. That professional authority is less than most professionals would like it to be is evident; nonetheless, it remains a critical element in the authority frame. Authority can not be negotiated away completely.

The conflict between these two models leaves the 1970s with a dilemma of justice (Rawls, 1971). Negotiation makes possible common definitions of justice, while authority always poses some unique and different understanding. Professional discretion values not necessarily the agreements that men mold but the insights that wisdom gives professionals. While the ultimate principles of justice derived from these two models might be the same, the processes of reaching these principles are different. For policy makers in education, the issues may involve clashes between wisdom of professionals and their senses of justice versus wisdoms of the publics and their senses of justice.

What we know about the impact of policy decisions on schools thus rests upon our explanatory frameworks and our sense of justice. From the standpoint of the systems analysis framework, policy is a set of straightforward answers to simple questions and notions of justice. From the standpoint of the negotiation frame, policy involves complex negotiations in which questions and answers often shift and our sense of justice might change over time. The authority frame suggests much negotiation but some preserve of professional discretion and sense of justice. In the 1960s the systems analysis framework was in fashion, but in the 1970s the negotiation and authority models are current. Standing in the midst of a complex world of educational policy, surrounded by negotiations and clashes over issues concerning professional discretion, the solutions of the 1960s seem simplistic. They appear to have been destined to fail.

Such a finding hardly deserves so much ink. To remind those around us and ourselves of the power of our paradigms for analysis and prescription, or of the time-and-place-bound sense of much of our thinking, verges on triviality. But a review of the impact of policy decisions on schools can not overlook these shifting senses of what constitutes *impact, policy decisions,* or *schooling,* or the senses of complexity and conflict which one era finds acceptable but an earlier era found so intolerable. The questions and answers of the 1960s do not look or feel like the questions and answers of the 1970s. Understanding that, and some of the differences, may alert us to our shortcomings or strengths.

Some Directions for Research

At least four concerns are evident from this review. First, nearly all of the studies reviewed concentrated on failure but ignored the possible benefits of failure. Second, unique student and teacher characteristics of the 1960s were all too often overlooked. Third, the linkages among a variety of educational systems and of these systems with their environments have drawn little interest. Fourth, the learnings of participants have been discounted.

The literature based on systems analysis of efforts to change schools generally is a litany of failures. The systems analysis perspective led nearly all studies to describe change as altering inputs to achieve some output that meshed with visions of a better tomorrow. The pattern traced the initial shock of bringing that vision to the world of school settings, through the casting off of a new vision and the return to older ways of doing things. The general task was the one of explaining failure.

Missing from the systems analysis literature on changing education is any sense of the possible benefits of failure (Hirschman, 1963). In his discussions of the failures of various economic development schemes, Hirschman discovered that attacking seemingly intractable problems often brings other, solvable, problems to the attention of decision makers. Alliances may form around the solvable problems that emerge in this fashion, and these alliances may then reconsider seemingly intractable problems. Finally, the very intractability of some problems may lead to increased pressure to take previously unpalatable actions.

For example, we could reconsider the failure of new math (Eddleman, 1975). The intent of its founders—the reshaping of the mathematics curriculum—has been embodied in many current textbooks. But overall the problems of new math seem to outweigh this incorporation. Problems, for instance, plague the assumption that math teaching would be easier if teachers explained the concepts of mathematics to students. Many teachers of mathematics at elementary and high school levels did not know the concepts involved and could not teach them with facility. Many students enjoyed the conceptual approach, but just as many were confused. Parents could not help their children with homework. The net outcome can be made to appear muddy, but in some sense new math must receive a grade of F. Nonetheless, the failure of new math brought clearly to the attention of educational policy makers a series of new problems. Curriculum materials alone seemed unable to improve educational practice. Materials based on larger and more theoretical patterns of reasoning did not necessarily produce greater student learning. All teachers do not have excellent methods of teaching or a firm grasp on the subject matter they present. Parental aid may be important in teaching some lessons. These new understandings of unanticipated problems were all provoked by the failure of new math. Solutions suggest further analysis and action on topics such as the linkage of curriculum materials and teaching styles, studies of student reasoning patterns, and understandings of how teachers "know" things. Thus failures can lead to improved problem solving.

A second concern arises from the general failure to account for unique characteristics of students and teachers in the 1960s. Many studies failed to account for patterns of student interaction within classrooms, among classrooms and outside of traditional classroom settings or in extracurricular activities. Nearly all studies assumed that students found the activities offered by teachers and classrooms to be critical. Often overlooked, however, was the importance of the student peer social system. Many studies also failed to account for mechanisms of recruitment by which students are sorted into various courses of study, or levels of courses, and the means of student control built into these sorting mechanisms (Erickson, 1972). Finally, demographic data about the students of the 1960s suggest that a unique place in society was assured students by their very numbers.

Demographic data about teachers in the 1960s, such factors as their age, sex, and experience distribution, have literally gone unexamined. Interactions of age and experience on teaching strategies have received some attention but are generally not linked to the age structure of the teaching profession. Fine-grained studies which document the willingness of the new or the recalcitrance of the old to try new ideas are lacking. Generally, there are gross and unexamined assumptions about levels of energy, availabilities of teaching techniques, and family life cycle problems. Serious considerations of the confounding influences on schools of not only more youth as students but also many more youthful and inexperienced teachers in the 1960s and early 1970s are needed. We must guard against the easy transfer of wisdom about students and teachers of this or other eras to present conditions. Studies of policy impact often fail to account for the uniqueness of either students or teachers in the crowded 1960s.

A third issue has to do with conceptualizing the relations among schools and their environments. The simplistic notion of environment used frequently by systems analysts seems heuristically sterile. Much of the current discussions of varieties of coupling seems to offer useful ways of thinking for educators (Pondy, n.d.). The notions of tight and loose coupling of organizations to environments, and of high and low variety in organizations, seem useful. It may be that schools are best viewed as larger systems whose subsystems have differing levels of variety (high to low) and different couplings (tight to loose) with different environments (turbulent to placid). Such lines of reasoning may suggest why some changes may occur in one area of a school and be rejected in other areas, and why the same information is viewed as useful to some and trivial to others.

The fourth issue is the marked lack of concern for how those who participated in the conception, birth, growth, and death of a policy decision or program implementation are affected. What has been "learned" by these participants about their job and career, the ways they can or cannot do their work, the rewards and frustrations of their efforts, or the values inherent in change or stability? Moreover, little interest has been paid to the development of new language schemes for discussing changes or for communicating learnings that may have occurred. For example, as open-space classes were proposed and implemented, few notions of vocabularies that may have been developed to deal with these new settings or of the ways this knowledge may have been codified became available. These efforts to formulate solutions may have led to new learnings and to patterns of deliberation far different from those used in traditional, self-contained classrooms. Little is known, finally, of how those who participated incorporated learnings and vocabularies into group norms.

It is easy to suggest that those who participated in earlier efforts are now abused and/or jaded. Unfortunately, it is just as easy to suggest that participants selectively have developed better teaching strategies or better ways of working with others. Participants over time may have learned, changed, and incorporated new wisdoms as guides for themselves and others. Few discussions of the learnings of participants seem to exist.

CONCLUSION

This review has suggested that two differing views of the impact of policy decisions on schools dominated the last two decades. The more conventional of these two views, during the 1960s, was the systems analysis approach. Policy developed on the assumptions of systems analysis held that educational systems operated as rational systems with tight linkages among inputs, conversion processes, and outputs, with operant feedback mechanisms. Unfortunately, the good intentions of federal policies were often weakened. They were bargained to the point that as policies they proposed weak (acceptable to all) treatments based on limited understandings of expected conversion processes. All too frequently the policies that were framed lacked detail and precision in understanding the multiple characteristics of different treatments, the usual ways of doing things in schools, and the interactions between schools and communities.

When these rationally conceived policy decisions interacted with school situations, the order of the day was limited effect only. The regularities of schools—commonplaces such as texts, buildings, scarce financial resources, and familiar and comfortably worn roles for students, teachers and grades—predominated. A well-understood system already existed, even if it did not look like the systems analysis model. What policy makers sought, what practitioners delivered, and what clients received were all moderated by local conditions, accented by personal tastes and differing aspirations and expectations about schooling, and refined by local loyalties. The universalistic solutions favored often were reshaped by local schools to meet particularistic goals.

By the early 1970s educational reform had failed, if reform was understood from the systems analysis perspective. A second model, one stressing negotiations–authority, seemed better suited to describe and prescribe educational change. This approach accepts different roles for diverse actors, such as policy makers, researchers, developers, disseminators, and clients. The relations among these groups now appear less clear and prescribed than in the systems analysis approach. Understandings of situations by various actors; their patterns of interaction or neglect; definitions of goals or senses of taboos; sanctions and rewards; and learning styles and nodalities are variables which are seen now as critical to educational change. Understandings among various actors, rather than conceptions of rational systems, appear important today.

From this vantage point, policies developed in the late 1970s will take into account extensive, and probably intense, negotiations among many groups. One core problem in these multiple-negotiation activities will be definitions of the range of professional discretion and authority. The limits of professional judgment, discretion, and authority undoubtedly will shift over the next decade as various groups negotiate and renegotiate their rights and prerogatives. The typography of new professional domains is not yet charted. But regardless of the shortsightedness of the viewer, policies developed to deal with the critical issue of professional authority will not look like the policy landscape of the 1960s.

An observer with an even longer historical perspective might suggest that we could safely forecast a revival of a more universalistic, rational pattern in the late 1980s or early 1990s. Notions such as efficiency, directives, order, precision, and improvement of national resources are just as much a part of the heritage of American schools as are the notions of humaneness, negotiations, complexity, serendipity, and enhancement of local talent. Our heritage as a nation attests to the value of discrepancies among our fundamental guiding principles (Turner, 1968). Reforms of the schools move between universal and particular poles. This should alert those who wish to keep score that they need to know which inning it is and who is at bat. In the 1960s the universalistic notions had their turn. The 1970s are visibly more particularistic. Nonetheless, it does not appear to be the last turn at bat for either side.

REFERENCES

Allison, G. T. *Essence of decision: Explaining the Cuban missile crisis.* Boston: Little, Brown, 1971.

Anton, T. J. The imagery of policy analysis: Stability, determinism, and reactions. *Policy Studies Journal,* 1975, *3,* 225-233.

Averch, H. A., Carroll, S. J., Donaldson, T. S., Kiesling, H. J., & Pincus, J. *How effective is schooling? A critical review and synthesis of research findings* (Report No. R-956-PCSF/RC). Santa Monica, Cal.: Rand, 1972.

Berke, J. S., & Kirst, M. W. *Federal aid to education: Who benefits? Who governs?* Lexington, Mass.: D. C. Heath, 1972.

Berkson, L. Post conversion analysis. *Policy Studies Journal,* 1974, *2,* 316-321.

Biderman, A. D. Information, intelligence, enlightened public policy: Functions and organization of societal feedback. *Policy Sciences,* 1970, *1,* 217-230.

Bredo, A. E., & Bredo, E. R. *A case study of educational innovation in a junior high school: Interaction of environment and structure* (R & D Memorandum No. 132). Stanford, Cal.: Stanford Center for Research and Development in Teaching, February 1975.

Burnett, J. H. Ceremony, rites and economy in the student system of an American high school. *Human Organization,* 1969, *28,* 1-10.

Callahan, R. E. *Education and the cult of efficiency: A study of the social forces that have shaped the administration of the public schools.* Chicago: University of Chicago Press, 1962.

Campbell, R. F., & Bunnell, R. A. (Eds.) *Nationalizing influences on secondary education.* Chicago: Midwest Administration Center, University of Chicago, 1963.

Campbell, R. F., Cunningham, L. L., McPhee, R. F., & Nystrand, R. O. *The organization and control of American schools* (2nd ed.). Columbus, Ohio: Charles E. Merrill, 1970.

Center for Educational Research and Innovation. *Case studies of educational innovation: III. At the school level.* Paris: Organization for Economic Cooperation and Development, 1973.

Charters, W. W., Jr., & Pellegrin, R. Barriers to the innovation process: Four case studies of differentiated staffing. *Educational Administration Quarterly,* 1972, *9,* 3-14.

Cicourel, A. V. *Organizational processes in educational research: Some suggestions for basic field research.* Unpublished paper, University of California, San Diego, 1975.

Cohen, D. K. The value of social experiments. In A. M. Rivlin and P. M. Timpane (Eds.), *Planned variation in education: Should we give up or try harder?* Washington, D.C.: Brookings Institution, 1975.

Cohen, M. D., & March, J. G. *Leadership and ambiguity: The American college president.* New York: McGraw-Hill, 1974.

Cohen, M. D., March, J. G., & Olsen, J. P. A garbage can model of organizational choice. *Administrative Science Quarterly,* 1972, *17,* 1-25.

Coleman, J. S., Campbell, E. Q., Hobson, C. J., McPartland, J., Mood, A. M., Weinfeld, F. D., & York, R. L. *Equality of educational opportunity.* Washington, D.C.: U.S. Government Printing Office, 1966.

Cusick, P. A. Adolescent groups and the school organization. *School Review,* 1972, *82,* 116-26.

Cyert, R. M., & March, J. G. *A behavioral theory of the firm.* Englewood Cliffs, N.J.: Prentice-Hall, 1963.

Deal, T. E. *An organizational explanation of the failure of alternative schools* (R & D Memorandum No. 133). Stanford, Cal.: Stanford Center for Research and Development in Teaching, February 1975.

Derthick, M. *New towns in-town: Why a federal program failed.* Washington, D.C.: Urban Institute, 1972.

Downs, A. *Inside bureaucracy.* Boston: Little, Brown, 1967.

Dreeben, R. The school as a workplace. In R. M. W. Travers (Ed.), *Second handbook of research on teaching.* Chicago: Rand McNally, 1973.

Dyer, H. S. The measurement of educational opportunity. In F. Mosteller and D. P. Moynihan (Eds.), *On equality of educational opportunity.* New York: Vintage Books, 1972.

Easton, D. *A systems analysis of political life.* New York: Wiley, 1965.

Eddleman, W. *Possible benefits of failure.* Unpublished paper, University of Illinois, 1975.

Elboim-Dror, R. Some characteristics of the education policy formation system. *Policy Sciences,* 1970, *1,* 231-253.

Elboim-Dror, R. The management system in education and staff relations. *Journal of Educational Administration and History,* 1971, *4,* 37-45 and 1972, *5,* 47-56.

Erickson, D. A. Moral dilemmas of administrative powerlessness. *Administrator's Notebook,* 1972, *20,* 1-4.

Firestone, W. A. The balance of control between parents and teachers in co-op free schools. *School Review,* 1977, *85,* 264-286.

Frank, A. G. Goal ambiguity and conflicting standards: An approach to the study of organization. *Human Organization,* 1958-59, *17,* 8-13.

Freidson, E. The impurity of professional authority. In H. S. Becker, B. Geer, D. Riesman, & R. S. Weiss (Eds.), *Institutions and the person: Papers presented to Everett C. Hughes.* Chicago: Aldine, 1968.

Fullan, M. Overview of the innovative process and the user. *Interchange,* 1972, *3,* 1-46.

Fullan, M., & Pomfret, A. *Review of research on curriculum implementation.* Toronto: Ontario Institute for Studies in Education, Department of Sociology in Education, April, 1975.

Gittell, M., & Hollander, T. E. *Six urban school districts: A comparative study of institutional response.* New York: Frederick A. Praeger, 1968.

Glass, G. V. Primary, secondary, and meta-analysis of research. *Educational Researcher,* 1976, *5,* 3-8.

Gross, N., Giacquinta, J. B., & Bernstein, M. *Implementing organizational innovations: A sociological analysis of planned educational change.* New York: Basic Books, 1971.

Grumm, J. G. A test for the existence of feedback in state legislative systems. In S. C. Patterson & J. C. Wahlke (Eds.), *Comparative legislative behavior: Frontiers of research.* New York: Wiley-Interscience, 1972.

Grumm, J. G. The analysis of policy impact. In F. I. Greenstein & N. W. Polsby (Eds.), *Policies and policymaking* (Vol. 6), *Handbook of Political Science.* Reading, Mass.: Addison-Wesley, 1975.

Hanson, M., & Ortiz, F. I. The management information system and the control of educational change: A field study. *Sociology of Education,* 1975, *48,* 257-275.

Hiner, N. R. An American ritual: Grading as a cultural function. *Clearing House,* 1973, *47,* 356-361.

Hirschman, A. O. *Journeys toward progress: Studies of economic policymaking in Latin America.* New York: 20th Century Fund, 1963.

Hirschman, A. O., & Lindblom, C. E. Economic development, research and development, policy making: Some converging views. *Behavioral Science,* 1962, *7,* 211-222.

House, E. R. *The politics of educational innovation.* Berkeley, Cal.: McCutchan, 1974.

Iannaccone, L., & Lutz, F. W. *Politics, power and policy: The governing of local school districts.* Columbus, Ohio: Charles E. Merrill, 1970.

James, H. T. *The new cult of efficiency and education.* Horace Mann Lectures, 1968. Pittsburgh: University of Pittsburgh Press, 1969.

Jencks, C., Smith, M., Acland, H., Bane, M. J., Cohen, D., Gintis, H., Heyns, B., and Michelson, S. *Inequality: A reassessment of the effect of family and schooling in America.* New York: Basic Books, 1972.

Katz, D., & Kahn, R. L. *The social psychology of organizations.* New York: Wiley, 1966.

Kirst, M. W. The rise and fall of PPBS in California. *Phi Delta Kappan,* 1975, *56,* 535-538.

Kritek, W. J. Lessons from the literature on implementation. *Educational Administration Quarterly,* 1976, *12,* 86-102.

Levinson, E. *The Alum Rock voucher demonstration: Three years of implementation* (Rand Paper Series, P-5631). Santa Monica, Cal.: Rand, 1976.

Light, R. J., & Smith, P. V. Accumulating evidence: Procedures for resolving contradictions among different research studies. *Harvard Educational Review,* 1971, *41,* 429-471.

Litt, E. Civic education, community norms, and political indoctrination. *American Sociological Review,* 1963, *28,* 69-75.

Lortie, D. C. *School-teacher: A sociological study.* Chicago: University of Chicago Press, 1975.

Mann, D. *The policies of administrative representation: School administrators and local democracy.* Lexington: D. C. Heath, 1976.

March, J. G., & Olsen, J. P. *Ambiguity and choice in organizations.* Bergen, Norway: Universitetsforlaget, 1976.

McKinney, W. L., & Westbury, I. Stability and change: The public schools of Gary, Indiana, 1940-1970. In W. A. Reid & D. F. Walker (Eds.), *Case studies in curriculum change: Great Britain and the United States.* Boston: Routledge & Kegan Paul, 1975.

Michael, D. N. *On learning to plan and planning to learn.* San Francisco: Jossey-Bass, 1973.

Murphy, J. T. Title I of ESEA: The politics of implementing federal education reform. *Harvard Educational Review,* 1971, *41,* 35-63.

Ortiz, F. I. *Workshops as socialization mechanisms.* Paper presented at the American Educational Research Association Annual Meeting, Chicago, April 1974.

Ostrom, E. The need for multiple indicators in measuring the output of public agencies. *Policy Studies Journal,* 1973, *2,* 85-92.

Parelius, R. J. Conflict over educational change in an economically depressed Negro community. In D. Street (Ed.), *Innovation in mass education.* New York: Wiley-Interscience, 1969.

Peshkin, A. Whom shall the schools serve? The dilemmas of local control in a rural school district. *Curriculum Inquiry,* 1977, *6,* 181-204.

Piele, P. K., & Hall, J. S. *Budgets, bonds, and ballots: Voting behavior in school financial elections.* Lexington, Ky.: D. C. Heath, 1973.

Pondy, L. R. *Two faces of evaluation.* Unpublished paper, University of Illinois, 1976.

Porter, D. O., with Warner, D. C., & Porter, T. W. *The politics of budgeting federal aid: Resource mobilization by local school districts.* Sage Professional Papers in Administrative and Policy Studies (Vol. 1, Series No. 03-003). Beverly Hills, Cal.: Sage, 1973.

Pressman, J. L., & Wildavsky, A. *Implementation: How great expectations in Washington are dashed in Oakland.* Berkeley, Cal.: University of California Press, 1973.

Rawls, J. *A theory of justice.* Cambridge, Mass.: Harvard University Press, 1971.

Reid, W. A. The changing curriculum: Theory and practice. In W. A. Reid and D. F. Walker (Eds.), *Case studies in curriculum change: Great Britain and the United States.* Boston: Routledge & Kegan Paul, 1975.

Rosenthal, R. A., & Weiss, R. S. Problems of organizational feedback processes. In R. A. Bauer (Ed.), *Social indicators.* Cambridge, Mass.: M.I.T. Press, 1966.

Rossi, P. H. Testing for success and failure in social action. In P. H. Rossi & W. Williams (Eds.), *Evaluating social programs: Theory, practice, and politics.* New York: Seminar Press, 1972.

Salisbury, R. H. The analysis of public policy: A search for theories and roles. In A. Ranney (Ed.), *Political science and public policy.* Chicago: Markham, 1968.

Shaver, J. P. Reflective thinking, values, and social studies textbooks. *School Review,* 1965, *73,* 226-257.

Sieber, S. D. Organizational influences on innovative roles. In T. L. Eidell & J. M. Kitchel (Eds.), *Knowledge production and utilization in educational administration.* Eugene: University of Oregon Press, 1968.

Spring, J. *The sorting machine: National educational policy since 1945.* New York: David McKay, 1976.

Steinberg, L. S. *Parent resistance to educational innovation.* Paper presented at the American Educational Research Association Annual Meeting, Chicago, April 1972.

Strauss, A., Schatzman, L., Ehrlich, D., Bucher, R., & Sabshin, M. The hospital and its negotiated order. In F. G. Castle, D. J. Murray & D. C. Potter (Eds.), *Decision, organizations and society: Selected readings.* Middlesex, England: Penguin Books, 1971.

Summerfield, H. L. Cuing and the open system of educational politics. *Education and Urban Society,* 1971, *3,* 425-439.

Timpane, M., Abramowitz, S., Bobrow, S. B., & Pascal, A. *Youth policy in transition.* (Report No. R-2006-HEW). Santa Monica, Cal.: Rand, 1976.

Turner, V. Mukanda: The politics of a non-political ritual. In M. J. Swartz (Ed.), *Local-level politics: Social and cultural perspectives.* Chicago: Aldine, 1968.

van Geel, T. PPBES and district resource allocation. *Administrator's Notebook,* 1973, *22,* 1-4.

Voege, H. W. The diffusion of Keynesian macroeconomics through American high school textbooks, 1936-1970. In W. A. Reid & D. F. Walker (Eds.), *Case studies in curriculum change: Great Britain and the United States.* Boston: Routledge & Kegan Paul, 1975.

Warner, W. K., & Havens, A. E. Goal displacement and the intangibility of organizational goals. *Administrative Science Quarterly,* 1968, *12,* 539-555.

Weiner, M. *The politics of scarcity: Public pressure and political response in India.* Chicago: University of Chicago, 1962.

Wiggins, T. W. Why our urban schools are leaderless. *Education and Urban Society,* 1970, *2,* 169-177.

Wilson, J. Q. Necessity versus the devil. In W. A. Hill & D. M. Egan (Eds.), *Readings in organization theory: A behavioral approach.* Boston: Allyn Bacon, 1967.

IV

MEASUREMENT AND EVALUATION

7

Test Theory

MICHAEL J. SUBKOVIAK and FRANK B. BAKER
University of Wisconsin

In the light of recent general surveys of the test theory literature by Bock and Wood (1971) and Lumsden (1976), this review will focus on particular topics of current interest. The chapter begins with an overview of general references in educational measurement and then considers the application of test theory to problems in three categories: criterion-referenced measurement, test bias, and latent trait estimation. The review is largely confined to the period January 1970 to January 1976.

SELECTED REFERENCES IN EDUCATIONAL MEASUREMENT

While the publication of Lord and Novick's *Statistical Theories of Mental Test Scores* (1968) predates the specified period of this review, failure to mention the text would constitute a significant omission. It has clearly become the bible of most theorists, and for good reason. As will become obvious, the portions of the book dealing with item sampling (chap. 11), latent trait theory (chap. 17-20), and binomial error models (chap. 23) constitute the basis for a number of current developments in educational measurement. However, from a pedagogical point of view, the book is somewhat less successful. Nonmathematical students with a genuine interest in advanced educational measurement typically find the volume quite difficult, due at least in part to a degree of notational complexity and occasional textual brevity not encountered in introductory texts. It is unfortunate that such students remain largely cut off from information that would significantly improve the quality of their applied work.

Hunter Breland, Educational Testing Service, Jason Millman, Cornell University, and Michael I. Waller, Educational Testing Service, were the editorial consultants for this chapter.

At a more elementary level, the individual chapters of Thorndike's (1971) *Educational Measurement* provide an expanded treatment of basic measurement topics covered in introductory texts. Particularly noteworthy in this regard are: Henryssen's chapter (5) on item analysis; Jones's chapter (12) on the nature of measurement; Stanley's chapter (13) on reliability; Cronbach's chapter (14) on validity; and Angoff's chapter (15) on scales, norms, and equivalent scores—most of which fall in Part III of the book (measurement theory). In addition, Parts I, II, and IV contain a wealth of other information on less theoretic topics such as stating objectives, writing items, and administering tests.

At the opposite end of the continuum from Lord and Novick is a host of introductory works, some of which appeared for the first time and others of which were newly revised during the period of this review (Ahmann & Glock, 1975; Aiken, 1976; Anastasi, 1976; Biggs & Lewis, 1975; Brown, 1976; Chase, 1974; Ebel, 1972; Gronlund, 1976; Lien, 1976; Mehrens & Lehmann, 1973; Noll & Scannell, 1972; Nunnally, 1972; Payne, 1974; Sax, 1974; Stanley & Hopkins, 1972; Thorndike & Hagen, 1977; Tuckman, 1975; Wick, 1973). While a number of these texts adequately present the basics, Mehrens and Lehmann's *Measurement and Evaluation in Education and Psychology,* emphasizing teacher-made tests, and Anastasi's *Psychological Testing,* emphasizing standardized tests, might be singled out as models of clarity, completeness, and currentness.

Other significant publications to appear during the review period include Buros's *Seventh Mental Measurements Yearbook* (1972) and *Tests in Print II* (1974), and a revision of the *Standards for Educational and Psychological Tests* (1974) by a Joint Committee of APA, AERA, and NCME. Analogous to preceding volumes, the *Seventh Mental Measurements Yearbook* covers the period 1964 to 1970; lists some 1,000 tests, of which over 500 are reviewed; and also lists and reviews over 600 books on testing. The companion work *Tests in Print II* is an annotated bibliography of the roughly 2,500 in-print tests listed in all seven *Mental Measurements Yearbooks;* separate indices list tests by title, by publisher, and by type. Finally, the revised *Standards for Educational and Psychological Tests* is now clearly intended to educate consumers, as well as publishers, regarding the qualities that a standardized test should possess. Accordingly, a new 18-page section on "Standards for Test Use" has been added that will be of particular interest to teachers and administrators. Perhaps the next order of business for the Joint Committee should be to consider methods of reaching parents and students, many of whom remain in the dark regarding the limitations and the potentialities of standardized tests.

The Dependability of Behavioral Measurements by Cronbach, Glaser, Nanda, and Rajaratnam (1972) is another contribution of the period that deserves special acknowledgement. This book summarizes the concept of generalizability, which is an extension of the traditional notion of reliability. In classical reliability theory, a person's observed score is viewed as one of a number of different outcomes that might have occurred for that person on various parallel tests, where the term *parallel* implies that a person's true ability score is the *same* across the various test forms. The reliability coefficient is then defined as the proportion of variance in observed scores for a group that is due to the variance of true scores for the group.

In generalizability theory, a person's observed score is viewed as one of a universe of outcomes that might have occurred for that person on various nonparallel tests, ratings, and so on; that is, the tests may differ in difficulty and may even tap slightly different ability dimensions so that the person has *different* true scores on the various test forms. However, each person has a single universe score which is his or her average score across the universe of observed outcomes on the various forms. A generalizability coefficient is then analogously defined as the proportion of variance in observed scores for a group due to the variance of universe scores for the group. Thus, generalizability theory is an extension of classical reliability theory in which alternate test forms are not strictly parallel. As such, generalizability is of value to test publishers and users who are interested in the extent to which members of a group will be ordered in the same way on nonparallel tests. In truth, this description of generalizability is suggestive rather than complete. More generally, conditions such as time and place can vary in addition to test forms and persons; and the user can determine which sources of variation in the data are to be considered error and which are not.

CRITERION-REFERENCED MEASUREMENT

Criterion-Referenced vs. Norm-Referenced Tests

Suppose a test is to consist of 10 addition items like the following: $a + b = $ _____, where both a and b can assume the values $0,1,...,9$. Since there are potentially 100 such items, there are $\binom{100}{10} = (100!)/(90! \times 10!)$ different sets of 10 items that could be included on the test, depending upon the particular purpose for which scores are to be used. Furthermore, a set of 10 items that is ideally suited for one purpose may not be well suited for another. For example, scores on such a test might be used to order persons relative to one another; or a score might be used to estimate what percent of the larger item pool an individual can answer correctly. The basic distinction between criterion-referenced tests (CRTs) and norm-referenced tests (NRTs) is one of different purposes, and thus different ideal sets of, say, 10 items.

Speaking generally, scores on a criterion-referenced test indicate what tasks an individual can or cannot perform (Glaser & Nitko, 1971, pp. 652-661).

As indicated in the example above, scores on 10 addition items might be used to estimate the overall proportion of problems in the well-defined pool of 100 that an individual can correctly answer. Thus an ideal set of 10 items would consist of a *representative* sample from the pool (Ebel, 1962; Harris & Stewart, 1971; Hively, Maxwell, Rabehl, Sension, & Lunden, 1973; Osborn, 1968). The term *domain-referenced test* (DRT) has been used to describe such instruments (Millman, 1974).

Test users frequently want to compare an individual's score to a previously defined criterion score. Again a criterion-referenced interpretation is desired, since the purpose is to make a judgment about the individual's level of functioning in an absolute sense. In this case, a different set of 10 items—items that can discriminate whether an individual is above or below the criterion score—is ideal. Such tests are commonly referred to as *mastery tests.*

Still another use of test scores might be to order individuals from high to low. Score interpretations that emphasize the relative ordering of examinees are called norm-referenced. Items that discriminate among individuals are ideal for making norm-referenced interpretations.

While a single set of items might conceivably be used for all of the above purposes, it can easily be demonstrated that one set would not be optimal in all cases. For example, Table 1 shows the scores for 10 hypothetical students on a DRT of 10 randomly selected addition items from the previously described pool. Also shown are each student's total score for the 10 items, the percent correct estimated from total score, and the true percent correct based on an administration of all 100 items in the pool.

The estimated percent correct differs from the true percent by only about 10% on the average, indicating that the small sample of items is reasonably well suited for this purpose. However, the variance of total scores in Table

TABLE 1
Scores on 10 Randomly Selected Items in a Domain-Referenced Test

Student	Item 1	2	3	4	5	6	7	8	9	10	Total Score*	Estimated Percent Correct	True Percent Correct
1	1	1	1	1	1	1	1	1	1	1	10	100	90
2	1	1	1	0	1	0	1	1	1	1	8	80	90
3	1	1	1	1	1	1	1	1	1	1	10	100	80
4	1	1	1	0	0	1	1	1	1	1	8	80	80
5	1	1	1	1	1	0	0	0	1	1	7	70	80
6	1	1	1	1	1	1	1	0	1	0	9	90	70
7	1	1	1	0	1	1	1	0	1	1	8	80	70
8	1	1	1	1	1	1	1	1	0	0	8	80	70
9	0	1	1	0	0	0	1	0	1	0	4	40	60
10	1	1	0	0	1	1	0	0	0	1	5	50	50

* Variance = 3.41.

1 is only 3.41. By contrast, the variance of total scores in Table 2 is 13.21 for the same students on a NRT of 10 discriminating items, that is, items which the better students tend to get right and the poorer students tend to get wrong. Thus the scores of Table 2 provide wider separations or cleaner distinctions between students than those in Table 1. However, as might be expected, the estimated and true percents of Table 2 differ by almost 30% on the average, which is about three times larger than the average difference of Table 1. Thus the items of Table 2 are less useful for estimating percent correct. (In fact, there is a systematic tendency in Table 2 to overestimate the true percent correct for the better students and to underestimate it for the poorer students. Items in the pool that nearly everyone gets right, including the poorer students, or items that nearly everyone gets wrong, including the better students, are deliberately omitted because such items do not discriminate between better and poorer students.)

A fair amount of debate among test theorists has revolved around whether or not separate methodologies are needed for constructing and evaluating DRTs and NRTs. For example, see the exchange between Woodson (1974a, 1974b) and Millman and Popham (1974) over the issue of item and test variance for DRTs as opposed to NRTs. Tables 1 and 2 illustrate the advantages that flow from such separateness. In summary, the DRT items of Table 1 are randomly selected; and as a result, total scores provide accurate estimates of true percent correct but a weak ordering of individuals, due to small score variability. On the other hand, the NRT items of Table 2 discriminate between the better and poorer students; and as a result, total scores provide a clean ordering but inaccurate estimates of true percent correct.

There are also other important distinctions between NRTs and CRTs beyond the particular item sets involved. For example, reliability in the case

TABLE 2
Scores on 10 Discriminating Items in a Norm-Referenced Test

Student	1′	2′	3′	4′	5′	6′	7′	8′	9′	10′	Total Score*	Estimated Percent Correct	True Percent Correct
1	1	1	1	1	1	1	1	1	1	1	10	100	90
2	1	1	1	1	1	1	1	1	1	1	10	100	90
3	1	1	1	1	1	0	1	1	1	1	9	90	80
4	1	1	1	1	1	1	1	1	0	0	8	80	80
5	1	0	1	1	1	0	0	1	1	1	7	70	80
6	0	0	0	1	0	1	1	0	0	0	3	30	70
7	0	0	0	0	1	0	0	1	0	0	2	20	70
8	1	0	0	0	0	0	0	0	1	0	2	20	70
9	0	0	1	0	0	0	0	0	0	0	1	10	60
10	0	0	0	0	0	0	1	0	0	0	1	10	50

* Variance = 13.21.

of a NRT refers to the consistency of the obtained ordering of persons across repeated testing, as measured by the correlation between scores on two equivalent testings or by a single administration estimate of that quantity such as Cronbach's alpha or a Kuder-Richardson coefficient. However, reliability in the context of CRTs depends upon the test purpose and can refer to the consistency of individuals' percent correct estimates over repeated testing or to the consistency with which individuals score above or below the criterion over repeated testing. Millman (1974) has reviewed procedures for estimating the reliability of CRTs and other such issues basic to the construction of CRTs. The following overview attempts to supplement and extend Millman's earlier work in the light of recent developments in the area of criterion-referenced testing. Procedures related to specifying the item pool, selecting test items, setting passing standards, estimating degree of mastery, computing reliability, and establishing validity for CRTs are discussed below. Parallel procedures related to the development of NRTs can, of course, be found in any of the basic references cited earlier.

Universe Definition

If a score on a CRT is to reflect a domain of tasks that a student can or cannot perform, it is essential that the relevant universe of tasks or potential item pool be clearly defined. This need has quite naturally stimulated interest in algorithms for generating item populations, such as $a + b = \underline{\quad}$ where a and b assume the values 0,1,...,9. Bormuth (1970), Guttman (1969), Hively et al. (1973), and Osburn (1968) have all suggested definitional schemes involving specification of the constant and the variable elements of the item pool. For example, in the $a + b = \underline{\quad}$ algorithm, the addition of two digits is constant, while the digits are free to vary from 0 through 9. Of course, most curricular domains cannot be defined as efficiently as basic addition. In fact, one of the common criticisms of criterion-referenced testing is the difficulty, if not impossibility, of specifying algorithms for more complex domains. Popham (1974; 1975, chap. 7) suggests the use of *amplified objectives* as a practical substitute for detailed algorithms, where an amplified objective is a statement delimiting the appropriate item stems and corresponding options for testing a particular instructional objective, plus a sample test item. However, any loss of domain specificity accruing from the latter approach is naturally accompanied by a commensurate loss of interpretability as to exactly what it is that a student can or cannot do. Thus the search for more general algorithms and procedures continues.

Item Selection

As illustrated in Table 1, a representative sample of test items from a well-defined pool is optimal for estimating the proportion of the item domain that an individual can correctly answer (DRT). If the items in the pool can be represented by an algorithm such as $a + b =$ ____ (where $a, b = 0, 1, ..., 9$), or exhaustively listed in some other fashion, then the selection of a representative sample is a relatively straightforward process. For example, a simple random sample of 10 of the 100 potential addition items was drawn in Table 1. An even better way to ensure the representativeness of the sample would be to stratify the 100-item pool according to difficulty, content, or other relevant facet, and then to randomly sample a proportion of the required 10 items from each stratum. For example, the 100-item pool could be partitioned into a stratum of 64 easy items that sum to 10 or less (so that students could obtain the answers by counting on their fingers) and a stratum of 36 difficult items that sum to more than 10 (requiring the use of both fingers and toes if the counting approach is taken). Thus, if six and four items, respectively, are randomly sampled from the easy and difficult strata, both item types will be represented in the test sample in about the same proportions as in the overall pool.

Unfortunately, as noted in the discussion of universe definition, many interesting domains cannot be specified as precisely as the example above, and if an item pool is only loosely defined, then the question of what constitutes a representative sample is ambiguous. Starting with a fuzzy blueprint of an item pool, different item writers will tend to generate test samples that differ in difficulty, content, and so forth; that is, the samples will actually represent somewhat different domains. Consequently, the conclusions drawn regarding a student's proficiency will vary from easy samples to more difficult ones. However, this problem is due primarily to imprecise universe definition rather than to faulty item selection procedures, the topic of the present section.

Assuming a representative item sample has been drawn for a DRT, the question arises of whether the items should be piloted and item responses analyzed. The answer, contrary to the advice of some proponents of criterion-referenced testing, is emphatically yes. However, the analyses should be directed toward the elimination of item flaws, such as unintended clues or ambiguities, rather than the elimination of items, since the latter could affect the representativeness of the test sample.

The best form of analysis is yet to be determined, but certain recommendations are possible. For example, the persons on whom the test is piloted might be asked to point out item defects (Millman, 1974). If, in the process, students complain that an item tests a concept to which they were not exposed, the universe definition, and not the test, may require revision.

More objective forms of analysis also seem possible. An item containing a flaw should produce a response pattern that deviates from the patterns obtained for equivalent, unflawed items. For example, if an item contains an unwarranted clue to the correct answer, then the difficulty index for that item should fall in the upper tail of the distribution of difficulties for unflawed items like that one. Similarly, the index for an ambiguous item should fall in the lower tail of the distribution of difficulties. However, the fact that an item has a deviant difficulty index merely identifies the item for further scrutiny and does not indicate the presence of a defect. An extreme index may also be due to over- or underlearning resulting from varying instructional emphases. Again, instructional considerations may suggest a redefinition of the item domain or universe. While the previously described procedure would require a priori grouping of like test items, more general methods for detecting deviant response patterns seem possible.

When the purpose of a test is to discriminate between different groups, like masters and nonmasters, conventional forms of analysis can be used in the item selection and revision process. Specifically, a set of items, each of which is answered correctly by half of the persons whose ability level is at the criterion, is optimal for distinguishing between masters and nonmasters. In practical terms, this means that the item responses should discriminate maximally between masters and nonmasters; for example, the correlation between item scores and mastery states, scored 0 for nonmasters and 1 for masters, should be positive and as large as possible.

Obviously, before one can begin to select items that discriminate between masters and nonmasters, one must first identify members of both groups on which to pilot potential items. A very direct method of doing so is to start with a core of representative items, like those that would appear on a DRT, and to define the mastery and nonmastery groups on the basis of performance on this core. Next, other purposefully selected items thought to discriminate between masters and nonmasters would be added to the pilot sample. Finally, the most discriminating items would be retained for the final test. Brennan (1972), Cox and Vargas (1972), Crehan (1974), and Haladyna and Roid (1976) provide discussions of various discrimination indices that might be used.

While the use of a representative item core is perhaps the best way to define masters and nonmasters, preexisting groups, such as instructed and uninstructed persons, might also serve as proxies (Haladyna, 1974; Millman, 1974). In this case, the test constructor need only be concerned with purposefully selecting and piloting potentially discriminating items on the preexisting groups. Millman also discusses a procedure suggested by Darlington (1970) that avoids having to identify mastery and nonmastery groups, provided one is willing to make some statistical assumptions about the performance of such groups.

Setting Passing Standards

It should be clear from Table 1 that criterion scores are not required for DRTs. Thus before setting a passing standard, the user should decide if one is even needed. If a criterion is desired (for example, to distinguish between masters and nonmasters), several methods have been suggested for determining rational passing standards (as opposed to merely arbitrary or traditional levels like 75 or 85 percent correct). Both Millman (1973) and Crambert (1976) have reviewed a number of such procedures. As will become apparent in the discussion that follows, some of these procedures rely heavily on human judgment and may lead to variable outcomes, while others are quite analytical. (Note that some of these procedures involve norm-referenced comparisons to a greater or lesser extent.)

One approach is to have a judge determine the amount of credit a minimal master or minimally acceptable person would earn on each test item, based on the judge's experience with such persons. The passing standard is then the *total expected credit across all items.* However, rather than estimate the expected credit for each item directly, Angoff (1971) suggests that the judge think of a number of minimal masters and then estimate the proportion of such persons that would correctly answer a particular item. The expected credit for the item is then the product of that proportion (i.e., the probability of a correct response by a minimal master) and the credit given for a correct item response.

If the items are multiple choice (or other supplied-response type), an approach suggested by Nedelsky (1954) is applicable. For each item, the judge identifies those distractors that a minimal master could eliminate. The reciprocal of the remaining options (including the keyed option) is the probability of a correct response, which is then multiplied by the credit of the item. If all the items are worth one point, the expected total score for a minimal master is simply the sum of the reciprocals. In addition, since the expected total for a minimal master is due in part to guessing among the options not eliminated, it may be desirable to increase the passing standard by adding to the expected total some multiple of the standard deviation of possible test scores for a minimal master (see Nedelsky, 1954). Another obvious refinement is to use the average passing standard across a representative group of judges to compensate for the subjectivity involved in the process.

A different method is to administer the test to a group already "certified" in the skill of interest and to set the cut-off at a particular percentile of the obtained score distribution, such as the 10th percentile. However, the resulting standard will vary with the choice of different percentiles and different certification groups.

Still another approach is to consider the educational consequences of a particular passing standard. For example, Block (1972) found (as might be expected) that a 95% criterion resulted in greater subsequent achievement in mathematics than lower criterion levels. Block also suggested that other levels may optimize succeeding attitudes toward math.

More analytical procedures for determining passing standards are also available, if certain types of information and certain assumptions are granted. For example, Huynh (1976c, pp. 76-77) has proposed a procedure for determining the cutting score that minimizes the financial or psychological costs associated with incorrect mastery and nonmastery classifications. His method requires that the ratio of two fixed costs be specified: the cost of granting mastery to a person who subsequently fails on an external performance criterion and the cost of granting nonmastery to a person who subsequently succeeds. Novick and Lewis (1974) suggest 2 to 1 or 3 to 1 as reasonable choices for this ratio.

Huynh's approach assumes that: (1) the distribution of the true ability scores for testees is a member of the beta family (for illustrations see LaValle, 1970, p. 256), (2) the distribution of observed scores for persons with the same fixed true score is binomial, and (3) the probability of success on the external performance criterion increases with true score and is logistic in form (generally S-shaped). Extensions of this procedure to the determination of cutting scores for hierarchically arranged instructional units has also been discussed (Huynh & Perney, 1976). Kriewall (1969) has likewise proposed an analytical approach for determining the passing score that minimizes the costs of misclassifying masters and nonmasters, given the degree to which such errors will be tolerated. Such procedures will undoubtedly become more commonplace as knowledge is acquired regarding misclassification costs and as the mathematical assumptions become more general (or are shown to be robust).

One final procedure which cannot be generally recommended because of its restrictive assumptions is found in Emrick (1971). Specifically, mastery is assumed to be an all-or-none affair, so that items missed by masters and items gotten by nonmasters are considered instances of measurement error rather than partial knowledge. Such an assumption is simply not realistic in the usual context of varying *degrees* of mastery (Ebel, 1971). See also the critique of Emrick's model in Wilcox and Harris (1977).

Estimating Degree of Mastery

Given a representative sample *(n)* of items on a DRT, a number of methods are available for estimating the proportion *(p)* of items in the domain that a person can answer, based upon the number of test items correctly answered *(X)*. The simplest and most obvious estimate is the observed proportion correct on the test given by:

$$\hat{p} = X/n \tag{1}$$

However, this estimate tends to be rather unstable over repeated testing of the same person(s) when the number of items is small, particularly when a person's proportion correct over the entire item domain is near $p = .50$.

A more stable estimate, because it takes into account information about the scores of the group to which a person belongs as well as the individual's score, is given by:

$$\hat{p} = \rho \cdot (X/n) + (1 - \rho)\ (\mu/n) \tag{2}$$

where ρ and μ are respectively the norm-referenced reliability coefficient and the mean of the test scores for the group (Lord & Novick, 1968, p. 65). An assumption underlying Equation 2, however, is that the score, X, is part of a single distribution with mean μ and reliability ρ; that is, there is a single group present of which the individual is a member. Blind use of this equation in the presence of groups having distinct score distributions and thus different means and reliabilities can lead to erroneous p estimates, such as various grade levels or widely disparate mastery and nonmastery groups. In the case of multiple groups, separate equations like 2 can be derived using the mean and reliability of each group, assuming the various groups of examinees are clearly distinguishable.

Novick, Lewis, and Jackson (1973) have proposed an analogous procedure for estimating p that capitalizes on group information and assumes each individual is a member of the same group. A highly readable account of the latter procedure has been provided by Millman (1974).

If the purpose of the test is to distinguish persons whose true scores *(T)* are above a predetermined criterion score *(C)* from those below, then an individual's observed score *(X)*, which generally differs from his or her true score due to measurement error, must be used to determine the category that most likely contains the true score. Of course, the observed score, X, could be used directly as an estimate of the true score, T, just as X/n is used as an estimate of the true proportion correct, p, in Equation 1. Classification decisions would then be made according to on which side of C the observed score, X, lies.

However, a more accurate estimate of true score is given by $\hat{T} = \rho X + (1 - \rho)\mu$, which is an analog of Equation 2 in regard to the symbolism employed and to the assumptions underlying its use. Such $\hat{T}$ estimates would be compared to C in determining mastery and nonmastery.

Hambleton and Novick (1973) and Swaminathan, Hambleton, and Algina (1975) have outlined another procedure for making classification decisions that considers not only on which side of the criterion, C, an individual's true score, T, is likely to lie, but also the relative (financial and psychological) costs of misclassifying a true nonmaster *(T < C)* as a master or a true master *(T ≥ C)* as a nonmaster. In this approach the decision to classify a student as a master or nonmaster is determined not only by his or her test performance but also by the costs of misclassification errors. Thus, if the cost of misclassifying a true nonmaster is large (relative to the cost of misclassifying a true master), then a true score estimate, $\hat{T}$, well above the criterion, C, is needed to bring about a mastery decision; that is, $\hat{T} = C$ does not necessarily grant mastery, since cost is also a factor.

Guessing.   In the above discussion, the observed score, X, was defined as the number of test items that an individual *answers* correctly. If the test is of the supplied-option type (e.g., multiple choice or true-false) where guessing is a significant factor, X generally differs from the number of items an individual actually *knows* to be correct. In this case, one might subtract the number of items guessed correct from the observed score before proceeding to estimate the proportion (known) correct or the mastery level. The standard formula for achieving this correction is:

$$X = R - \frac{W}{o-1},$$

where X now represents the number of items known correct and where R, W, and o are, respectively, the number answered right, the number answered wrong (not counting omissions), and the number of response options.

However, the correction formula is based on the assumption that guessing is a purely random behavior. In practice, risk-takers "beat" the formula and add to their scores by using partial information to make educated guesses; timid individuals in effect penalize themselves by not guessing. Crocker and Benson (1976) explicitly advise against employing this formula in the context of criterion-referenced testing, since it seems to inhibit testees from making use of partial information, thereby reducing their scores.

Reliability

The reliability of a DRT refers to the *consistency* of an individual's proportion-correct estimates (e.g., see Equations 1 and 2) over repeated administrations of the same or equivalent tests. As such, the standard deviation of an individual's distribution of scores over repeated testings is a natural index of reliability in this context, and the square root of the average individual variance is a comparable group coefficient. In other words, if there are N persons in a group and if the ith person's proportion-correct estimates, $\hat{p}_i$, have variance σ_i^2 over repeated testing, a group index of consistency is given by:

$$S = \sqrt{\frac{1}{N}\sum_{i=1}^{N}\sigma_i^2}, \tag{3}$$

which is simply the standard error of measurement of classical theory as applied to proportions.

In the case of exactly two test administrations, Equation 3 simplifies to

$$S = \sqrt{\frac{1}{2n^2N}\sum_{i=1}^{N}(X_i - X_i^{i\cdot})^2},$$

where X_i and X_i' are the number correct on the first and second administrations, respectively, and n and N are the number of items and persons (see Lord & Novick, 1968, pp. 154-155). Thus if the test of Table 1 were administered twice, as shown in Table 3,

$$\hat{S} = \sqrt{\frac{1}{2 \cdot 10^2 \cdot 10}} \ (45) = .15,$$

indicating that on the average an individual's $\hat{p}_i$ estimates over repeated testing tend to differ from the mean of these estimates by .15.

If a test is administered only once, the analog of Equation 3 is $S = (\sigma/n)\sqrt{1 - \rho}$, where σ and ρ are, respectively, the group standard deviation and the single-administration (norm-referenced) reliability of total test scores, and where n is the number of items. For the X_i scores of Table 3, $\sigma = \sqrt{3.41} = 1.85$, the KR20 reliability is $\rho = .60$, and $n = 10$. Thus $\hat{S} = (1.85/10)\sqrt{1 - .60} = .12$, which is reasonably close to the two-administration estimate (.15).

When the purpose of the test is to classify individuals into mastery or nonmastery groups, reliability refers to the consistency or stability of such classifications over repeated testings. Swaminathan, Hambleton, and Algina (1974) have thus proposed that the proportion of individuals consistently classified as master/master or nonmaster/nonmaster on two testings be used as a group index of reliability for mastery tests. In other words, if X_i and X_i' are the scores of the ith person on two testings, and if C is the criterion score, the reliability index is:

$$P_C = P(X_i < C, X_i' < C) + P(X_i \geq C, X_i' \geq C), \tag{4}$$

where $P(X_i < C, X_i' < C)$ and $P(X_i \geq C, X_i' \geq C)$ are, respectively, the proportion of individuals classified as nonmaster/nonmaster and as master/master on the two test administrations. For example, if $C = 8$ in Table 3, two students (9 and 10) are consistently classified as nonmaster on both tests; and five students (1, 2, 3, 4, and 8) are consistently classified as master. Thus, $P_8 = 2/10 + 5/10 = .70$.

Recently a number of single-administration analogs of Equation 4 have also been proposed (Huynh, 1976a; Marshall & Haertel, 1976; Subkoviak, 1976). All of these procedures substitute assumptions for the missing second test, but the Huynh procedure seems to be the most mathematically tractable. Basically, the Huynh approach assumes that *if* a second test were administered, the bivariate distribution of total scores on the two tests would be negative hypergeometric in form, where the negative hypergeometric family of distributions includes both unimodal and bimodal forms. This assumption

TABLE 3
Scores on Two Administrations of a Domain-Referenced Test

Student (i)	X_i	X_i'	$(X_i - X_i')^2$
1	10	10	0
2	8	10	4
3	10	8	4
4	8	8	0
5	7	9	4
6	9	5	16
7	8	6	4
8	8	8	0
9	4	7	9
10	5	3	4

$$\sum_{i=1}^{10} (X_i - X_i')^2 = 45$$

tends to follow if a test consists of items randomly sampled from a homogeneous item pool and if the items are scored 0 or 1.

Under this assumption, a single-administration estimate of the proportion of consistent nonmaster/nonmaster and master/master outcomes is given by:

$$P_C = \sum_{X=0}^{C-1} \sum_{X'=0}^{C-1} f(X,X') + \sum_{X=C}^{n} \sum_{X'=C}^{n} f(X,X'). \tag{5}$$

In Equation 5, $f(X,X')$ represents the proportion of persons that would obtain score pair (X,X') if two tests were administered, and the summations on the right side of the equation are, respectively, the proportion of consistent nonmastery/nonmastery and mastery/mastery outcomes that would occur.

The quantities $f(X,X')$ in Equation 5 can be estimated from scores on one test administration in the following way (see Huynh, 1976a, pp. 254-255):

1. Compute the mean, μ, variance, σ^2, and KR21 coefficient, $\alpha_{21} = [n/(n-1)][1 - \mu(n-\mu)/(n\sigma^2)]$ for the scores on a single testing.
2. Compute parameters $\alpha = (-1 + 1/\alpha_{21})\mu$ and $\beta = -\alpha + n/\alpha_{21} - n$, which define a particular negative hypergeometric distribution of score pairs (X,X') that would occur if two tests were administered.
3. Compute $f(0,0) = \prod_{i=1}^{2n} \dfrac{2n+\beta-i}{2n+\alpha+\beta-i} =$
$$\frac{2n+\beta-1}{2n+\alpha+\beta-1} \times \frac{2n+\beta-2}{2n+\alpha+\beta-2} \times \cdots \times \frac{2n+\beta-2n}{2n+\alpha+\beta-2n},$$
which is the proportion of persons that would obtain a score of zero on both tests.

4. Other values required by Equation 5 can be obtained from the relation
$f(X+1, X') = f(X,X')[(n-X)(\alpha+X+X')]/[(X+1)(2n+\beta-X-X'-1)]$ and the fact that $f(a,b) = f(b,a)$. For instance, $f(1,0) = f(0,0)$ $[n\alpha/(1)(2n+\beta-1)]$,
where $f(0,0)$ is computed in Step 3. Also, $f(0,1) = f(1,0)$.

For example, the X scores on the $n=10$ item test of Table 3 have mean $\hat{\mu} = 7.7$, variance $\hat{\sigma}^2 = 3.41$, and KR21 coefficient $\hat{\alpha}_{21} = [10/9] [1 - (7.7)(10-7.7)/(10 \times 3.41)] = .53$. The parameters of the negative hypergeometric distribution are thus $\hat{\alpha} = (-1+1/.53)(7.7) = 6.83$ and $\beta = -6.83 + (10/.53) - 10 = 2.04$. Following Steps 3 and 4 above, the quantities required by Equation 5 are: $f(0,0) = \prod_{i=1}^{20} \dfrac{20+2.04-i}{20+6.83+2.04-i} = .00001;$

$$f(1,0) = (.00001) [(10)(6.83)/(1)(20+2.04-1)] = .00003;$$

and so on. Finally, if the criterion is set at $C = 8$ in Equation 5, then the proportion of consistent classifications is $P_8 = .26 + .47 = .73$, which compares favorably in this instance to the dual-administration estimate (.70), in spite of the small item and subject samples.

If one is willing to replace the negative hypergeometric assumption underlying Equation 5 with the somewhat more restrictive assumption that the distribution of scores on two tests is bivariate normal (often reasonable when $n > 10$), then the labor involved in computing the single-administration coefficient is greatly reduced (see Huynh, 1976a; Subkoviak, 1976). The Huynh procedure is as follows.

1. Compute the mean, μ, standard deviation, σ, coefficient, α_{21}, and parameter, α, for a single test administration, as discussed above. Let C be the criterion score.
2. Compute a new mean, $\mu' = \sin^{-1} \sqrt{\mu/n}$; standard deviation, $\sigma' = \sqrt{[(\alpha_{21}+1)/(\alpha+n)]}$; coefficient, $\rho' = \alpha_{21}\sqrt{(n-1)/(n+\alpha_{21})}$; and criterion, $C' = \sin^{-1}\sqrt{(C-.5)/n}$. These parameters describe the roughly normal distribution that would be obtained if an arc sin transformation were applied to the test scores. The transformation thus normalizes the raw data and appears to provide good results if $.15 \leq \mu/n \leq .85$ and $n \geq 8$.
3. Compute $z = (C'-\mu')/\sigma'$. Then obtain the probability, $F(z)$, that a standardized normal variable is less z, using tables of the normal distribution found in most statistical texts. Also obtain the probability, $F(z,z)$, that two standardized normal variables, correlated ρ', are both less than z, using tables of the bivariate normal distribution (Gupta, 1963; *Tables of the Bivariate Normal Distribution*, 1959).
4. Finally, substitute $F(z)$ and $F(z,z)$ into the following equation to obtain the proportion of consistent decisions that would occur on two testings:

$$P_C = 1 - 2[F(z) - F(z,z)] \tag{6}$$

For the X scores of Table 3, $n = 10$; $\hat{\mu} = 7.7$; $\hat{\sigma} = 1.85$; $\hat{\alpha}_{21} = .53$; $\hat{\alpha} = 6.83$; and $C = 8$. Thus the new parameters after transformation are $\hat{\mu}' = \sin^{-1}\sqrt{7.7/10} = 1.07$; $\hat{\sigma}' = \sqrt{(.53 + 1)/(6.83 + 10)} = .30$; $\hat{\rho}' = .53$ $\sqrt{(10 - 1)/(10 + .53)} = .49$; $C' = \sin^{-1}\sqrt{(8 - .5)/10} = 1.05$; and $z = (1.05 - 1.07)/.30 = -.07$. Tables of the univariate and bivariate normal distribution indicate that $F(-.07) = .47$ and $F(-.07, -.07) = .31$. By Equation 6, the estimated proportion of consistent outcomes is $P_8 = 1 - 2[.47 - .31] = .68$, which again compares well to the dual-administration estimate (.70).

As previously discussed, the coefficient P_C determined by Equations 4-6 represents the proportion of consistent mastery/mastery and nonmastery/nonmastery classifications expected on two testings. However, a certain proportion of the consistent decisions would be expected even if tests X and X' were operating independently—just as heads might be observed on two independent flips of a coin. This "chance" proportion of consistent decisions is a function of the proportions of masters and nonmasters in the group tested, i.e., $P_{\text{chance}} = P(X < C) \times P(X' < C) + P(X \geq C) \times P(X' \geq C)$. Coefficient kappa, defined as $\kappa = (P_C - P_{\text{chance}})/(1 - P_{\text{chance}})$, represents the proportion of consistent, nonchance decisions expected on two testings (Huynh, 1976a; Swaminathan et al., 1974).

For example, in Table 3 the dual-administration estimate of consistent decisions was computed by Equation 4 to be $P_8 = 2/10 + 5/10 = .70$, where $C = 8$. In this case the proportion due to chance is $P_{\text{chance}} = (3/10)$ $(4/10) + (7/10)(6/10) = .54$. Thus, the nonchance proportion is $\kappa = (.70 - .54)/(1 - .54) = .35$.

Obviously, coefficients P_C and κ have different interpretations, and they also have different statistical properties. For instance, if the criterion, C, is set at different points across the range of test scores, and if both P_C and κ are computed at each point, then the point at which P_C attains its *minimum* value is often the point at which κ attains its *maximum* value. Also, P_C assumes values between P_{chance} and 1, whereas κ varies between 0 and 1. Finally, P_C has a smaller associated standard error of estimate than κ. Thus, the user should not choose blindly between these or other coefficients, but rather should consider the properties of each coefficient in relation to the intended application. For further discussion of this issue, see Goodman and Krushal (1954) and Subkoviak (1977).

Essentially, the coefficients represented by Equations 4-6 indicate the consistency of dichotomous outcomes, mastery $\equiv 1$ and nonmastery $\equiv 0$, over repeated testing. However, if a user were interested in distinguishing various *degrees* of mastery and nonmastery (i.e., exactly how far above or below the criterion a person's ability lies), an index proposed by Brennan and Kane (1977) might be more appropriate. Basically, their coefficient reflects the stability of score deviations about the criterion over repeated testing, that is, the dependability of distances between test scores and criterion.

Test Length

In the preceding section, the X scores of a group on an $n = 10$ item DRT (see Table 1 or 3) were used in conjunction with Equation 3 to compute a reliability estimate, $\hat{S} = .12$. In this section it will be shown that this procedure can also be reversed; that is, given the desired reliability in the planning stages of a test, say $S = .12$, Equation 3 can be used to compute the number of test items, n, needed to attain that reliability.

The procedure outlined here assumes that an individual's proportion-correct scores, $\hat{p}_i$ over repeated testing follow a binomial distribution, with mean p_i (which is the individual's true percent-correct score) and variance $\sigma^2(\hat{p}_i) = p_i(1 - p_i)/n$, where n is the number of test items (Lord & Novick, 1698, chap. 21). If $\sigma^2(\hat{p}_i) = p_i(1 - p_i)/n$ is substituted into Equation 3, the unknown n can be expressed as follows:

$$n = \frac{\mu(1 - \mu) - (\sigma^2 + S^2)}{S^2} \tag{7}$$

In Equation 7, S is the desired reliability, and μ and σ^2 are the expected mean and variance of *proportion-correct* scores for the group to be tested. Estimates of the quantities μ and σ^2 are based upon (previous) knowledge of the distribution of ability for the group to be tested. (Note that the *observed* variance, σ^2, should always be greater than or equal to the *error* variance, S^2, in Equation 7, since σ^2 is composed of true plus error variance.)

For example, suppose a test constructor expects the *proportion-correct* scores for the group to be tested to have mean $\hat{\mu} = 7.7/10 = .77$ and variance $\hat{\sigma}^2 = 3.41/10^2 = .0341$, like the proportions of Table 1, and suppose the test constructor wants to achieve a reliability of $S = .12$. How many items will be required? By Equation 7, the projected number is $n = [.77(1 - .77) - (.0341 + .12^2)]/.12^2 \doteq 9$.

Before leaving this example, a couple of points are worth noting. First, usable estimates of variance, $\hat{\sigma}^2$, in Equation 7 might be obtained from the expected range, r, of observed proportions for the group to be tested; for example, $\hat{\sigma}^2 \doteq (r/6)^2$ for a normal distribution of observed proportions; $\hat{\sigma}^2 \doteq (r/4)^2$ for a uniform distribution; and $\hat{\sigma}^2 \doteq (r/2)^2$ for a symmetric, bimodal distribution. Second, as previously mentioned, the observed variance, σ^2, cannnot be less than the specified error variance, S^2, in Equation 7.

Both Millman (1973) and Novick and Lewis (1974) have addressed the question of estimating test length for mastery tests, and Meskauskas (1975) has discussed the relative merits of the two approaches.

Millman, for example, provides tables of the number of items needed to assure that a desired proportion of individuals, each having the same true score, will be correctly classified on the basis of observed scores (e.g., correctly classified as master if their true score exceeds the criterion). Thus, Millman relates test length to the proportion of correct decisions made about persons having a particular true score.

However, Millman's tables do not directly relate test length to the overall classification accuracy for a group having a given *range* of true scores. Novick and Lewis (1974, p. 142) also point to the fact that these tables report the probability of a correct classification given a particular true score, whereas in practice one is interested in probability of a correct classification, given a particular observed score.

Accordingly, Novick and Lewis have provided their own tables of test length. In order to use the latter, one must be able to specify three types of information: (1) certain properties of the distribution of true scores for the group to be tested; (2) the (financial and psychological) cost of an incorrect mastery decision relative to the cost of an incorrect nonmastery decision, for example, 2 to 1 or 3 to 1; and (3) the criterion score for the test. In return, the tables provide the test length which will minimize the costs associated with incorrect mastery and nonmastery decisions. Naturally, the required test length varies according to the three types of information specified above, so one must make wise choices. On the other hand, one might specify conservative information so as to overestimate the required test length.

More recently, Wilcox (1976) has described a method based on Fhanér (1974) for determining the length of a mastery test and has provided a small table of test lengths to illustrate the procedure. The user enters the table by specifying (1) the criterion score, (2) a small "interval of indifference" bracketing the criterion score—incorrect decisions are tolerated for persons whose true scores lie within this interval, and (3) the desired probability of making a correct decision about persons whose abilities are not in the "interval of indifference." The table, in turn, provides the user with the required number of items and the appropriate criterion score for the test.

All of the above approaches are aimed at determining the test length necessary to obtain a desired degree of classification accuracy. One might also determine mastery test length so as to assure a desired level of reliability. For example, one might use Equation 6 in reverse. Suppose the distribution of *proportion-correct* scores for the group to be tested is expected to be *normal,* with estimated mean $\hat{\mu} = .77$ and variance $\hat{\sigma}^2 = .0341$ (as in Table 1); and suppose a reliability $P_C = .70$ is desired when the criterion is .75. It follows that the standardized criterion score associated with Equation 6 is $z = (.75 - \mu)/\sigma = (.75 - .77)/\sqrt{.0341} = -.11$; and the tabled probability of a standardized normal variable, z, being less than $z = -.11$ is $P_z = .46$. Substituting $P_C = .70$ and $P_z = .46$ into Equation 6 and solving for P_{zz} leads to $P_{zz} = (P_C + 2P_z - 1)/2 = (.70 + 2 \times .46 - 1)/2 = .31$, which is the probability that two standardized normal variables are less than $z = -.11$. But tables of the bivariate normal distribution indicate that when $z = -.11$ and $P_{zz} = .31$, then the correlation between the two variables is .60. This correlation (.60) can be taken as an estimate of the KR21 coefficient.

Finally, the formula for KR21 can be solved for n, the required number of test items, as follows:

$$n = \frac{\mu(1 - \mu) - \sigma^2 \alpha_{21}}{\sigma^2(1 - \alpha_{21})}, \tag{8}$$

where μ and σ^2 are the expected mean and variance of proportion-correct scores and α_{21} is the KR21 coefficient. Since $\hat{\mu} = .77$, $\hat{\sigma}^2 = .0341$, and $\alpha_{21} = .60$ in the example, $n = [.77(1 - .77) - .0341 \times .60]/[.0341(1 - .60)] \doteq 11$.

A few points are worth noting in regard to this procedure. First, the specified magnitude of the desired reliability can never be less than $P_C = .50$, which is the minimum value that P_C can assume in theory (Huynh, 1976b). Second, since the distribution of scores is assumed to be normal, an estimate of the variance, σ^2, in Equation 8 is $\sigma^2 = (r/6)^2$, where r is the expected range of proportion-correct scores.

Validity

The *Standards for Educational and Psychological Tests* (1974) distinguishes among three well-known types of validity—content, construct, and predictive—corresponding to the different purposes for which a test may be used. Since scores on a DRT are supposed to indicate the proportion of a well-defined item pool that a student can correctly answer, content validity is important. Content validity, of course, refers to the degree to which test items are a representative sample from the universe of relevant tasks. In establishing content validity, curriculum or measurement specialists generally pass judgement on the adequacy of the various stages involved in the development of a DRT, such as domain definition and item sampling (Cronbach, 1971).

However, Cronbach notes that content validity might also be analyzed statistically. Two forms of a DRT test could be *independently* constructed using the same blueprint (domain definition, sampling procedure, etc.) and administered to the same group. The discrepancy between the scores X and X' on the two forms is then an index of content validity. Specifically, if the test plan is sufficiently refined, then the mean of the squared differences $(X - X')^2$ should not exceed the sum of the error variances of the two test forms (Cronbach, 1971, p. 456). In terms of Equation 3 and Table 3, this is equivalent to comparing the two-form estimate of error variance, S^2, for equality to the average of two single-form estimates of error variance. Unfavorable results would indicate that aspects of the test plan, such as domain definition or sampling procedure, are too vague to provide a valid content interpretation for the test scores. Favorable results would offer assurance regarding the representativeness of test items and the interpretability of percent correct scores.

When a test is designed for the purpose of classifying individuals as masters or nonmasters, there generally is the belief that the test results are related to outcomes on other variables such as success or failure in subsequent endeavors. Thus, predictive validity, or the strength of relation between test results and other outcomes, is a primary consideration.

Both Millman (1974) and Harris (1974, pp. 109-113) have reviewed predictive validity in this context, and Cronbach (1971) provides a thorough discussion of the concept in general. In particular, Millman notes that the degree of relationship between the test and a criterion variable might be summarized as a Pearson product-moment, point-biserial, or phi correlation—depending upon whether the test and criterion are expressed as continuous scores or discrete categories. Harris additionally suggests the potential usefulness of conditional probabilities as measures of predictive validity, for example, the proportion of test masters who subsequently succeed on the criterion.

TEST BIAS

Research on test bias has predominantly focused on bias in individual test items, or bias in hiring or selecting applicants on the basis of total scores. Accordingly, this section considers significant developments in these two areas. While some progress has been made in each, particularly in regard to defining problems and understanding the limitations of proposed solutions, current knowledge is far from definitive. The extent of test bias (or lack thereof) has yet to be clearly established, and the latest methods for dealing with bias have yet to be tested. Therefore no attempt has been made to review the topic exhaustively.

Item Bias

Anastasi (1966; 1976, p. 191) notes that the usefulness of a test for predictive or other purposes may be limited by efforts to include *only* skills common to all subgroups. Test items should tap all relevant skills. However, the important part that tests now play in certification and selection for educational and occupational roles further demands that some attempt be made to identify and eliminate possible individual item bias.

For example, consider the following item, which might appear on a test of educational and psychological measurement:

The Miss America Contest is a norm-referenced activity (true or false).

The fact that this item is more difficult for non–U.S. citizens than U.S. citizens (where difficulty refers to the percent passing in each group) might simply reflect a difference in knowledge of the "apparent" content, the concept of norm-referenced (see Hawkes, Lindquist & Mann, 1936, pp. 66-81, for further distinction between "apparent" and "functioning" content). If so, the item would serve the purpose of the test and might be retained in its present form. Similarly, Scheuneman (1976) found that Orientals could not discriminate L and R sounds as well as other groups—a skill that might be relevant for certain test purposes.

However, in the case of the true-false item above, the difference in difficulty might well be due to the unfamiliarity of non–U.S. citizens with the nature of the Miss America Contest, the "functioning" content. If so, it would seem necessary to replace the Miss America Contest with a more commonly known norm-referenced activity like the Olympic games or to substitute another item tapping the same skill.

A number of techniques have been proposed for detecting performance differences between various subgroups, as in the example above (Rudner, 1976). However, it should be noted at the outset that none of these procedures distinguishes between relevant or irrelevant item content as the source of such differences (e.g., norm-referenced vs. Miss America Contest). Identifying sources of item bias remains a matter of human judgment, based on psychological analysis of student thought processes.

As noted above, the fact that an item is more difficult for one group than another may simply reflect a difference in relevant knowledge or skill— a difference that may also be reflected on other items of the test. However, if the *difficulty difference* for a particular item is noticeably *larger* than the difference for other items, the added dose of difficulty for that particular item may be due to bias, such as irrelevant item content. On the other hand, the larger difference might also be due simply to exceptionally large group differences in relevant item content. (Disproportionately *small* difficulty differences might likewise be due either to group equality on relevant content or to an unintended ambiguity or clue that equalizes performance.)

Cleary & Hilton (1968), Angoff & Ford (1973), and Echternacht (1972) have all used significant *between-group difficulty difference* as an indicator of possible item bias. Cleary and Hilton, for example, used analysis of variance to examine the interaction between items and racial groups on the Preliminary Scholastic Aptitude Test (PSAT), and also the interaction between items and socioeconomic status within each race. While both interactions were statistically significant, due to large sample sizes, neither interaction accounted for an appreciable percentage of total variance (e.g., less than 2% in all cases). It was concluded that for practical purposes, the items were not biased for the black and white groups considered.

Angoff and Ford used a somewhat different approach to answer the same basic question. They plotted (transformed) item difficulties on the PSAT for blacks versus whites. The points of the scatterplot generally fell along a straight line representing a correlation in the low .90s between black and white item difficulties. In addition, a few items fell some distance from the plot line. These items were regarded as potentially biased, since they represented items that are especially more difficult for one group than for the other.

In a similar manner, Green (1976) and Green and Draper (1972) have used between-group item discrimination differences (which generally reflect item difficulty differences) as indicators of potential item bias.

An interesting finding of particular relevance for the above procedures is that item by group interaction (in the above sense) tends to decrease noticeably when comparison groups are matched on ability, indicating that such interaction is due at least in part to group ability differences—not solely to item bias (Angoff & Ford, 1973; Jensen, 1973). Accordingly, Scheuneman (1975, 1976) and Lord (1977) have proposed item detection procedures that are relatively independent of group ability. Basically, both approaches amount to a comparison of the black and the white item-characteristic curves obtained by plotting the proportion of blacks *at each possible total score* that answer the item correctly and doing the same for whites. If the two curves differ greatly, the item is potentially biased. Since each item characteristic curve is independent of the particular distribution of total scores for the black or white group, this procedure may be more *directly* sensitive to potential item bias than previous approaches.

Angoff (1976) has further noted a circularity involved in all of the above forms of internal analysis. That is, the bias of a particular item is determined via other items or total scores whose bias is also in question. Nevertheless, internal analyses of the type discussed above have proved useful in the past and may do so again.

Finally, Tittle, McCarthy, and Steckler (1974) offer some commonsense advice for constructing minimal-bias tests: assemble heterogeneous committees to define test objectives and write items; require heterogeneity among test administrators and proctors; ensure adequate numbers of each subgroup in the pilot sample to detect possible item bias; and so forth. While there seems to be no published evidence that such practices actually reduce bias, these suggestions are food for thought.

Bias in Selection

The entire Spring 1976 issue of the *Journal of Educational Measurement* is devoted to the topic of bias in selection. The leading article by Petersen and Novick (1976) is a review of current procedures for culture-fair selection: Cleary (1968), Cole (1973), Darlington (1971), Einhorn and Bass (1971), Linn (1973), and Thorndike (1971).

Certain logical inconsistencies are noted for the Cole, Linn, and Thorndike methods. For example, consider the Thorndike model. Figure 1 represents

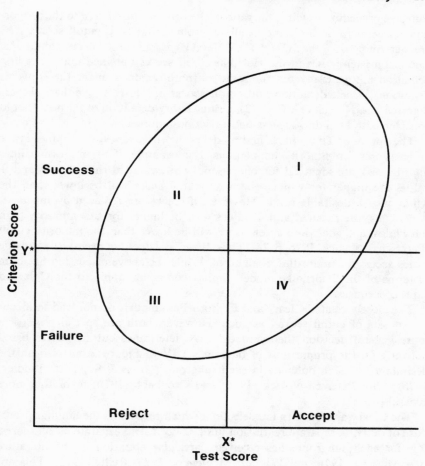

Figure 1.   Bivariate distribution of test and criterion scores.

the bivariate distribution of scores on a test and on a criterion for a single subgroup, for example, entrance examination scores and subsequent grade point averages for blacks. Applicants with test scores above the cutoff score X^* are considered acceptable for admission, while the others are not. Similarly, persons with criterion scores above Y^* are successful; and the others are not. Thorndike stated that a selection procedure is fair if the ratio of the proportion *selected* to the proportion *successful* is the same in all subgroups, that is, if a different cutoff, X^*, is determined for each subgroup so that $(I + IV)/(I + II)$ is constant across all subgroups.

However, looking at Figure 1 using identical logic, one might define a converse procedure as fair if the ratio of the proportion *rejected* to the proportion *unsuccessful* is the same in all subgroups, that is, if cutoff scores X^{**} are determined so that $(III + II)/(III + IV)$ is constant across subgroups. The inconsistency lies in the fact that cutoff scores obtained under the first definition are generally not the same as those obtained under the converse definition. Which definition and cutoff scores are correct? Neither, suggest Petersen and Novick (1976, p. 22); a satisfactory definition of fairness should consider both selection-success and rejection-failure.

The appeal of Thorndike's first model is that it *generally* determines lower cutoff scores for minority populations. For example, if the regression lines for Figure 1 are identical for blacks and whites, and if the mean X and Y values are higher for whites, the black cutoff score will be lower than the white one—a desirable result. However, if blacks are replaced by Japanese-Americans, the mean X and Y values may be higher for this minority than for whites, and the white cutoff score will be lower than the minority cutoff (Petersen & Novick, 1976, p. 24). Thus, the model does not necessarily provide easier access for minorities in all cases. While the above discussion has been in terms of the Thorndike model, similar comments apply to the Cole and Linn procedures.

The closely related Cleary and Einhorn-Bass models do not lead to inconsistent sets of cutoff scores, as such. However, both are special cases of a more general decision theory model that determines cutting scores based not only on the proportions of outcomes I-IV in Figure 1 but also on the desirability of each outcome in each subgroup (Gross & Su, 1975; Lindley, 1976). Both Petersen-Novick (1976) and Cronbach (1976) favor this more general procedure.

The Cleary approach to fair selection, which represents the familiar procedure of deriving separate regression lines, Y on X, and separate cutoff scores, X^*, for each subgroup, has received particular attention in the literature (see Anastasi, 1976, pp. 171-197; McNemar, 1975; Reilly, 1973). This approach is fair in the sense that the applicants with the highest predicted criterion scores (based on separate regression equations) are the ones that are selected. The Cleary (and Einhorn-Bass) procedure implicitly tends to give equal and total weight to outcome I across all subgroups (Cronbach, 1976, p. 38)—an approach that does not provide compensation by attaching more importance to outcome I for a minority subgroup than for a majority. This does not mean that a model should necessarily provide such compensation, but rather that previous models have not made their underlying assumptions and priorities explicit. For further discussion of the implicit assumptions underlying various selection models, see the paper by Hunter and Schmidt (1976).

Clearly then, we are just beginning to understand the strengths, weaknesses, and implications of the various methods proposed for item bias detection and fair personnel selection. Lord (1977) and Petersen and Novick (1976) seem to provide promising procedures in these two areas, respectively; but as noted previously, such techniques await further confirmation.

LATENT TRAIT THEORY

Latent trait theory has been threaded through the history of educational measurement. Its origins can be found in the work of the early psychophysicists as the phi-gamma hypothesis and in the work of Binet and Simon in the form of item-characteristic curves. The former has become the basis for much of the field of scaling and is presented in depth by Torgerson (1958). The latter became the curve-fitting approach to item analysis; a historical account of this development has been given by Baker (1965). Although its basic concepts have been used since the turn of the century, the first comprehensive presentation of latent trait theory, in the context of mental testing, appeared in Lord and Novick (1968). The next three-year period was an especially active one in the development of latent trait theory and has been thoroughly reviewed by Bock and Wood (1971). Consequently, the present review attempts to start where the Bock and Wood review terminated. To do so is similar to entering a play in the second act. Thus certain developments prior to 1970 are also included for the sake of clarity.

An unavoidable characteristic of latent trait theory is that its mathematical level is considerably higher than that encountered in standard measurement tests. As a result, advances in the field have had little immediate impact upon routine testing practice. Hence, a major purpose of this section is to make the nature of these advances and their implications available to a wider audience. (The Spring 1977 issue of the *Journal of Educational Measurement* gives another readable account of latent trait theory.) Progress has occurred in three areas: extensions of the item-characteristic curve model, estimation procedures and associated computer programs, and testing procedures capitalizing on the properties of the latent trait model. Each of these is discussed below.

Item-Characteristic Curve Models

The psychological theory underlying norm-referenced testing postulates that people possess certain characteristics, called traits, that account for their behavior. While these traits, such as intelligence and perceptiveness, have considerable intuitive meaning, they cannot be observed directly; hence they are underlying, or latent, traits. In the context of mental testing, such traits have been given the label, *ability,* and this term is used interchangeably with *latent trait* in the literature.

An item-characteristic curve is a function relating the probability of choosing a particular item response to the ability scale. If the response of interest is the correct response, the item-characteristic curve would be a monotonically increasing function of ability. Readers unfamiliar with the item characteristic-curve model are referred to Baker (1964, 1977), Henryssen (1971), and Lord and Novick (1968, chap. 16). Item-characteristic curves are typically assumed to have the form of either a normal or a logistic ogive. Both ogives represent families of cumulative distribution curves defined by two parameters, one of location and one of scale.

In item analysis usage, the *location* parameter is the mean of the ogive and specifies the point on the ability scale where the probability of choosing the item response is .50 (for persons at that point on the ability scale). In an attempt to be compatible with the more common classical approach to item analysis, this parameter is often referred to as the difficulty parameter. However, the concepts of location and difficulty are not completely interchangeable. The *scale* parameter is the reciprocal of the standard deviation of the ogive and reflects the steepness of the central portion of the ogive. This parameter is a direct analogy to the usual item-criterion correlation used as a discrimination index. An item-characteristic curve with a location parameter of —.5 and a scale parameter of +1.2 is shown in Figure 2a.

As traditionally formulated, the item-characteristic curve model has been employed with dichotomously scored items. However, in a bioassay context, Atichison and Silvey (1957) and Gurland, Lee, and Dahm (1960) extended the model to the case of graded responses. Somewhat later, Samejima (1969) made a similar extension in the context of test theory. Samejima (1973b) has carried this case to its theoretical limit—a continuum of graded responses. In a subsequent paper (Samejima, 1974), the concept was further extended to the situation where more than one ability or latent trait is involved.

In the graded-response type of item, the several response categories are considered to be ordered along the latent trait scale. Thus, low-ability persons should choose, say, high-numbered categories. If the item functions as expected, location parameters, one for each category, should be properly ordered along the ability scale. In addition, all the categories share a common discrimination (scale) index. Since the response categories are mutually exclusive and exhaustive, the sum of the probabilities of choosing the r response categories is unity, at any given point on the ability scale. Thus, given the first $r - 1$ probabilities, the rth probability is determined. To cope with this dependency, an item-characteristic curve model is used that relates the probability of choosing all categories, up to and including the one of interest, to the ability scale. Thus, the item-characteristic curves correspond to the boundaries between categories rather than the categories per se. The result is that there is one less item-characteristic curve than there are item-response categories, and the lack of independence has been taken into account. Figure 2c depicts the item-characteristic curves for an item having graded responses.

While the work on graded responses provides a model for items whose

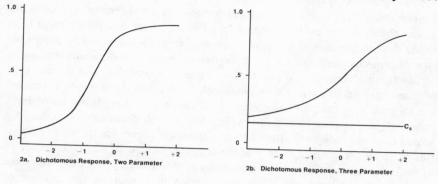

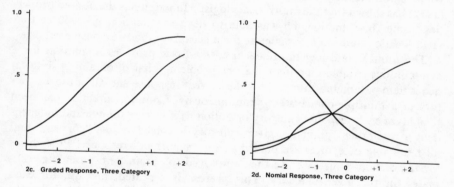

Figure 2. Item-characteristic curves.

response categories from an ordinal scale, Bock (1972) has provided a model for items whose response categories form an unordered or nominal scale. In this case, the item-response categories do not possess an ordering over the ability scale. An item represented by such a model could have several response choices, all of which are correct. For example, an item could deal with a counseling situation, and the several response categories could be typical counselor reactions, all of which are correct.

In the nominal response case, the item-response categories are mutually exclusive and exhaustive, but they are nonordered. However, the technique used to take the lack of independence into account in the graded case is not appropriate. If one considers only a single item-response category, the item-characteristic curve relating the probability of choosing that category to the ability scale can take one of two forms. These two forms have been called the monotone and nonmonotone item-response curves. The monotone type of item-characteristic curve for the category is a monotonically increasing (or decreasing) function of ability, as shown in Figure 2a. The second type of item-characteristic curve is one in which the probability of response reaches a maximum at some point along the ability scale and then decreases to zero; hence, it is a nonmonotone curve. In the case of items having nominally scored response categories, the item-characteristic curves for the set of categories must be some mixture of these two types. Figure 2d illustrates a set of item-characteristic curves for a nominally scored item having three response categories. Samejima (1972) has an extended discussion of the mixture of item-characteristic curves possible in the case of nominally scaled item-response categories.

The nominal-response case presents a very difficult problem in terms of finding a mathematical model that provides the proper mixture of curves while simultaneously coping with the lack of category independence. Bock (1972) has shown that the multivariate logistic function has the desired properties; using this function, he was able to derive estimation procedures that yield location and scale parameters for a set of nominal response categories.

The multivariate logistic model used by Bock provides a solution for a common but troublesome item analysis problem—that of obtaining simultaneous item parameter estimates for the correct response and all of the distractors of a multiple-choice item simultaneously. Common practice has been to analyze each response category or option as if it were unique and independent of the other options. A given category is considered as "correct," and all remaining categories are pooled as the "incorrect" response. Procedures for the dichotomous case are then employed to obtain item parameter estimates for the given category. This process is repeated, in turn, for each response category. Baker and Martin (1969), for example, have implemented such a procedure. However, it is obvious that under this approach the item parameter estimates for the several categories are not independent. Consequently, Bock's nominal-response model is the correct one to use when analyzing all responses to a multiple-choice item.

The item-characteristic curve models for the dichotomous, graded, and nominal scoring of an item have been integrated into a general model by Samejima (1972). In her scheme the graded case is subdivided into a homogeneous case and a heterogeneous case. Under the former, the item-characteristic curves for $r - 1$ item-response category boundaries share a common scale parameter. Under the latter, they do not; and this is the same as nominal scoring, except that the location parameters are ordered. The nominal case places no restrictions on the pattern of location and scale parameters. Samejima's contribution in this area has been to formalize the underlying mathematical conditions needed to justify the item-characteristic curve models used in conjunction with the various item-scoring procedures.

Under all three approaches to scoring an item, the item-characteristic curves employed have been two-parameter (scale and location) models. In recent years, much attention has been devoted to logistic models for dichotomously scored items with either *one* parameter or *three* parameters. Birnbaum (1968) introduced a third parameter to the logistic model, often called a guessing parameter. It provides a lower bound to the item-characteristic curve that is greater than zero, i.e., low-ability subjects have a nonzero probability of getting an item correct. This model is depicted in figure 2b. Using a very large sample of SAT data (103,275 subjects), Lord (1970a) showed a very good fit between this three-parameter logistic model and empirical item-response data.

The one-parameter logistic model, known as the Rasch model, is simply the two-parameter logistic model with the item discrimination index arbitrarily set equal to unity. When this is done, a considerable simplification in the parameter estimation procedure occurs, and both item difficulty and raw test scores acquire some desirable statistical properties. The basic Rasch model for dichotomously scored items has been extended to the graded-response case by Anderson (1973a). Independent of Bock (1966, 1972), he applied the multivariate logistic function to items having graded responses, but he employed fewer parameters and placed different restrictions on the parameters in the estimation process.

In summary, the extension of the item-characteristic curve model to the graded- and nominal-response cases accomplishes two ends. First, it extends latent trait theory to a wider range of item-scoring schemes. Second, it provides a theoretically sound basis for performing item analysis on item styles that were previously handled on an ad hoc basis. The provision of one- and three-parameter models for item-characteristic curves provides further flexibility in dealing with data sets. In addition, the one-parameter Rasch model provides conceptual simplification that has appeal to practitioners.

Estimation

The item-characteristic curve models employed under latent trait theory relate an underlying latent trait to the probability of a particular response to an item. Since this underlying trait is a hypothetical construct and is not observable, recent emphasis within latent trait theory has been on the estimation of an examinee's latent trait or ability score from the information provided by the item-response data. Obtaining ability estimates has considerable importance, since such estimates are direct measures of the variable of interest and their availability eliminates the need for indirect measures such as raw scores. One could readily conceive of reporting standardized test results in terms of such estimates. In addition, there is a theoretical advantage in employing ability estimates. Given a population of items measuring a particular trait, the ability estimates are invariant with respect to the particular set of items used to obtain the estimates. Thus, one should obtain statistically equivalent ability estimates for a given person from two or more different sets of items taken from the item pool. While this invariance holds in theory, it is difficult to obtain in practice in all but highly specialized situations (see Baker, 1974, for a discussion of the invariance issue in the context of computer-aided test construction).

A major emphasis in recent years has been deriving procedures for the joint estimation of item parameters and examinee ability levels. In this context, Bock and Lieberman (1970) have made an important distinction between conditional and unconditional parameter estimation. In the case of conditional estimation, one set of parameters is known, such as the item parameters, while the other set, such as the examinee ability levels, is estimated. Unconditional estimation makes distributional assumptions about one set of parameters (usually ability) and removes the parameters mathematically from the estimation process for the other set. In practice, only the former (conditional) approach is practical, and it is implemented in currently available computer programs.

The basic cyclic estimation paradigm was introduced by Birnbaum (1968) in conjunction with a three-parameter model and by Wright and Panchapakesan (1969) for the one-parameter (Rasch) model. Under this approach, an examinee's test score or some function of the test score is taken as the true ability score. Using these ability scores, item parameters are estimated, item by item. Then, the obtained item parameter estimates are considered as true parameter values, and ability scores are estimated. This back-and-forth procedure is repeated until a stable set of values is obtained for both sets of parameters. In the sense of Bock and Lieberman (1970), this is clearly a conditional estimation procedure. The mathematical basis for the estimation procedures is maximum likelihood, and it is well known that this technique can fail under certain conditions. In fact, Samejima (1973a) has shown that the three-parameter logistic model can encounter examinee response patterns for which the ability estimator is either not unique or does not exist. In a data set analyzed by Lord (1974b), no such problem was encountered. Waller (1974), however, has found such a case.

Under this estimation paradigm, the measurement scale obtained for the latent trait and for the item parameters is indeterminant; that is, the origin and unit of measurement are arbitrarily determined. The scale yielded by the estimation process is a function of the set of items, the group of subjects, and the techniques used to "anchor" or define the origin and determine the unit of measurement.[1] A number of different techniques have been proposed to resolve this indeterminancy (see Andersen, 1973a; Wingersky & Lord, 1973; Wright & Douglas, 1975). Whitely and Dawis (1974) indicated that under the Rasch model estimates could be anchored to a particular set of items or to a particular group of persons; however, the interpretation of such estimates would then be linked to these anchor points. The net effect would be measurements that are meaningful only within a specific context.

Lord (1975) has encountered an additional estimation problem related to the latent trait metric. For a particular set, he found a correlation between the estimates of the scale (discrimination) and location (difficulty) parameters of the items. Through the definition of a new metric he was able to eliminate this correlation.

Omitted item responses represent another problem area. The three-parameter Birnbaum paradigm has been modified by Lord (1974b) to take omitted responses into account. He employed a scoring formula of 1 for a correct response, 0 for an incorrect response, and C for an omitted response, where $C \equiv 1/A$ and A is the number of response alternatives. However, the modification resulted in parameter estimates that were not maximum likelihood estimates. As a check on the reasonableness of this approach, the characteristics of the obtained item parameter and ability estimates were compared with those yielded by the maximum likelihood procedure, with omitted responses randomly filled in. Two sets of test results were used in the study, and the results showed the ability estimates yielded by the two estimation procedures were very similar. An artificial data set was also analyzed to compare item parameter estimates; again, the two approaches produced comparable results.

The proper procedure for handling guessing in latent trait theory has also received some attention. Birnbaum's so-called guessing parameter, C_g, places a lower bound on the item characteristic curve; however its exact relationship to guessing is unclear. Wingersky and Lord (1973) used a complex set of rules to decide whether the estimate of C_g for a particular item was reasonable. If not, they replaced it by the median estimated C_g value for all items.

Waller (1974) has taken quite a different approach to taking the effects of guessing into account in estimating examinee ability. He has labeled his approach *ability removing random guessing* (ARRG). Under this procedure, the probability of a correct response to an item is estimated as a function of an examinee's ability. It is assumed that there exists a probability, P_c, dividing all item responses into two groups. The first group includes responses made on the basis of a subject's ability. The second group of responses are made on the basis of random guessing. If the estimated probability of a correct response for a given person on a given item exceeds P_c, the person's item response is retained. If it is less than P_c, the item response is scored as incorrect. Waller's procedures for item parameter and ability estimation take this rescoring into account. In an empirical study, simulated data sets containing guessing and no guessing were analyzed under the two-parameter, the three-parameter, and the ARRG approaches. The results showed that the ARRG procedure was able to identify data sets free of guessing as well as provide the best fit to the data, when the value of P_c matched the proportion of guessing built into the data. Of course, with actual data, this proportion of guessing, P_c, is not known, but the pattern of χ^2 goodness-of-fit indices may be used in determining P_c. Waller (1976) also extended the ARRG approach to handle ability estimation under the Rasch model.

Estimation procedures for the one-parameter logistic (Rasch) model have received considerable attention during the period under review. Wright and Douglas (1975) have provided a long overdue exposition of the equations and back-and-forth maximum likelihood estimation paradigm implemented by Wright and Panchapakesan (1969) for the Rasch model. A correction factor used to eliminate bias in the item difficulty estimator, but not specifically mentioned by Wright and Panchapakesan, was also explained. In addition, Wright and Douglas have developed an approximate estimation procedure (PROX) that is computationally less expensive than the original maximum likelihood approach (UCON). Through a series of analyses of artificial data they found the approximate procedure yielded estimates comparable to those from the maximum likelihood procedure. In addition, Andersen (1970, 1972, 1973a) has employed conditional maximum likelihood estimation as the basis for parameter estimation under the Rasch model. He has also provided a χ^2 test of goodness of fit between the obtained estimates and the actual data (Andersen, 1973b). However, Wright and Douglas reported Andersen's estimation procedures for dichotomously scored items were prone to accumulation of round-off error and were not useful in practice.

A common deficiency of the maximum likelihood estimation procedures used in conjunction with the Rasch model is that infinite parameter estimates are obtained for items answered correctly by everyone or by no one, and for persons with zero or perfect scores. The CALFIT computer program (Wright and Mead, 1975) has an edit feature that automatically eliminates such items and persons before the estimation process begins.

As previously noted, the Rasch model assumes that all items have a discrimination index of unity. However, Bock and Wood (1971) indicate this assumption can be relaxed to one of equal discrimination, if the metric of the ability scale is adjusted in an appropriate manner. Since experience has shown that item discrimination indices vary considerably across items within a test, there is some concern as to the appropriateness of the Rasch model. The CALFIT program calculates a statistic to measure the fit of an actual item to the model. Items not fitting the model can be removed from the data and the whole estimation process repeated until a reduced set of items fitting the model is found.

Mandeville and Smarr (1976) used the CALFIT program to analyze two tests used in a statewide testing program. They reported only 2 of the 48 items in the first test and none of the items in the second test fit the Rasch model. More encouraging results were obtained when the sample was divided by sex and by high-low score groups. In these subgroups, roughly half the items fit the model. In addition, they analyzed a classroom test constructed to fit the model and found 46 of the 50 items fit. Whitely and Dawis (1974) conducted a similar study using three different arrangements: odd-even, easy-hard, and random division of 60 test items. They found 23 percent of the easy items and 57 percent of the hard items did not fit the model. They concluded the equal discrimination index requirement was crucial to the Rasch model. They also observed, as did Andersen (1973b), that the Rasch model requires relatively large numbers of persons within each total score group. The empirical results related to the Rasch model indicate that one should use a test construction process which will lead to items with common item discrimination index values. To do so is not difficult, but it involves a restriction in the basis upon which items are retained for inclusion in the item pool.

Computer Programs

The statistical sophistication of the item-characteristic curve models and the maximum likelihood estimation of item and ability parameters makes the use of digital computers a necessity. Fortunately, a number of computer programs using the latent trait approach have been reported. Kolakowski and Bock (1973a) developed a computer program called LOGO based upon the two-parameter logistic model which yields item parameter and ability estimates for the graded- and nominal-response cases. For a test of 38 five-choice items and 700 subjects, the nominal response case required six minutes of IBM 360/65 time per cycle and four to six cycles to perform the estimation process. These same authors produced another computer program called NORMOG (Kolakowski & Bock, 1973b) for maximum likelihood estimation of item parameters under the normal ogive model for dichotomously scored items. They include a guessing parameter capability similar to Birnbaum's but require the user to specify its value for each item. The program also produces ability estimates. In contrast to LOGO, the latter program is relatively fast, requiring only 55 seconds per cycle of the estimation process. Both of these programs are available commercially.[2]

A computer program implementing Birnbaum's three-parameter logistic model when there are omitted responses has been developed by Wingersky and Lord (1973). It will accommodate 3,000 persons and up to 96 items. Using an IBM 360/65, a test of 90 items and 994 examinees required 70 seconds per cycle and between 30 and 40 cycles to converge.

Wright and his students have developed a number of computer programs for the Rasch model, the most recent of which is CALFIT (Wright & Mead, 1975). This program implements both the approximation procedure (PROX) and the maximum likelihood procedure (UCON). Running times were not reported, but given the mathematical simplicity of the Rasch model, the time per cycle should be less than those reported above.

The rather lengthy nature of the computer runs associated with the conditional estimation procedures is the result of a number of factors. First, large numbers of item parameters and ability estimates are being produced. Second, the mathematical computations are much more complex than those involved in traditional item analysis programs. Third, the back-and-forth conditional estimation paradigm must converge for both item and subject parameter estimates. Finally, the computer programs tend to employ definitional rather than computational forms of the estimation equations. Following the lead of Wright and Douglas (1975), clever approximation methods should be developed to reduce both computer costs and to increase the capacity of such computer programs.

Applications

As noted above, advances in this area have been primarily in theory and in estimation procedures. However, Lord (1974a) has discussed the potential of latent trait theory in individualized instruction. One very interesting application has been to what Lord (1970b) calls *tailored testing*. The basic idea is to estimate a person's ability with a small set of sequentially administered items that are tailored to a given person. The approach rests upon the item invariant properties of ability estimates under latent trait theory. That is, if an item's scale and location parameters are known, a subject's ability can be estimated from responses to an arbitrary set of items. However, the precision of the ability estimate is improved if the items selected have location parameters (difficulty) matching the subject's ability. Thus, a fundamental prerequisite of tailored testing is that the item pool be precalibrated; that is, item parameters should be predetermined from response data for a large norm group. It is also assumed that the person being tested is a member of the population from which the norm group was selected. Under the tailored testing paradigm, if an examinee answers an item correctly, the next item administered will be more difficult. The converse holds if the item is incorrectly answered. Items are administered sequentially until a reasonably accurate estimate of the subject's ability is obtained. Using this paradigm, tailored testing attempts to achieve as precise an estimate of ability over a range of the ability scale as conventional tests achieve at only the mean ability level.

A basic issue in such sequential testing procedures is the step size, the difference between the subject's estimated ability and the location parameter of the next item to be administered. Lord (1971a) has performed an extensive investigation comparing a fixed step size with a shrinking step size, known as the Robbins-Munro procedure. Under the latter approach, the initial step sizes are large and are intended to bracket the examinee's ability. At each successive stage a smaller step size is used to refine the ability estimate increasingly. Of concern is the relative effectiveness of the two approaches, with item economy being a basic issue. The fixed step size requires that a pool of $m(m+1)/2$ items be available to draw upon at each stage, where m is the number of stages; whereas the shrinking step size requires $2^m - 1$ items at each stage. Lord (1971a) compared the two-step size conventions under a wide variety of conditions—choice of initial items, initial step size, and the presence of guessing. His general conclusion was that the shrinking step size procedure had some advantages over fixed step sizes. However, these advantages were counterbalanced by the requirement for larger item pools if more than six stages were needed to estimate an examinee's ability level.

Lord's initial work in tailored testing has led to a variety of adaptations of the basic idea. These variations differ primarily in the nature of the strategy used to select the next item to be administered. Flexilevel testing (Lord, 1971b) employs an item pool rank ordered by difficulty (location parameter). The first item administered is at the median difficulty. Following each correct response, the next available, more difficult item is administered. The converse is true in the case of an incorrect response. The net effect is a back-and-forth convergence to a subject's ability.

A number of other single- and multiple-stage strategies have been developed and are reviewed by Weiss (1974). Weiss and his students have performed extensive investigations of what he has called *adaptive testing,* using actual items and persons as well as computer simulations. This line of inquiry has resulted in a series of research reports over the period 1972-1975 (see Weiss, 1976, for a bibliography). Under one of these strategies, the stradaptive approach, the item pool is stratified by location parameters, and within strata the items are rank ordered by discrimination index. The strategy is to switch from stratum to stratum as a function of an examinee's response and to use the items in rank order within each stratum.

Most of the work to date on adaptive testing has been performed under rather constrained circumstances involving assumptions such as equally discriminating items, no guessing, and so forth. Thus, although the results are encouraging, they lack generality (see comments by Bock and Linn in Weiss, 1975). Consequently, additional research will be needed to develop a more complete picture of the potential of adaptive testing.

In a somewhat different application, latent trait theory has been used by Lord (1973) to estimate the total test score of examinees who were not given sufficient time to complete a power test, that is, who were mistimed. The item parameters for the 90-item test were estimated from the item-response data of 994 subjects, including 21 who were mistimed. Using these item parameter estimates, the ability of the examinees who were mistimed was estimated. In addition, Lord was able to estimate their number-right test scores. A scattergram of the total sample showed very good agreement between the actual and estimated number-right test scores. On the basis of this agreement, he felt justified in predicting the total test score of the 21 students who were mistimed.

Summary of Latent Trait Theory

It is clear that latent trait theory is rapidly achieving the status of a comprehensive test theory. The recent extensions of the item-characteristic curve model to the cases of graded and nominal responses are particularly significant. In addition, considerable attention is now being focused upon the role of latent trait theory in estimating underlying ability. Current computer procedures enable one to routinely estimate a subject's ability as well as item parameters, opening the possibility of test results being reported as estimated ability rather than as raw or transformed test scores. By taking advantage of some rather basic properties of latent trait theory, a number of testing strategies have evolved. These tailored and adaptive strategies are well suited to interactive computing, and one can foresee the growth of computer-aided testing based upon this approach.

Latent trait theory has not yet permeated the widely used measurement texts. Yet it provides a more comprehensive conceptualization of the role of items in test theory than do the classical notions of item difficulty and item-criterion correlation. Undoubtedly the mathematical level of the current latent trait literature stands as a barrier to popularization of the approach. However, elementary exposition of latent trait theory, coupled with readily available computer programs, may yet translate the theoretical gains into better practice.

CONCLUSION

This chapter has reviewed topics of current interest in educational measurement, with particular attention to the period 1970-1976.

First, criterion-referenced measurement was discussed. A distinction was made between domain-referenced and mastery tests; and item selection, reliability, validity estimation, and so on were considered separately for each type of test. Second, the issue of test bias was considered. Here, a distinction was made between item bias and selection bias, and promising approaches in each area were identified. Finally, latent trait theory was reviewed. The concept of an item-characteristic curve was introduced; procedures for estimating associated parameters were noted; and test applications of latent trait theory were provided.

NOTES

1. It is of interest to note that both the iterative paradigm and the indeterminancy of the resulting ability scale are also encountered in individual-differences scaling procedures (Torgerson, 1968).

2. Source for the computer programs is National Educational Resources, Inc., 215 Kenwood Avenue, Ann Arbor, Michigan 48103.

REFERENCES

Ahmann, J. S., & Glock, M. D. *Evaluating pupil growth: Principles of tests and measurements* (5th ed.). Boston: Allyn & Bacon, 1975.

Aiken, L. R., Jr. *Psychological testing and assessment* (2nd ed.). Boston: Allyn & Bacon, 1976.

Anastasi, A. Some implications of cultural factors for test construction. In A. Anastasi (Ed.), *Testing problems in perspective.* Washington, D.C.: American Council on Education, 1966.

Anastasi, A. *Psychological testing* (4th ed.). New York: Macmillan, 1976.

Andersen, E. B. Asymptotic properties of conditional maximum-likelihood estimators. *Journal of the Royal Statistical Society, Series B,* 1970, *32,* 283-301.

Andersen, E. B. The numerical solution of a set of conditional estimation equations. *Journal of the Royal Statistical Society, Series B,* 1972, *34,* 42-45.

Andersen, E. B. Conditional inference for multiple choice questionnaires. *British Journal of Mathematical and Statistical Psychology,* 1973, *26,* 31-44. (a)

Andersen, E. B. A goodness of fit test for the Rasch model. *Psychometrika,* 1973, *38,* 123-140. (b)

Angoff, W. H. Scales, norms, and equivalent scores. In R. L. Thorndike (Ed.), *Educational measurement* (2nd ed.). Washington, D.C.: American Council on Education, 1971.

Angoff, W. H. *General considerations in the study of test bias when the criterion is absent.* Paper presented at the annual meeting of the American Educational Research Association, San Francisco, April 1976.

Angoff, W. H., & Ford, S. F. Item-race interaction on a test of scholastic aptitude. *Journal of Educational Measurement,* 1973, *10,* 95-106.

Atichison, J., & Silvey, S. D. The generalization of profit analysis to the case of multiple responses. *Biometrika,* 1957, *44,* 131-140.

Baker, F. B. An intersection of test score interpretation and item analysis. *Journal of Educational Measurement,* 1964, *1,* 23-28.

Baker, F. B. Origins of the item parameters X_{50} and β as a modern item analysis technique. *Journal of Educational Measurement,* 1965, *2,* 167-180.

Baker, F. B. The roles of statistics. In G. Lippey (Ed.), *Computer-assisted test construction.* Englewood Cliffs, N.J.: Educational Technology Press, 1974.

Baker, F. B. Advances in item analysis. *Review of Educational Research,* 1977, *47,* 151-178.

Baker, F. B., & Martin, T. J. FORTAP: A FORTRAN test analysis package. *Educational and Psychological Measurement,* 1969, *29,* 159-164.

Biggs, D. L., & Lewis, E. L. *Measurement and evaluation in the schools.* Boston; Houghton Mifflin, 1975.

Birnbaum, A. Some latent trait models and their use in inferring an examinee's ability. In F. M. Lord and M. R. Novick, *Statistical theories of mental test scores.* Reading, Mass.: Addison-Wesley, 1968.

Block, J. H. Student learning and the setting of mastery performance standards. *Educational Horizons,* 1972, *50,* 183-190.

Bock, R. D. *Estimating multinomial response relations* (Research Memorandum No. 5). Chicago: Statistical Laboratory, Department of Education, University of Chicago, 1966.

Bock, R. D. Estimating item parameters and latent ability when responses are scored in two or more nominal categories. *Psychometrika,* 1972, *37,* 29-51.

Bock, R. D., & Lieberman, M. Fitting a response model for n dichotomously scored items. *Psychometrika,* 1970, *35,* 179-197.

Bock, R. D., & Wood, R. Test theory. *Annual Review of Psychology,* 1971, *22,* 193-224.

Bormuth, J. R. *On the theory of achievement test items.* Chicago: University of Chicago Press, 1970.

Brennan, R. L. A generalized upper-lower item discrimination index. *Educational and Psychological Measurement,* 1972, *32,* 289-303.

Brennan, R. L., & Kane, M. T. An index of dependability for mastery tests. *Journal of Educational Measurement,* 1977, *14,* 277-289.

Brown, F. G. *Principles of educational and psychological testing* (2nd ed.). New York: Holt, Rinehart, & Winston, 1976.

Buros, O. K. (Ed.) *The seventh mental measurements yearbook.* Highland Park, N.J.: Gryphon Press, 1972.

Buros, O. K. (Ed.) *Tests in print II.* Highland Park, N.J.: Gryphon Press, 1974.

Chase, C. I. *Measurement for educational evaluation.* Reading, Mass.: Addison-Wesley, 1974.

Cleary, T. A. Test bias: Prediction of grades of Negro and white students in integrated colleges. *Journal of Educational Measurement,* 1968, *5,* 115-124.

Cleary, T. A., & Hilton, T. L. An investigation of item bias. *Educational and Psychological Measurement,* 1968, *28,* 61-75.

Cole, N. S. Bias in selection. *Journal of Educational Measurement,* 1973, *10,* 237-255.

Cox, R. C., & Vargas, J. C. *A comparison of item selection techniques for norm-referenced and criterion-referenced tests.* Paper presented at the annual meeting of the American Educational Research Association, Chicago, February 1972.

Crambert, A. C. *Use of mastery cutoff scores in criterion-referenced measurement.* Paper presented at the annual meeting of the American Educational Research Association, San Francisco, April 1976.

Crehan, K. D. Item analysis for teacher-made mastery tests. *Journal of Educational Measurement,* 1974, *11,* 255-262.

Crocker, L., & Benson, J. Achievement, guessing, and risk-taking behavior under norm referenced and criterion referenced testing conditions. *American Educational Research Journal,* 1976, *13,* 207-215.

Cronbach, L. J. Test validation. In R. L. Thorndike (Ed.), *Educational measurement* (2nd ed.). Washington, D.C.: American Council on Education, 1971.

Cronbach, L. J. Equity in selection—where psychometrics and political philosophy meet. *Journal of Educational Measurement,* 1976, *13,* 31-44.

Cronbach, L. J., Glaser, G. C., Nanda, H., & Rajaratnam, N. *The dependability of behavioral measurements: Theory of generalizability for scores and profiles.* New York: John Wiley, 1972.

Darlington, R. B. Some techniques for maximizing a test's validity when the criterion variable is unobserved. *Journal of Educational Measurement,* 1970, *7,* 1-14.

Darlington, R. B. Another look at "cultural fairness." *Journal of Educational Measurement,* 1971, *8,* 71-82.

Ebel, R. L. Content standard test scores. *Educational and Psychological Measurement,* 1962, *22,* 15-25.

Ebel, R. L. Criterion-referenced measurements: Limitations. *School Review,* 1971, *79,* 282-288.

Ebel, R. L. *Essentials of eductional measurement.* Englewood Cliffs, N.J.: Prentice-Hall, 1972.

Echternacht, G. J. *A quick method for determining test bias* (Research Bulletin 72-17). Princeton, N.J.: Educational Testing Service, 1972.

Edwards, A. L. *Techniques of attitude scale construction.* New York: Appleton-Century-Crofts, 1957.

Einhorn, H. J., & Bass, A. R. Methodological considerations relevant to discrimination in employment testing. *Psychological Bulletin,* 1971, *75,* 261-269.

Emrick, J. A. An evaluation model for mastery testing. *Journal of Educational Measurement,* 1971, *8,* 321-326.

Fhanér, S. Item sampling and decision making in achievement testing. *British Journal of Mathematical and Statistical Psychology,* 1974, *27,* 172-175.

Glaser, R., & Nitko, A. J. Measurement in learning and instruction. In R. L. Thorndike (Ed.), *Educational measurement* (2nd ed.). Washington, D.C.: American Council on Education, 1971.

Goodman, L. A., & Krushal, W. H. Measures of association for cross-classifications. *Journal of the American Statistical Association,* 1954, *49,* 732-764.

Green, D. R. *Reducing bias in achievement tests.* Paper presented at the annual meeting of the American Educational Research Association, San Francisco, April 1976.

Green, D. R., & Draper, J. F. *Exploratory studies of bias in achievement tests.* Paper presented at the annual meeting of the American Psychological Association, Honolulu, August 1972.

Gronlund, N. E. *Measurement and evaluation in teaching* (3rd ed.). New York: Macmillan, 1976.

Gross, A. L., & Su, W. Defining a "fair" or "unbiased" selection model: A question of utilities. *Journal of Applied Psychology,* 1975, *60,* 345-351.

Gupta, S. S. Probability integrals of multivariate normal and multivariate *t. Annals of Mathematical Statistics,* 1963, *34,* 792-828.

Gurland, L., Lee, I., & Dahm, P. A. Polychotomous quantal response in biological assay. *Biometrics,* 1960, *16,* 382-398.

Guttman, L. Integration of test design and analysis. In *Proceedings of the 1969 invitational conference on testing problems.* Princeton, N.J.: Educational Testing Service, 1969.

Haladyna, T. M. Effects of different samples on item and test characteristics of criterion-referenced tests. *Journal of Educational Measurement,* 1974, *11,* 93-99.

Haladyna, T. M., & Roid, G. H. *The quality of domain-referenced test items.* Paper presented at the annual meeting of the American Educational Research Association, San Francisco, April 1976.

Hambleton, R. K., & Novick, M. R. Toward an integration of theory and method for criterion-referenced tests. *Journal of Educational Measurement,* 1973, *10,* 159-170.

Harris, C. W. Some technical characteristics of mastery tests. In C. W. Harris, M. C. Alkin, and W. J. Popham (Eds.), *Problems in criterion-referenced measurement* (CSE Monograph Series in Evaluation No. 3). Los Angeles: University of California at Los Angeles, Center for the Study of Evaluation, 1974.

Harris, M. L., & Stewart, D. M. *Application of classical strategies to criterion-referenced test construction.* Paper presented at the annual meeting of the American Educational Research Association, New York, March, 1971.

Hawkes, H. E., Lindquist, E. F., & Mann, C. R. *The construction and use of achievement examinations.* Boston: Houghton Mifflin, 1936.

Henryssen, S. Gathering, analyzing, and using data on test items. In R. L. Thorndike

(Ed.), *Educational measurement.* Washington, D.C.: American Council on Education, 1971.

Hively, W., Maxwell, G., Rabehl, G., Sension, D., & Lunden, S. *Domain referenced curriculum evaluation: A technical handbook and a case study from the Minnemast Project* (CSE Monograph Series in Evaluation No. 1). Los Angeles: University of California at Los Angeles, Center for the Study of Evaluation, 1973.

Hunter, J. E., & Schmidt, F. L. Critical analysis of the statistical and ethical implications of various definitions of *test bias. Psychological Bulletin,* 1976, *83,* 1053-1071.

Huynh, H. Reliability of decisions in domain-referenced testing. *Journal of Educational Measurement,* 1976, *13,* 253-264. (a)

Huynh, H. *On the reliability of multiple classifications.* Paper presented at the joint meeting of the Psychometric Society and the Mathematical Psychology Group, Murray Hill, N.J., April, 1976. (b)

Huynh, H. Statistical consideration of mastery scores. *Psychometrika,* 1976, *41,* 65-78. (c)

Huynh, H., & Perney, J. *Determination of mastery scores when instructional units are linearly related.* Paper presented at the annual meeting of the American Educational Research Association, San Francisco 1976.

Jensen, A. P. *An examination of culture bias in the Wonderlic Personnel Test.* Berkeley: University of California, 1973. (ERIC Document Reproduction Service No. ED 086 726)

Kolakowski, D., & Bock, R. D. *LOGO: Maximum likelihood item analysis and test scoring-logistic model for multiple item responses.* Ann Arbor: National Educational Resources, 1973. (a)

Kolakowski, D., & Bock, R. D. *NORMOG—Maximum likelihood item analysis and test scoring: Normal ogive model.* Ann Arbor: National Educational Resources, 1973. (b)

Kriewall, T. E. Application of information theory and acceptance sampling principles to the management of mathematics instruction (Doctoral dissertation, University of Wisconsin, 1969). *Dissertation Abstracts International,* 1970, *30,* 5344. (University Microfilms No. 69-22417)

LaValle, I. H. *An introduction to probability, decision, and inference.* New York: Holt, Rinehart & Winston, 1970.

Lien, A. J. *Measurement and evaluation of learning* (3rd ed.). Dubuque, Ia.: William C. Brown, 1976.

Lindley, D. V. A class of utility functions. *Annals of Statistics,* 1976, *4,* 1-10.

Linn, R. L. Fair test use in selection. *Review of Educational Research,* 1973, *43,* 139-161.

Lippy, G. (Ed.). *Computer-assisted test construction.* Englewood Cliffs, N.J.: Educational Technology Press, 1974.

Lord, F. M. Item characteristic curves estimated without knowledge of their mathematical form: A confrontation of Birnbaum's logistic model. *Psychometrika,* 1970, *35,* 43-50. (a)

Lord, F. M. Some test theory for tailored testing. In W. H. Holtzman (Ed.), *Computer-assisted instruction, testing, and guidance.* New York: Harper & Row, 1970. (b)

Lord, F. M. Robbins-Munro procedures for tailored testing. *Educational and Psychological Measurement,* 1971, *31,* 3-31. (a)

Lord, F. M. The self-scoring flexilevel test. *Journal of Educational Measurement,* 1971, *8,* 147-151. (b)

Lord, F. M. Power scores estimated by item characteristic curves. *Educational and Psychological Measurement,* 1973, *33,* 219-224.

Lord, F. M. Estimation of latent ability and item parameters when there are omitted responses. *Psychometrika,* 1974, *39,* 247-264. (a)

Lord, F. M. Individualized testing and item characteristic curve theory. In D. H. Krantz, R. C. Atkinson, R. D. Luce, & P. Suppes (Eds.), *Contemporary developments in mathematical psychology.* San Francisco: W. H. Freeman, 1974. (b)

Lord, F. M. The 'ability' scale in item characteristic curve theory. *Psychometrika,* 1975, *40,* 205-218.

Lord, F. M. *A study of item bias using item characteristic curve theory.* In Y. H. Poortinga (Ed.), *Basic problems in cross-cultural psychology.* Amsterdam: Swets & Zeitlinger, 1977.

Lord, F. M., & Novick, M. R. *Statistical theories of mental test scores.* Reading, Mass.: Addison-Wesley, 1968.

Lumsden, J. Test theory. *Annual Review of Psychology,* 1976, *27,* 251-280.

Mandeville, G. K., & Smarr, A. M. *Rasch model analysis of three types of cognitive data.* Paper presented at annual meeting of the American Educational Research Association, San Francisco, April 1976.

Marshall, J. L., & Haertel, E. H. *The mean split-half coefficient of agreement: A single-administration index of reliability for mastery tests.* Unpublished manuscript, University of Wisconsin, 1976.

McNemar, Q. On so-called test bias. *American Psychologist,* 1975, *30,* 848-851.

Mehrens, W. A., & Lehmann, I. J. *Measurement and evaluation in education and psychology.* New York: Holt, Rinehart & Winston, 1973.

Meskauskas, J. A. Evaluation models for criterion-referenced testing: Views regarding mastery and standard setting. *Review of Educational Research,* 1975, *46,* 133-158.

Millman, J. Passing scores and test lengths for domain-referenced measures. *Review of Educational Research,* 1973, *43,* 205-216.

Millman, J. Criterion-referenced measurement. In W. J. Popham (Ed.), *Evaluation in education: Current applications.* Berkeley, Cal.: McCutchan, 1974.

Millman, J., & Popham, W. J. The issue of item and test variance for criterion-referenced tests: A clarification. *Journal of Educational Measurement,* 1974, *11,* 137-138.

Nedelsky, L. Absolute grading standards for objective tests. *Educational and Psychological Measurement,* 1954, *14,* 3-19.

Noll, V. H., & Scannell, D. P. *Introduction to educational measurement* (3rd ed.). New York: Houghton Mifflin, 1972.

Novick, M. R., & Lewis, C. Prescribing test length for criterion-referenced measurement. In C. W. Harris, M. C. Alkin, and W. J. Popham (Eds.), *Problems in criterion-referenced measurement* (CSE Monograph Series in Evaluation No. 3). Los Angeles: University of California at Los Angeles, Center for the Study of Evaluation, 1974.

Novick, M. R., Lewis, C., & Jackson, P. H. The estimation of proportions in *m* groups. *Psychometrika,* 1973, *38,* 19-46.

Nunnally, J. C. *Educational measurement and evaluation* (2nd ed.). New York: McGraw-Hill, 1972.

Osburn, H. G. Item sampling for achievement testing. *Educational and Psychological Measurement,* 1968, *28,* 95-104.

Payne, D. A. *The assessment of learning: Cognitive and affective.* Lexington, Mass.: D. C. Heath, 1974.

Petersen, N. S., & Novick, M. R. An evaluation of some models for culture-fair selection. *Journal of Educational Measurement,* 1976, *13,* 3-29.

Popham, W. J. Selecting objectives and generating test items for objectives based tests. In C. W. Harris, M. A. Alkin, and W. J. Popham (Eds.), *Problems in criterion-referenced measurement* (CSE Monograph Series in Evalution No. 3). Los Angeles, Center for the Study of Evaluation, 1974.

Popham, W. J. *Educational evaluation.* Englewood Cliffs, N.J.: Prentice-Hall, 1975.

Reilly, R. R. A note on minority group test bias studies. *Psychological Bulletin,* 1973, *80,* 130-132.

Rudner, L. M. Approaches toward biased item identification. Manuscript submitted for publication, 1976.

Samejima, F. Estimation of latent ability using a response pattern of graded scores. *Psychometrika,* 1969, *34* (Pt. 2), 1-97. (Monograph)

Samejima, F. A general model for free response data. *Psychometrika,* 1972, *37* (4, Pt. 2), 1-68. (Monograph)

Samejima, F. A comment on Birnbaum's three-parameter logistic model in the latent trait theory. *Psychometrika,* 1973, *38,* 221-233. (a)

Samejima, F. Homogeneous case of the continuous response model. *Psychometrika,* 1973, *38,* 203-219. (b)

Samejima, F. Normal ogive model on the continuous response level in the multidimensional latent space. *Psychometrika,* 1974, *39,* 111-121.

Sax, G. *Principles of educational measurement and evaluation.* Belmont, Cal.: Wadsworth, 1974.

Scheuneman, J. *A new method of assessing bias in test items.* Paper presented at the annual meeting of the American Educational Research Association, Washington, D.C., April 1975.

Scheuneman, J. *Validating a procedure for assessing bias in test items in the absence of an outside criterion.* Paper presented at the annual meeting of the American Educational Research Association, San Francisco, April 1976.

Standards for educational and psychological tests. Washington, D.C.: American Psychological Association, 1974.

Stanley, J. C., & Hopkins, K. D. *Educational and psychological measurement and evaluation.* Englewood Cliffs, N.J.: Prentice-Hall, 1972.

Subkoviak, M. J. Estimating reliability from a single administration of a criterion-referenced test. *Journal of Educational Measurement,* 1976, *13,* 265-276.

Subkoviak, M. J. Reliability for criterion-referenced tests: Some additional comments (Laboratory of Experimental Design, Occasional Paper No. 17). Unpublished manuscript, University of Wisconsin-Madison, 1977.

Swaminathan, H., Hambleton, R. K., & Algina, J. Reliability of criterion-referenced tests: A decision-theoretic formulation. *Journal of Educational Measurement,* 1974, *11,* 263-268.

Swaminathan, H., Hambleton, R. K., & Algina, J. A Bayesian decision-theoretic procedure for use with criterion-referenced tests. *Journal of Educational Measurement,* 1975, *12,* 87-98.

Tables of the bivariate normal distribution and related functions. Washington, D.C.: U.S. Government Printing Office, 1959.

Thorndike, R. L. Concepts of culture-fairness. *Journal of Educational Measurement,* 1971, *8,* 63-70

Thorndike, R. L. (Ed.). *Educational measurement* (2nd ed.). Washington, D.C.: American Council on Education, 1971.

Thorndike, R. L., & Hagen, E. *Measurement and evaluation in psychology and evaluation* (4th ed.). New York: John Wiley, 1977.

Tittle, C. K., McCarthy, K., & Steckler, J. F. *Women and educational testing.* Unpublished manuscript, Educational Testing Services, 1974.

Torgerson, W. S. *Theory and methods of scaling.* New York: John Wiley, 1958.

Torgerson, W. S. "Scaling." *International Encyclopedia of Social Sciences* (Vol. 14, pp. 25-28). Crowell, Collier & Macmillan, 1968.

Tuckman, B. W. *Measuring educational outcomes: Fundamentals of testing.* New York: Harcourt Brace Jovanovich, 1975.

Waller, M. I. *Removing the effects of random guessing from latent trait ability estimates* (Research Bulletin RB-74-32). Princeton, N.J.: Educational Testing Service, 1974.

Waller, M. I. *Estimating parameters in the Rasch model: Removing the effects of random guessing* (Research Bulletin RB-76-8). Princeton, N.J.: Educational Testing Service, 1976.

Weiss, D. J. *Strategies of adaptive measurement* (Research Report 74-5). Minneapolis: Psychometric Methods Program, Department of Psychology, University of Minnesota, 1974.

Weiss, D. J. (Ed.). *Computerized adaptive trait measurement: Problems and perspectives* (Research Report 75-5). Minneapolis: Psychometric Methods Program, Department of Psychology, University of Minnesota, 1975.

Weiss, D. J. *Computerized ability testing* (Final Rep.). Minneapolis: Psychometric Methods Program, Department of Psychology, University of Minnesota, 1976.

Whitely, S. E., & Dawis, R. V. The nature of objectivity with the Rasch model. *Journal of Educational Measurement,* 1974, *11,* 163-177.

Wick, J. W. *Educational measurement: Where are we going and how will we know when we get there?* Columbus, Ohio: Charles E. Merrill, 1973.

Wilcox, R. R. A note on test length and passing score of a mastery test. *Journal of Educational Statistics,* 1976, *1,* 359-364.

Wilcox, R. R., & Harris, C. A. On Emrich's "An evaluation model for mastery testing." *Journal of Educational Measurement,* 1977, *14,* 215-218.

Wingersky, M. S., & Lord, F. M. *A computer program for estimating examinee ability and item characteristic curve parameters when there are omitted responses* (Research Memorandum 73-2). Princeton, N.J.: Educational Testing Service, 1973.

Woodson, M. I. C. E. The issue of item and test variance for criterion-referenced tests. *Journal of Educational Measurement,* 1974, *11,* 63-64. (a)

Woodson, M. I. C. E. The issue of item and test variance for criterion-referenced tests: A reply. *Journal of Educational Measurement,* 1974, *11,* 139-140. (b)

Wright, B. D., & Douglas, G. A. *Better procedures for sample-free item analysis* (Research Memorandum 20). Chicago: Statistical Laboratory, Department of Education, University of Chicago, 1975.

Wright, B. D., & Mead, R. J. *CALFIT: Sample-free item calibration with a Rasch measurement model* (Research Memorandum 18). Chicago: Statistical Laboratory, Department of Education. University of Chicago, 1975.

Wright, B. D., & Panchapakesan, N. A procedure for sample-free item analysis. *Educational and Psychological Measurement,* 1969, *29,* 23-48.

8

Making Sense of Curriculum Evaluation: Continuities and Discontinuities in an Educational Idea

DAVID HAMILTON
Centre for Applied Research in Education
University of East Anglia
Norwich, England

At first encounter the reviewer's task for this chapter appears impossible. Curriculum evaluation is a field which lacks a strong sense of boundary. The growing corpus of published and unpublished material tends to foster feelings of unease and incompetence rather than insight and optimism. The more secluded corners of the academic garden seem to offer a greater sense of security.

Further reflection, however, indicates the shallowness of such withdrawal. Disengagement is neither a solution to the problems of the researcher nor an adequate representation of the process of intellectual inquiry. Curriculum evaluation—like any other educational activity—is guided by the accumulated experience (or inexperience) of its participants and focused by their individual or group aspirations. The purpose of this chapter is to examine the conventional, but often tacit, wisdom of curriculum evaluation. In short, it is an attempt to demystify the invisible college.

Two broad strategies are open to a reviewer. The first is to adopt the style of a 19th-century anthropologist and set out, as it were, to unearth the totality of cultural artifacts embedded in a bygone age. Unfortunately, however, product-centered reviews of this type are often trapped by their own rhetoric. By claiming to provide an exhaustive account they also become

ROBERT STAKE, University of Illinois, Urbana, and HERBERT J. WALBERG, University of Illinois, Chicago Circle, were the editorial consultants for this chapter.

Note: The author would like to thank colleagues at the Centre for Applied Research in Education (University of East Anglia, Norwich, England) and the Center for Instructional Research and Curriculum Evaluation (University of Illinois, Urbana) for their material and intellectual assistance with this chapter.

impossible to complete. Posthumous or partial publication is their most conspicuous outcome.

The second strategy is to focus upon the processes of research. Reviews of this type make no particular claim to catalog the myriad manifestations of an endeavor but rather seek to characterize the generative elements that help to create them.

This chapter follows the second strategy. Its aim is to make sense of the present through an appraisal of the past. A historical perspective is believed to be a valid and useful heuristic for establishing the processes that activate curriculum evaluation. No claim is made that this account provides an all-embracing history of evaluation. Indeed, to do so would be to switch to the encyclopedic stance of the erstwhile anthropologist.

There is also a more profound sense in which this account cannot be complete. As a recurrent feature of educational life, curriculum evaluation necessarily prefigures a past that has yet to come. Thus, insofar as the interpretations of this paper are sensitive to the future as well as to the past, they must remain, in Cronbach's cautionary phrase, "more provocative rather than authoritative" (1963, p. 672).

Guided by these initial assumptions, this chapter is divided into four sections. The first part, "Some Perspectives for the Study of Curriculum Evaluation," offers a set of conceptual prisms for differentiating the relatively unchanging features of curriculum evaluation. Primarily, its purpose is to delimit the concerns of this review. The second part, "The Origins of Curriculum Evaluation," outlines the beliefs and practices which came to dominate evaluation research after World War II, arguing that many of these concerns had remained unaltered since the 19th century. The third part, "Curriculum Evaluation and the Image of Consensus," considers the incorporation of these earlier ideas into the education reform movements of the 1960s and early 1970s. It focuses on the relationship between evaluation as course improvement and evaluation as social auditing. The fourth part, "Curriculum Evaluation and the Image of Pluralism," documents and comments upon some of the contrary perspectives that have arisen along with the consensus assumptions of the 1960s. Accordingly, it suggests that recent developments reveal the existence of a major disjunction in both the theory and practice of curriculum evaluation.

Overall, the aims of this chapter are to distill the ideas and events of the past 150 years and to provide a parsimonious yet comprehensive review of contemporary practice in curriculum evaluation.

SOME PERSPECTIVES FOR THE STUDY OF CURRICULUM EVALUATION

The substance of this review is held together by a number of different unifying ideas. These relate to evaluation as a form of practical morality, evaluation and social change, evaluation and curriculum development, the internal and external dynamics of evaluation, the politics of evaluation, and evaluation and pluralism.

The foremost assumption of this chapter is that curriculum evaluation falls within the sphere of practical morality. As such, it responds not only to the ethical question "What should we do?" but also to the empirical question "What can we do?" Traditionally, however, these two questions have been held at arm's length by the educational research community. Value statements have been regarded as something quite different from factual statements. As Scriven (1974, p. 4) has noted, many of the debates surrounding curriculum evaluation have been created through the interpenetration of these hitherto separately considered concerns.

The second assumption is that societal concern for evaluation is heightened, if not created, by the facts of social change. Evaluation is meaningless without the possibility or requirement of alternative courses of action. Almost by definition, social change engenders such options. Evaluative actions are as old as social life. They occur whenever there is a social setting and someone in a position to change it. Curriculum evaluation takes place at all levels in the education system. A kindergarten child's decision to do math rather than painting is, in principle, just as much an evaluation as a superintendent's decision to spend more money on science and less on the arts. In each of these examples, a choice is made by weighing the options against a set of criteria. These illustrations, however, indicate only part of the story. Throughout the history of schooling continuous attempts have been made to translate these informal decision processes into explicit rules and formal procedures. Governments have made evaluation compulsory; federal agencies have formulated guidelines; universities have trained evaluators; textbooks have supplied methodologies; journals have established accepted practices. And so on. Thus social change creates not only new options but also new traditions and institutions.

The third assumption is that curriculum evaluation can be seen as functionally related to curriculum development. For instance, if curriculum developers attend to the production of instructional packages, evaluators seem to respond in analogous fashion (e.g., the "Product Evaluation Profile" in Scriven, 1974). If, however, development becomes the preparation of delivery systems, then procedures developed for the evaluation of packages may become devalued and inoperative.

The fourth assumption is that curriculum evaluation has both an internal and external dynamic. It can be discussed, for instance, within the restricted concerns of program operation as well as within the broader boundaries of social policy. These overlapping realms of thought and action do not always operate in concert. There is always the possibility of disagreement among the various parties to the evaluation, such as researchers, sponsors, and audiences.

A fifth assumption is that evaluation is directly linked to the distribution of resources in the education system. As such it is essentially a political process. The history of curriculum evaluation can be seen as part of the struggle by different interest groups—educationalists, teachers, administrators, industrialists—to gain control and exercise power over the forces that shape the practices of schooling. In these terms, a review of curriculum evaluation has also to be concerned with the distribution of power in the education system.

The final assumption of this review relates to the idea of evaluation as a social process. As indicated above, evaluations conducted by individuals with respect to their own practice are usually based on a single set of criteria. If, however, more than one person is involved, the process takes on a completely different complexion. The participants may not agree upon the selection of criteria. Consensus can no longer be assumed. To this extent, value differences are crucial to the organization and enactment of educational change. They figure prominently in this review.

THE ORIGINS OF CURRICULUM EVALUATION

An appropriate starting point is the work of John Stuart Mill (1806-1873). In the first half of the 19th century Mill laid down some of the most important ground rules of Western thought. Together with the ideas of colleagues and contemporaries like Bentham, Carlyle, Whewell, Herschel, Comte, and de Tocqueville, Mill's notions have exerted a major, though often unrecognised, influence on 20th-century social philosophy. As a journal editor and member of parliament, and as a philosopher and economist, Mill was a pivotal figure in the linking of scientific practice to social administration. His writings—notably *A System of Logic* (1843), *Principles of Political Economy* (1848) and *Utilitarianism* (1861)—were both a defense and an elaboration of the liberal ideologies that took shape during the periods of revolutionary social change in North America and Western Europe. They were an "attempt . . . to embody and systematize" the "best ideas of the epoch" (*A System of Logic,* preface). Although more than a century has passed since Mill reached the height of his career, the issues he addressed are still a source of contention among theorists, administrators, and politicians.

Mill's impact on curriculum evaluation can be traced to three related concerns. First, he provided a coherent rationale for the conduct of the social sciences. Second, he developed a naturalistic (i.e., empirically rooted) theory of ethics. And third, he laid the philosophic foundations for what would now be termed the *welfare state.*

Science, Values, and State Intervention

A System of Logic was published in eight editions during Mill's life time. It was the first comprehensive formulation of the newly fashionable empirical method, and the "best attacked" book of the time (Nagel, 1950, p. xvii). In the final section ("On the Logic of the Moral Sciences") Mill sought to rescue the "proper study of mankind" from what he regarded as the inadequacies of philosophy and theology. He emphasized that the moral (i.e., social) sciences should follow the same methods and strive for the same goals as the natural sciences. By this reasoning, Mill articulated what would now be called the *scientific approach* (Kerlinger, 1964) to the study of social phenomena.

Mill's utilitarian theory of ethics was directly related to his views on scientific and logical method. In its most general form utilitarianism embodies two assumptions: first, that principles of conduct can be adduced from the canons of experimental inquiry, and second, that social behavior can be unequivocably judged against an overarching (and "self-evident") moral principle. These assumptions enabled Mill to measure morality against a one-dimensional ordinal scale. The "Greatest Happiness" can be established unequivocally by reference to what "competent judges" consider to be "desirable" (*Utilitarianism,* part 2). By adopting this form of moral yardstick Mill was able to overcome what would now be called the criterion problem in evaluation:

There must be some standard by which to determine the goodness or badness, absolute or comparative, of ends or objects of desires. And whatever that standard is, there can be but one; for if there were several ultimate principles of conduct, the same conduct might be approved by one of these principles and condemned by another; and there will be needed some more general principle as umpire between them (*A System of Logic,* final chapter).

Mill's views on the state also drew support from his moral precepts. He believed that in certain areas of social life (e.g., elementary education, the alleviation of poverty), the free-trade assumptions of laissez-faire government were contrary to the overall "Greatest Happiness" of society. As a result, Mill held that the welfare state should act as a counterbalancing force by supporting the charitable efforts of "private and voluntary agency" (*Principles of Political Economy,* Book 5, Chapter 11; there were seven editions during Mill's lifetime).

In 1859, the publication of Charles Darwin's *The Origin of Species* gave Mill's methodological and political ideas a fresh lease on life. The Darwinian precept that differences between members of the same species provide the mainspring of biological evolution gave a new impetus to the empirical study of human characteristics. Soon after Mill's death in 1873, Francis Galton began a series of anthropometric and psychometric surveys which helped to establish not only a psychology of individual differences but also a new inferential calculus (correlational analysis) for the codification of empirical associations (see Hamilton, 1974). The United States first learned of Galton's ideas—and those of his associate Karl Pearson—through the efforts of J. McKeen Cattell, who coined the term *mental test* in 1890, and Edward L. Thorndike, who used their ideas in the construction of achievement tests (see Joncich, 1968, pp. 290-293).

Although Mill and Galton shared a common belief in the scientific methods of the 19th century, their political theories were mutually at variance. Mill stressed the shaping influence of environmental forces; Galton emphasized the primary importance of heredity. Nevertheless, the methodological unity of the two schools of thought meant that their ideas could be tested using the same equipment and procedures. A rash of social investigations in late 19th-century Britain were the outcome of this common concern. The crucial question was whether social assistance increased or decreased the self-help capacities of the urban poor.

One of the most prominent investigators of the time was Charles Booth, a wealthy shipping magnate. Booth conducted a series of inquiries which were reported in the 17 volumes of *Life and Labour of the People of London* (1889-1903). Although he began his research by siding with Galton, Booth later came out in favor of state intervention in the affairs of the "helpless and incompetent" (Webb, 1926, pp. 260-261). Booth and his assistants used questionnaires, official census data and "personal (i.e., participant) observation" to document and portray the extent of poverty in London. Furthermore, part of their work focused on the preparation of a "social diagnosis" (or evaluation) of various "experiments" in poor-law relief. The influence of Booth's work, like that of Galton, also spread to the United States, giving strong support to the settlement movements in Chicago and New York (see Cremin, 1961, chap. 3).

Pragmatism and Social Change in the United States

By the end of the 19th century the social and economic forces which had made Britain the world's leading industrial power began to stir more vigorously in the United States. In the wake of the Civil War, Darwin's ideas—transposed to the realm of social evolution by Herbert Spencer—were the focus of long and vigorous debate. The dominant viewpoint was that "survival of the fittest" (Spencer's term) should be retained, through laissez-faire government, as the most efficient mechanism for social improvement. Other commentators—notably the pragmatists—took a position that was close to Mill's (William James's *Pragmatism* was dedicated to J. S. Mill). They felt that Spencer's evolutionist views were a one-sided interpretation of Darwinism and, moreover, a thinly disguised biological apology for the excesses of laissez-faire government. Above all, they rejected the assumption that the social environment was outside the realm of human control. If Spencer offered a philosophy of inevitability, the pragmatists replied with a vision of possibility (see Hofstadter, 1955, p. 103). In an era of rapid social change, characterized by such movements as accelerating urbanization, massive immigration, economic boom and bust, and labor unrest, they put forward proposals which could serve to coordinate the disparate elements of an ungainly social system. Education rather than competition was advocated as the most effective instrument of social improvement (Feinberg, 1973).

The major architect of practical pragmatism was John Dewey. Like Mill, Dewey addressed a wide range of concerns in the realms of social science, ethics, and government policy. Briefly, he believed that logic could be redefined as the theory of inquiry, that moral knowledge was a species of empirical knowledge, and that social life could be enhanced through the use of a political technology (see White, 1972, p. 277 ff).

During his stay at the University of Chicago (1896-1904), Dewey not only founded the Laboratory School (1896) but also developed his education theories within a new philosophical and psychological framework. For instance, in his 1899 presidential address to the American Psychological Association ("Psychology and Social Practice," 1900) Dewey argued for a "fuller" understanding of the relationship between the "new education" and the elements of "psycho-physical mechanism." Through its new-found knowledge, psychology provided education with a "statement of mechanism" through which "ethical ends" could be "realized" (p. 121):

. . . the more thorough-going and complete the mechanical and causal statement, the more controlled, the more economical are the discovery and realization of human aims. It is not in spite of, nor in neglect of, but because of the mechanical statement that human activity has been freed, and made effective in thousands of new practical directions, upon a scale and with a certainty hitherto undreamed of. (p. 118)

Dewey's rhetoric resonated not only with the aspirations of an emerging industrial society but also with the debates taking place inside education, such as the NEA's "Committee of Ten" on colleges and secondary schools, initiated in 1892, and the "Committee of Fifteen" on elementary education, initiated in 1893. The established curriculum of the 19th-century secondary school was based on faculty psychology and the related concept of transfer of training. By the last decade of the century faculty psychology was forced onto the defensive (see Krug, 1969, chaps. 1 & 2). Criticism came from two sides. Psychologists such as Thorndike and Woodworth, at the conference presided over by John Dewey, claimed that there was limited experimental evidence for transfer of training from the old disciplines such as Latin to the new ones. The other attack came from those inside and outside education who wanted the curriculum to respond more adequately to the social efficiency movements gaining ground in the spheres of industrial and administrative life.

Evaluation and the Cult of Efficiency

In due course, the education system responded to these concerns with a welter of innovations. Examinations began to replace school accreditation as a means of selecting students for college (the College Entrance Examination Board, for example, was founded in 1900). Individualization became a key concept of school theory and practice (Joncich, 1968, p. 311); age-grade statistics were collected to measure the productive quality of school systems (Tyack, 1974, p. 199 ff.); mental tests were used to categorize school children (Karier, 1973, p. 115); and industrial and vocational schooling came into greater prominence (Lazerson, 1971, chaps. 5-7).

The net result of these developments was the centralization of education, locally and nationally, and the growth of an administrative and managerial elite—many of whom were recruited from expanding graduate institutions like Teachers College, Columbia, the University of Chicago, and Stanford University (Joncich, pp. 216-231; Tyack, pp. 182-198). The rallying cry and self-justification of these "administrative progressives" (Tyack's term) was that streamlined efficiency would be achieved in all spheres of education through a more rigorous application of the scientific method.

As the new century grew a little older, school superintendents began to see themselves more as business executives than as scholars or statesmen (Callahan, 1962, pp. 7-8). The practical consequences of this trend took various forms. For instance, the National Education Association appointed four committees between 1904 and 1911 to study the classification and progress of children; E. L. Thorndike published his first achievement scale (on handwriting) in 1908; and New York City established a Bureau of Research in 1912 to conduct a continuous built-in survey of the school system, using "the new measurement techniques" (Seguel, 1966, p. 75). In turn, the administration of education shifted from a rural model of lay community control toward one that stressed professional training and bureaucratic expertise (see Tyack, 1974, passim). The control of the school curriculum underwent a similar change. In the late 19th century curriculum and pedagogical decisions rested with two agencies: local school boards and college accreditation committees, initiated by the University of Michigan in 1871. By 1910, the impact of the reform movement in schooling meant that the school curriculum fell increasingly under the influence of the business ethic. It spoke for the captains of industry, and their lieutenants, the superintendents, and not for the below-decks personnel such as parents, teachers, and students.

A further wave of support for the scientific movement followed the publication of F. W. Taylor's *The Principles of Scientific Management* (1911). Taylor's ideas were brought to the attention of educational administrators through *The Supervision of City Schools,* The 12th Yearbook of the National Society for the Study of Education (1913). The yearbook's editor was Franklin Bobbitt, who in later years began to focus more specifically on the organization of school subjects (e.g., *The Curriculum*, 1918; and *How to Make a Curriculum*, 1924). Bobbitt's interests were shared by W. W. Charters (e.g., *Curriculum Construction*, 1923), who, unlike Bobbitt, came to curriculum design from an interest in teaching rather than administration.

Bobbitt and Charters developed a conveyor-belt system of curriculum making. They believed, following Taylor, that educational efficiency could be increased through a detailed analysis of the skills a child must acquire to become a socially mature adult. Further, they held that educational goals could be established by reference to "common aims" (Bobbitt, 1913, quoted in Seguel, 1966, p. 99) rather than to the concerns of any particular interest group such as principals or teachers.

By this appeal, Bobbitt and Charters were able to unite teachers and administrators in a common technological task—the facilitation of effective schooling. In one respect, therefore, they were successful in taking politics out of the curriculum. In another respect, they also enhanced the value-neutral image of research. Evaluation of a scholastic activity could be regarded as a technical achievement equivalent to the evaluation of a mathematical expression.

Within the rhetoric of educational efficiency, the main purpose of curriculum construction was to facilitate the production (or reproduction) of an ideal adult. For their curriculum blueprints, Bobbitt and Charters looked to the superintendents and teachers; for their quality control they looked to the growing measurement community.

Evaluation and Curriculum Design

Both Bobbitt and Charters had connections with the University of Chicago. Charters had been a graduate student of John Dewey, and Bobbitt was to serve the university as a professor of educational administration from 1912 to 1941 (Jackson, 1975). In 1919 Charters became director of a research bureau for retail training at the Carnegie Institute of Technology in Pittsburgh. The strong vocational concerns of the bureau (and the availability of federal grants for trade and industrial training under the Smith-Hughes Act, 1917) allowed Charters to extend his earlier pedagogic enquiries toward the analysis of adult occupations and the construction of suitably related curricula and teaching methods. After a second period at Chicago in the 1920s, Charters moved to the directorship of the Bureau of Educational Research at Ohio State University.

While at Ohio State, Charters shared his job analysis interests with Ralph Tyler, a former doctoral student at the University of Chicago. Tyler's crucial contribution to the work of the bureau derived from his graduate training. Unlike many earlier researchers, he combined expertise in both testing theory (the responsibility of psychologists) and curriculum construction (the responsibility of administrators and teachers). The title of Tyler's 1927 doctoral thesis—"Statistical Methods for Evaluating Teacher-Training Curricula"—symbolizes this unification.

Tyler's complementary interests were successfully combined when he became research director of the Committee on Evaluation and Recording of the Eight-Year Study (1932-40). This was a curriculum experiment commissioned at the height of the Great Depression by the Progressive Education Association (honorary president, John Dewey) and supported by private funds from the Carnegie Foundation and the Rockefeller-initiated General Education Board. Over 300 colleges agreed with the PEA to relax their formal entrance requirements, and 29 experimental schools reciprocated by redesigning their curricula along "progressive" lines. Tyler's evaluation rationale was that an "appraisal of an educational institution is fundamentally only the process by which we find out how far the objectives of the institution are being realized" (Tyler, in Smith & Tyler, 1942, p. 5).

The first half of the study followed this "objectives" model. The evaluation staff was "primarily concerned with developing means by which the achievement of students in the schools could be appraised" (p. 5). The second half used a different rationale. The relative merits of progressive and traditional courses were adduced by means of a comparative design. The college careers of the participating students were compared with those of a matched sample of 1,475 nonexperimental students. To practising educationalists the apparently favorable results of the Eight-Year Study indicated the efficacy of progressive methods. To the research community, they signaled the emergence of a sophisticated paradigm for the design and evaluation of school and college curricula (Tyler, 1949).

Tyler's specific contributions to the Eight-Year Study reflected both his training and his experience. As a colleague of Charters, he placed high priority on the analysis of curriculum goals and activities (see Charters, 1926). As a recently trained psychologist, he argued that objectives should be prespecified in behavioral terms (see Anderson, 1975, p. 143). And as a witness to the industrial collapse of the depression he held to a much broader conception of education—one that included affective as well as cognitive and vocational components (see Cremin, 1961, chap. 7; Smith & Tyler, 1942).

After World War II the public success of the Eight-Year Study stimulated other cooperative investigations of a similar kind, such as the American Council on Education Project on Evaluation in General Education (McKim, 1957; Taylor & Cowley, 1972). Tyler's concern for schoolwide behavioral objectives received a fresh boost in 1956 with the publication of Handbook 1 of the *Taxonomy of Educational Objectives* (Bloom, 1956). This short but seminal work was the result of a seven-year collaborative project set up in 1949 by two of Tyler's co-workers: J. Thomas Hastings, of the University of Illinois, and Benjamin S. Bloom, of the University of Chicago. In a sense the encyclopedic efforts of Bloom and his colleagues marked both a beginning and an end. Their work had an air of completeness and finality about it. Yet, in combination with the postwar growth of factor analysis (Thurstone & Thurstone, 1941), psychometric theory (Lindquist, 1951), and experimental design (Stanley, 1966), it also offered an awesome prospect for the future.

This section has sketched some of the recurrent themes and precipitating events that accompanied educational change and evaluation in the period prior to the mid-1950s. At the risk of underestimating the influence of countercurrents, it has argued that the dominant ideas of the day were translated into educational terms by John Dewey, fostered by private and state investment in education, operationalized (not always with Dewey's approval) by Thorndike, Bobbitt, and Charters, and reproduced by the generations of administrators and professors who passed through the portals of Teachers College, Chicago, Stanford, and elsewhere.

The ideas of the founding fathers were clearly articulated and efficiently disseminated. Relatively little, however, is known about the translation of their prescriptions into the realm of classroom practice. Given the "lack" of "empirical studies on the conduct of evaluation during this period" (Lortie, 1970, p. 155), the stipulation remains clearer than the deed. It is also probably true, though perhaps a little unjust, that the founding fathers are better remembered by their technologies than by their aspirations.

In these terms, the new wave of educational evaluators created in the late 1950s and 1960s had much to contend with. The groundwork had been done; a plateau had been reached (see Taylor & Cowley, 1972, p. 1). In some senses, then, the history of evaluation had drawn to a close. From another standpoint, however, it had hardly begun.

CURRICULUM EVALUATION AND THE IMAGE OF CONSENSUS

The ethos of the Eight-Year Study carried through into the postwar years. But, according to Hagen and Thorndike (1960), there was a shift from a *"research oriented* attempt to develop new and better evaluation procedures to an *action research oriented* attempt to involve school personnel in evaluating their own educational programs" (1960, p. 482, emphasis in original; see Smith & Tyler, 1942, p. 30). In time, however, this new "school of thought" (Cronbach, 1963, p. 674) came under sharp attack. It was claimed for instance that general academic standards were being eroded and, more specifically, that the average college entrant's performance had begun to decline. From a vocational perspective, it was also claimed that colleges were failing to fill the demand for scientific personnel in industry (Cremin, 1961, chap. 9). The response to this "crisis in popular schooling" (Cremin's phase) was slow but sure. In 1951, for example, the University of Illinois Committee on School Mathematics received funds from the Carnegie Corporation to enable faculty members to give guidance to high school teachers. Similar stirrings occurred within other specialized fields (Goodlad, 1966). In the process, curriculum development shifted away from the techniques of course construction toward a concern for the substance of course content. The new curriculum mandarins were drawn from the ranks of subject specialists, not management technologists or educational psychologists.

This emphasis on discipline-centered curriculum reform eventually received official and financial recognition from Congress (Hurd, 1969, p. 14). In 1958 the sputnik-prompted National Defense Education Act released federal funds to the National Science Foundation for the improvement of science, mathematics, and (in part) social science curricula.

Evaluation and Course Improvement

The circumscribed nature of curriculum development's funding and the materials-based character of its commitments meant that it gradually became synonymous with program development. Task forces of specialists were convened to produce packages of ideas and procedures which, if required, could be transmitted intact to the farthest corners of the school system. At first the overall merit of the revised curricula was taken to be self-evident. Evaluation remained an informal iterative process directed toward course improvement and conducted by members of the subject team in association with teachers in trial schools. Command of the endeavor remained in the hands of subject specialists. The superior intellectual prestige of the pure sciences enabled the developers to be a self-policing, self-evaluating community. Curriculum projects tended to reject or ignore the conventional wisdom of the evaluation traditions that had flowered in the 1930s (Atkin, 1963).

In the early 1960s evaluation issues began to be raised more sharply as the earlier curriculum projects penetrated through the school system. A typical complaint was that the new schemes had no visible impact (Goodlad, 1968; Provus, 1971, Chap. 1). In this respect, doubt was cast upon the pedagogical rather than the intellectual viability of the programs. Merit could no longer be taken for granted; it had to be made manifest. Insignificant or equivocal results made curriculum developers more willing to enlist the support of ideas from within the realms of behavioral research (see Weir's account of the Biological Science Curriculum Study project, 1976). At that time the educational research community was dominated by psychologists trained in the experimental or individual-differences traditions. Not surprisingly, therefore, these traditions began providing the basic blueprints used in curriculum evaluation. Concern about the visibility of programs also influenced the organization of curriculum research: Evaluation gradually became a specialist activity.

Evaluation and Social Auditing

In 1965 the emergent evaluation community received a boost when continued financial support under Title 1 and Title 3 of the Elementary and Secondary Educational Act was made contingent upon submission of evaluation reports by local program operators. With this administrative device, consolidated and extended in subsequent legislation, curriculum evaluation took a new turn. Its major concern ceased to be course improvement and became instead educational auditing. The range of objectives to be scrutinized was much more limited than the "comprehensive" range of objectives envisaged by Tyler in *Basic Principles of Curriculum and Instruction* (1949, p. 5 ff.). At the same time, de facto control of the curriculum was taken out of the hands of subject specialists and located closer to the heart of the federal administration, itself undergoing a period of reappraisal.

In the early 1960s, Secretary of Defense Robert McNamara, newly recruited from the Ford Motor Company, introduced a form of evaluation termed Planning, Programming, Budgeting System into the decision-making processes of his own department. The essential feature of this innovation was that it shifted the basis of decision making from input to output budgeting—that is, from indices such as class size to measurements such as pupil performance. In 1965 this type of cost-effective appraisal was extended to all federal departments and agencies (Williams & Evans, 1969). Until that time most federal and local educational agencies had evaluated the results of their endeavors using the same internally organized procedures as curriculum developers used. Both groups saw their primary task as the production of a visible program; every dollar spent on evaluation was a dollar lost to program development (McDill, McDill, & Sprehe, 1972, p. 148).

As suggested above, the legislation of the mid-1960s foreshadowed a rapid growth of administrative involvement in evaluation. This interest was particularly evident with respect to poverty programs funded under the Economic Opportunity Act of 1964 and with respect to the growth of statewide accountability schemes and the nationwide Program for the Assessment of Educational Progress. From its inception, the Office of Economic Opportunity (OEO) contained a section for Research Plans, Programs and Evaluation (Glennan, 1972, p. 188). The evaluation efforts of this section during its early years were directed toward servicing the requests of program participants and consumers. No attempts were made to question the existence of any given program.

In 1966 (presumably in response to the introduction of PPBS) the Research Plans, Programs, and Evaluation (RPP&E) office began a series of program evaluations. These studies were precipitated by an internal request for evidence which could assist with decisions over the alteration, curtailment, or discontinuation of programs. Whatever its espoused intention, this request had the effect of luring the evaluators' allegiances from the concerns of the program teams to those of the program sponsors. In effect, the evaluation agency was charged with the task of eliciting visible results which could be displayed in the company prospectus and itemized in the annual balance sheet. In such a climate, it is not surprising that evaluators became more concerned with visible products than inferred processes.

These social auditing concerns were formalized in an OEO "instruction" of March 1968 which established a major component of evaluation as "determining the extent to which programs are successful in achieving basic objectives" (Glennan, 1972, p. 189). Specific responsibility for this evaluation strategy was invested in RPP&E, which was established as a separate division of OEO in 1967. The separation between outcome evaluation and program development was also formalized in a decision that RPP&E should automatically receive a small proportion (0.16%) of any program budget (Glennan, 1972, p. 190).

This division of labor soon provoked its own contradiction. When asked to design an evaluation of Head Start, the RPP&E evaluators, who needed data for decision making, came into conflict with program staff, who believed the evaluators' proposals were too narrow. After "much internal debate" the director of OEO "ordered" the study. A contract was made with the Westinghouse Learning Corporation and Ohio University in June 1968. Eight months later (i.e., prior to the completion of this study), former President Richard Nixon's economic opportunity message to Congress revealed that the long-term effect of Head Start appeared to be "extremely weak" (Williams & Evans, 1969, p. 124). This statement provoked a storm of controversy. In its wake, the population at large became more aware that social scientists were divided among themselves as to the implications of the Westinghouse-Ohio results. Along with controversies about the relationship between schooling and educational achievement (Coleman, Campbell, Hobson, McPartland, Mood, Weinfeld, & York, 1966; Jensen, 1969), the Head Start investigation did little to validate the activities of professional evaluators. Nevertheless, as Nixon's statement suggests, the research community's power to legitimate political decision making remained as strong as ever.

Thus, despite its evident technical shortcomings, the Ohio-Westinghouse study increased rather than decreased the attention focused on curriculum evaluation. As the Vietnam War drew to an end and no new revenue was made available for federal spending (see Glazer, 1973), evaluation began to serve more sharply in an auditing function. At a time of economic stagnation it became an agent of program contraction (or rationalization) rather than a patron of program promotion.

Monitoring the Curriculum

Statewide accountability schemes were a further instance of centralized monitoring of the curriculum. Educational accountability, as it developed in the 1970s (see Sciara & Jantz, 1972), rested upon the logic that educational processes—rather like productive mechanisms—can be broken down into their constituent parts and specified in terms of operational criteria. Uniform and heightened efficiency was taken to be the end which justifies the means. As in the days of Bobbitt and Charters, educational technology of this kind had strong links with business management and centralized control. Just as the earlier generation appealed to the division of labor, so their descendants utilized the language of cybernetics. Assistant Commissioner of Education Leon M. Lessinger's references in 1970 to logistics, systems analysis and human factors engineering are examples (see Popkewitz & Wehlage, 1973, p. 49).

The National Assessment of Education Progress (NAEP) took shape in the mid-1960s. In 1965 an exploratory committee (under the chairmanship of Ralph Tyler, and supported by the Carnegie Corporation and the Ford Foundation) set out to prepare educational objectives and assessment procedures which would embrace the entire school curriculum (Flanagan, 1969, p. 223). The goal of the NAEP was to develop indices of educational output, like economic indices such as the gross national product, which might serve as a basis for social planning.

The first results of NAEP were announced in 1970. They had been generated by a national sample of about 100,000 children and adults who had responded to test items drawn from 460 exercises in science, citizenship, and writing. A significant feature of the NAEP is that its indices do not refer to particular students, classes, schools, or school systems, but rather to the overall (aggregate) attainment of a large number of people. To this extent, the information directly serves the generalized interests of administrative bureaucracies, not the specific concerns of students, teachers, or schools. As with the utilitarian theory of J. S. Mill, the needs of the system are held to be congruent with the needs of the individual (Britton, 1969, p. 53).

Educational Research and Curriculum Evaluation

Confronted with the problems and opportunities offered by these wider developments, the educational research community reacted with not unsurprising speed. In 1964 (i.e., before evaluation was mandated by the Elementary and Secondary Education Act) L. J. Cronbach, then the president of the American Educational Research Association, appointed an ad hoc committee to study the contribution the association could make to the growing interest in evaluation. A year later, President Benjamin S. Bloom commissioned a committee to develop evaluation guidelines and model procedures. The following year's committee (extended by President Julian S. Stanley) rejected Bloom's concerns in favor of a more eclectic stance. One of the outcomes of these deliberations was the *AERA Monograph Series on Curriculum Evaluation,* seven volumes of which were published between 1967 and 1974 (see Stake, 1967b, pp. 8-12).

The Monograph Series bears witness to the diversity of opinions expressed within the research community. In the early days there were two competing schools of evaluation thought. On the one hand there were those (like Cronbach) who argued in favor of a modified Tylerian rationale (see Tyler, 1949), whereby a study is made of the "post-course performance of a well described group with respect to many important objectives and side effects" (Cronbach, 1963, p. 676). On the other hand, there were those (like Stanley) who advocated comparative studies which used control and treatment groups (see Campbell & Stanley, 1963).

Although the experimental model had the most persuasive scientific appeal, few studies of the new curricula achieved the required levels of randomization and control. According to Welch and Walberg (1974), only 4 out of 46 government-sponsored course development projects had used "true" experiments in their evaluation strategies by 1969 (p. 113). Nevertheless, the comparative assumptions of the experimental paradigm still served to underpin the "two most frequently used models in large-scale program evaluation" (Light & Smith, 1970, p. 9). The first of these models—post hoc quasiexperimentation, as in the Head Start evaluation—establishes experimental and control groups after the treatment has been applied. The second model—post hoc sample surveying, as in the Coleman report (1966)—relies on a large data base which, because of its size and variability, can be subsequently analyzed to account for the various designated treatments.

Comparative versus Tylerian Rationales

Objections to the comparative model (Cronbach, 1963; Guba, 1969) rested on the argument that it was both technically and philosophically inappropriate to the nature of curriculum evaluation. Cronbach and Guba, for instance, maintained, like J. S. Mill, that group comparisons may give equivocal results if more than one variable is studied (i.e., the control group may appear superior on one variable, the experimental group on another). Other critics (e.g., Walker & Schaffarzick, 1974) argued against comparative evaluation designs on the grounds that the new curricula set their own goals and standards. In principle, Tylerian evaluation models avoid these problems: The innovative curriculum is measured against agreed internal standards, not against the results achieved by another (possibly nonequivalent) program.

Scriven identified some of the epistemological weaknesses of the Tylerian and comparative rationales in the first AERA Monograph (Scriven, 1967). The Tylerian approach does not solve the comparison problem since, as in the Eight-Year Study, curriculum objectives are always established by reference to (or in reaction to) the objectives and achievements of other programs and sets of standards. In effect, Scriven demonstrated that the question "Does it meet the standards laid down by program staff?" is, in principle, no different from the question "Is it better than Brand X?" Scriven also reiterated the argument that two-group comparative designs give ambiguous results in that there is no intrinsic mechanism for separating the impact of the actual treatment from that of the associated Hawthorne and John Henry effects (p. 68).

By analyzing the complementary weaknesses of the preeminent rationales, Scriven was able to outline some possible solutions. First, he maintained that the opinion of subject specialists should count more heavily in the validation of Tylerian objectives and criteria. Second, he suggested that simple designs based on experimental versus control groups should be replaced by designs with more than one experimental group. Finally, Scriven offered a solution to J. S. Mill's multiple-criterion problem by arguing that individual criteria could be differentially weighted and then combined to form a single criterion measure.

Scriven's theoretical appraisal of the criterion problem was both elegant and appropriate. In 1970, however, Glass claimed that the practical implementation of Scriven's solution required "evaluation techniques still not discovered" (p. 23). Glass examined possible procedures (such as minimax techniques) but was unable to devise a further technique for choosing among them. He concluded that "human judgment" (p. 29) was the only valid arbiter.

Although the science of human conduct had come a long way since the days of John Stuart Mill, it continued to run aground on the shifting sands of human values.

Confronted by such a tangle of epistemological, empirical, and statistical problems (Lord, 1967; Campbell & Erlebacher, 1970), certain educationists began to look for evaluation models beyond the conventional boundaries of postwar educational research. Among the more successful forays have been those into the realms of management theory, literary criticism, jurisprudence, and consumer science.

Evaluation and Management Theory

Management models for evaluation (Provus, 1969; Rippey, 1973; Stufflebeam, Foley, Gephart, Guba, Hammond, Merriman & Provus, 1971) are program, organization, or system centered. They take as their basic aim the improvement of rational decision making. Evaluations are designed to reduce "institutional conflict" (Rippey, p. 14), to "facilitate quality control and improvement" (Stufflebeam et al., p. 217), or to "determine whether to improve, maintain or terminate a program" (Provus, p. 245). Although their methodologies may vary, the data and performance criteria of management models relate to the "total system" (Stufflebeam et al., 1971, p. 238) rather than to individual pupils or teachers. As such, they reflect the aspirations of personnel with programwide responsibility, not the immediate concerns of classroom practitioners.

Management-oriented evaluation models hark back to Bobbitt's writings on the administration of school systems. Bureaucratic (i.e., management) efficiency tends to be blended with educational efficiency. In Provus' revealing formulations, the evaluator is like a "management engineer" (p. 245), and the evaluation functions as a "watchdog of program management" (p. 260).

Evaluation and Literary Criticism

The influence of literary criticism as a role model for evaluation (Eisner, 1972; Kelly, 1971) also grew out of dissatisfaction with existing paradigms. Evaluations of this kind—a "supplement to the use of scientific procedures" (Eisner, 1975)—draw upon an artistic tradition of "connoisseurship and criticism." They incorporate ways of seeing rather than ways of measuring. The evaluator (or "critic") aims to sensitize the individual practitioner (or reader) by "rendering" an account of the program, using the "vehicles" of "suggestion, simile, and metaphor" (Eisner, 1972, p. 586). Nevertheless, despite these important methodological differences, Eisner's "new" approach was, in essence, just as much an abstruse technology (with specialist training, journals, books, studentships) as the procedures it sought to supplement (see Eisner, 1975). This is not altogether surprising, since Eisner's concern for "judgment . . . grounded in reasons" harks back to Dewey, whom he quotes approvingly, just as Cooley and Lohnes' (1976) call, equally Dewey-inspired, for evaluation research that is "multi-variate, large-sample and longitudinal" (p. 5). Eisner also solves the criterion problem in a way that is similar to the manner of Cooley and Lohnes. Judgments are established externally—by reference to prior "human needs" (Cooley & Lohnes, p. 13) or values derived from "tradition and habit" and "the nature of artistic virtue" (Eisner, 1975).

Evaluation and Jurisprudence

Legal or adversary models for evaluation (Kourilsky, 1973a; Levine, 1973b; Wolf, 1974) use the notion that courts of law have well-established principles of procedure which can be used to regulate and administer the processes of decision making. They can be seen as an attempt by the evaluation community to institutionalize the kind of debates that typically occur following the publication of an evaluation report. The most significant theoretical feature of these models is that they legitimate the existence of discrepant accounts presented by advocates and adversaries. Different models, however, embody different concepts of decision making. Kourilsky (1973b) saw the "goal" of adversary evaluation as the generation of "properly informed" decisions, whereas Levine (1973a) regarded the adversary model simply as a means of conducting debates about educational programs. Kourilsky focused on the "technology" of decision making, such as "selecting appropriate information" (1973a, p. 4), or "empanelling jurors" (see Wolf, 1974, preface). Levine emphasized the "politics of decision making" (1973b, p. 8; Levine, 1974). As shown below, such a distinction is crucial to this review.

Evaluation and Consumer Science

Consumer science provides a model for evaluation in cases where the curriculum is studied in terms of its value to the user, rather than in terms of the intentions (or goals) of the producer. Consumption is the ultimate criterion, not production. Evaluations of this kind examine payoffs rather than precepts. By comparison with the Tylerian rationale, the *"actual* effects" of the program are given priority over its objectives or *"alleged* effects" (Scriven, 1972b, p. 2, emphasis in original). In these instances the judgmental criteria are not prespecified by the curriculum developer. They are applied post hoc by the evaluator who uses external "standards of merit" derived from "the needs of the nation" (Scriven, 1972b, p. 2). Scriven (1972b) coined the term *Goal Free Evaluation* to describe this type of study. However, its ancestry stretches back through the evaluation of broad-aim programs of social action (see Weiss & Rein, 1969) to the social diagnoses conducted by Booth and others in the 19th century (see Caro, 1971).

Evaluation and the Problem of Consensus

Despite superficial differences, the evaluation models discussed in this section share a number of attributes. Each one draws upon a consensual image of social life. They assume that, in principle, the goals of a curriculum and the criteria for its success can be agreed upon. Their credibility rests on the stability of this assumption.

In practice, consensus is usually arrived at by allowing surrogate interest groups, such as the evaluation community, to speak for the "welfare of society as a whole" (Scriven, 1967, p. 81). Whether consent is in fact assumed or established will vary from case to case. In most instances, however, there seems to be a tendency for course developers and evaluators to play a particularly strong role. The Tylerian tradition, for example, relies heavily upon the "curriculum maker" for its objectives (Tyler, 1949, passim; Stake, 1970, p. 187). Likewise, Scriven's comparative evaluation model uses criteria validated by "highly qualified experts" and "professionally competent evaluators" (1967, pp. 58, 53). The national assessment program follows a similar pattern. It utilizes objectives identified by committees of "subject matter specialists" sprinkled with "thoughtful lay-persons" (Merwin & Womer, 1969, p. 315). Management systems approaches also subscribe to a similar view of consensus. Responsibility for defining performance criteria is delegated to "skilled operating personnel" (Rippey, 1973, p. 13) or to the "program manager" (Provus, 1969, p. 251).

Even the literary criticism, legal, and consumer models take an equivalent stance. Eisner, for instance, looks to "connoisseurship" for his ultimate criteria; decision-oriented legal models are suffused with the consensus image of unanimous verdicts (see Wolf, 1974, p. 62 ff.); and goal-free evaluation allows the evaluator to infer the "goals of the consumer or the funding agency" (Scriven, 1972b, p. 2).

Given the assumption of goal consensus, the implementation of an evaluation rationale hinges upon the comparison of various means to achieve such ends. From John Stuart Mill and John Dewey, to Ralph Tyler and Michael Scriven, the possibility of realizing a theory of evaluation rested upon this assumption. For them, the dualistic separation of fact and value is incorrect and unacceptable. From Mill's "Greatest Happiness" principle to Scriven's "system of principles aimed at maximizing long-run social utility" (1967, p. 81), the assumptions and logic have remained essentially the same. Throughout, this vision of consensus has been well formulated, overtly rational, and immensely powerful.

All the evaluation models discussed in this section stress the importance of agreement about objectives and/or criteria. As a consequence, they tend to play down the possibility that criteria might be mutually exclusive. This does not mean, of course, that they ignore areas of antagonism—merely that they regard them as potentially or pragmatically resolvable. Although Scriven, for instance, has acknowledged that different individuals may have an "opposite preference" (1972b, p. 2), his main thrust has been that evaluators should focus preferentially upon areas of agreement (1972a, p. 84). Stufflebeam et al. (1971) made a similar point. They proposed that the decision maker should go into the "value web of the larger world only as far as necessary to find a common value among his constructs" (p. 116).

Both these strategies presume that values which are shared are more significant than discrepant values. There is no logical reason why this should be the case. Such a presumption may offer an expedient solution to the criterion problem, but it has difficulty in resolving the prior value question, Who decides that consensus has been achieved? As this suggests, consensus models tend to be justified by appeals to representative democracy, yet, as in the days of J. S. Mill, it is still not clear in each case whether everyone has achieved the right to vote or to sit on the jury panel.

CURRICULUM EVALUATION AND THE IMAGE OF PLURALISM

Just as Herbert Spencer raised objections to Mill's social theories, and various contemporaries of Bobbitt and Charters expressed concern with the curriculum-building model (e.g., Rugg, 1931), so certain commentators articulated doubts about the consensus assumptions of recent evaluation theories. Ideas about pluralism and politics were brought to the forefront.

A connection between consensus and politics was clearly identified by the early critics. For instance, in a review of "Research Styles in Science Education," Atkin (1967-68) noted that one of the "major shortcomings" of the systems model of curriculum development was its reluctance to "recognize the competition among diverse value systems and power groups" (p. 341). Around the same time Stake's "The Countenance of Evaluation" (1967a) paper included the pluralist argument that "part of the responsibility of evaluation is to make known which standards are held by whom" (p. 535).

In retrospect, developments of this kind can be seen as a turning point in the recent history of evaluation. Atkin and Stake (both at the University of Illinois) were accepted leaders in, respectively, the fields of curriculum development and curriculum evaluation. It was as if the winners of the tournament had suddenly begun to question the rules that had made them victorious.

The rediscovery of values was also fueled by Scriven's contemporaneous argument that "evaluation proper" must also include the "evaluation of goals." The idea that goal evaluation should be an "equal partner with the measuring of performance against goals" implied a radical shift of concern (Scriven, 1967, p. 52). Within Scriven's rationale, evaluation was not merely "the process of determining to what extent the educational objectives are being realized" (Tyler, 1949, p. 105); it also included the post hoc scrutiny of the prespecified objectives.

Value Analysis and Value Pluralism

The possibilities of value analysis and value pluralism opened up new perspectives and new problems for curriculum evaluation. The major premise that evaluation is the ascription of worth with reference to a given set of standards was joined by a new assumption: that a uniformity of standards may not be attainable in social situations. The introduction of this second assumption nullified the conventional wisdom of earlier theory. The notion of evaluator as "watchdog" became difficult to advocate, since its flavor was too reminiscent of autocratic, hired-hand research. Likewise, evaluators could no longer claim to provide categorical answers acceptable to all parties or to furnish prepackaged instruments suitable for every occasion. A long-established technology became unwieldy, if not unsafe.

In the search for more "democratic" models (see MacDonald, 1976) certain evaluators sought to redefine the evaluation problem, renegotiate their role, and reformulate their strategies for information gathering and data analysis. The new perspectives tended to acknowledge that evaluation is as much a sociopolitical as a methodological process (e.g., "The Process and Ideology of Valuing in Educational Settings," Apple, 1974; *School Evaluation: The Politics and the Process,* House, 1973; "Racism and Educational Evaluation," Jenkins, Kemmis, MacDonald, & Verma, 1977; and "Politics, Ethics and Ideology," Sjoberg, 1975).

At the present time, evaluation models with a pluralistic concern are still relatively limited in their impact. They occupy either an interstitial or a subordinate status in the education system. In the former case they tend to be employed (and funded) where Tylerian and experimental models are empirically, financially, or politically less attractive—as in studies of alternative schools (Black & Geiser, 1971), programs in aesthetic education (Stake, 1975), extracurricular activities (Stake & Gjerde, 1974) and multicultural projects such as the Teacher Corps (Fox, 1976). The second context for the utilization of pluralist models is as a complement to Tylerian or experimental designs, as in the evaluation of Home Start (Love, Nauta, Coelen, Hewett, & Rupp, 1976) and the evaluation of a school-based computer-aided instruction curriculum (Smith & Pohland, 1974). In these latter cases, however, the pluralist assumptions were overshadowed by the consensus concerns of the dominant models. Despite a declared eclecticism, the conflicting priorities of consensus and pluralist models are rarely (if at all) resolved in a manner that honors the aspiration of all parties (see, e.g., Wehlage, 1976).

In practical terms, pluralist evaluation models (Parlett & Hamilton, 1972; Patton, 1975; Stake, 1967a) can be characterized in the following manner. Compared with the classical models, they tend to be more extensive (not necessarily centered on numerical data), more naturalistic (based on program activity rather than program intent), and more adaptable (not constrained by experimental or preordinate designs). In turn they are likely to be sensitive to the different values of program participants, to endorse empirical methods which incorporate ethnographic fieldwork, to develop feedback materials which are couched in the natural language of the recipients, and to shift the locus of formal judgment from the evaluator to the participants.

Problems of Pluralism

At first, such models were rarely self-conscious or explicit about their pluralism. They were more likely to emerge in isolation as a response to the methodological weaknesses of the traditional models. Through time, however, they began to develop an epistemological and logical identity of their own: a theory *about* evaluation rather than a theory *of* evaluation. This, in turn, raised a series of specific problems for pluralist practitioners.

One such difficulty stemmed from the separation of program development from program evaluation. What role, for instance, can a pluralist evaluation play with regard to a Tylerian rationale which has as one of its "basic assumptions" that "an educational program is appraised by finding out how far the objectives of the program are actually being realized" (Tyler, in Smith & Tyler, 1942, p. 12)? The evaluation team would be predisposed to scrutinize the objectives of the program—something that the development team would consider to be illegitimate. How can such a tension be resolved?

The possibility of practitioner disagreement over curriculum objectives also means that pluralist evaluations are likely to work from program practices to program goals. In effect, a figure-ground reversal takes place. As in the case of goal-free evaluation, the learning milieu is regarded as containing the substance of educational innovation, not, as is sometimes implied, its pale or distorted shadow. The program shapes the evaluation methodology, not vice versa. As noted above, this can create serious difficulties, since it is no longer possible to prescribe specific methodological procedures without a knowledge of the context in which they are to be used. The preparation of training programs for pluralist evaluators is vitiated by this problem. In what sense is it possible to talk about a methodology in the absence of a complementary theory of the situation?

A third issue resulting from the adoption of pluralist evaluation models relates to the establishment of evaluative criteria. Given the unacceptability of standards unilaterally offered by "experts," the problem facing the evaluator is not so much which criteria and how as it is whose criteria and why.

A fourth issue hinges on the interpretation of *pluralist*. In the extreme, pluralist evaluation models could be taken to mean that all viewpoints are equally valid, and all interest groups are equally powerful. This position creates profound problems, since the very essence of evaluation is making statements about the relative merits of different perspectives. To espouse this cause is to be committed to a relativist, value-free evaluation (see Nowell-Smith, 1971).

A Pluralist Theory of Evaluation?

Doubts about relativism lie at the heart of debates about pluralist evaluation: In what sense is a pluralist evaluation possible? Will objective data be honored? In what sense can a pluralist evaluation be fair to all parties? Whose logic will be followed? These questions were posed very sharply in "Justice and Evaluation" (House, 1976). Although critical of the utilitarian basis of consensus models, House noted the absence of an explicit pluralist theory of evaluation. His paper offered such a theory, using notions derived from *A Theory of Justice* (Rawls, 1971).

If J. S. Mill claimed that "utility" should be the "first principle" of ethics, Rawls countered with the concept of "justice as fairness." The value of a curriculum is not measured against its effectiveness, as with aggregate changes in test score, but against its fairness. Furthermore, individual persons are taken to be the basic focus of analysis, rather than social institutions such as "schools and colleges," as in the Eight-Year Study (see Smith & Tyler, 1942, p. 5) or "geographic regions," as in the National Assessment Educational Progress (see Education Commission of the States, 1974, p. 2). This last point allows for the fact that different individuals can pursue a "plurality of ends" (House, 1976, p. 97). Justice as fairness aspires to be the pluralist counterpart of utilitarianism.

In these terms House confronted the problem of relativism by arguing that the viewpoint of the "least advantaged" (p. 84) should be given priority over the values of other groups. House had already tested these ideas in his evaluation of the Michigan Accountability System (House, Rivers, &

Stufflebeam, 1974). This evaluation was commissioned by certain recipients of the scheme (the NEA), rather than by its originators (Michigan Department of Education). House acknowledged that his analysis "ignored" some of the "philosophic difficulties" (p. 98) surrounding the notion of justice as fairness (e.g., it presupposes the existence of a consensus in favor of pluralism). Nevertheless, his paper had the important distinction of forcing the relativism problem out into the open.

Other models of pluralist evaluation have tried to resolve the relativist dilemma by stressing the information-gathering rather than the judgment-making aspects of evaluation. Still others have idealized the evaluator as a free-floating, independent intellectual. Both these positions (reviewed in House, 1976) are weak and unsatisfactory. At root they embody a kind of concealed consensus. The former comes very close to the hired-hand role of management-oriented evaluation, and the latter, by its appeal to expertise, is highly reminiscent of elitist variants of the consensus model.

One final and perhaps more coherent response to the problems of pluralist evaluation has been to hand over responsibility for the control of an evaluation to those who have to live with its consequences. Evaluation is conducted by the participants rather than for the participants. Models of this kind, such as Black & Geiser's (1971) notion of "peer research," and Scheyer & Stake's (1976) image of a "self-evaluation portfolio," undermine the de facto hierarchical and bureaucratic processes of consensus evaluation. They respond to an alternative conception of accountability—one that locates community rather than centralized control at its core. They imply that lifelong experience of social relationships in inner-city schools may generate a more sophisticated account of educational practice than proficiency at multivariate analysis. And they also imply that the tacit knowledge of practitioners may be more significant to program operation than the generalized statements of theoreticians.

In a sense, the history of curriculum evaluation has come full circle. Just as the curriculum was taken out of lay control in the 19th century, so, at a new level, demands are heard for its restoral. Curriculum evaluation has played a part in both these movements.

SUMMARY AND CONCLUSIONS

In his introduction to a 1970 review symposium on educational evaluation, Denny (1970) noted the absence of investigations into the "historical growth of evaluation methodology." This chapter, written by a participant rather than a bystander, has tried to respond to that shortcoming. Through an examination of the historical forms embraced by curriculum evaluation, it has related some of their more fundamental features. At the same time, it has suggested that recent events indicate a crucial differentiation of these institutional forms.

On the one hand, there are evaluation models which rely for their coherence on notions of consensus; on the other, there are others (here termed *pluralist*) which treat consensus as a problematic assumption.

As befits their origins in 19th-century liberal and pragmatic thought (Gouldner, 1971, passim; Karier, 1974, p. 280), consensus models are strong on technology, reformism, and social engineering. They regard evaluation as a technical accomplishment: the demonstration of empirical/logical connections between what is and what (we all agree) ought to be. If an evaluation is to be successful, there has to be "consensus on the key issues of the hierarchy of purposes of education and the rules of evidence" (Cooley & Lohnes, 1976, p. 5). The internal logic of these models guarantees the strength of their truth statements. Given agreement on educational ends, the unambiguous selection of appropriate means (i.e., the curriculum) is simply a technical problem. A crucial feature of pluralist models, however, is that they are skeptical of these "preconditions" (Cooley & Lohnes, p. 5). To this extent, the differences between consensus and pluralist models are epistemological rather than methodological.

One explanation for the emergence of pluralist theories is that, as in the 1930s, they reflect a general crisis in the realm of social values. They are an expression of doubt and reflection rather than certainty and action. As such, they tend to be strong on conflicting interpretations, value differences, and incomplete closure. Evaluation is offered as an unfinished blueprint rather than a perfected technology. It generates issues, not solutions. It is about information rather than confirmation.

By their openness, however, pluralist models also leave a number of questions unanswered. Is pluralism consonant with an overarching theory of values? Or is it incompatible with such a universalistic notion? Is the rise of pluralism a temporary phase? Will it be replaced by a new consensus? Or has crisis become a necessary feature of any social system that has gone "beyond the stable state" (Schon, 1971)?

To address questions such as these is to reach out far beyond the problems of research technique and goal identification. Yet, if acts are best comprehended by establishing their context, then tasks of this magnitude are essential to an adequate understanding of curriculum evaluation.

REFERENCES

Anderson, S. B., Ball, S., & Murphy, R. T. (Ed.). *Encyclopedia of educational evaluation.* San Francisco: Jossey-Bass, 1975.

Apple, M. W. The process and ideology of valuing in educational settings. In M. W. Apple, M. J. Subkoviak, & H. S. Lufler (Eds.), *Educational evaluation: Analysis and responsibility.* Berkeley, Cal.: McCutchan, 1974.

Apple, M. W., Subkoviak, M. J., & Lufler, H. S. (Eds.). *Educational evaluation: Analysis and responsibility.* Berkeley, Cal.: McCutchan, 1974.

Atkin, J. M. Some evaluation problems in a course content improvement project. *Journal of Research in Science Teaching*, 1963, *1*, 129-132.

Atkin, J. M. Research styles in science education. *Journal of Research in Science Teaching*, 1967-68, *5*, 338-345.

Black, S., & Geiser, K. *The Watertown Home Base School evaluation methodology report*. Watertown, Mass.: Home Base School, 1971. (mimeo)

Bloom, B. S. (Ed.). *Taxonomy of educational objectives: The classification of educational goals. Handbook 1: Cognitive domain*. London: Longmans Green, 1956.

Britton, K. *John Stuart Mill*. New York: Dover, 1969.

Callahan, R. G. *Education and the cult of efficiency: A study of the social forces that have shaped the administration of the public schools*. Chicago: University of Chicago Press, 1962.

Campbell, D. T., & Erlebacher, A. How regression artifacts in quasi-experimental evaluations can mistakenly make compensatory education appear harmful. In J. Hellmuth (Ed.), *Disadvantaged Child* (Vol. 3). New York: Brunner/Mazel, 1970.

Campbell, D. T., & Stanley, J. C. Experimental and quasi-experimental designs for research on teaching. In N. L. Gage (Ed.), *Handbook of research on teaching*. Chicago: Rand McNally, 1963.

Caro, F. G. Evaluation research: An overview. In F. G. Caro (Ed.), *Readings in evaluation research*. New York: Russell Sage Foundation, 1971.

Charters, W. W. Review and critique of curriculum making for the vocations. In G. M. Whipple (Ed.), *The foundations and technique of curriculum construction*. 26th Yearbook of the NSSE. Bloomington, Ill.: Public School Publishing Company, 1926.

Coleman, J. S., Campbell, E. Q., Hobson, C. J., McPartland, J., Mood, A. M., Weinfeld, F. D., & York, R. L. *Equality of educational opportunity*. Washington, D.C.: U.S. Government Printing Office, 1966.

Cooley, W. W., & Lohnes, P. R. *Evaluation research in education*. New York: Irvington Publishers (John Wiley), 1976.

Cremin, L. A. *The transformation of the school: Progressivism in American education, 1876-1957*. New York: Alfred A. Knopf, 1961.

Cronbach, L. J. Course improvement through evaluation. *Teachers College Record*, 1963, *64*, 672-683.

Denny, T. Foreword to a series of review articles on educational evaluation. *Review of Educational Research*, 1970, *40* (2), Foreword.

Dewey, J. Psychology and social practice. *Psychological Review*, 1900, *7*, 105-124.

Education Commission of the States. *Questions and answers about the National Assessment of Educational Progress*. Denver, Colo.: Education Commission of the States, 1974.

Eisner, E. Emerging models for educational evaluation. *School Review*, 1972, *80*, 573-590.

Eisner, E. *The perceptive eye: Toward the reformation of educational evaluation*. Paper presented at the meeting of the American Educational Research Association. Washington, D.C., 1975.

Feinberg, W. Ethics and objectivity: The effects of the Darwinian revolution on educational reform. *Educational Theory*, 1973, *23*, 294-302.

Flanagan, J. C. The uses of educational evaluation in the development of programs, courses, instructional materials and equipment, instructional and learning procedures, and administrative arrangements. In R. W. Tyler (Ed.), *Educational evalua-*

tion: New roles, new means, 69th Yearbook of the NSSE, Pt. 2. Chicago: University of Chicago Press, 1969.

Fox, J. T. (Ed.). *The 1975 CMTI impact study.* Madison: University of Wisconsin, School of Education, 1976. (mimeo)

Glass, G. V The growth of evaluation methodology. Boulder, Colorado: Laboratory of Educational Research, 1970. (mimeo)

Glazer, N. Social policy in America. *New Society,* April 5, 1973, pp. 9-11.

Glennan, T. K. Evaluating federal manpower programs: Notes and observations. In P. H. Rossi & W. Williams (Eds.), *Evaluating social programs.* New York: Seminar Press, 1972.

Goodlad, J. I. *The changing school curriculum.* New York: Fund for the Advancement of Education, 1966.

Goodlad, J. I. Thought, invention and research in the advancement of education. *Educational Forum,* 1968, *33,* 7-18.

Gouldner, A. W. *The coming crisis of Western sociology.* London: Heinemann, 1971.

Guba, E. Significant differences. *Educational Researcher,* 1969, *20,* 4-5.

Hagen, E. P., & Thorndike, R. L. Evaluation. In C. W. Harris (Ed.), *Encyclopedia of educational research.* New York: Macmillan, 1960.

Hamilton, D. *Educational research and the shadows of Francis Galton and Ronald Fisher.* Unpublished paper, 1974 (mimeo). To appear in W. B. Dockrell & D. Hamilton (Eds.), *Rethinking educational research.* London: Hodder & Stoughton, in press.

Hofstadter, R. *Social Darwinism in American thought, 1860-1915.* Philadelphia: University of Pennsylvania Press, 1955.

House, E. (Ed.). *School evaluation: The politics and process.* Berkeley: McCutchan, 1973.

House, E. Justice in evaluation. In G. V Glass (Ed.), *Evaluation studies review annual.* Beverly Hills, Cal.: Sage, 1976.

House, E. R., Rivers, W., & Stufflebeam, D. L. An assessment of the Michigan accountability system. *Phi Delta Kappan,* 1974, *55,* 663-669.

Hurd, P. D. *New directions in teaching secondary school science.* Chicago: Rand McNally, 1969.

Jackson, P. W. Shifting visions of the curriculum: Notes on the ageing of Franklin Bobbitt. *Elementary School Journal,* 1975, *75,* 119-133.

Jenkins, D., Kemmis, S., MacDonald, B., & Verma, G. Racism and educational evaluation. In G. Verma & C. Bagley (Eds.), *Race, education and identity.* London: Heinemann, 1977.

Jensen, A. R. How much can we boost IQ and scholastic achievement? *Harvard Educational Review,* 1969, *39,* 1-123.

Joncich, G. *The sane positivist: A biography of Edward L. Thorndike.* Middletown, Conn.: Wesleyan University Press, 1968.

Karier, C. J. Testing for order and control in the corporal liberal state. In C. Karier, P. Violas, & J. Spring, *Roots of crisis: American education in the twentieth century.* Chicago: Rand McNally, 1973.

Karier, C. Ideology and evaluation: In quest of meritocracy. In M. W. Apple, M. J. Subkoviak, & H. S. Lufler (Eds.), *Education evaluation, analysis and responsibility.* Berkeley, Cal.: McCutchan, 1974.

Kelly, E. *Curriculum evaluation and literary criticism: The explication of an analogy.* Unpublished doctoral dessertation, University of Illinois at Champaign–Urbana, 1971.

Kerlinger, F. N. *Foundations of behavioral research.* New York: Holt, Rinehart & Winston, 1964.

Krug, E. A. *The shaping of the American high school, 1880-1920.* Madison, Wis.: University of Wisconsin Press, 1969.

Kourilsky, M. An adversary model for educational evaluation. *Evaluation Comment,* 1973, *4* (2), 3-6. (a)

Kourilsky, M. The Levine adversary model: An adversary comment. *Evaluation Comment,* 1973, *4* (2), 6-7. (b)

Lazerson, M. *Origins of the urban school: Public education in Massachusetts, 1870-1915.* Cambridge, Mass.: Harvard University Press, 1971.

Levine, M. The Kourilsky adversary model: An adversary comment. *Evaluation Comment,* 1973, *4* (2), 8. (a)

Levine, M. Scientific method and the adversary model. *Evaluation Comment,* 1973, *4* (2), 1-3. (b)

Levine, M. Scientific method and the adversary model. *American Psychologist,* 1974, *29,* 661-677.

Light, R. J., & Smith, P. V. Choosing a future: Strategies for designing and evaluating new programs. *Harvard Educational Review,* 1970, *40,* 1-28.

Lindquist, E. F. (Ed.). *Educational measurement.* Washington, D.C.: American Council on Education, 1951.

Lord, F. M. A paradox in the interpretation of group comparisons. *Psychological Bulletin,* 1967, *68,* 304-305.

Lortie, D. C. The cracked cake of educational custom and emerging issues in evaluation. In M. C. Wittrock & D. E. Wiley (Eds.), *The evaluation of instruction: Issues and problems.* New York: Holt, Rinehart & Winston, 1970.

Love, J., Nauta, M., Coelen, C., Hewett, K., & Rupp, R. *National Home Start evaluation: Final report.* Ypsilanti, Mich.: High/Scope Educational Research Foundation; Cambridge: Abt Associates Inc., 1976.

MacDonald, B. Evaluation and the control of education. In D. Tawney (Ed.), *Curriculum evaluation today: Trends and implications.* London: Macmillan, 1976.

McDill, E. L., McDill, M. S., & Sprehe, J. T. Evaluation in practice. In P. H. Rossi & W. Williams (Eds.), *Evaluating social programs.* New York: Seminar Press, 1972.

McKim, M. G. Curriculum research in historical perspective. In *Research for curriculum improvement.* 1957 Yearbook of the Association for Supervision and Curriculum Development. Washington, D.C., 1957.

Merwin, J. C., & Womer, F. B. Evaluation in assessing the progress of education to provide bases of public understanding and public policy. In R. W. Tyler (Ed.), *Educational evaluation: New roles, new means.* 68th Yearbook of the NSSE, Pt. 2. Chicago: University of Chicago Press, 1969.

Nagel, E. (Ed.). *John Stuart Mill's philosophy of scientific method.* New York: Hafner, 1950.

Nowell-Smith, P. H. Cultural relativism. *Philosophy of Social Science,* 1971, *1,* 1-17.

Parlett, M., & Hamilton, D. *Evaluation as illumination: A new approach to the study of innovatory programs.* Occasional Paper No. 9, University of Edinburgh Centre for Research in the Educational Sciences, 1972. (Reprinted in G. V Glass (Ed.), *Evaluation studies review annual.* Beverly Hills, Cal.: Sage, 1976.)

Patton, M. Q. *Alternative evaluation research paradigm.* Grand Forks, N.D.: North Dakota Study Group on Evaluation, 1975.

Popham, W. J. (Ed.). *Evaluation in education.* Berkeley, Cal.: McCutchan, 1974.

Popkewitz, T. S., & Wehlage, G. G. Accountability: Critique and alternative perspective. *Interchange,* 1973, *4* (4), 48-62.

Provus, M. Evaluation of ongoing programs in the public school system. In R. W. Tyler (Ed.), *Education evaluation: New roles, new means.* 68th Yearbook of the NSSE, Pt. 2. Chicago: University of Chicago Press, 1969.

Provus, M. *Discrepancy evaluation.* Berkeley, Cal.: McCutchan, 1971.

Rawls, J. *A theory of justice.* Cambridge, Mass.: Belknap, 1971.

Rippey, R. M. (Ed.). *Studies in transactional evaluation.* Berkeley, Cal.: McCutchan, 1973.

Rugg, H. O. *Culture and education in America.* New York: Harcourt Brace, 1931.

Scheyer, P., & Stake, R. E. *A program's self-evaluation portfolio.* Center for Instructional Research and Curriculum Evaluation, University of Illinois at Champaign–Urbana, 1976. (mimeo)

Schon, D. A. *Beyond the stable state: Public and private learning in a changing society.* London: Temple Smith, 1971.

Schutz, R. E. Methodological issues in curriculum research. *Review of Educational Research,* 1969, *39,* 359-366.

Sciara, F. J., & Jantz, R. K. (Eds.). *Accountability in American education.* Boston: Allyn & Bacon, 1972.

Scriven, M. The methodology of evaluation. In *AERA Monograph Series on Curriculum Evaluation* (No. 1). Chicago: Rand McNally, 1967. Pp. 39-83.

Scriven, M. An introduction to meta-evaluation. In P. A. Taylor & D. M. Cowley (Eds.), *Readings in curriculum evaluation.* Dubuque, Iowa: William C. Brown, 1972. (a)

Scriven, M. Pros and cons about goal-free evaluation. *Evaluation Comment,* 1972, *3,* 1-4. (b)

Scriven, M. Evaluation perspectives and procedures. In W. J. Popham (Ed.), *Evaluation in education.* Berkeley, Cal.: McCutchan, 1974.

Seguel, M. L. *The curriculum field: Its formative years.* New York: Teachers College Press, 1966.

Sjoberg, G. Politics, ethics and evaluation research. In E. L. Struening & M. Guttentag (Eds.), *Handbook of evaluation research* (Vol. 2). Beverly Hills, Cal.: Sage, 1975.

Smith, E. R., & Tyler, R. W. *Appraising and recording student progress.* New York: Harper & Bros., 1942.

Smith, L. M., & Pohland, P. A. Education, technology and the rural highlands. In *AERA Monograph Series on Curriculum Evaluation* (No. 7). Chicago: Rand McNally, 1974.

Stake, R. E. The countenance of educational evaluation. *Teachers College Record,* 1967, *68,* 523-540. (a)

Stake, R. E. Toward a technology for the evaluation of educational programs. In *AERA Monograph Series on Curriculum Evaluation* (No. 1). Chicago: Rand McNally, 1967. (b)

Stake, R. E. Objectives, priorities, and other judgment data. *Review of Educational Research,* 1970, *40,* 181-212.

Stake, R. E. (Ed.). *Evaluating the arts in education: A responsive approach.* Columbus, Ohio: Charles E. Merrill, 1975.

Stake, R., & Gjerde, C. An evaluation of TCITY, the Twin City Institute for Talented Youth. In *AERA Monograph Series on Curriculum Evaluation* (No. 7). Chicago: Rand McNally, 1974.

Stanley, J. C. The influence of Fisher's "The Design of Experiments" on educational research thirty years later. *American Educational Research Journal,* 1966, *3,* 223-229.

Stufflebeam, D. L., Foley, W. J., Gephart, W. J., Guba, E. G., Hammond, R. L., Merriman, H. O., & Provus, M. M. *Educational evaluation and decision making.* Itasca, Ill.: F. E. Peacock, 1971.

Taylor, F. W. *The principles of scientific management.* New York: Harper & Bros., 1911.

Taylor, P. A., & Cowley, D. M. New dimensions in evaluation. In P. A. Taylor & D. M. Cowley (Eds.), *Readings in curriculum evaluation.* Dubuque, Iowa: William C. Brown, 1972.

Taylor, P. A., & Cowley, D. M. (Eds.). *Readings in curriculum evaluation.* Dubuque, Iowa: William C. Brown, 1972.

Thurstone, L. L., & Thurstone, T. G. *Factorial studies of intelligence.* Chicago: University of Chicago Press, 1941.

Tyack, D. B. *The one best system: A history of American urban education.* Cambridge, Mass.: Harvard University Press, 1974.

Tyler, R. W. *Basic principles of curriculum and instruction.* Chicago: University of Chicago Press, 1949.

Tyler, R. W. (Ed.). *Educational evaluation: New roles, new means.* 68th yearbook of the NSSE, part 2. Chicago: University of Chicago Press, 1969.

Walberg, H. J. (Ed.). *Evaluating educational performance: A sourcebook of methods, instruments, and examples.* Berkeley: McCutchan, 1974.

Walker, D. F., & Schaffarzick, J. Comparing curricula. *Review of Educational Research,* 1974, *44,* 83-111.

Webb, B. *My apprenticeship.* Harmondsworth, England: Penguin Books, 1971. (Originally published, 1926.)

Wehlage, G. *The ethics and politics of evaluation: Patrons, clients and casualties.* Paper presented at the meeting of the American Educational Research Association, San Francisco, April, 1976.

Weir, E. An experimental approach to curriculum evaluation: The BSCS population genetics field trial. In R. E. Stake (Ed.), *Case studies in the evaluation of educational programmes.* Paris: Organization for Economic Cooperation and Development, 1976.

Weiss, R. S., & Rein, M. The evaluation of broad-aim programs: A cautionary case and a moral. *Annals,* 1969, *385,* 133-142.

Welch, W. W., & Walberg, H. J. A course evaluation. In H. J. Walberg (Ed.), *Evaluating educational performance.* Berkeley, Cal.: McCutchan, 1974.

White, M. G. *Science and sentiment in America: Philosophical thought from Jonathan Edwards to John Dewey.* New York: Oxford University Press, 1972.

Williams, W., & Evans, J. W. The politics of evaluation: The case of Head Start. *Annals,* 1969, *385,* 118-132.

Wolf, R. L. *The application of select legal concepts to educational evaluation.* Unpublished doctoral dissertation, University of Illinois at Champaign–Urbana, 1974.

V

METHODOLOGY

9

Integrating Findings: The Meta-Analysis of Research

GENE V GLASS
University of Colorado

Maccoby and Jacklin's (1974) review of research on the psychology of sex differences encompassed 1,600 works published before 1973. Considering the literature on that topic since 1973, and the fact that many other studies that are not focused specifically on sex differences may contain data on the question, a population of over 5,000 studies on sex differences can be imagined. There are dozens of educational problems on which the research literature is comprised of several hundred articles: ability grouping, reading instruction, programmed learning, instructional television, integration, and so on.

Educational research and evaluation is a large and widely scattered enterprise. On problems of importance, it produces literally hundreds of studies in less than five years. The research techniques used, the measurements taken, the types of person studied—all may vary from one study to the next, even though the topic is the same. The research enterprise in education and the social sciences is a rough-hewn, variegated undertaking of huge proportions. Determining what knowledge this enterprise has produced on some question is itself a genuinely important scholarly endeavor.

The evolution of style of research integration has been shaped by the size of the research literature. In the 1940s and 1950s, a reviewer contributing to the *Review of Educational Research* or *Psychological Bulletin* might find one or two dozen studies on a topic. A narrative, rhetorical integration of so few studies was probably satisfactory. By the late 1960s, the research

DAVID BERLINER, University of Arizona, was the editorial consultant for this chapter.

This paper was prepared while the author was a visiting researcher at the Max-Planck Institute for Psychiatry, Munich, Germany.

The preparation of this chapter was supported in part by a grant from the Spencer Foundation.

literature had swollen to gigantic proportions. Although scholars continued to integrate studies narratively, it was becoming clear that chronologically arranged verbal descriptions of research failed to portray the accumulated knowledge. Reviewers began to make crude classifications and measurements of the conditions and results of studies. Typically, studies were classified in contingency tables by type and by whether outcomes reached statistical significance.

Integrating the research literature of the 1970s demands more sophisticated techniques of measurement and statistical analysis. The accumulated findings of dozens or even hundreds of studies should be regarded as complex data points, no more comprehensible without the full use of statistical analysis than hundreds of data points in a single study could be so casually understood. Contemporary research reviewing ought to be undertaken in a style more technical and statistical than narrative and rhetorical. Toward this end, I have suggested a name to make the needed approach distinctive; I referred to this approach as the *meta-analysis* of research (Glass, 1976). I have no stake in the use of this term; it sounds pretentious, but is only incidentally so. It was chosen to suggest the analysis of analyses, i.e., the statistical analysis of the findings of many individual analyses. The term *integrative analysis* might serve as well. But *secondary analysis* is imprecise to the point of being misleading and should not be used interchangeably with these terms; it connotes an altogether different activity (Cook, 1974).

Educational researchers have apparently thought little about the methodological and technical problems of research integration. Light and Smith (1971) first gave serious attention to these problems. Their paper is a careful treatment of the inadequacies of simple methods of research integration. Their proposed solution—the cluster approach—is in the spirit of the solution recommended here, but it is more conservative: ". . . little headway can be made by pooling the *words in the conclusions* of a set of studies. Rather, progress will only come when we are able to pool, in a systematic manner, the original data from the studies" (Light & Smith, p. 443). This assumption and the methods based on it probably discard far too many informative studies for which the data are no longer available, though the summary findings remain. (Wolins, 1962, once wrote to 37 authors requesting data from their studies published between 1959 and 1961. The results: 5 authors did not reply, 21 reported the data lost or destroyed, 2 claimed proprietary rights to the data. Of the nine who sent their data, four sent it too late to be useful.) Rosenthal (1976) integrated several hundred studies of experimenter expectancy effects in behavioral research. The techniques he employed and the accompanying discussion of methodological issues are remarkably like those presented by Glass and Smith (1976) in their meta-analysis of psychotherapy research, though the two efforts proceeded quite independently.

PROBLEMS OF ACCESS, REWARDS, AND ORGANIZATION

I have no particular insight into many of the problems of research integration. Certain nontechnical problems of access to documents, professional rewards, publication, and standardization of methods seem particularly important. I commend them to the attention of others more experienced in these areas. However, my personal experiences in attempting to integrate research in a few fields have left me with some opinions on these problems.

Access

Modern libraries and document retrieval systems (e.g., ERIC, Dissertation Microfilms) are extremely important resources. They are clearly earning their current levels of support. Educational research lacks a regular compendium of abstracts of the archival literature with backward and forward citations. One is needed. In my opinion, any attempts to control the quality of what goes into retrieval systems such as ERIC would be mistaken.

Rewards

The integration of published research is not a highly valued contribution in most fields. Where problems are sharply defined and techniques are standardized (as in molecular biology or physiology), the meaning of multiple studies is obvious. They form a ladder, with each rung leading toward an indistinctly envisioned goal. Biologists purchase materials from one or two major suppliers, and it was not uncommon a few years ago for a Ph.D. candidate to open a journal and find his thesis problem newly solved and published. Such tidy fields face fewer problems of fitting together a sprawling and seemingly contradictory research literature. For these reasons, perhaps, research review and integration have lacked prestige. The fiction that science progresses along a string of dramatic, critical experiments dies hard. For educational research, the priorities need to be changed. The integration of research studies requires the best minds. It should be valued more highly than many forms of original research.

Standardization Methods

When confronted by the cluttered appearance of the educational research literature, the initial, angry reaction may be to decry the unstandardized methods and reporting forms. There may be merit to standardizing some areas of educational research, but my experiences with commissions and committees that attempt to impose order in this small corner of chaos leave me pessimistic. The attempt assumes a centralization of authority which is noticeably missing. Educational research is scattered among nearly a hundred journals and many more short-lived newsletters and technical report series.

It emanates from research centers and laboratories, universities, school districts, and professional organizations which operate quite independently. Without authority, standards are wish lists, situated on the margins which are cut first when the demands of time and money begin to press.

Even if the use of standard research methods and materials could be enforced, to do so would exert a conservative drag on inquiry. Lack of standardization is most acutely felt in measurement. But this is probably the most labile and rapidly developing area of research and evaluation. New developments in testing occur quickly (criterion-referenced testing; frequent revision of achievement tests; affective measures of creativity, self-concept, internal-external control; and so on), and to freeze the technology of measurement at a 1975 or a 1980 stage would be unwise. It is better to accept graciously the rugged and irregular character of educational research and work with it.

Journals

A journal editor exercises a great deal of authority, though it extends only over those who seek publication in the editor's own journal. This amounts to tremendous influence in fields with one or two major outlets, such as the *American Mathematical Monthly* or *Physical Review* and *Physical Review Letters*. But the education literature is spread among literally dozens of journals, and the editors have virtually no contact with one another. To my knowledge, the editors of journals who publish empirical educational research have never met to consider the form and detail of research reporting which would serve the interests of research integration—which, incidentally, are nearly identical with the interests of any reader trying to make genuine sense of a report. Those editors who are sensitive to the significance of the problem of research integration can do something to make the situation better. They could require authors to submit original data which would be kept on file or mailed at cost to researchers wishing to check findings or make new calculations. This plan would raise sticky questions of proprietary rights to data, but in the interests of the field, the questions must be resolved. Editors could ensure that meaningful data were reported in journal articles. The lowly mean and variance are nearly essential in understanding an article and absolutely essential in research integration. There is a fine line between reporting too much and too little data, and, from the looks of the published literature, too few authors and editors know where that line should be drawn.

CONCEPTS IN META-ANALYSIS OF RESEARCH

"Studies"

It is ironic that the basic unit of the research and evaluation enterprise, namely the *study,* is so vaguely and ambiguously specified. In some narrowly circumscribed areas of research, studies come to have a standard size, duration, and materials, whether through custom or conscious planning. However, across a broad field of interest, a "study" may represent anything from an afternoon dalliance with a dozen subjects to an enormous field trial lasting months. The mythology of Neyman-Pearsonian power calculations and the proscriptions of elementary research methods textbooks aside, the design of a *study* is a complex judgmental process that produces as many different studies as there are researchers and settings in which they work.

The semantics are further tangled when one realizes that one study can produce more than one finding; indeed, sometimes it may produce dozens. A philosophical analysis of *study* and *finding* is probably not called for here. It is sufficient, perhaps, to recognize that the basic units on which a meta-analysis is carried out are essentially undefined terms. One must trust in a relatively widely shared understanding of the words *study* and *finding*. Furthermore, the common conception of these terms is sufficient to indicate the nature of the technical problem that arises: Should a "study" with ten times as many subjects as another study be given greater or equal weight in a composite? And, if greater, should the weighting factor be n, $\sqrt{n}$, and so on? Should each "finding" from a study be entered as an observation into a composite, or should "findings" be averaged within studies? These questions have implications which will be examined more closely in later sections.

Criticism and Integration

Research criticism has taken an unhealthy turn. It has become confused with research design. The critic often reads a published study and second guesses the aspects of measurement and analysis that should have been anticipated by the researcher. If a study "fails" on a sufficient number of these criteria—or if it fails to meet conditions of which the critic is particularly fond—the study is discounted or eliminated completely from consideration. Research design has a logic of its own, but it is not a logic appropriate to research integration. The researcher does not want to perform a study deficient in some aspect of measurement or analysis, but it hardly follows that after a less-than-perfect study has been done, its findings should not be considered. A logic of research integration could lead to a description of design and analysis features and study of their covariance with research findings. If, for example, the covariance is quite small between the size of an experimental effect and whether or not subjects were volunteers, then the force of the criticism that some experiments used volunteers is clearly diminished.

Obviously, studying the covariation between design characteristics and findings can lead to better designs. In the meta-analysis of psychotherapy outcome studies reported elsewhere (Glass & Smith, 1976), a judgment to eliminate all studies not having control groups was made at the outset. In

356 Review of Research in Education, 5

retrospect, it would have been wiser, perhaps, to include "experiments" that comprised only pretesting and posttesting a single group of subjects. Such a design—as primitive as it is—is nonetheless adequate *if* the treated group members' pretreatment status is a good estimate of their hypothetical post-treatment status in the absence of treatment. And in any area of research, this is an empirical question. By including pretest-posttest only designs and comparing their findings with the findings of better designed experiments, we might have substantially expanded the data base or determined something about the sensitivity of the phenomena to design features like maturation or testing effects. This can be done without in any way condoning future experiments that have weaknesses of design, analysis, or measurement.

An early attempt at meta-analysis was characterized somewhat cynically by a critic as follows: "Although no single study was well enough done to prove that psychotherapy is effective, when you put all these bad studies together, they show beyond doubt that therapy works." This skeptical characterization with its paradoxical ring is a central thesis of research integration. In fact, many weak studies can add up to a strong conclusion. Suppose that, in a group of 100 studies, studies 1-10 are weak in representative sampling but strong in other respects; studies 11-20 are weak in measurement but otherwise strong; studies 21-30 are weak in internal validity only; studies 31-40 are weak only in data analysis; and so on. But imagine also that all 100 studies are somewhat similar in that they show a superiority of the experimental over the control group. The critic who maintains that the total collection of studies does not support strongly the conclusion of treatment efficacy is forced to invoke an explanation of multiple causality (i.e., the observed difference can be caused either by this particular measurement flaw *or* this particular design flaw *or* this particular analysis flaw *or* . . .). The number of multiple causes which must be invoked to counter the explanation of treatment efficacy can be embarrassingly large for even a few dozen studies. Indeed, the multiple-defects explanation will soon grow into a conspiracy theory or else collapse under its own weight. Respect for parsimony and good sense demands an acceptance of the notion that imperfect studies can converge on a true conclusion.

Integrating "Different" Studies

In combining or integrating studies, the worry is often encountered that incommensurable studies are being forced together, or different studies are being made to answer the same question, or apples are being mixed with oranges. Implicit in this concern is the belief that only studies that are the *same* in certain respects can be aggregated. "A study's dependent variables and those independent variables which are measured must be measured in the same way as, or in a way subject to a conversion into, those employed in the rest of the studies" (Light & Smith, 1971, p. 449). This thesis should be clarified in at least two ways: *Same* is not defined, and the respects in which comparable studies must be the same are unspecified. The claim that only studies which are the same in *all* respects can be compared is self-contradictory; there is no need to compare them, since they would obviously have the same findings within statistical error. The only studies which need to be compared or integrated are *different* studies. Yet it is intuitively clear that some differences among studies are so large or critical that no one is interested in their integration. What, for example, is to be made of study 1, which demonstrates the effectiveness of disulfiram in the treatment of alcoholism, and study 2, which demonstrates the benefits of motorcycle helmet laws? Not much, I suppose. But it hardly follows that the integration of study 3 on lysergide treatment of alcoholism and study 4 on "controlled drinking" is meaningless; we are understandably concerned with which treatment has a greater cure rate. Is the essential difference between the two examples that in the former case the *problems* addressed by the studies are different, but the *problem* is the same in the latter example? *Problem* is no better defined than *study* or *findings,* and invoking the word clarifies little. It is easy to imagine the Secretary of Health, Education, and Welfare comparing 50 studies on alcoholism treatment with 50 studies on drug addiction treatment or 100 studies on the treatment of obesity. If the two former groups of studies are negative and the latter is positive, the Secretary may decide to fund only obesity treatment centers. From the Secretary's point of view, the *problem* is public health, not simply alcoholism *or* drug addiction.

Suppose a researcher wished to integrate existing studies on computer-assisted instruction (CAI) and cross-age tutoring (CAT) to obtain some notion of their relative effectiveness. That studies 1 and 2 on CAI used different standardized achievement tests to measure progress in mathematics is a difference that should cause little concern, considering the basic similarity of most standardized achievement tests. Whoever would object to integrating the findings from these two studies must face a succession of difficult questions, beginning with whether to accept as comparable two studies using *different* forms of the *same* test, or whether to accept as equal two average scores which were achieved by *different* patterns of item responses to the *same* form of the *same* test.

Imagine further that of 100 CAI studies, 75 were in math and 25 in science, whereas of the 100 CAT studies, 25 were in math and 75 were in science. Are the aggregated data on effectiveness from 100 studies each of CAI and CAT meaningfully comparable? It depends entirely on the exact form of the question being addressed. If CAI is naturally much more frequently applied to math instruction than to science (and vice versa for CAT), then the simple aggregation of effectiveness measures may most meaningfully answer the question of what benefits could be expected by a typical school from installing CAI (and using it in the natural manner, which means three times more extensively in math than in science) instead of instigating CAT. If, however, we were more interested in the question of whether CAI was a more effective *medium* than CAT, then such a comparison ought not to be confounded with problems of the difficulties of learning math versus science. In these circumstances, a straightforward aggregation of the findings in each set of 100 studies would not be most meaningful. To compare the media independently of subject taught, we could calculate effectiveness measures separately for math and science within either CAI or CAT. Then total effectiveness measures for CAI and CAT would be constructed by some appropriate method of proportional weighting, for example, Tukey's "balancing" (Maxwell & Jones, 1976).

The tough intellectual work in many applied fields is to make incommensurables commensurable, in short, to compare apples and oranges. In fields where many things "work," determining what works best is the primary task. It requires a librarian's temperament and solid technical expertise.

The "Voting Method" and Simpson's Paradox

The most commonly used method of integrating research studies is what Light and Smith (1971) referred to as the *voting method*. There exists a virtually huge number of such reviews, and no purpose would be served by citing examples here. Light and Smith characterized the voting method in these words:

All studies which have data on a dependent variable and a specific independent variable or interest are examined. Three possible outcomes are defined. The relationship between the independent variable and the dependent variable is either significantly positive, significantly negative, or there is no significant relationship in either direction. The number of studies falling into each of these three categories is then simply tallied. If a plurality of studies falls into any one of these three categories, with fewer falling into the other two, the modal category is declared the winner. This modal categorization is then assumed to give the best estimate of the direction of the true relationship between the independent and dependent variable. (p. 433)

Light and Smith pointed out that the voting method of study integration disregards sample size. Large samples produce more "statistically significant" findings than small samples. Suppose that nine small-sample studies yield not quite significant results, and the tenth large-sample result is significant. The vote is one "for" and nine "against," a conclusion quite at odds with one's best instincts. So much the worse for the voting method. Precisely what weight to assign to each study in an aggregation is an extremely complex question, one that is not answered adequately by suggestions to pool the raw data (which are rarely available) or to give each study equal weight, regardless of sample size. If one is aggregating arithmetic means, a weighting of results from each study according to $\sqrt{n}$ might make sense, reasoning from an admittedly weak analogy between integrating study findings and combining independent random samples from a population. The problems of proper integration of statistical findings are not simply problems of sample size; if pursued for long, they lead back to the ambiguities of the concept of a "study."

Some of the complications of sample size can be avoided post hoc if the sample size, n, of studies is not systematically related to the magnitude of the findings of the studies, for example, mean differences or correlation coefficients. Glass and Smith (1976) found for over 800 measures of the experimental effect of psychotherapy versus a control condition that the effect size had a linear correlation of only $-.10$ with n and essentially no curvilinear correlation. Smaller size studies tended to show slightly larger effects, but the relationship was so weak that it is doubtful that any weighting of findings would make any difference in the aggregation.

A serious deficiency of the voting method of research integration is that it discards good descriptive information. To know that televised instruction beats traditional classroom instruction in 25 of 30 studies—if, in fact, it does—is not to know whether TV wins by a nose or in a walkaway. One ought to integrate measures of the strength of experimental effects or relationships among variables (according to whether the problem is basically experimental or correlational). Researchers commonly believe that significance levels are more informative than they are. Tallies of statistical significance or insignificance tell little about the strength or importance of a relationship.

An example will demonstrate that the aggregation of even simple statistical information can create unexpected difficulties. There exists a paradox attributed to E. H. Simpson by Colin Blyth (1972) which has a counterpart in aggregating research results. Imagine that researcher A is conducting a study of the effect of amphetamines on hyperactivity in sixth-grade children. (It is alleged that amphetamines act as depressants on prepubescent children.) In A's study, 110 hyperactive children receive the amphetamine, and 70 receive a placebo. After six weeks' treatment, each child is rated as either *improved* or *worse*. The following findings are obtained:

Study A

	Amphetamine	Placebo	
Improved	50	30	80
Worse	60	40	100
	110	70	180

The improvement rate for the amphetamines exceeds that for the placebo: .45 vs. .43.

Suppose researcher B is studying the same problem at a different site and obtains the following results:

Study B

	Amphetamine	Placebo	
Improved	60	90	150
Worse	30	50	80
	90	140	230

Again, the improvement rate for amphetamines is superior to that for the placebo: .67 vs. .64.

By the voting method of aggregation, the score would be 2-0 in favor of amphetamines. However, an aggregation of the raw data produces the opposite conclusion:

Studies A & B Combined

	Amphetamine	Placebo	
Improved	110	120	230
Worse	90	90	180
	200	210	410

The improvement rate for placebo now exceeds that for amphetamines: .55 for amphetamines vs. .57 for placebo.

Which method of aggregation is correct? Obviously they cannot both be correct, since they lead to contradictory conclusions. In pondering this paradox and its implications for research integration, it is helpful to note that (1) the paradox has nothing whatever to do with statistical significance, (2) the sizes of the differences in rates could be made as large or small as one wished by juggling the figures, (3) the basic problem is related to the problems of unbalanced experimental designs (Simpson's paradox could not occur if amphetamine and placebo groups were of equal size within each study), and (4) the practical consequences of the paradox are not negligible—it occurred, for example, in a study of sex bias in graduate school admissions (see Bickel, Hammel, & O'Connell, 1975; Gardner, 1976).

Integrating Significance Tests

Some researchers have set forward as the principal problem of research integration the combining of significance levels into a joint test of a null hypothesis. Gage (1976) contributed a considered and illuminating paper on integrating studies on teaching. Following an astute critique of the voting method, he posed the aggregation problem as a problem in determining whether several individual studies, many of which showed no significant correlation, constituted in the aggregate sufficient evidence to reject the null hypothesis at a high level of significance. He employed the chi square method of K. Pearson (1933) and E. S. Pearson (1938) via Jones and Fiske (1953). If k independent studies yield significance levels, $p_1, p_2, \ldots, p_k$, then under the common null hypothesis tested in each study:

$$-2 \sum_{i=1}^{k} \log_e p_i \sim \chi^2_{2k}$$

This approach seems defensible and more powerful than a binomial test— testing whether the probability of "positive" findings is different from .5— where statistical hypothesis testing is a genuine concern. For most problems of meta-analysis, however, the number of studies will be so large and will encompass so many hundreds of subjects that null hypotheses will be rejected routinely. Perhaps it is more realistic to think of the typical meta-analysis problem as residing in that vicinity the statistician calls "the limit," where all null hypotheses are false and inferential questions disappear. The statistical integration of studies probably ought to fulfill descriptive purposes more than inferential ones, though obviously it may fulfill both.

If the Pearson χ^2 test of combined results begins to play an increasingly important role in research integration, methodologists will need to scrutinize its assumptions and properties. It is probably quite sensitive to nonindependence of studies (cf. Jones & Fiske, 1953, pp. 377-381). Furthermore, the extreme tails of distributions are exotic places about which more would have to be learned. For example, violation of normality assumptions has little effect on 95th and 99th percentiles of t and F distributions, but conceivably it can change a p of .001, under normality, to a p of .0001, which is a disturbance in natural logarithms from −6.91 to −9.21.

Delimiting an Area of Research

Areas of research are not surveyed and platted into neat adjacent lots. One typically approaches the meta-analysis of research with a casually formulated conception of the topic: initial reading instruction, methods of school desegregation, or the effects of "mainstreaming." Studies are soon encountered which lie neither clearly inside nor outside the field of study: How many hours per day must EMH pupils work in regular classrooms to be "mainstreamed"? If EMH pupils are grouped by ability in regular classrooms, does the arrangement still qualify as "mainstreaming"? Should the reassignment of EMR pupils to EMH classes be regarded as "mainstreaming"? I know of no general principles that resolve such problems; any cutting of the cloth will soon fray at the edges. But two considerations might help. A topic that is defined broadly at the stage of literature collection can be narrowed safely at the stage of data analysis. Furthermore, the features of a study that characterize its distance (in a sense) from the focal point of the topic under consideration can be quantified as part of its description. In effect, then, the marginal studies can be tagged and analyzed separately; or better, it can be determined whether the features of studies that distinguish them by type are related in important ways to the research findings.

When one construes a research topic broadly, he may find that the literature on the subject runs to a few thousand studies. A recent check on the literature in psychopharmacology revealed several thousand controlled, double-blind experiments on psychoactive drugs. The practical difficulties of collecting and reading so many articles are obvious. Some of these difficulties might be alleviated by constructing a sampling design and selecting only a portion of the studies for analysis. Two hundred representative studies will give the same answer as two thousand, provided one simple question has been asked. Rosenthal (1976, p. 445) identified over 300 studies of the experimenter effect in behavioral research but could not examine all of them, since calculations had to be made for each study read. He stratified the population of 300 studies by research topic and then drew a random sample of 75 for thorough analysis.

Considerations such as these naturally lead to the question of how many studies are needed to perform a meta-analysis. It is the type of question to which statisticians are expected to give answers, and they probably cannot. The number of studies needed is a matter of how many questions will be addressed with the data. Very likely, any investigator will find a large number of irresistible questions to try to answer in a meta-analysis. Even if he collects and analyzes over a thousand studies, he will still attempt to answer questions which will stretch the available data very thin. In this regard, more studies are better than fewer.

An ensuing question—what is the smallest number of studies required for a meta-analysis?—ought to be rephrased. The spirit of meta-analysis is that statistical methods aid perception; tables, graphs, simple descriptive measures of location and spread, scatter diagrams, and regression surfaces reveal information not apparent to otherwise unaided perception. The question then becomes, How many studies can be read and integrated without resorting to statistical methods to reveal aggregate findings and relationships? The number is probably very small.

THE FORM OF META-ANALYSIS RESULTS

The meta-analysis of research on a topic is directed toward a quantitative aggregation of findings and the description of the relationships among findings and characteristics of the studies. In a meta-analysis of psychotherapy outcome studies (Glass & Smith, 1976), a common measure of treatment effectiveness was first defined. This measure, called the *effect size,* was defined as the difference between the means of the psychotherapy and the control group, divided by the control group standard deviation. Across nearly 400 controlled outcome studies yielding over 800 effect-size values (since in some studies more than one outcome variable was observed on more than one occasion), the average effect size was 0.68, i.e., the average person receiving some form of psychotherapy was about two-thirds standard deviation more improved on an outcome measure than the average control group member, as depicted in Figure 1. The relationships between the effect-size measure and characteristics of the studies were examined by graphing and tabulating various crosscuts of the data. For example, when the effect-size measures were averaged separately by type of outcome assessed, the results in Table 1 were obtained. There one sees that psychotherapy works large and nearly equal effects on reducing fears and enhancing self-esteem but much smaller effects on achievement, generally as measured by school grades or supervisor's ratings.

As informative as good graphs and tables may be, ultimately they lack the concentrated descriptive force of more sophisticated statistical techniques such as multiple regression analysis. In Glass & Smith, regression techniques were employed to describe the decay of psychotherapy effects over time. Each effect-size measure was coded with the number of months elapsing between the termination of therapy and the assessment of the outcome. About 200 studies of a therapy derived from learning theory, known as systematic desensitization, were selected for this analysis. A graph was drawn of the

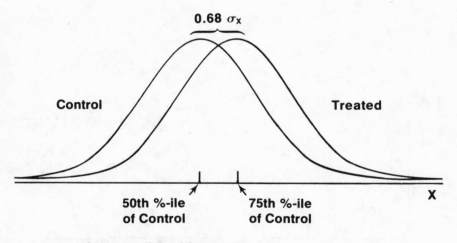

Average Effect Size: 0.68σ_x
Standard Deviation of Effect Size: 0.67 σ_x

Figure 1.   Normal curves illustrating the aggregate effect of psychotherapy in relation to untreated control groups. Data were based on 833 effect-size measures from 375 studies, representing about 40,000 treated and untreated subjects.

TABLE 1
Average Sizes of Psychotherapy Effects for Three Types
of Outcome (in standard deviation units)

Type of Outcome	No. of Effect-Size Measures	Average Effect size[a]
Reduction of fear and anxiety	261	.97 ± .04
Increase in self-esteem	53	.90 ± .08
Improved achievement in school or at work	145	.31 ± .05

[a] With an indication of the approximate standard error of the average. Thus the interval indicated has a confidence coefficient of about two-thirds.

relationship between size of effect and the number of months after therapy for measurement of effect, the latter variable hereafter referred to as *Mos. Post.* The scatter diagram showed a clear curvilinear relationship—an initial sharp decline, giving way to a gradual approach to an asymptote. Consequently, the dependent variable, effect size, was regressed onto the square root of the independent variable, *Mos. Post,* as in Figure 2. This shows that systematic desensitization therapy produces an immediate effect of .90, which decays to .80 at four months and .70 at 16 months.

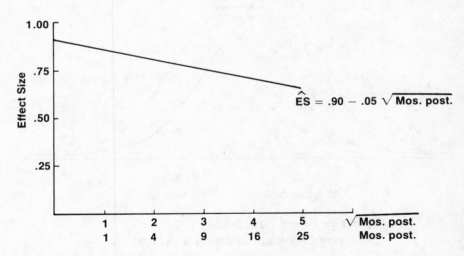

Figure 2.   Regression of psychotherapy effect onto the time (square root of months) elapsing between therapy and assessment of outcomes for systematic desensitization therapy.

PROBLEMS OF QUANTIFICATION AND MEASUREMENT

The quantification of the findings and features of research studies and the analysis of their relationships raise several technical problems. None is unique to the meta-analysis of research, although some of them may demand renewed attention because of the need to integrate rapidly growing research literatures. These technical questions can be grouped under the headings of quantification and measurement of study characteristics, of experimental outcomes, of correlational outcomes, and problems of statistical inference.

Study Characteristics

To make full use of statistical methods in describing study findings and accounting for their variance, the features of the research problem and setting which might mediate results must be measured or otherwise expressed in quantitative terms. Some of these characteristics can be measured on familiar scales: hours of treatment, years of teaching experience, IQ of pupils, time of follow-up measurement. Other features will be nonordinal characteristics which can be coded by "indicator variables" and entered into regression analyses: type of treatment, ethnic group of subjects, type of outcome (e.g., speed, comprehension, or interest). In some few instances, it may be worthwhile to attempt to bridge the gap between nominal and quantitative characteristics by means of scaling techniques. For example, Glass and Smith (1976) attempted to simplify twelve psychotherapies to first four and then two clusters through a multidimensional scaling of clinicians' judgments of similarities.

The quantification of study characteristics presents many practical problems. Reports of studies frequently omit important information about the setting, subjects, or techniques. At the meta-analysis stage, "missing data" methods are necessary. Other quantification problems verge on questions of definition. Suppose one wishes to quantify the amount of psychotherapy in hours that subjects receive in an experiment. It is a simple matter when a therapist meets a client one hour each Wednesday morning for three months. But suppose the subject in a study is a psychotic in a hospital ward being treated by a form of behavioral therapy in which each of his attempts at conversation is rewarded with some privilege off the ward. Does the subject receive 16 hours of treatment per day? Or if one day he performs no rewarded act, has he received no treatment that day? The complexity and variety of what we seek to study permit no simple answers.

Consider a related problem. In a meta-analysis of methods of math instruction, one might find that in study 1 pupils were taught by computer for ten hours in five two-hour sessions within a single week, whereas in study 2 pupils were taught one hour per week for ten consecutive weeks. Is it sufficient to record each study as having encompassed ten hours of instruction? It is difficult to know in advance. Fortunately, one can adopt a tactical approach to sidestep the problem. One can safely make distinctions where there are no genuine differences, then later obscure the distinction when it becomes apparent that important practical differences do not exist. In the hypothetical example with math instruction, one could classify each study by total number of hours of instruction and also by number of days or weeks from the beginning to the end of instruction. The two variables together capture most of what one means by "pace of instruction." If across dozens of studies the two variables correlate very highly, one could be eliminated (probably the latter) for the sake of simplicity and accuracy of estimation of regression weights. In an elaborate and complex domain, a factor analysis of study characteristics may even be indicated prior to analyses relating study results to characteristics.

Outcomes of Experimental Studies

The description of findings in experimental studies so that results can be aggregated and their variability studied presents several technical problems. The findings of comparative experiments are probably best expressed as standardized mean differences between pairs of treatment conditions. It will seldom be satisfactory to express experimental findings as a measure of association between several levels of an independent variable and a metric dependent variable. Such association measures (e.g., ω^2) are descriptive of a complete, somewhat arbitrary, set of experimental conditions an investigator chooses to investigate in a single study. For example, if one wished to determine the comparative effects of computer-assisted and traditional foreign language instruction, then it is irrelevant that a televised instruction condition was also present in a study, and one would not want a quantitative measure of effect to be influenced by the irrelevant condition (Glass & Hakstian, 1969).

In what follows, reference will be made to the comparison of a particular experimental condition with a control group. Of course, there may be no "control" group in a traditional sense, and one could imagine that two different experimental conditions are compared. The most informative and straightforward measure of experimental *effect size* is the mean difference divided by within-group standard deviation:

$$ES = \frac{\bar{X}_E - \bar{X}_C}{s_x}.$$

The meaning of *ES* is readily comprehended and, assuming some distribution form, can be translated into notions of overlapping distributions of scores and comparable percentiles. For example, suppose that a study of the effect of ritalin versus placebo on reducing hyperactivity reveals an *ES* of −1.00. One knows immediately that the average child on ritalin shows hyperactivity one standard deviation below that of the average child on placebo; thus, assuming normality, only 16 percent of the placebo children are less hyperactive than the average child on the drug, and so on. *ES* has been used by Rosenthal (1976, p. 444) in his meta-analysis of research on experimenter effects in behavioral research and is the form of the findings on psychotherapy in several of the examples given above.

Although *ES* is simple, it can present many difficulties in both conception and execution. Many research reports do not contain the means and standard deviations of experimental conditions. Where there are more than two experimental conditions and means are not reported, there is little hope of ever recovering an *ES* from the report. There are several circumstances of incomplete data reporting in which a harmless assumption and some simple algebra will make it possible to reconstruct *ES* measures:

1. One knows the value of t and whether $\bar{X}_E$ or $\bar{X}_C$ is larger.
2. One knows the significance level of a mean difference and the two sample sizes.
3. One knows $\bar{X}_{E_1}$, $\bar{X}_{E_2}$, . . . , and the value of F.
4. One knows $\bar{X}_E$ and $\bar{X}_C$ and the value of some multiple comparisons statistics such as Tukey's q or Dunn's or Dunnett's statistics.

One example worked out in detail should suffice to illustrate how to proceed in these general circumstances. The report of an experiment contains J means $\bar{X}_1$, $\bar{X}_2$, . . . , $\bar{X}_J$, the sizes of each group $(n_1, \ldots, n_J)$, and an F statistic. Suppose that $\bar{X}_1$ is the mean of the experimental condition of interest and that a second condition is a control yielding $\bar{X}_C$.

The value of the F statistic was calculated by the original investigator from the following formula:

$$F = \frac{\Sigma n_j(\bar{X}_j - \bar{X})^2/(J-1)}{\Sigma(n_j - 1)s^2_j/(N-J)} = \frac{MS_B}{MS_W},$$

where the only symbol which might not be obvious is N, which equals $n_1 + n_2 + \ldots + n_J$. Under the assumption that the variance, s^2_j, in each group is the same, the above expression can be readily solved to obtain s^2_x, the assumed homogeneous variance:

$$s^2_x = \frac{MS_B}{F}.$$

The effect size follows directly:

$$ES = \frac{\bar{X}_1 - \bar{X}_C}{s_x}.$$

How to calculate *ES* when s^2_j is not homogeneous and how to define s_x in multifactor experimental designs are more than simple technical questions.

As will be seen later in this section, they raise basic concerns about the definition and meaning of *ES*.

One commonly encountered method of reporting results presents unique difficulties. Reports sometimes give only the sample sizes and an indication of whether a mean difference was statistically significant at a customary level. A conservative approximation to the *ES* can be derived by setting a *t*-ratio equal to the critical value corresponding to the reported significance level and solving for $(\overline{X}_E - \overline{X}_C)/s_x$, under the assumption of equal within-group variances. For example, suppose that a report contains only the information that the mean of the n_1 experimental subjects exceeded the mean of the n_2 control subjects at the .05 level of significance. At the very least, then,

$$t = \frac{\overline{X}_E - \overline{X}_C}{\sqrt{s_x^2 \left(\frac{1}{n_1} + \frac{1}{n_2} \right)}} = 1.96.$$

Clearly,

$$ES = \frac{\overline{X}_E - \overline{X}_C}{s_x} = 1.96 \sqrt{\frac{1}{n_1} + \frac{1}{n_2}}$$

gives a conservative estimate of the experimental effect. This small bit of algebra also indicates how one obtains *ES* when given only *t* and n_1 and n_2:

$$ES = t \sqrt{\frac{1}{n_1} + \frac{1}{n_2}}.$$

Nonparametric statistical techniques similarly hide essential information about the magnitude of effects, since they are not built on basic concepts of means and variances but instead are constructed primarily for inferential purposes. Since they do yield significance levels for distribution differences, one could equate the α level to that of a parametric *t* test and employ the techniques set forth in the above paragraph. This method would be doubly conservative, for the reason already indicated for the *t* test and also because the nonparametric test is likely to be less powerful.

Experimental outcomes are frequently measured in crude dichotomies where refined metric scales do not exist: dropped out vs. persisted in school, remained sober vs. resumed drinking, convicted vs. not convicted of a crime. It seems inappropriate with such data to calculate means and standard deviations and take a conventional ratio. One approach to this problem is to attempt to recover underlying metric information. Suppose that with respect to some underlying but unobservable metric (e.g., motivation to stay in school), the experimental and control groups are distributed normally as in Figure 3. It is assumed that there exists a cut-off point, C_x, such that if motivation to stay in school falls below C_x, the pupil will drop out. What can be observed are the proportions p_E and p_C of the groups which fall below C_x. Under the normal distributions assumption,

$$p_E = \int_{-\infty}^{z_E} \frac{1}{\sqrt{2\pi}}\, e^{-z^2/2} dz,$$

where

$$z = \frac{X - \bar{X}_E}{s_E}.$$

Clearly, z_E is simply the standard normal deviate which divides the curve at the $100p_E$th percentile and can be obtained from any table of the normal curve. Likewise, z_C is that value of the standard normal variable which cuts off the bottom $100p_C$ percent of the distribution. Since,

$$z_E = \frac{C_x - \bar{X}_E}{s_E}$$

and

$$z_C = \frac{C_x - \bar{X}_C}{s_C},$$

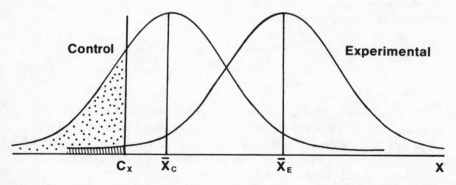

Figure 3.   Model of the recovery of metric effect-size measures from dichotomous findings.

it can be shown under the assumption of homogeneous variances that

$$z_C - z_E = \frac{\bar{X}_E - \bar{X}_C}{s_x} = ES.$$

Thus, effect-size measures on hypothetical metric variables can be obtained simply by differencing the standard normal deviates corresponding to the percentages observed in the experimental and control groups. The reasoning followed here is essentially the same as that which underlies *probit analysis* in biometrics (see Finney, 1971). Where the unobservable metric distributions ought to be assumed skewed in an expected direction, the methods of *logit transformation* will be more appropriate (Ashton, 1972). The problematic case of *p* equal to one or zero was addressed by Fisher (1935).

The transformation of dichotomous information to metric information via probits or logits makes it possible to expand greatly the data base of a meta-analysis. Frequently, studies on a single topic will encompass both metric and dichotomous measurement of outcomes. Having to integrate findings separately by type of outcome measurement is inconvenient as well as less than the broadest, most comprehensive integration of research possible.

The definition of *ES* appears uncomplicated, but heterogeneous group variances cause substantial difficulties. Suppose that experimental and control groups have means and standard deviations as follows:

	Experimental	Control
Means	$\bar{X}_E = 52$	$\bar{X}_C = 50$
Standard deviations	$s_E = 2$	$s_C = 10$

The measure of experimental effect could be calculated either by use of s_E or s_C or some combination of the two, such as an average or the square root of the average of their squares or whatever. The differences in effect sizes ensuing from such choices are huge:

Basis of Standardization	Effect Size
s_E	1.00
s_C	0.20
$(s_E + s_C)/2$	0.33

The third basis of standardization—the average standard deviation—probably should be eliminated as merely a mindless statistical reaction to a perplexing choice. It must be acknowledged that both the remaining 1.00 and 0.20 are *correct;* neither can be ruled out as false. It is true, in fact, that the experimental group mean is one standard deviation above the control group mean in terms of the experimental group standard deviation; and, assuming normality, the average subject in the control group is superior to only 16 percent of the members of the experimental group. However, the control group mean is only one-fifth standard deviation below the mean of the experimental group when measured in control group standard deviations; thus, the average experimental group subject exceeds 58 percent of the subjects in the control group. These facts are neither contradictory nor inconsistent; rather they are two distinct features of a finding which cannot be captured by one number. Scale transformations that make variances equal could help resolve the problem, but they have other drawbacks. In a meta-analysis of psychotherapy experiments, the problem of heterogeneous standard deviations was resolved from a quite different direction. Suppose that methods A, B, and Control are compared in a single experiment, with the following results:

	Method A	Method B	Control
Means	50	50	48
Standard deviations	10	1	4

If effect sizes are calculated using the standard deviations of the "method," then ES_A equals 0.20 and ES_B equals 2.00—a misleading difference, considering the equality of the method means on the dependent variable. Standardization of mean differences by the control group standard deviation at least has the advantage of allotting equal effect sizes to equal means. This seems reason enough to resolve the choice in favor of the control group standard deviation.

None of these deliberations helps resolve an even more perplexing situation that is likely to arise. We might want to summarize a collection of experiments in which methods A and B are compared to an untreated control condition, in order to determine which is more effective. Experiments are certain to turn up in which A and B are compared without a control. Such experiments may be quite informative but do not permit calculation of effect sizes of methods vis-à-vis the missing control condition. A certain percentage of "pseudo-effects" constructed along the following lines seems tolerable. Suppose an experiment comparing only A and B yields a difference in favor of A of .50 standard deviations, and assume that all other available comparisons of A and B with the control condition yield average effect sizes of 2.00 and 1.00, respectively. Then assigning effect-size measures of 1.75 to A and 1.25 to B has the advantage of being closest to the respective average effects, while corresponding to the difference obtained in the experiment in question. (The problem of heterogeneous variances remains and has no clear answer.)

A final consideration will illustrate how complex and intricate the description of experimental findings can be. The size of "within-group" variance is affected by the homogeneity of the experimental subjects and the number of classificatory factors in the design, among other things. For example, suppose that the Initial Teaching Alphabet *(ITA)* method of reading instruction is approximately 10 points superior to traditional *(T)* instruction on some measure of achievement. If Jones performs an experiment with a typical group of first-grade pupils whose standard deviation on the outcome measure is 20 points, he will obtain an effect size for *ITA* vs. *T* of 0.50. However, if Brown conducts a similar experiment but with a more homogeneous group of pupils (e.g., with a standard deviation of 5), an effect size of 2.00 will be obtained. This is clearly not a situation in which only one study is valid. A similar set of circumstances may be encountered in a single study. An investigator compares *ITA* and *T* methods of reading instruction and reports findings in a two-factor analysis of variance design, Method × Intelligence. What is the proper standard deviation to use in calculating the effect size: the standard deviation within cells of the factorial design, or the standard deviation within methods but crossing intelligence levels? The difference between the effect-size measures calculated by the two methods might be substantial. If some attempt is not made to deal with this problem, a source of inexplicable and annoying variance will be left in a group of effect-size measures. At least two techniques can help reduce the problem. If the scale of measurement of the outcome variables is familiar, it may be possible to calculate all effect-size measures using the known population standard deviation. For example, if the outcomes of reading instruction studies are measured with standardized reading tests in grade-equivalent units, the experimental vs. control mean difference can be divided by $\sigma_x = .5$ in grades 1 and 2, by $\sigma_x = 1.0$ in grades 3 and 4, and by $\sigma_x = 1.5$ in grades 5 and 6. An alternative approach based on less bold assumptions and requiring less a priori knowledge is to regard the homogeneity of the subjects as a characteristic of the studies. Effect-size measures could then be tagged as having arisen from studies with low, average, or highly homogeneous subjects, for example. One can then examine the covariance of *ES* with the homogeneity of the subjects used in the experiment.

Outcomes of Correlational Studies

In the meta-analysis of correlational studies, one is integrating correlation coefficients descriptive of the relationship between two variables, such as achievement and socioeconomic level, or teacher personality and pupil learning. The quantitative description of findings from correlational studies presents fewer complications than do experimental studies.

Illustrations of the integrative analysis of correlational studies will be drawn from a study of the relationship between pupils' socioeconomic status (SES) and their academic achievement. White (1976) collected over 600 correlation coefficients from published and unpublished literature. The coefficients were analyzed to determine how their magnitude was related to varying definitions of SES, different types of achievement, age of the subjects, and so on. White found that the 636 available correlations of SES and achievement averaged .25 with a standard deviation of about .20 and positive skew. Thus, SES and achievement correlation is below what is generally believed to be the strength of association of the two variables. The correlation diminished as students got older, r decreasing from about .25 at the primary grades to around .15 late in high school. SES correlated higher with verbal than math achievement (.24 vs. .19 for 174 and 128 coefficients, respectively). When White classified the SES and achievement correlations by the type of SES measure employed (see Table 2), SES measured as income correlated more highly with achievement than either SES measured by the education of the parents or the occupational level of the head of household. Several reliable trends in the collection of 600 coefficients could help methodologists designing studies and sociologists constructing models of the schooling-social system.

It probably matters little whether analysis is carried out in the metric of r_{xy}, r_{xy}^2 or Fisher's Z transformation of r_{xy}. The final results ought to be expressed in terms of the familiar r_{xy} scale, however. There appears to be no good reason to transform r_{xy} to Fisher's Z at the intermediate stages of aggregation and analysis, though this is sometimes recommended. Fisher's transformation was developed to solve an inferential problem, and it would be an unlikely happenstance if it proved to be the method of choice for combining correlation measures from several studies. It is frequently recommended that two or more r_{xy}'s be squared, averaged, and the square root taken rather than averaged directly. However, it is fairly easy to show that the choice seldom makes a practical difference. A little algebra applied to the ratio of $(r_1 + r_2)/2$ to $\sqrt{r_1^2 + r_2^2}/2$ will show that the discrepancy between the two depends primarily on the size of the difference between r_1 and r_2 and that they must be enormously different for the two averaging methods to differ in any important way. For example, the three coefficients—.20, .30, and .40—average .30 directly; and they average .31 if first squared and averaged, and the square root is taken. A gap of approximately more than .50 between r_1 and r_2 is needed to separate $(r_1 + r_2)/2$ and $\sqrt{r_1^2 + r_2^2}/2$ by more than .05. The researcher can safely decide whether the scale of r_{xy} or r_{xy}^2 is more meaningful to him and work in that metric throughout an integration of correlational studies.

The correlational studies referred to here deal with ordinal, metric variables. Correlational results which involve genuine dichotomies or polychoto-

TABLE 2
Average Correlation between SES and Achievement for Different Kinds of SES Measure

SES Measure	Average r_{xy}[a]
Indicators of parents' income	.315 (19)
Indicators of parents' education	.185 (116)
Indicators of parents' occupation level	.201 (65)

[a] Number of coefficients averaged in parentheses.

mies (e.g., sex, ethnic group) should be recast into more informative descriptive measures such as standardized differences among means, and the techniques of "effect-size" measurement discussed above may then be applied. Where the two variables correlated are conceived of as having metric properties—even if the technology of measurement at the time fell short of actual metric measurement—then one ought to seek to transform all correlation measures to the scale of Pearson's product-moment correlation coefficient.

When a large field of correlational research is collected, a bewildering variety of statistics is encountered: biserial and point-biserial correlation coefficients, rank-order correlations, phi coefficients, contingency coefficients, contingency tables with chi square tests, t-tests, analyses of variance, and more. In White's analysis of SES and achievement correlation, a variety of methods of reporting what was basically a correlational finding was encountered. Of

TABLE 3
Guidelines for Converting Various Summary Statistics into Product-Moment Correlations

Summary Statistic	Transformation to r_{xy}	References
a. Point-biserial correlation, r_{pb}	$r_{xy} = r_{pb}\sqrt{n_1 n_2}/(un)$	Glass & Stanley (1970, p. 171)
b. $t = \dfrac{\bar{X}_1 - \bar{X}_2}{\sqrt{s_{\bar{x}}^2\left(\dfrac{1}{n_1} + \dfrac{1}{n_2}\right)}}$	$r_{pb} = \sqrt{\dfrac{t^2}{t^2 + (n_1 + n_2 - 2)}}$ then convert r_{pb} to r_{xy} via *a* above.	Glass & Stanley (1970, p. 318)
c. $F = MS_b/MS_w$ for $J = 2$ groups	$\sqrt{F} = |t|$ then proceed via *b* above.	
d. $F = MS_b/MS_w$ for $J > 2$ groups	1. Collapse J groups to 2 and then proceed via *c* above, or 2. $r_{xy} = \eta = \sqrt{SS_b/(SS_b + SS_w)}$	Hays (1973, pp. 683–684)
e. χ^2 only (i.e., no frequencies reported) for a contingency table	$r_{xy} = \left(\dfrac{\chi^2}{\chi^2 + n}\right)^{1/2}$	Kendall & Stuart (1967, p. 557 ff)
f. 2×2 contingency table	Calculate tetrachoric r_{xy} from tables	Glass & Stanley (1970, p. 165 ff)
g. $R \times C$ contingency table	Collapse to a 2×2 table and proceed via *f* above.	
h. Spearman's rank correlation, r_s.	$r_{xy} = r_s$, since the translation of r_s to r_{xy} under bivariate normality is nearly a straight line.	Kruskal (1958)
i. Mann-Whitney U.	Convert U to a t statistic having the same level of significance, then proceed via *b* above.	

143 studies, 37 reported t or F statistics, 71 reported Pearson r's, 8 reported chi square or nonparametric statistics, and 27 presented only graphs or tables of means.

There usually is an algebraic path from the reported statistics to a Pearson correlation coefficient or an approximation to one. Some signposts along the paths are set out in Table 3, where it is indicated how one might travel from particular forms of reported data to a product-moment correlation measure.

PROBLEMS OF STATISTICAL INFERENCE

Whether the findings from a collection of studies are regarded as a sample from a hypothetical universe of studies, or they are in fact a sample from a well-defined population, problems of statistical inference arise. Significance tests or confidence intervals around estimates of averages or regression planes will indicate where the research literature is conclusive on a question and where the aggregated findings still leave doubts—at least insofar as sampling error is concerned.

The inferential statistical problems of the meta-analysis of research are uniquely complex. The data set to be analyzed will invariably contain complicated patterns of statistical dependence. "Studies" cannot be considered the unit of data analysis without aggregating findings above the levels at which many interesting relationships can be studied. Each study is likely to yield more than one finding. An experiment comparing heterogeneous and homogeneous ability grouping might produce effect-size measures on three types of school achievement at four points in time; thus, 12 of the several hundred effect-size measures in an aggregate data set would have arisen from a single study. There is no simple answer to the question of how many independent units of information exist in the larger data set. One might attempt to impose some type of cluster or multiple-stage sampling framework on the data, but in the end this will probably restrict the movement of an imaginative data analyst. Two resolutions of the problem can be envisioned: one risky, the other complex.

The simple (but risky) solution is to regard each finding as independent of the others. The assumption is untrue, but practical. All inferential calculations could proceed on this independence assumption. The results (standard errors of means, of correlations, and of regression coefficients) could be reported with the qualification that they were calculated under the assumption of independence. This procedure might be useful because the effect of the dependence is almost surely to increase standard errors of estimates above what they would be if the same number of data points were independent. Thus, if 50 effect-size measures from 30 studies yielded an unsatisfactorily large standard error for the mean effect size, then it could be assumed safely that the standard error would be even larger if the complex dependence in the data were accounted for properly.

An inferential technique which takes account of the interdependencies in a large set of findings in a meta-analysis is Tukey's jackknife method (Mosteller & Tukey, 1968). Space does not permit a basic exposition of the jackknife technique. One suggestion and an example must suffice. In calculating the "pseudovalues" in the jackknife method, some portion of the data set is discarded, and the sample estimate of the parameter of interest is calculated. In a meta-analysis, the portion of data eliminated should correspond to all those findings (e.g., effect sizes or correlation coefficients) arising from a particular study. Thus there will be as many pseudovalues as there are studies. The method will be illustrated on a small portion of the data from a meta-analysis of psychotherapy outcome studies.

The data in Table 4 represent 39 effect-size measures from 26 experimental studies in which behavioral and nonbehavioral psychotherapies were compared for their effects on fear and anxiety. The effect-size measure was defined as $ES = (\bar{X}_{\text{beh.}} - \bar{X}_{\text{nonbeh.}})/s_x$. For example, study 1 produced two measures of experimental effect, the first of which shows the nonbehavioral therapy as slightly superior to the behavioral therapy, and the second of which shows the behavioral therapy nearly three-fourths of a standard deviation superior to the nonbehavioral therapy. The first step in establishing a jackknife confidence interval on the mean effect size is to average the 39 effect-size measures to obtain $\bar{X}$. Second, 26 partial means, $\bar{X}_{-i}$, are calculated by eliminating each study in turn; for example, the first partial mean is based on the 37 effect-size measures remaining after the effect sizes from study 1 ($-.10, .74$) are removed. Third, 26 pseudovalues are calculated as follows: $\hat{\theta}_i = 26\bar{X} - 25\bar{X}_{-i}$. The 26 pseudovalues can safely be regarded as a sample of observations of normally distributed independent variables, with expected value approximately equal to the true mean effect size and variance $\sigma_{\hat{\theta}}^2$. Thus, the set of pseudo values, $\hat{\theta}_i$, can be treated as an ordinary sample of data to which t-distribution methods can be applied. The right-hand side of Table 4 lists the calculations for the 95% confidence interval on the true effect size; the interval does not quite span zero, indicating a statistically reliable superiority of the behavioral therapies. By comparison, a t-method 95% confidence interval on the population mean effect size calculated from the 39 effect-size measures, assuming independent observations, extends from $-.10$ to $+.50$.

Statistical inferential methods on the type of data illustrated here could play a role in directing future research. From standard errors of averages and confidence regions around regression planes, one can determine where parameters are sharply estimated by the current body of research studies and where sample estimates remain poor. The simple cross-tabulation of the characteristics of studies completed is helpful for the same purpose. How-

TABLE 4
Illustration of Application of the Jackknife Technique of Interval Estimation of Mean Effect Size

Study No.	Effect-Size Measures	Pseudo Values $\hat{\theta}_i = 26\bar{X} - 25\bar{X}_i$	Calculations
1	− .10		
	.74	.366	$N = 39$ effect-size measures
2	.43		$n = 26$ studies
	.45	.528	
3	.65	.493	$\bar{X}_{\hat{\theta}} = .186$
4	.52	.407	
5	.20	.197	$s_{\hat{\theta}} = .457$
6	− .16	−.040	
7	− .50	−.264	
8	3.35		
	−2.82	.291	95% jackknife confidence
9	.18	.184	interval on μ:
10	.51	.278	
11	− .39	−.191	$_{.975}t_{25} = 2.06$
12	− .95	−.560	
13	.33	.282	
14	.12	.144	$\bar{X}_{\hat{\theta}} \pm ts_{\hat{\theta}}/\sqrt{n} =$
15	.08	.118	$.186 \pm (2.06)(.457)/\sqrt{26} = (.002, .371)$
16	1.90	1.315	
17	− .44	−.224	
18	−1.00	−.593	
19	.06		
	.20		
	.10		
	.00	−.097	
20	.64	.486	
21	.59		
	.96	.980	
22	.05		
	.20	.102	
23	.01	.072	
24	.12		
	.00		
	.14		
	− .28	−.368	
25	− .22	−.079	
26	1.28		
	.24		
	.24	1.016	

ever, it must be pointed out that the number of studies needed to estimate accurately an aggregate effect size is partly a function of the variance of effect sizes. For example, 5 studies may determine accurately the effect of amphetamines on hyperactive 8-year-olds, whereas 20 studies may be needed to achieve the same accuracy with 12-year-olds if the effects are fundamentally more variable for older children.

CONCLUSION

Apprehending the meaning of the collected research on an educational problem has become a technical problem. The findings of studies are too varied and numerous to be grasped readily, as for example one might understand a theory simply by reading it. The confusion that grows from irregularity and sheer multiplicity is tamed by coding, ordering, and arranging instances in search of patterns and gross features. Statistical methods are techniques found generally useful for revealing unity in numerosity or patterns in irregularity. Modern methods are quantitative and complex. To use them fully requires technical skill.

I have attempted to describe and illustrate some techniques for the integration of research findings. The techniques are part of the stock-in-trade of any methodologist and most empirical researchers. They are the same techniques commonly applied by researchers in analyzing their primary data. Their application to the analysis of the results of many primary analyses may raise new questions about measurement and statistical description.

REFERENCES

Ashton, W. D. *The logit transformation.* London: Charles Griffin, 1972.

Bickel, P. J., Hammel, E. A., & O'Connell, J. W. Sex bias in graduate admissions: Data from Berkeley. *Science,* 1975, *187,* 398-404.

Blyth, C. R. On Simpson's paradox and the sure-thing principle. *Journal of the American Statistical Association,* 1972, *67,* 364-366.

Cook, T. D. The potential and limitations of secondary evaluations. In M. W. Apple, M. J. Subkoviak, & H. S. Lufler (Eds.), *Educational evaluation: Analysis and responsibility.* Berkeley, Cal.: McCutchan, 1974.

Finney, D. J. *Probit analysis* (3rd ed.). Cambridge: Cambridge University Press, 1971.

Fisher, R. A. Appendix to C. I. Bliss. The case of zero survivors. *Annals of Applied Biology,* 1935, *22,* 164-165.

Gage, N. L. *The scientific basis of the art of teaching.* New York: Teachers College Press (in press).

Gardner, M. Mathematical games. *Scientific American,* August 1976, pp. 119-122.

Glass, G. V Primary, secondary and meta-analysis of research. *Educational Researcher,* 1976, *5,* 3-8.

Glass, G. V, & Hakstian, A. R. Measures of association in comparative experiments: Their development and interpretation. *American Educational Research Journal,* 1969, *6,* 403-414.

Glass, G. V, & Smith, M. L. *Meta-analysis of psychotherapy outcome studies.* Paper presented at the Annual Meeting of the Society for Psychotherapy Research, San Diego, Cal., June 1976.

Glass, G. V, & Stanley, J. C. *Statistical methods in education and psychology.* Englewood Cliffs, N.J.: Prentice-Hall, 1970.

Hays, W. L. *Statistics for the social sciences.* New York: Holt, Rinehart & Winston, 1973.

Jones, L. V., & Fiske, D. W. Models for testing the significance of combined results. *Psychological Bulletin,* 1953, *50,* 375-382.

Kendall, M. G., & Stuart, A. *The advanced theory of statistics* (Vol. 2, 2nd ed.). New York: Hafner, 1967.

Kruskal, W. H. Ordinal measures of association. *Journal of the American Statistical Association*, 1958, *53*, 814-861.

Light, R. J., & Smith, P. V. Accumulating evidence: Procedures for resolving contradictions among different research studies. *Harvard Educational Review*, 1971, *41*, 429-471.

Maccoby, E. E., & Jacklin, C. N. *The psychology of sex differences.* Stanford, Cal.: Stanford University Press, 1974.

Maxwell, S. E., & Jones, L. V. Female and male admission to graduate school: An illustrative inquiry. *Journal of Educational Statistics*, 1976, *1*, 1-37.

Mosteller, F. M., & Tukey, J. W. Data analysis, including statistics. In G. Lindzey and E. Aronson (Eds.), *Handbook of social psychology* (2nd ed.). Reading, Mass.: Addison-Wesley, 1968.

Pearson, E. S. The probability integral transformation for testing goodness of fit and combining independent tests of significance. *Biometrika*, 1938, *30*, 134-148.

Pearson, K. On the method of determining whether a sample of size *n* supposed to have been drawn from a parent population having a known probability integral has probably been drawn at random. *Biometrika*, 1933, *25*, 379-410.

Rosenthal, R. *Experimenter effects in behavioral research.* New York: Irvington, 1976.

White, K. R. *The relationship between socioeconomic status and academic achievement.* Unpublished doctoral dissertation, University of Colorado, 1976.

Wolins, L. Responsibility for raw data. *American Psychologist*, 1962, *17*, 657-658.

Name Index

Subject Index

Ability: *see* achievement, group ability, IQ., latent trait theory, tracking

Accountability, 129-30, 156, 157, 341; and state, 331-2; definition of, 129

Achievement: and ability, 99 (*see also* latent trait theory); and attitude, Table 106; 173, 180, 255, 265; and classroom ecology paradigm, 176-88; and classroom language, 109-15; and classroom mediators, 183-5; and educational equality, 238; and environment, 323; and formal classrooms, 158; and genetic background, 115, 323; and grades, 257-8; and Head Start, 331; and income, 212; and individual differences, 172, 180-1; and instructional materials, 172-4; and IQ, 230, 363, 372; and occupational status, 212; and psychotherapy, Table 364; and race, 331-2; and school characteristics, 90-159; and socioeconomic status, 372-5; and standards, 333-4; and teacher ability, 100, Table 106; and teacher behavior, 171-2; and teacher variables, 165-8, 173, 177-8, 187-8; and teaching style, 139-42, 165-6; and testing, 294-6, 323; and time, 117, 121-6, Table 123; 130, 155, 168-9, 174, 180, 365-6; and tracking, 100, 116, 143-50, Table 145; 158; by districts, 96; verbal, 93; *see also* learning, performance, retention, tests

Achievement gain, 98-103, 115

Achievement scale, 325

Adaptive testing, 309

Administrative progressives, 325

Affective entry behavior: definition of, 120

Algorithm, 9, 51, 60, 72, 73-4, 280-1

Alum Rock voucher experiment, 251-2

Amplified objectives: definition of, 280

Anxiety, 37-8

Attention and preattention, 55-7

Attitude: and achievement, Table 106; 173, 180, 255, 265

Attribute organization, 18-9

Binomial error models, 275

Birnbaum's model, 305, 307

Calligraphy, 78

Cartesian graphs, 50, 69

Cartography, 74-5

Chains of opportunity, 202-3, 233-4; *see also* mobility

Charts, 63-8

Civil Rights Act of 1964, 249

Classroom composition, 118-9; *see also* educational inequality, equality of educational opportunity

Classroom discourse, 110-2, 156

Classroom ecology paradigm, 165, 176-88

Classroom environment, 178-9, 221, 225-6

Classroom interaction, Table 106; 109-15, Table 111; 154-5, 169, 178-82, 185-6, 221, 225-6, 257, 265; definition of, 108

Classroom instruction, 89-159, 183-5; models, 102-50

Classroom language, 109-15, 184-5

THE BOOK MANUFACTURE

Computer-assisted composition (RCA VideoComp 800), offset printing, and binding of *Review of Research in Education, 5,* were by Kingsport Press. The paper is Glatfelter Litho. Internal and cover design were by John Goetz. The type is Times Roman with Helvetica display.